CULTURAL POLITICS IN FIFTEENTH-CENTURY ENGLAND

BRILL'S STUDIES IN INTELLECTUAL HISTORY

CULTURAL POLITICS
IN FIFTEENTH-CENTURY
ENGLAND

The Case of Humphrey, Duke of Gloucester

BY

ALESSANDRA PETRINA

BRILL
LEIDEN · BOSTON
2004

This book is printed on acid-free paper.

Library of Congress Cataloging-in-Publication Data

Petrina, Alessandra.
  Cultural politics in fifteenth-century England : the case of Humphrey, Duke of Gloucester
/ by Alessandra Petrina.
    p. cm. — (Brill's studies in intellectual history, ISSN 0920-8607 ; v. 124)
  Includes bibliographical references and index.
  ISBN 90-04-13713-0 (alk. paper)
    1. Humphrey, Duke of Gloucester, 1391-1447. 2. Great Britain—History—Lancaster and
York, 1399-1485—Biography. 3. Great Britain—Politics and government—1399-1485. 4.
Authors and patrons—England—History—To 1500. 5. Book
collecting—England—History—To 1500. 6. England—Intellectual life—1066-1485. 7.
Nobility—Great Britain—Biography. 8. Humanists—England. I. Title. II. Series.

  DA247.H8P48 2004
  942.04'092—dc22

                                                                            2003069556

ISSN   0920-8607
ISBN   90 04 13713 0

PRINTED IN THE NETHERLANDS

CONTENTS

FOREWORD

The picture on the cover of this book shows a fifteenth-century patron, sitting on what seems to be a very stylised high-backed chair or a throne, surrounded by a number of people; one of them kneels before the central figure, presenting him with a book; the others, standing around this central group, look at the donor. The picture, a fifteenth century Flemish miniature, bears no direct relation to Duke Humphrey of Gloucester; indeed, the patron portrayed here might even be one of Humphrey's many enemies. But it has been chosen for its symbolic significance, representing a scene that seems to be typical of the relations between patron and poet in the fifteenth century. There are manuscripts, particularly presentation copies, in which the same scene is proposed, more or less skilfully, with Humphrey as the receiver of the book; what fascinated me about this particular, anonymous image was that the two central actors, poet and patron, are surrounded by a number of other figures, who have arranged themselves so as to form a circle around the patron. Who were they? Other poets, or simple courtiers? Or both?

This image haunted me while I was researching and writing this book. For it seemed to me that an exploration of the Duke of Gloucester's role and his contribution to the first generation of English humanism, did not consist solely in a reconstruction of his indefatigable activity as a book collector and donor. It was necessary to reconcile two different, occasionally contrasting images: Humphrey the ambitious but unsuccessful politician, Humphrey the wise and (occasionally) generous patron. At the same time those figures standing around the patron could belong to both worlds: a poet could also be, indeed needed sometimes to be, finely attuned to the political changes of his own time; a courtier, a nobleman, an abbot could also be an avid reader, fascinated by the immense heritage of medieval learning but also by the novelties proposed by Italian humanism, which were beginning to make themselves perceived in northern Europe.

As chapter 1 shows, there has been a certain amount of research on Duke Humphrey and his activity as a book collector, especially in the past seventy years; posterity has perhaps been kinder to the

Duke than he might have any right to expect, and sometimes much, perhaps too much, has been made of his contribution to English intellectual life. Yet most studies on Humphrey, and on early fifteenth-century English humanism, have been especially interested in the relationship of the patron with Italian humanists, and the achievements of English writers and scholars have always been measured against the achievements of contemporary Italian literature and thought. This, though an indispensable part of the research on the duke and his circle, has condemned both to a sort of dependence on an implicitly superior model. Perhaps there was something to be gained by analysing the English side of Humphrey's intellectual activity, and its relation with a political role that set the Duke at the centre of the stage in the most difficult years of the Lancastrian reign.

This is what I have set out to do with this book. I have deliberately devoted less attention to the relationship between the duke and a number of Italian humanists with whom he corresponded or who entered his service, and focused instead on his political and intellectual activity in his country: his skilful use of propaganda, his collection of books (especially against the background of a bibliophilia shared by his brothers, and perhaps his nephew), his role in the development of a university library in Oxford.

This book has accompanied me for the last three years, and many friends and colleagues have walked with me for part of the way. To acknowledge one's debts in this case also means looking back on months of exciting, if sometimes exhausting, research, fascinating discussions, surprising discoveries. I have first of all a debt with the two institutions that have given me the necessary time and resources to complete this work: the University of Padova and the Warburg Institute. Both have funded my research and, in the case of the former, granted me the occasional leave from teaching duties. I am very grateful to my Department for its material and intellectual support, and especially to Giuseppe Brunetti, who beside guiding me in all my years of work there also read the finished manuscript of this book, correcting mistakes and suggesting improvements with meticulous kindness. Mario Melchionda directed my initial efforts, and has always been ready to support and spur me on. To them, and all my other colleagues, my thanks. The Warburg Institute, by awarding me a Brian Hewson Crawford Fellowship in 2002, has allowed me to work in one of the most fascinating libraries in the world, with the active and constant help of its staff, fellows, students and readers; to be part of this scholarly community is indeed a privilege. I wish to thank Charles Hope for inviting me to give a Director's seminar in which I could test my hypotheses on a very responsive audience, J.B. Trapp who gave me invaluable suggestions, Elizabeth McGrath and Ian Jones who helped me find my way in the Photographic Collection and give a face and a setting to the many figures of my pages; very special thanks are due to Jill Kraye, who so generously put at my disposal her knowledge and her dialectical skills, and always been near me with her assistance and friendship. Martin Davies kindly let me read and quote from his doctoral dissertation, and together with Jill has engaged me in challenging discussions on Italian and English humanism; John Burrow signalled to me some very useful unpublished material; Benedek Láng drew my attention to a fascinating and half-forgotten detail of Duke Humphrey's activity; Maura Bridget Nolan, beside sending me a copy of her article, also discussed and clarified for me a number of puzzles in Lydgate's work; Rosalynn Voaden, by inviting me to the 2001 Medieval Translator congress, allowed me to discuss a number of questions concerning the Middle English translation of Palladius's *De Agricultura*, later developed in an article she edited. David Rundle has discussed with me innumerable major and minor points of Duke Humphrey's intellectual activity and patronage, and allowed me to read and quote from his unpublished work; his scholarship is only matched by his generosity. The staff of a number of libraries have been kind and helpful even with my most puzzling requests; thanks are due to the librarians and assistants of the Bodleian Library, the British Library, the Warburg Institute Library, the Biblioteca Apostolica Vaticana, the Biblioteca Braidense, York University Library and Cambridge University Library.

My family has been a constant support, and I am grateful in particular to Giovanni Petrina for his unfailing assistance and his Latin scholarship. A number of friends have been patient as well as supportive, offering me assistance, encouragement, and dinners. Mario Varricchio helped me at a particularly critical stage of my bibliographical research; Mary Laven and Jason Scott-Warren, beside putting their house at my disposal on a number of occasions, also advised me and helped me to find my way among the intricacies of the English language. Oscar Meana has been near me in moments of happiness and discouragement, and seen the work take shape almost page by page. This book is dedicated to him.

David Rundle warned me that there is a controversy on the correct spelling of the name of the protagonist of this volume. For practical considerations, I have decided to use the spelling "Humphrey" for the Duke of Gloucester, and "Humfrey" for the library that commemorates his achievements and generosity. Quotations in languages other than English are translated in the footnotes.

LIST OF ILLUSTRATIONS

Cover illustration: Georges Hurtrel, "Scribe writing and the author presenting his book" (detail). Washington, National Gallery of Art, Rosenwald Collection. Image © Board of Trustees.

A DEFINITION OF HUMANISM
IN EARLY FIFTEENTH-CENTURY ENGLAND

The century itself defies definition. There is something deeply contradictory about the English fifteenth century, and even more, about the modern scholar's perception of it. From the historian's point of view, it is a time fraught with interest: it is during this century that the English nation finds its modern identity and is ultimately released, even through the endless vicissitudes of the Hundred Years' War, from its connection with France and the French crown; meanwhile, the deposition of an anointed king, Richard II, introduces a time of almost frenetic dynastic changes, concluding with the ascent to the throne of the first Tudor king and the beginning of a very long period of relative political stability; the political turmoil has an equally relevant religious counterpart with the Wycliffite movement and the subsequent diffusion of Lollardy, which anticipates in a number of ways much of the religious dissension to come, and its brutal repression on the part of both Church and State. Contemporary events such as the development of the press (William Caxton set up the first press in Westminster in 1476) and the establishment of the vernacular as the language of Chancery provide just as much scope to the intellectual historian. It is a period of great changes and contradictions, heralding the more apparent but possibly no deeper changes of the sixteenth century.

If the historian can find matters of great interest in an even superficial analysis of the English fifteenth century, the literary critic appears decidedly less happy about it, and the reason is obvious, at least at a first glance. Sandwiched between Geoffrey Chaucer and the many splendours of the Elizabethan age, this century is apparently reduced to relying on a few, decidedly dull Chaucerians and a handful of talented Scots. If C.S. Lewis's definition of the early sixteenth century, "the Drab Age",[1] brilliant if imprecise, has unfortunately

---

[1] C.S. Lewis, *English Literature in the Sixteenth Century Excluding Drama*, Oxford: Clarendon Press, 1954. "The Drab Age" is used as a title to the relevant section.

stuck, H.S. Bennett in the companion volume on the fifteenth century was even less charitable:

> The fifteenth century is by no means as barren of poetry as it used to be fashionable for critics to believe; nevertheless, the glory had departed, and the story of fifteenth-century poetry in England is largely the story of 'the shades of that which once was great', though momentary flashes reveal the fires underneath.[2]

Most books dedicated to the literature of the fifteenth century begin on the same complaining tone: as C. David Benson wittily observes, "we have all been taught from our first medieval survey that Lydgate's works form the Valley of Poetic Despair, and their only function is to connect the two Delectable Mountains of Chaucer and Shakespeare".[3] More recent criticism has done very little to restore the balance; it is a curious trait of a number of books devoted to the literature of the period that their tone should become at times intensely apologetic, underlining the (admittedly numerous) instances of pedantic imitation of former poets or even of non-English classics, rather than the genuine attempts at creative originality. Most studies on fifteenth-century literature, though perceptive in many respects, tend to confine their scope to the concept of imitation of the master Chaucer, and to dwell very little on original contributions. A significant instance of this ambivalent attitude can be found in A.C. Spearing's essay "The Chaucerian Tradition",[4] as well as in his *Medieval to Renaissance in English Poetry*, where the critic writes: "The persistent distortion of Chaucer's achievement that is represented by the poetry of most of his disciples meant that the work of the literary Renaissance, which Chaucer had begun single-handed, had to be done all over again in the sixteenth century".[5] Derek Pearsall's work on John Lydgate, though it remains one of the most important contributions of recent scholarship on this poet, maintains

---

[2] H.S. Bennett, *Chaucer and the Fifteenth Century*, Oxford: Clarendon Press, 1947, p. 96.
[3] C. David Benson, *The History of Troy in Middle English Literature: Guido Delle Colonne's Historia Destructionis Troiae in Medieval England*, Woodbridge: D.S. Brewer, 1980, p. 97.
[4] In his *Medieval Dream-Poetry*, Cambridge: Cambridge University Press, 1976, pp. 171–218.
[5] A.C. Spearing, *Medieval to Renaissance in English Poetry*, Cambridge: Cambridge University Press, 1985, p. 120.

a curiously regretful tone, invoking, for "the discrepancy between Lydgate's general reputation in his own day, and his general reputation now" a number of historical and cultural factors that he would have had no reason to invoke in the case of Geoffrey Chaucer.[6] This attitude may help explain the difficulty in granting canonical status to a number of literary works belonging to this period.[7] Much of its written production can be described as literary only with some controversy, since in many cases it consists of translations, commentaries, or works of scientific or practical value. For all these reasons, the fifteenth century's "received reputation"[8] of dullness appears to resist even its exegetes.[9]

Yet it is not easy to dismiss this period, if only because so many things happened to change the course of English intellectual life, and consequently of English letters. N.F. Blake notes how, setting literary achievements apart,

> in certain cultural activities [the fifteenth century] is also a period of progress: a specifically English style of architecture led to the building of many fine churches; music flourished; and art and manuscript illumination reached an advanced stage.[10]

The library of the University of Oxford, for example, may be said to have found its core and asserted itself as a centre of lay learning, after a period of decline, in the fifteenth century, thanks to Duke

---

[6] See his *John Lydgate*, London: Routledge & Kegan Paul, 1970, pp. 4ff. Revealing remarks upon the modern critics' attitude towards the fifteenth century can be found in David Lawton, "Dullness and the Fifteenth Century", *English Literary History* 54 (1987), pp. 761ff. For a useful, if by now slightly dated, discussion on this point, see also N.F. Blake, "The Fifteenth Century Reconsidered", *Neuphilologische Mitteilungen* 71 (1970), pp. 146–57. See also Helen Cooper, "Introduction", in *The Long Fifteenth Century. Essays for Douglas Gray*, ed. H. Cooper and S. Mapstone. Oxford: Clarendon Press, 1997: 1–14, pp. 1–2.

[7] Significantly, there is practically no mention of the century in either *The Oxford* or *The Norton Anthology of English Literature*. A solitary exception is made in the case of Thomas Malory, who tends to be considered not as a single author, but as the conclusion of a cycle, the last and all-embracing representative of the Arthurian tradition.

[8] David Lawton's phrase, from his "Dullness and the Fifteenth Century", p. 761.

[9] I have deliberately kept out drama from my survey. Indeed, the best literary production of the fifteenth century in England is to be found among the miracle, mystery and morality plays, and it would be absurd to call "dull" a century which saw the rise of the Wakefield Master. Yet drama in this century has little to do with courtly literature, with perhaps the solitary exception of John Lydgate.

[10] Blake, p. 147.

Humphrey of Gloucester's munificent donations, while it was to be neglected almost to the point of extinction in the early sixteenth, being half-destroyed by Edward VI's protestant reformers: its donations drastically diminished, Oxford University as a whole was to be caught in the religious turmoil of the time (much more so than Cambridge), while very little money would be spent in the acquisition of new books.[11] Furthermore, during the reigns of Henry V and Henry VI a determined and conscious effort was made to raise English intellectual life to the level of the famous European centres of learning by inviting Italian humanists to work in a number of noble households, and by introducing into England and systematically translating into the vernacular classical and humanist texts; at the same time, the Lancastrian political power attempted to organise the production of writing within the intellectual framework of a political ideology. It was thus that the basis of a national culture, that might find a definition within national structures of power, was first set. Whether its results be meagre or not (the relation between the interference of political power and the meagreness of the results is still a matter of debate), it is impossible to dismiss the fifteenth century as a dull and unproductive age, or to judge it only from short-term results. If it does not find adequate expression in the equivalent of Chaucer or of the *Gawain*-poet, it prepares the terrain for a radical change in British intellectual life—a change that was to affect the literary output of the following century not only in terms

---

[11] The first signs of trouble had already appeared during the reign of Henry VIII, but Edward VI further tightened state control over university matters, particularly as concerned the fellows' and students' observance of protestant rites. The "dissolution year" brought a destruction of most of the manuscripts and books preserved in the colleges maintained in Oxford by the Benedictines (Canterbury College alone, before ceasing to exist in 1540, suffered the loss of about 300 manuscripts), while the University library experienced a serious decline: "The university library ceased to have an obvious function soon after it was built. It did not attract gifts and it did not have money to buy books and so it became a closed and out-of-date collection in the four decades after 1500 during which printed books took the place of manuscripts in other libraries" (N.R. Ker, "The Provision of Books", in *The History of the University of Oxford, vol. 3, The Collegiate University*, ed. by J. McConica, Oxford: Clarendon Press, 1987: 441–77, p. 465). "The library had entirely disappeared by 1556 and the library furniture was sold" (Elisabeth Leedham-Green, "University Libraries and Book-sellers", in *The Cambridge History of the Book in Britain, vol. 3: 1400–1557*, ed. by L. Hellinga and J.B. Trapp, Cambridge: Cambridge University Press, 1999: 316–53, p. 317). For further information on this point see also Claire Cross, "Oxford and the Tudor State from the Accession of Henry VIII to the Death of Mary", in McConica, pp. 117–49.

of models or genres, but also in terms of language. More important still, even if it was not a century of great original writers, it certainly seems to have been a century of great readers, translators and commentators—a characteristic it shares with the Italian fifteenth century.

It remains to be seen whether these changes can go under the name of humanism, or create a situation in any way comparable with the wider phenomenon of Italian humanism. The comparison has been attempted before, often resulting in a sort of intellectual match between England and Italy whose results inevitably spelled defeat for the latter. This is, for instance, what Fritz Caspari wrote in 1954:

> Throughout most of the fifteenth century, humanism in England was predominantly a formal, scholarly movement modeled on the imitation of Ciceronian Latin which then flourished in Italy. In this outward form it found a limited degree of acceptance. Thus, the new Latin style became increasingly the language of diplomacy, and men who could write and speak it could hope for employment in diplomatic functions. The inner core of humanism, the ethical, pedagogical, and political values that had so vitally affected Italian life, was but dimly perceived. Humanism did not play a decisive part in English intellectual life until, toward the end of the fifteenth century, these values began to be assimilated, and, in the sixteenth century, took a firm root as a definite body of doctrine.[12]

Seen in these terms, indeed, the comparison has no point and sheds no light on the state of English letters. Besides, it forces us to a very narrow perspective, forgetting the contribution of other European countries such as France, setting the Italian courts and scholars as a model, and the achievements of England as worthy of being measured only in terms of a closer or farther approach to this goal. But a different perspective may be useful. It is true that, if there was a form of humanism in fifteenth-century England, it expressed itself, at least in its early stages, mainly as an imitation of the achievements of Italian humanists. When Henry Beaufort, meeting Poggio Bracciolini at the Council of Constance, invited him to become a member of his retinue, or Duke Humphrey, with a less glamorous move, made Tito Livio Frulovisi his Latin secretary, they both attempted to transplant the intellectual atmosphere of Italian humanism onto English

---

[12] Fritz Caspari, *Humanism and the Social Order in Tudor England*, Chicago: University of Chicago Press, 1954, p. 1.

soil.[13] It must be admitted that the disappointment was severe on both sides—we read of Bracciolini often lamenting the poverty of English libraries (and the foulness of the English weather), while his patron plainly saw little use for his new follower.[14] The concern of the English aristocracy at this stage was more with individual humanists that might help further their patrons' political or personal advancement than with an abstract concept of humanism.

Six centuries later, however, historians can observe this intellectual movement in a unifying perspective, as a progress culminating in the truly golden Henrician era, and see, beyond the similarities between Italian and English humanism (similarities mainly acquired by imitation), differences that might be even more telling, and allow us a re-definition of the movement in England. We can also avoid the tendency, manifested even by modern scholars, towards a universalism of the spirit where European humanism is concerned. The predominance of Italian humanism, and its spreading towards the rest of Europe with a vehemence that had been rarely known before, occasionally make us forget the importance of regional differences.[15]

---

[13] The date of Bracciolini's arrival in England (c. 1418–22) was first chosen by Roberto Weiss as symbolic of the beginning of English humanism (*Humanism in England during the Fifteenth Century*, Oxford: Blackwell, 1941 (3rd ed. 1967), p. 7), and there seems to be no reason to change it; in a recent study, Clare Carroll chooses the same date, adding an equally symbolic date to mark the end of this phase, that is, Bishop William Waynflete's founding of Magdalen College School at Oxford (1480). See her "Humanism and English Literature in the Fifteenth and Sixteenth Centuries", in *The Cambridge Companion to Renaissance Humanism*, ed. by J. Kraye, Cambridge: Cambridge University Press, 1996, p. 246.

[14] As for Tito Livio Frulovisi, he was obviously not in the same league as Bracciolini, if the Latin works he has left are any guide (see, for instance, *Titi Livii Forojuliensis Vita Henrici Quinti*, ed. by T. Hearne, Oxoniae, 1716; for occasionally dismal instances of his Latin, see his comedies, published in *Opera Hactenus Inedita T. Livii de Frulovisiis de Ferraria*, ed. by C.W. Previté-Orton, Cambridge: Cantabrigiae typis Academiae, 1932). However, he did not seem completely happy about his situation either, though his complaints mainly concerned money and status.

[15] It is possible to apply to the English humanism an important observation Paul Oskar Kristeller made when defining the Italian Renaissance, stressing the uniqueness of the process Italy underwent in the Middle Ages in comparison with other European countries: "Scholars have become so accustomed to stress the universalism of the medieval church and of medieval culture and also to consider the Italian Renaissance as a European phenomenon that they are apt to forget that profound regional differences existed even during the Middle Ages". Paul Oskar Kristeller, "Humanism and Scholasticism in the Italian Renaissance," *Byzantion* 17 (1944–45), pp. 346–75, reprinted in *Renaissance Thought and its Sources*, ed. by M. Mooney, New York: Columbia University Press, 1979, p. 86.

They should be kept in mind when analysing the phenomenon of humanism in England, since they allow us to view it as the unique product of a unique situation rather than as a passive, imperfect and belated imitation of the superior Italian model.[16] To do so, it is indispensable to see this intellectual process against the background of the political system that saw its birth and supported it. As in the case of Italy, some of the key-figures of English humanism were not scholars or writers, but princes and politicians—Duke Humphrey of Gloucester being the most notable example. If he apparently surrounded himself with mediocre scholars and unremarkable poets (yet this, too, is a debatable point, as I shall try to show in this book), the long-range effects of his work show us that there were deeper reasons and a more complex plan underlying his patronage than a simple desire to enhance his status.

On the other hand, since the idea of humanism can be evaluated in its concurrent causes but must be seen especially in its output, an analysis of the writings the English fifteenth century produced is indispensable to give, quite simply, a *raison d'être* to this work. I have used the word 'writings' on purpose, preferring it to the more obvious expression 'literary production', because the latter choice of words forces us to take into consideration a modern concept of literature that has been often superimposed to the more catholic, medieval one.[17] Fifteenth-century poetry may have been for the greatest part imitative, academic, often dull. As for prose, it may tend to exclude originality altogether. What the modern literary critic tends to forget is that side by side with a disappointing poetic production there were translations, theological commentaries, scientific works, manuals, whether in prose or verse: books that sit uneasily within the boundaries of the modern definition of literature and that were,

---

[16] In the case of English humanism, as hinted at before, we may also allow for other factors, such as non-Italian influences: "probably some of the influences were French, coming already from the curia at Avignon" (Margaret Harvey, *England, Rome and the Papacy 1417–64. The Study of a Relationship*, Manchester: Manchester University Press, 1993, p. 40). This point, however, will be discussed in a later section.

[17] As John A. Burrow notes: "Modern canons of literature [. . .] have increasingly tended to exclude sermons, treatises, travel books, autobiographies, and other such specimens of non-fictional prose. In the case of Middle (and Old) English the strict application of this fictivity test would leave almost no prose literature at all" (*Medieval Writers and Their Work*, Oxford: Oxford University Press, 1982, p. 17).

besides, not necessarily written in English, but in any one of the three languages that were used in England at the time. The reduction of the terms of the discussion to what we would accept as literature (probably limiting our acceptance to literature in the vernacular), prevents us from seeing the intellectual activity of the century in its entirety: its extraordinary variety, its intricate link with contemporary politics, and its difficult relationship with the establishment of a national language; a few decades earlier, John Gower's trilingual tour de force had already presented an outstanding example of the latter attitude. Besides, in the European Middle Ages even poetry was often considered a means rather than an end, particularly by its makers. When Dante Alighieri wrote his *Divine Comedy*, his intent was clearly didactic and theological, poetry being the most adequate, elegant form in which to present his 'sublime' meditations. The fact that he is now read for his poetry, and very little for his theology, has nothing to do with the author's intentions, or even with the attitude of the audience for whom the poem was intended. By the same token, John Lydgate, by implication almost the literary spokesman of the century in England, can be read less as an inevitably dull poet and more as a translator, an erudite explorer of foreign texts or a willing spokesman for the powers that be. If his output in poetical terms is not to be compared with Dante's, they share a concept of poetry as a style equally suitable to scholarship as well as celebration, used to express an acknowledgement of the worth of their master (whether it was God or King Henry) as well as a lyric expression of their inner self. This does not make Lydgate a great poet, but it forces us to re-consider our perspective, and particularly the meaning we give to the concept of poetry in the Middle Ages, evidently different from the modern concept of poetry.[18]

By an analogous process, we are forced to reconsider the significance and range of humanism as a concept. This can be done by going back to the original meaning of the word *humanist*, and widening our range of observation. In the fifteenth century it had a decidedly narrow, almost practical use, as Nicholas Mann reminds us:

---

[18] It may be noted here that even in the recent work of a scholar such as Derek Brewer the misconception on the primary function of poetry is maintained. Brewer assumes a specific utilitarian role for prose in medieval literature, thus implicitly delegating the function of entertainment to verse. See his *English Gothic Literature*, London: Macmillan, 1983, p. 241.

The term *umanista* was used, in fifteenth-century Italian academic jargon, to describe a teacher or student of classical literature and the arts associated with it, including that of rhetoric. The English equivalent 'humanist' makes its appearance in the late sixteenth century with a very similar meaning.[19]

The association of the term with an activity, and not with a cultural idea, is very suggestive: to be a humanist was a profession, not a vocation, and the concept of humanism was linked with teaching and with rhetoric, not with philosophy and scholarship—a difference that should help us be rid of many prejudices associated with the role of humanists, whether in Italy or in England. As somebody who lived by his learning and wit, the humanist had to follow the times and go where his services might be required. On the other hand, as in Italy culture was being gradually detached from the hands of the ecclesiastical power, the humanist knew that his abilities might no longer be profitably employed in the monastery: "the future was with the courts, the cathedral schools and the cities".[20] In this perspective, it is not the humanists that determine the progressive secularisation of culture in fifteenth-century Italy: rather, events force the humanists to adapt themselves to a new course. Ideology and its practical consequences shape culture, rather than the other way round.

Thus, a different political situation may have determined a different version of humanism, and a different role for the humanist—which may explain why a comparison between England and Italy on this ground is largely useless, since history was shaping a very different course for the two countries. Once again, then, we find that history plays a relevant role in determining modes and contents of cultural investigation. This concerns not only the humanist as a man of

---

[19] Nicholas Mann, "The Origins of Humanism", in *The Cambridge Companion to Renaissance Humanism*, ed. by J. Kraye, Cambridge: Cambridge University Press, 1996, p. 1. I have quoted Mann as being one of the most recent contributions on the subject, but a very similar observation can be found, for instance, in Kristeller, p. 99. Significantly, Elizabeth Cox Wright makes the same point as concerns English humanism when she writes that it was "essentially not concerned with the arts, but practical in the sense of being applied to conduct, to religion, to reform and amelioration" ("Continuity in Fifteenth-Century English Humanism," *Publications of the Modern Language Association of America* 51: 1936, 370–6, p. 374). See also the definition proposed by J.B. Trapp in his "The Humanist Book", in *The Cambridge History of the Book in Britain, vol. 3: 1400–1557*, ed. by L. Hellinga and J.B. Trapp, Cambridge: Cambridge University Press, 1999: 285–315, p. 285.

[20] Mann, p. 4.

letters, but the humanist as a supporter of an ideology. We should distinguish between the long-term effects of humanism, and the activities that mainly occupied humanists or gave them standing, reputation, and a means of living. If philology was the highest achievement of the greatest among the humanists, their everyday activity concerned rather the field of rhetoric, thus marking, incidentally, their closeness with their medieval forefathers. Eloquence was not only part of their education, but also one of their fundamental tools, and doubtless the study of classical texts was at least initially undertaken as a means towards a very different end.[21] Modern students of humanism inevitably tend to concentrate on the philological study and on the discoveries of Latin and Greek classical texts, regardless of whether it was a means or an end, since it is this side of the humanists' activity that has carried the weightiest consequences. But even this activity may be better understood if we analyse the cultural context in which humanists moved, their motivations, their immediate aims, and particularly if we concentrate on their main fields of activity, that is, rhetoric, grammar and education.

The idea that rhetoric and grammar were the fields in which humanism found its origin and initial scope is important in our definition of this cultural movement. It allows us to get rid of some misconceptions about the humanists' scientific or philosophical activity (an activity that Kristeller already reduced considerably in size in his 1944 article), and to see them not as all-curious scholars, freelance writers naïvely fascinated by every branch of human knowledge, but as professionals operating in a very specific field. Above all, it allows us to re-define their role in the politics of their day. While we tend to have no delusions about the importance and the role of ideologues in modern politics, an almost Platonic confidence in the power of philosophers has often led us to overestimate the humanists' role and influence, and to confuse their intellectual activity, particularly if undertaken at the service of ideology, with philosophical speculation aimed at a definition of politics. But once again, this was not the concern of humanists. As James Hankins rightly observes,

> Unlike modern political scientists or medieval scholastic philosophers, Renaissance humanists were not occupied with political theory as such.

---

[21] Kristeller, p. 90.

> Professionally, humanists acted as teachers, diplomats, political propa-
> gandists, courtier and bureaucrats.[22]

Under this perspective, this seems an activity on the narrow rather
than the wide range, concerning immediate and day-to-day business
rather than higher issues. There are, both in England and in Italy,
humanist texts concerned with politics, but, particularly at this stage,
they deal almost exclusively with individual matters, appearing at the
same time heavily influenced by the political position of the present
patron. We will see in the following chapters how a good part of
Lydgate's production constitutes a very apt example of this attitude,
on a par with the writings of many Italian humanists. A study of
fifteenth-century humanist texts dealing with politics thus may give
us vital clues on the political currents of the day, and on the movements and ideas that concurred to the making of European history,
but we should not therefore believe that there was a structured intellectual activity having as its main purpose the construction of an
ideology. Rather, the humanist went in the direction he was required
to go, or where he believed it useful for his advancement to go,
employing his talents as they were required but barely believing he
was dealing with something more than historical contingency.

The real, more practical concerns of many humanists, and the
real object of much of their activity, can sometimes be glimpsed in
their letters, such as the one written in 1444 by Pier Candido Decembrio to Duke Humphrey, after the latter had received Decembrio's
version of Plato's *Republic* and had offered him a (not excessively
generous) annual stipend if the humanist would accept to be permanently in the Duke's service. Decembrio reminds Humphrey of
his offer, punctiliously quoting from the Duke's letter, and adds:

> Demum additis: "quicquid in tua re nos iudicabis facturos, facile impe-
> trabis". Itaque ne forte silendo displicerem, scripsi dominationi tue me

---

[22] James Hankins, "Humanism and the Origins of Modern Political Thought",
in *The Cambridge Companion to Renaissance Humanism*, ed. by J. Kraye, Cambridge:
Cambridge University Press, 1996, pp. 118–141, p. 118. Hankins then continues:
"Most humanist writings on politics therefore took the form of moral admonition
to rulers or panegyrics of the *patria* and its leaders. On the few occasions when
analysis was called for, the tone was usually one of cool detachment and pragma-
tism, rather than fiery ideological commitment. In general, while humanists were
frequently called upon to act as propagandists, they were not ideologues in the
modern sense, that is, intellectuals committed to a single political ideology to the
exclusion of all others" (p. 120).

provisionem non admittere; narravi tam fideliter necessitatem meam,
et pretium ville olim Francisci Petrarce piis precibus ab eadem postulavi, non quidem eo pacto ut necessitatem ullam sibi imponeret, sed
ut sciret qua via mihi complacere posset, quemadmodum littere tue
continebant; quam postulationem cum duplicatis edidissem litteris, usque
in presentem diem responsione indignus habitus sum.[23]

Petitions for money, or even, as in this case, loud clamours for an
adequate recompense are often to be found in the humanists' correspondence. After all, they lived by their intellectual efforts. We
may rightly observe that their new, almost professional status required
corresponding emoluments, though Decembrio's tone is that of a
suppliant rather than a claimant. Humphrey's implicit refusal (the
letter, as far as it is possible to know, was never answered) marked
the conclusion of the relations between the humanist and his disappointing patron.[24] The letter, however, is useful to determine the gap
between the humanist's and his patron's consideration of the former's work, but also to understand Decembrio's view of his work as
a professional service, not a vocation.

As for the link between humanism and education, once again, it
should be reconsidered for a correct evaluation of the phenomenon.
Italian humanists, for instance, were involved in university education, generally occupying the chairs of grammar and rhetoric. In the
fifteenth century, education still concerned only a very limited part
of the population, and tended to be individually oriented, not directed
to a whole community. Even once it had left the cloister and turned

---

[23] "Then you said: 'You will obtain whatever you think we should do'. So, not
to displease you by my silence, I wrote to your highness that I did not agree with
your offer; I faithfully told you my needs, and prayed for the price of the house
once belonging to Petrarch, not requiring it of you in the name of that pact, but
so as you could know how to please me, just as your letters said; and though I
reiterated my request in my letters, so far I have been considered unworthy of an
answer". The letter in its entirety is to be found in Sammut, pp. 200–3; this excerpt
p. 201.

[24] It seems indeed that from this point of view Duke Humphrey could be a very
unsatisfactory patron, as is shown not only by Decembrio's letter, but also by Antonio
Beccaria's epigram, also quoted in Sammut, p. 165: "Saepe mihi dicis: 'Si quid,
Becaria, voles, me Mane petas, quoniam mane petita dabo'. Mane peto, sed me
capis, optime princeps. Ast ego nil capio ac vespere deinde petam. Vespere cumque
peto, te dicis mane daturum: Mane venit: nihil est quod mihi mane datur" (You
often tell me, "If you want anything, Beccaria, ask me in the morning, and I will
give it to you". I ask you, but you cheat me, great prince. But I receive nothing
in the evening, and when I ask, you say you will give it to me in the morning:
The morning comes: nothing is given to me in the morning).

towards a lay, city- or university-based ground, education was not intended to promote the intellectual welfare of a nation: part of its contents may have changed, but its main target was still a restricted group of future leaders. However, then as now, education, especially of the very young, was considered one of the most powerful tools in the hands of political power, and as such was shaped and exploited; a case in point concerns England, and the house of Lancaster. The education proposed by the humanists happened to meet the rulers' needs, or rather, "as in Italy, humanism took root in England at a time when the education it promoted was suited to the needs of the governing classes".[25] There is little doubt in this case that humanism and the governing classes met each other's needs thanks to the influential patronage exercised by some members of the latter, especially insofar as the structuring of education might concern future rulers; there are fifteen years in early fifteenth-century England, between 1422 and 1437, in which the country was only nominally ruled by a king, Henry VI, who was in his minority, and whose guardians might have striven to make his education an effective tool towards the shaping of this king's future politics. Since Henry was crowned king when he was only nine months old, his kingship-oriented education could start at a very early stage, and be carefully planned.[26] Thus, at least in part, the development of early humanism in England could be measured in terms of the shaping of ideology through the means of the education of the young King, and some of the books or translations which were commissioned to humanists at the time might have a very specific, didactic purpose.

We have quoted Clare Carroll on the relation between education and the needs of the governing classes. Carroll's article continues thus:

> Since, however, this humanist programme was also appropriated and deployed to produce great literary works, it can be said to have been much more than a mere pragmatic tool to attain influence and power. Indeed, humanist-inspired works of literature even allowed for scepticism about the principles underlying the primary realm of power—

---

[25] Carroll, p. 246.
[26] An interesting if occasionally controversial discussion on this point can be found in Susanne Saygin, *Humphrey, Duke of Gloucester (1390–1447) and the Italian Humanists*, Leiden: Brill, 2002.

the economy, politics, institutional religion—as well as criticism of the aims of humanism itself.[27]

It is true that, centuries later, we may form an estimate of humanism on the basis of literary works that were produced independently of the current principles of power, or even as a reaction to them— Lorenzo Valla remains to this day the symbol of the free-thinking humanist who is not afraid to attack power at its very core. This very consideration, however, forces us to study this uneasy relation between intellectual and political activity as the breeding ground of much that was produced in English humanism. If the political situation in fifteenth-century Italy is so confused and fragmented as to make such considerations extremely controversial, whatever their issue, it might be possible to draw clearer conclusions in the case of England, where the modern idea of nation had crystallised already, and any struggle for power, be it conducted from the ecclesiastical or from the lay side, had constantly to reckon with the establishment and the universally acknowledged existence of a reigning dynasty. Many forces might struggle for the control of power, but it seems that the symbolic centre of such power at least was, and is, clearly recognisable. Ecclesiastical hierarchies had, at least until 1534, another point of reference in the Roman Curia, but the lay nobility knew that in political affairs the ultimate decision would always rest within the royal court, even if not always with the actual King.

Intellectual history then might profit from a deeper analysis of political history. In particular, our knowledge of early English humanism, a phenomenon which is still so little known and even curiously amorphous in places, might certainly gain from a study of its relations with political power, and even of the struggles that were behind the patronage of Italian (as well as English) humanists in England. A number of points should be taken into account: for example, the fact that if we read English humanism as the transmission of Italian values into England (however limiting this choice be), then the Papal officials and the Englishmen who visited the Roman court or (at a later stage) attended Italian universities are a preferential channel. The coincidence between the early stages of humanism and the rise of the vernacular as the language of officialdom also deserves a closer

---

[27] Carroll, p. 246.

scrutiny. As we can see, politics, social history, and a very concrete analysis of the literary and non-literary texts still available should all concur to make the picture clearer for us.

The choice of focusing on a single relevant patron, Duke Humphrey of Gloucester, may make us lose sight of the general landscape; but Duke Humphrey, besides being the most prominent patron of writers and scholars at the time, and a munificent donor of books, may have been connected with the education of King Henry VI, in his role as Protector of England during the latter's minority. He became involved throughout his life in political competitions with ecclesiastical authority, and ultimately in a losing battle with his peers over the control of a still underage and weak king. After his death, he achieved a fame that went far beyond his political merits, and sometimes was wide of the mark as regards his political inclinations. Modern historiography tends to underestimate his role as a politician, while there is a certain unease about his actual importance as a patron of scholars and writers; it may be added that the two roles have very rarely been evaluated side by side. From the point of view of the modern intellectual historian, he is ideally placed to represent the achievements and the contradictions of English humanism in its early stages.

CHAPTER ONE

ROBERTO WEISS'S INHERITANCE
AND THE CURRENT STATE OF STUDIES

A survey of the critical literature on the fifteenth century shows us that English humanism is a subject of controversy as far as its very existence is concerned, and if no scholar disputes the claims and achievements of late humanism, that is, the period roughly spanning from William Caxton to Thomas More, the investigation of early humanism is still at a very tentative stage. While we are still discussing general issues connected with the idea of English humanism, and before observing in detail the activity of Duke Humphrey and of some of the scholars and writers he called to work near him, it would be useful to take as complete an account as possible of the critical debate on the subject, concentrating our attention roughly on the last hundred years. In doing so, it is inevitable to point to Roberto Weiss's work, and particularly to his 1941 book, *Humanism in England During the Fifteenth Century*, as a milestone—however much he may be criticised now, and however far scholarly investigation may have progressed, there is no doubt that Weiss marked an era in fifteenth-century studies, and scholars and critics after him have had to confront their results with his achievements, one way or another. It is perhaps to be regretted that no comprehensive study of English humanism has followed Weiss's, and that at the present moment the subject lacks the kind of updated reference guide that we can find for the phenomenon as it developed in other European countries. On the other hand, it may be interesting to see how far studies on early humanism and on the relevant texts had progressed before Weiss's contribution, even if in many cases the critical contributions of the first half of the twentieth century (generally concentrating upon individual writers, such as Lydgate or John Capgrave, and overlooking the link between intellectual and political history) resolved themselves in little more than a paving of the way. Accordingly, this chapter is divided in three sections—the last including a discussion not only on the aftermath of Weiss's achievements and on later reactions to his work, but on the more recent scholarly activity, so as to provide the reader with a perspective of the present situation of studies on early fifteenth-century humanism in England, and in particular on the role Duke Humphrey of Gloucester has been assigned in historical and critical studies on this movement.

Early studies on English humanism

The role Humphrey played in the re-birth of the University of Oxford has been acknowledged by scholars (as well as by the University itself) throughout the centuries; one early instance is the mention Humphrey receives towards the end of the eighteenth century in Thomas Warton's *History of English Poetry*.[1] Warton's definition of the Duke of Gloucester is "a singular promoter of literature, and, however unqualified for political intrigues, the common patron of the scholars of the times"[2]—an evaluation that has been repeated often in the following years. However, we begin to collect substantial evidence of the scholars' interest in Duke Humphrey of Gloucester and his literary entourage only in the late nineteenth century, when no less than two editions of the Middle English translation of Palladius's *De Re Rustica* were published; the later and better of them unhesitatingly linked this work with Duke Humphrey's cultural milieu, on the basis of precise references appearing in the text, and particularly in a prologue the translator had added to the original Latin text.[3] It might be said that the words of the anonymous Palladius translator, for the first time available to modern readers, evoked the image of a circle of scholars and writers, both English and Italian, gathered under the munificent protection of a patron who is depicted as adorned of every virtue and proficient in every branch of knowledge, to the point of correcting the writer's own metre. It seems apt, therefore, to quote the passage at the beginning of our investigation on the scholars' awareness of the development of humanism in England:

---

[1] Thomas Warton, *History of English Poetry from the Close of the Eleventh to the Commencement of the Eighteenth Century*, London, 1774–81, pp. 344–6.

[2] Warton, p. 344. Warton also assumes that Humphrey gave about 600 manuscripts to Oxford, and slightly exaggerates the role of the Italian humanists in the English courts.

[3] *Palladius on Husbondrie*, ed. by B. Lodge, Early English Text Society, London: Trübner, 1873, repr. 1988; *The Middle-English Translation of Palladius De Re Rustica*, ed. by M. Liddell, Berlin: E. Ebering, 1896.

For clergie, or knyghthod, or husbondrie,
That oratour, poete, or philosophre
hath tretid, told, or taught, in memorie
Vche lef and lyne hath he, as shette in cofre;
Oon nouelte vnnethe is hym to profre.
Yit Whethamstede, and also Pers de Mounte,
Titus, and Anthony, and y laste ofre
And leest. Our newe is old in hym tacounte

But that his vertu list vs exercise,
And moo as fele as kan in vertu do.
He, sapient, is diligent to wise
Alle ignoraunt, and y am oon of tho.
He taught me metur make, and y soso
Hym counturfete, and hope, aftir my sorow,
In God and hym to glade; and aftir woo,
To ioy, and aftir nyght, to sey good morow.[4]

Thus scholars and intellectual historians were faced with what seemed irrefutable evidence of the existence of humanism in early fifteenth-century England. It is perhaps to be regretted that Liddell's edition, based on the very reliable Fitzwilliam manuscript and presenting a far more complete text that Lodge's, should now be accessible only with some difficulty, while there have been numerous reprints of the inferior Early English Text Society edition. In a "Temporary Preface" to the 1896 volume, Liddell promised that a fuller discussion of the linguistic novelties in the text—and perhaps of their links with the cultural milieu from which this text originated—would appear in a second volume which was unfortunately never published (and possibly never written), and which might have constituted a very important contribution to the discussion on English humanism. The Palladius translation has subsequently been an object of interest, if only of a sporadic nature: a linguistic study of the text appeared between the publication of the two above-mentioned editions.[5] Unfortunately, as it referred to the earlier edition, deriving from an incomplete manuscript, it did not take into consideration the new elements, specifically

---

[4] Liddell, p. 22. A full discussion of this point is to be found in Alessandra Petrina, "The Middle English Translation of Palladius's De Agricultura", in *The Medieval Translator. Traduire au Noyen Age 8*, ed. by R. Voaden, R. Tixier, T. Sanchez Roura and J.R. Rytting, Turnhout: Brepols, 2003: 317–28.

[5] Carl Struever, *Die Mittelenglische Übersetzung des Palladius. Ihr Verhältnis zur Quelle und Ihre Sprache*, Halle: Ehrhardt Kanas, 1887.

concerning Duke Humphrey's milieu, that the second edition would bring to light.

In the same years in which the two modern editions of the Middle English Palladius were appearing, though independently from them, scholars began to feel some interest in Duke Humphrey's activity as a literary patron: historians such as Mandell Creighton, W.D. MacRay, Mario Borsa and W.L. Newman wrote articles on Humphrey's correspondence with Italian humanists, and particularly with Pier Candido Decembrio;[6] some Italian scholars devoted particular attention to the activity of the Duke's "poeta et orator", Tito Livio Frulovisi;[7] Humphrey's activity as a book collector was described by Paget Toynbee, particularly in connection with manuscripts of Italian works,[8] while the first tentative accounts on the size and the nature of Humphrey's library began to be drawn, on the basis of the extant lists of manuscripts donated to the University of Oxford.[9] The Duke's relations with contemporary English writers began to be investigated in particular by Eleanor Prescott Hammond, first in a series of articles appearing in *Anglia*,[10] then in her volume *English Verse Between Chaucer and Surrey*, an annotated anthology of fifteenth-century poets.[11] In her articles, Hammond appeared especially interested in the role of John Lydgate, putting his poetic production in historical perspective by

---

[6] Mandell Creighton, "Some Literary Correspondence of Humphrey, Duke of Gloucester", *English Historical Review* 10: 1895, 99–104; W.D. MacRay, "Early Dedications to Englishmen by Foreign Authors and Editors", *Bibliographica* 1: 1895, 324–47; Mario Borsa, "P.C. Decembrio e l'umanesimo in Lombardia", *Archivio Storico Lombardo* 20: 1893, 5–75, 358–441, and "Correspondence of Humphrey Duke of Gloucester and Pier Candido Decembrio", *English Historical Review* 19: 1904, 509–26; W.L. Newman, "The Correspondence of Humphrey, Duke of Gloucester, and Pier Candido Decembrio", *The English Historical Review* 20: 1905, 484–98.

[7] Remigio Sabbadini, "Tito Livio Frulovisio umanista del sec. XV", *Giornale Storico della Letteratura Italiana* 103: 1934, 55–73.

[8] Toynbee, Paget, *Dante in English Literature from Chaucer to Cary (c. 1380–1844)*, London: Methuen, 1909, pp. 20–22; "The Dante MSS. presented to Oxford by Duke Humphrey", *The Times Literary Supplement*, 18 March 1920, 187; "Duke Humphrey's Dante, Petrarch, and Boccaccio MSS.", *The Times Literary Supplement*, 22 April 1920, 256.

[9] H.H.E. Craster, "Index to Duke Humphrey's Gifts to the Old Library of the University in 1439, 1441, and 1444", *Bodleian Quarterly Record* 1: 1914–16, 131–35.

[10] "Lydgate and the Duchess of Gloucester", *Anglia* 27: 1904, 381–98; "Two British Museum Manuscripts (Harley 2251 and Adds. 34360). A Contribution to the Bibliography of John Lydgate", *Anglia* 28: 1905, 1–28, 143–44; "Poet and Patron in the *Fall of Princes*: Lydgate and Humphrey of Gloucester", *Anglia* 38: 1914, 121–36; "Lydgate and Coluccio Salutati", *Modern Philology* 25: 1927–8, 49–57.

[11] London: Duke University Press, 1927.

considering the patrons for whom he wrote, particularly Humphrey Duke of Gloucester; in referring to the Duke, Hammond calls him "the English Maecenas of the fifteenth century".[12] She also draws the reader's attention to Humphrey's first wife, Jacqueline of Hainault. The book, on the other hand, working on a wider perspective, analyses the phenomenon of fifteenth-century writing without being fettered by a restriction to a concept of literature as original production, but rather taking into consideration non-fictive texts such as translations, commentaries, books of nurture. The annotated anthology that is the result of this effort is a comprehensive mirror of fifteenth-century poetic writing, often discussing in its introductory notes to the individual writers the occasion that prompted a composition, and the role a patron might have had not only in deciding upon a text to be translated, but even in suggesting a metaphor or an allusion.[13] Both the book and the articles are of great interest to us as they indicate, in contrast with the attitude of many literary critics in the twentieth century, that the correct approach to fifteenth-century English literature might be from the point of view of intellectual history rather than of traditional literary criticism. But there was not as yet an attempt to see this cultural movement as an English variant of humanism, or to set it against the context of contemporary events such as the arrival of a number of Italian humanists in England, and the introduction of classical and Italian texts in English libraries.

Lewis Einstein's book, *The Italian Renaissance in England*,[14] published in the same years as Hammond's earliest work, marks what is probably the first attempt in the twentieth century to see in Duke Humphrey's work, and in the activity of his circle, the beginning of a cultural movement that would reach far into the sixteenth century. A great merit of Einstein's book is its treatment of various aspects of the Italian influence in England ("from the beginning of the fifteenth century until the death of Elizabeth"),[15] in order to provide an overall view of the movement, centring, in its early phase, upon the 'rebirth' of the University of Oxford. The main, ideological shortcoming of the book, on the other hand, is probably due to the view

---

[12] "Lydgate and the Duchess of Gloucester", p. 382.
[13] Possibly more exhaustively than Derek Pearsall's recent *Chaucer to Spenser. An Anthology of Writings in English 1375–1575*, Oxford: Blackwell, 1999.
[14] New York: The Columbia University Press, 1902.
[15] Einstein, p. vii.

taken in Einstein's times of a supposedly sharp separation between Middle Ages and Renaissance, and is evident in passages such as this:

> during the fifteenth century in England, learning was almost entirely confined to the universities, and to churchmen who for the most part had received their education in colleges.[16]

This dismissal of the ecclesiastical contribution to fifteenth-century culture in England, as we shall see, is one of the major blunders not only of Einstein's, but of a surprising part of twentieth-century criticism on the subject, resting as it does on a traditional division between *divinae* and *humanae litterae* that sees in humanism a staunch defender of the latter—an attitude associated with the equally traditional division between Middle Ages and humanism, the former considered as looking upon learning as "the handmaid to theology".[17]

As for the role of Humphrey of Gloucester, Einstein gives it almost dramatic relevance, associating it with a supposedly central role of the University of Oxford as representative of the cultural history of English Renaissance:

> In the early years of the fifteenth century, when the lowest depths of intellectual torpor had been reached in England, the efforts of a single man were to bring about a great change and introduce new rays of light. In Duke Humphrey of Gloucester, son of Henry the Fourth, and in the cultivated circle of his friends, the intellectual hopes of his country were centred.[18]

In spite of this solemn tone, Einstein later admits that Humphrey's influence, if momentarily of great impact, had little lasting effect, though he does not link this with Humphrey's alternating and finally declining political fortune. The Duke is devoted a dozen pages at the beginning of the book; then, Einstein adopts a synchronic approach to the issue, devoting each chapter to a different social or professional group—courtiers, merchants, travellers and so on—that might have reacted in various ways to the cultural changes of the English fifteenth century. It is rather surprising that Roberto Weiss, taking stock of previous critical literature before embarking on his groundbreaking work on English humanism, should not acknowledge Einstein's

---

[16] Einstein, p. 2.
[17] Einstein, p. 2.
[18] Einstein, p. 3.

contribution, shortly dismissing his book as "a short and superficial survey":[19] for all its approximation Einstein's work presents *in nuce* some of the intuitions that would afterwards constitute the backbone of subsequent work (including Weiss's own studies). Even Einstein's attempt to work through categories that might be affected by the new intellectual climate or by the increasing cultural exchange with Italy helps to throw new light on the movement, though some of his conclusions are indeed ingenuous.

The role of Humphrey as a patron of English poets was also recognised by Karl Julius Holzknecht in his *Literary Patronage in the Middle Ages*,[20] in which particular attention is paid to the literary production of John Lydgate, who had been dedicating poems to an extraordinary number of famous and less famous people, and of Thomas Hoccleve. Holzknecht, however, even if he correctly highlighted and in part analysed the corpus of *De Regimine Principum* literature produced at the time in England, and distinguished between the simple dedication and books written on request, did not further explore the connection between patronage and ideology. This seems to be a common trait of most early scholars investigating the English fifteenth century: Duke Humphrey is generally seen as an extraordinary and perhaps unmerited gift to the budding English humanists, and there is no further exploration into his motives apart from a generic admiration for his devoted activity:

> That he was a patron of letters and more than a dilettante is amply attested, and of his taste there can be no doubt. Nor was his patronage a pose adopted for the popularity it would bring. [. . .] Humphrey [. . .] occupies an interesting position in the Renaissance movement and the development of the nationalities in Europe, which is mirrored by the adoption of the vernacular languages for scholarly purposes.[21]

However, a decisive contribution to the evaluation of Duke Humphrey both as a politician and as a patron of humanists was to be given by the monumental, still unsurpassed biography written by Kenneth H. Vickers in 1907.[22] Vickers's work was clearly defined in scope,

---

[19] Roberto Weiss, *Humanism in England during the Fifteenth Century*, Oxford: Blackwell, 1941 (3rd ed. 1967), p. 5. Apart from any other consideration, to call "short" a 420-page survey seems rather far-fetched.

[20] New York: The Collegiate Press, 1923.

[21] Holzknecht, pp. 150-1.

[22] Kenneth H. Vickers, *Humphrey Duke of Gloucester. A Biography*, London: Constable, 1907.

since he had no intention to attempt an evaluation of the phenomenon
of English humanism. But his research on the fascinating and contradictory figure of the Duke of Gloucester allows us to consider the
politician along with the man of letters (Vickers presents the reader
with an extremely accurate survey of Humphrey's relations with both
Italian and English intellectuals), the ruthless if occasionally blundering man of ambition together with the legend that was created
around him after his rather mysterious death. It is probably because
Duke Humphrey is such a controversial figure to analyse that Vickers,
a historian rather than a literary scholar, can point to historical or
social events that were extremely significant for the development of
culture, and whose relevance the literary critic may not realise in
full. Introducing the period of bitter dissension in which Humphrey
lived with the words "no period of English history is less romantic
than that in which Humphrey of Gloucester's life was cast",[23] Vickers
contrasts this political turmoil with the intellectual fervour that, sweeping all over Europe, was bound to reach England too. In considering the phenomenon of Italian humanism, the historian reiterates
the division between Middle Ages and Renaissance that, as we have
seen in the introduction, has created an obstacle to a fuller understanding of both Italian and English humanism; at the same time,
however, his view of the cultural situation in England, in relation
with Humphrey's very singular personality, helps us in the reconstruction of an intellectual and social climate generated or at least
influenced by the echoes of humanism:

> Humphrey felt the full force of this movement: his life was moulded
> thereby. His activity and many-sided energy found their origin in this
> new spirit. His fervid imagination, which led him into impossible pro-
> jects, his love of display, above all, his desire to stamp his individual-
> ity on the politics of his country, all sprang from the new realisation
> which was vouchsafed to him—the realisation of his own individual-
> ity. In England, the new spirit was more manifest politically than in
> isolated individuals; the country was throwing off the feudal system,
> her merchants and traders were demanding the acknowledgement of
> their importance, peasants and townsmen alike were preparing for that
> long, uphill struggle which has culminated in the parliamentary sys-
> tem of the nineteenth century.[24]

---

[23] Vickers, p. 340.
[24] Vickers, p. 341.

The juxtaposition—Humphrey's determined individuality on one side, the ascent of a new class claiming political recognition on the other— would make, and perhaps does make, a rather anachronistic figure of Duke Humphrey: a nobleman fighting to uphold the vision of a splendid monarchy that, in the years between Agincourt and Henry VI's feeble reign, had lost most of its splendour. In spite of his popularity with Londoners (a popularity that, seen in retrospective, might look of more consequence than it was, since it greatly increased after his death, and may partly be connected with the mysterious rumours surrounding his downfall), Gloucester remained solidly linked to the court, and looked for alliances among his peers and the ecclesiastical hierarchies. Also, on more than one occasion he deliberately antagonised Parliament, and was relentless in his pursuits of Lollards, evidently blind to the social changes that this religious movement was bringing. He thus saw little of the social change in fifteenth-century England. Vickers's conclusion to the previously quoted passage is therefore apt: "Humphrey, with all his senses ready to receive the message of the Renaissance movement, did not, however, grasp its true significance in England."[25]

Along with Vickers's historical contribution, we can perhaps take into consideration another work that is not concerned specifically with English humanism but offers precious indications for a better understanding of the movement; I allude to Charles L. Kingsford's *English Historical Literature in the Fifteenth Century*,[26] published in 1913 and followed, first by *English History in the Fifteenth Century*[27] and, twelve years later, by what became an almost companion volume to the first, *Prejudice and Promise in Fifteenth Century England*.[28] Kingsford does not attempt anything but the most cursory literary evaluation of the texts he is surveying; he repeats the old cliché that "though, with the exception of Malory, there is no great literary name in the fifteenth century, that age was not barren,"[29] but he also correctly highlights the diffusion of the vernacular as "the common medium

---

[25] Vickers, p. 341.

[26] Charles L. Kingsford, *English Historical Literature in the Fifteenth Century*, Oxford: Clarendon Press, 1913.

[27] Charles L. Kingsford, *English History in the Fifteenth Century and the Historical Plays of Shakespeare*, London: National Home-Reading Union, 1914.

[28] Charles L. Kingsford, *Prejudice and Promise in Fifteenth Century England*, Oxford: Clarendon Press, 1925.

[29] Kingsford, *English History*, pp. 3–4.

of written intercourse,"[30] and insists on the importance of the study
of fifteenth-century chronicles and histories to gain a more correct
appreciation of later texts such as Shakespeare's history plays. His
1913 book in particular is a useful guide to a number of texts that are
largely ignored by the majority of literary critics and that can offer
a great help towards the understanding of the intellectual development and the concept of history in the late Middle Ages in England.
It is a careful survey of all the fifteenth-century historical literature
that is still extant: chronicles, biographies, letters, and even poems
and ballads containing historical allusions. Thus Kingsford can underline the role of Duke Humphrey as a collector of manuscripts, and
his munificence as a donor, but can also note how, with his correspondence with Italian humanists, "he established a link between the
revival of Letters on the Continent and in England."[31] Of particular
importance is his reading of Tito Livio Frulovisi's *Vita Henrici Quinti*
as having "a distinct influence in the development of English historical literature"[32]—a point that has often been made subsequently,
even if Frulovisi is far from claiming the title of first humanist historian in England, a title unanimously attributed to Polydore Vergil.

Kingsford's 1925 volume, originating from a series of lectures, does
not have the reference value of *English Historical Literature* but elabo-
rates on the material presented in the former book; some of the sections lay particular stress on the author's favourite motif of the
relationship between fifteenth-century chronicles and Shakespearean
drama, while in other cases the author's interest is more specifically
historical and sociological. When comparing the political ferment of
the age with its literary barrenness, he devotes a few lines to the
"zeal for learning" that found expression first in the English scholars visiting Italy, then in the role that the introduction of printing
had by the end of the century;[33] but he does not link this phenomenon with Humphrey's activity, or with the arrival of Italian
scholars in England.

There is no doubt, as I have observed above, that these studies,
though not specifically dealing with the concept of humanism in
England, helped its definition. This is clearly shown in the volume

---

[30] Kingsford, *English History*, pp. 3–4.
[31] Kingsford, *English Historical Literature*, p. 4.
[32] Kingsford, *English Historical Literature*, p. 5.
[33] Kingsford, *Prejudice and Promise*, p. 21.

that followed Einstein's work, twenty-nine years later, that is, Walter
Schirmer's *Der englische Frühhumanismus*,[34] once again attempting a thorough overview of the phenomenon and concentrating, rather than
on social or professional groups, on individual scholars and patrons.
Duke Humphrey duly appears in this volume, together with Henry
Beaufort and his circle, Bekynton and Whethamstede, and a number of other English humanists including the later Linacre, Grocin
and Latimer. Conversely, poets that had access to humanist circles
such as Lydgate or Capgrave receive only a cursory mention. The
author explicitly keeps the focus of his analysis on the relationship
between Italian and English humanism; on the other hand, his work
is probably the first survey on the subject that is so comprehensive
and scholarly, and that can be used as a reference even today,
though, as Weiss would observe later, too little attention is paid to
manuscript sources. A later study by the same scholar, centring on
the poet John Lydgate,[35] realises the union of literary criticism and
historical perspective that is still so rare in modern scholarly writing
on the subject. Schirmer's intuition in this case was that, whatever
the critical judgement on Lydgate's art, he was invaluable as a literary seismograph of his age, a receptive annotator of contemporary
events, and a flexible instrument for contemporary propaganda. Thus
his study of the poet presents a parallel survey of Lydgate's age, covering the years from Edward III's reign to Henry VI's. What we do
miss in Schirmer's analysis, perhaps, is a closer insight into the question of patronage.

Of later work, appearing before the publication of Weiss's main
volume, there is little to be said. Douglas Bush's *The Renaissance and
English Humanism*[36] did not take into account the early fifteenth century, believing that "the real character of English humanism did not
definitely emerge until the end of the fifteenth century",[37] and referring readers to Schirmer. On the other hand, Elizabeth Cox Wright,
in an article published in 1936 that reviewed Schirmer's work and

---

[34] Walter F. Schirmer, *Der englische Frühhumanismus. Ein Betrag zur Englischen Literatur-
Geschichte der 15. Jahrhundert*, Leipzig: Bernherd Tauchnitz, 1931.
[35] Walter F. Schirmer, *John Lydgate, a Study in the Culture of the Fifteenth Century*,
transl. Ann E. Knepp, London: Methuen, 1961 (the original, German edition was
published in 1957).
[36] Douglas Bush, *The Renaissance and English Humanism*, Toronto: The University
of Toronto Press, 1939.
[37] Bush, p. 70.

corrected some of its assumptions,[38] attempted a re-definition of English humanism. It was wrong, in Wright's view, to maintain a strict division between an early humanism characterised by the presence of patrons who would call scholars and writers to work at their court, and a late humanism marked by seekers, going after the new learning in Italy: "the facts are that the early seekers went to Italy during the period of Humphrey's and Bekynton's patronage, and that Grey and Tiptoft, although seekers, were also patrons."[39] Wright's revaluation of the third quarter of the fifteenth century, and her identification of a pattern of continuity between the early and the later period, give the reader a series of useful indications for a better understanding of the intellectual climate of the English fifteenth century: she correctly stresses the importance not only of the much-mentioned Council of Constance, but also of the later Council of Basel, and of the occasions the latter offered for the exchange of ideas and books. She also suggests that further light should be thrown upon a number of English scholars that have remained relatively obscure, such as Andrew Holes or Robert Fleming. Unfortunately, the brevity of Wright's essay does not allow for a detailed analysis on her part, but her contribution should not therefore be ignored.

Roberto Weiss

In his seminal work *Humanism in England during the Fifteenth Century*, Roberto Weiss attempted a definition of English humanism—if not for the first time, as we have seen in the previous section, yet with a range of observation and a depth of analysis that had never been used before. The work had started as a doctoral thesis in 1938, and became a book in 1941; a number of addenda were inserted in successive editions, and Weiss subsequently supplemented his work with a series of articles and essays;[40] besides, some of his unpublished

---

[38] Elizabeth Cox Wright, "Continuity in English Humanism", *Publications of the Modern Language Association of America* 51: 1936: 370–6.

[39] Wright, p. 371.

[40] Among the most significant are "New Light on Humanism in England during the Fifteenth Century," *Journal of the Warburg and Courtauld Institutes* 14: 1951, 21–33; "An Unnoticed MS of Humfrey, Duke of Gloucester," *The Bodleian Library Record* 5: 1955, 123–24; "Humphrey Duke of Gloucester and Tito Livio Frulovisi",

papers reveal that he was engaged upon further work on the subject before his death.[41] For the most part, however, these smaller contributions were little more than glosses to the main work, while many of the assumptions he included in the first book remained unchallenged in the following years and in later publications. If later scholarship has corrected some of Weiss's assumptions, updating or adjusting some of his notions and clearing minor as well as major matters, it must be admitted that his book has not been surpassed or even matched by anything of comparable magnitude, and that any scholar dealing with the English fifteenth century in terms of intellectual history must take it into account.

The first merit of Weiss's work is its sheer scope: his survey is accurate and complete, ranging from Poggio Bracciolini's meeting with Henry Beaufort, Bishop of Winchester, at the Council of Constance, to the accession of Henry VII, and focusing upon the transition from medieval to Renaissance culture in England; while following to a certain extent Schirmer's example as regards the structure of his work, Weiss certainly established less naïve boundaries than Einstein had done, since the latter linked the humanists' activity merely with the goodwill of individual patrons, rather than with wider political movements; his intuition as concerns the important role played by Lancastrian politicians in contemporary intellectual life has been subsequently confirmed by archival discoveries or philological studies; equally fundamental is his research into Anglo-Italian relationships and their consequences in cultural terms. Weiss focuses, besides, on a number of humanists in England, underlying the extent and originality of their contributions, and trying to identify a pattern of continuity throughout the century.

A discussion concerned not only with Weiss's contribution, but with the distance covered since, starts inevitably with a sentence

---

in *Fritz Saxl 1890–1948. A Volume of Memorial Essays from his Friends in England*, ed. by D.J. Gordon, London: Thomas Nelson, 1957: 218–27; "The Private Collector and the Revival of Greek Learning", in *The English Library before 1700*, ed. by F. Wormald and C.E. Wright, London, 1958: 112–35; "Portrait of a Bibliophile XI: Humphrey, Duke of Gloucester, d. 1447," *The Book Collector* 13: 1964, 161–70.

[41] See, for instance, a typescript with a partial transcription of Frulovisi's *Hunfroidos*, together with a communication of another scholar (probably Butler) to Weiss, entitled "Reflections on the work of a certain Tito Livio di Forlì by one who is of opinion that either the aforesaid Tito or he himself should never have been born", now at the Warburg Institute, London.

occurring in the opening paragraph of his book; it is a statement
that appears to have been quietly taken for granted in subsequent
studies, even in the sharp criticism later scholars have levelled at
Weiss's work. Weiss is here giving a definition of humanism:

> 'Humanism' will be understood to embrace the whole range of clas-
> sical studies and activities as conceived by the Italians from the days
> of Petrarch and by 'humanist' [is meant] the scholar who studied the
> writings of ancient authors without fear of supernatural anticiceronian
> warnings, searched for manuscripts of lost or rare classical texts, col-
> lected the works of classical writers, and attempted to learn Greek and
> write like the ancient authors of Rome.[42]

In itself, the definition is not explicitly concerned with England, and
may be simply read as an anticipation of what Kristeller would write
a few years after Weiss's book in an article I shall be discussing
shortly:

> By humanism we mean merely the general tendency of the age to
> attach the greatest importance to classical studies, and to consider clas-
> sical antiquity as the common standard and model by which to guide
> all cultural activities.[43]

Such a perspective is clearly concerned with one of the most important aspects of European humanism, and moreover with the aspect
that has meant more for the cultural development to come. It would
perhaps be better if the definition was not read to the exclusion of
everything else that constituted the phenomenon we know call humanism. Though, in comparison, Weiss's definition is a little more extreme,
it is adequately applicable to the Italian situation between the fourteenth and the fifteenth century, in spite of later tendencies on the
part of the scholarly community to highlight a pattern of continuity
between Middle Ages and humanism. Yet a serious fault of this
definition is that it is a description rather than a definition, and a
description of one of the possible forms of humanism. Once used as
a postulate and applied to a European perspective, it inevitably
describes the shortcomings of English humanism; it postulates Italy
as a model. The reference to classical studies and to the fear of

---

[42] Weiss, *Humanism in England*, p. 1.
[43] Paul Oskar Kristeller, "Humanism and Scholasticism in the Italian Renaissance,"
Byzantion 17: 1944–5, 346–75, reprinted in *Renaissance Thought and its Sources*, ed. by
M. Mooney, New York: Columbia University Press, 1979: 85–105, pp. 87–88.

"supernatural anticiceronian warnings" is very much out of place in fifteenth-century England; in particular, the distinction, implied by Weiss's formula, between classical and non-classical studies may be felt as a criticism of theological and scholastic studies that, throughout the Middle Ages, had shadowed or more often misinterpreted classical texts (the case of the *Ovide moralizée* being the most obvious). This perspective has now been for the most part refuted: making allowances for undiscovered manuscripts, it is unfair to accuse the Middle Ages of lack of interest in the classics, or worse, of an interest so biased as to see the classics merely *sub specie Christianitatis*. A very obvious fact should be remembered: the expression "middle Ages" covers over a millennium of European history, which means that cultural generalisations are even more dangerous in this case than with "the modern age" or any other such heading (which at least have the merit of encompassing a shorter period); besides, this millennium included centuries of startling intellectual fervour, such as the twelfth century, and slacker times, but a scholar would be hard put to demonstrate a dismissal of Latin classics on the part of medieval intellectuals at any given period. If Weiss's work has not been surpassed yet, we cannot say the same of his intellectual attitude.

Then perhaps the critical perspective Weiss employs should be referred not so much to a generic juxtaposition of Middle Ages and Renaissance, but to a narrower comparison between the Renaissance and what came immediately before it. Once again we are bound to do without separations and clear-cut oppositions: a mere survey of the fifteenth century, even in England, shows that a comparative scarcity of original literary production was abundantly compensated by scholarly research; the century presents a number of writers working on translations and commentaries, as if to prepare the way to what was to come in terms of creative writing, or to what a modern critic would consider 'real' literature. Such a description would fit both England and Italy, setting aside different methodologies and cultural policies. It is therefore mainly on this point that our confutation of Weiss's view revolves.

In the case of English humanism, however, a further distinction should be made. The situation Weiss described, implying the rediscovery and fervent study of a wealth of classical works and even of those "lost or rare manuscripts" now presumably no longer lost, is hardly applicable to England, whatever we may think of it in the case of Italy. We have Poggio Bracciolini's own evidence on this

point, as Weiss himself underlines: his activity as a book hunter during his English years concentrated on apparently unlikely texts of
Fathers of the Church which he found in monastic libraries, but he
focused on them for other reasons besides the lack of classical texts:
"Poggio's interest in patristic literature did reflect the availability of
texts, but it was a change that he found congenial."[44] Once again,
thus, we find circumstances shaping the humanist's career, and
Bracciolini's attitude forces us to reconsider the established definition
of the humanist as a strenuous defender of *humanae litterae*—a point
that shall be taken up more at length in the next chapter. Weiss not
only left this dichotomy unexplained, but represented Poggio's failure to have a noticeable impact on English culture in terms of the
distance between the Italian humanists and the milieu in which he
worked for four years: "he was too eager about his intellectual pursuits, not to have helped improve the state of English classical scholarship had he found opportunities and encouragement".[45] The reduction
of the definition of humanism to the revival of classical scholarship
thus runs a double risk: on the one hand, Poggio's interest in patristic literature must be perforce underestimated; on the other, the failure of England to produce classical texts, or to show an adequate
interest in them, automatically makes the country unworthy of the
humanist's attention. The perspective offered by Weiss in these terms
is deliberately simplistic, and exaggerates the importance that a single humanist, however famous and intellectually equipped, could have
upon a community which shared neither this scholar's interests nor
his language.

As for the contribution of Duke Humphrey, it is seen as the necessary means for England to pass from a state of cultural stagnation
to an adoption of "humane standards". There is perfect awareness,
on Weiss's part, of Humphrey's shortcomings as a scholar: the rather
unfortunate appointment of Tito Livio Frulovisi as the Duke's Latin
secretary, in spite of the weakness of his qualifications, is explained
as a result of Humphrey's inability to evaluate correctly the intel-

---

[44] Rundle, David, "On the Difference between Virtue and Weiss: Humanist Texts
in England during the Fifteenth Century", in *Courts, Counties and the Capital in the
Later Middle Ages*, ed. by D.E.S. Dunn. New York: St Martin's Press, 1996: 181–203,
p. 186. In this essay, Rundle corrects Weiss's attitude as far as English humanism
is concerned on a number of points.
[45] Weiss, *Humanism in England*, p. 21.

lectual resources (and the Latin prose) of his employee. Humphrey's relations with a number of Italian humanists—not only Frulovisi and the other members of his household but also his correspondents, such as Decembrio and Bruni—is thoroughly analysed. One perhaps might wish for more attention directed towards the nobleman's relations with English scholars, many of whom were part of his entourage: a small but significant instance is the fact that Signorelli is mentioned as the Duke's physician, while Gilbert Kymer is never alluded to, in spite of the notable role of the latter, a former Oxford student, who would become chancellor to the University in Humphrey's lifetime (often acting as an intermediary between the Duke and the University on the occasions of the latter's pleas for support) and write a medical treatise directly connected with the person of the Duke. The same happens in the case of John Whethamstede, who is discussed more as a correspondent of Leonardo Bruni than as one of Humphrey's closest friends and counsellors. We then see how, even in the analysis of the first Englishman that, according to Weiss, brought a decisive contribution to English humanism, much stress is laid upon his role as a cultural intermediary between Italy and England: the benefit Oxford received from Humphrey's donations is justly highlighted, but the latter's contacts with English intellectuals are almost ignored, as is demonstrated by the critic's conclusive evaluation of the patron:

> His employment of Italians as secretaries, his relations with Bruni and Decembrio, his bibliophile activities, his efforts to advance learning in Oxford, show the direction of his intellectual leanings. The translations from the Greek which Bruni and Decembrio made at his request suggest some attraction to political philosophy, while the contents of his library hint to the catholicity of his reading.[46]

It is an evaluation with which the modern scholar undoubtedly agrees, yet which seems to forget a whole circle of English scholars and poets that was likewise working under Humphrey's directions, or in any case benefiting from his patronage, and who might have been equally instrumental to the advancement of learning in England. They are indeed mentioned even when the connection with Duke Humphrey is tenuous: a few pages are devoted to Thomas Bekynton, Vincent Clement, Andrew Holes and Adam de Moleyns, but once

---

[46] Weiss, *Humanism in England*, pp. 67–8.

again what is underlined is that it was thanks to Humphrey's patron-age that Thomas Bekynton, for instance, had the opportunity of meeting Frulovisi and other Italian humanists and thus come "under their influence".[47] There is very little reference to any original con-tribution on the part of the English writers or scholars.

Weiss's later articles and essays sometimes help to expand on details that had been left unexplained in his major work. Such an instance may be found in his 1964 article, published in *The Book Collector*. Revising his view of the Duke of Gloucester and consider-ing him in the role of book-lover rather than of politician or patron, Weiss writes an interesting portrait that sets the Duke against a fam-ily background of book-lovers, adding:

> Yet as book lovers Henry IV, Henry V, and John of Bedford, were really typical of their own time, that is to say they delighted in beau-tifully decorated books of devotion, accepted quite willingly the dedi-cation of literary works, showed some interest in chronicles or romances, and were ready to present volumes to deserving institutions like Oxford University with a vague intention to encourage learning.[48]

It is on the basis of this difference that Weiss concludes that "as bibliophiles Henry IV, Henry V, and Bedford belonged to the Middle Ages, while Humfrey was a typical Renaissance book lover".[49] Though the factual premises are correct, the conclusion is, one feels, rather too pat. It is a clear indication of the conception of humanism towards which Weiss was working: humanism is identified with the moment in which the book is no longer an object valuable in itself, whether because of its rich decorations and gilding, or because of its power to entertain, delight or elevate the individual reader, but assumes a significance that goes beyond its intrinsic value. Humphrey's activity as a patron is then showed as mainly aiming at such acts as the successive donations of manuscripts to Oxford, donations which spring "from the desire to improve learning and particularly Latin learning in Oxford, that is to say in England".[50] The book becomes then an instrument, and the humanist bibliophile does not collect

---

[47] Weiss, *Humanism in England*, p. 71.
[48] Roberto Weiss, "Portrait of a Bibliophile XI: Humphrey, Duke of Gloucester, d. 1447," *The Book Collector* 13: 1964, 161–70, p. 161.
[49] Weiss, "Portrait of a Bibliophile", p. 162.
[50] Weiss, "Portrait of a Bibliophile", p. 169.

books simply for the pleasure of possessing them (Weiss rightly underlines the fact that many of Duke Humphrey's manuscripts had an inconspicuous appearance, though he might be wrong in his supposition that the Duke employed no illuminators), but as a means towards the advancement of learning for the scholarly community. On the other hand, there is no doubt that Humphrey's collection did present notable differences from either his father's or his brothers'. Yet such differences deserve a more detailed analysis. For instance, the Duke of Bedford's attempts to build a library, using the extraordinary resources of the library in the Louvre, and even to patronise three different universities in France and England (Paris, Caen, and Oxford), were doomed to repeated disappointments; therefore, it is rather difficult for the modern scholar to understand what the extent of Bedford's cultural activity might have been.

The debt later students of English humanism have towards Weiss's works is undoubtedly enormous; in no other text are we presented with such an accurate and complete survey, one of whose many merits is its plain and accessible style. However controversial his conclusions and interpretations may be, there is no doubt that throughout his work Weiss is scrupulously faithful to historical truth, so that even as a simple account of the cultural activity in fifteenth-century England the book is invaluable. As we have seen, we might occasionally quarrel with the scholar's bias for Italy as the source of any humanistic activity, and his almost complete disregard for the notable literary production in the vernacular that was the result, directly of indirectly, of Humphrey's patronage and of his acquisition of manuscripts. Weiss's conclusions faithfully reflect his initial assumptions: English humanism, even in its later development, is analysed in its difference from the Italian ideal. What is possibly lacking in a survey that we can only praise for its accuracy is, however, an account of fifteenth-century English literature, or, more simply, of the production in the vernacular, which Weiss very rarely mentions. Another serious shortcoming of Weiss's work, and of the definition of English humanism that derived from it, is the scholar's complete overlooking of the literary contribution of France. This is a contribution that must be analysed in linguistic terms first: if Latin was the language of communication for Italian humanists, their English readers may have had some difficulty with it. This appears evident in the case of Duke Humphrey himself, who allegedly preferred to read Livy in a French translation, as is shown in a letter he wrote to the King of Naples, accompanying the same French version of Livy's *History*,[51] but also in the case of John Lydgate, who translated Boccaccio's *De casibus virorum illustrium* via Laurent de Premierfait's French version. France, however, played an important role during the fifteenth century also as concerns the transmission of manuscripts. If its role has been underestimated in Weiss's works, one consequence has certainly been a general underestimation of this point on the part of most later studies.

After Weiss: reactions, refutations, continuations

Scholarly reactions to Weiss's work, though mostly limited to a series of re-discussions of individual points, have been numerous, while practically every book even marginally concerned with English humanism refers back to Weiss as a matter of course; in this section I mean to discuss the most significant trends of these reactions, together with the studies on English humanism (and occasionally, on the literary fifteenth century) that appear to enter different fields from those explored by the Anglo-Italian scholar. In many cases we have a rather passive following of Weiss's footsteps, or taking for granted of his assumptions: such is the case, for example, with Fritz Caspari's *Humanism and the Social Order in Tudor England*,[52] or with an essay written as late as 1989 by Douglas Gray,[53] and more specifically with R.C. Simonini's *Italian Scholarship in Renaissance England*.[54] In retracing the roots of English Renaissance to the early fifteenth century, Simonini might be quite correct, though we should be wary of an evaluation of any given cultural period that finds its justification in the literary or artistic production of the period that followed.[55] The

---

[51] "Quapropter, cum [. . .] forte Titi Livii libros ex latino in gallico sermone conversos legerem . . ." (Therefore, as I was reading Lyvy's books translated from Latin into French . . .). The letter is quoted in Sammut, pp. 215–6.

[52] Fritz Caspari, *Humanism and the Social Order in Tudor England*, Chicago: The University of Chicago Press, 1954.

[53] Gray, Douglas, "Humanism and Humanisms in the Literature of Late Medieval England", in *Italy and the English Renaissance*, ed. by S. Rossi and D. Savoia. Milano: Unicopli, 1989: 25–44.

[54] R.C. Simonini, *Italian Scholarship in Renaissance England*, Chapel Hill: The University of North Carolina, 1952.

[55] N.F. Blake, in his "The Fifteenth Century Reconsidered" (*Neuphilologische*

critic also highlights what he calls a unique characteristic of early English humanism, when he defines it "a utilitarian impulse to bend the 'new learning' to practical ends". I am not sure, however, whether the definition, used in the rest of the passage as a postulate, could not be equally well applied to humanism as a whole, rather than considered a peculiarity of the English movement. The quotation continues:

> Interest in humanism came almost entirely from the standpoint of politics, theology, philosophy, or science; culture was not thought of as an end in itself. English statesmen, scholars, schoolmen, and ecclesiastics in general realized the practical potentialities of humanism and exploited it as such [. . .] Humanism in England, in truth, began in an almost haphazard and casual way. It was the work of pioneers, a series of individual endeavors that were eventually to revolutionize English scholarship. Oxford University seems to have been the first center of humanistic scholarship in England during the fifteenth century.[56]

The choice of "haphazard and casual" to describe the beginning of humanism does not seem particularly happy in this instance, since it solves the problem of political inference into cultural development as being simply the result of chance, and really leaves no possibility of investigation for the cultural historian.

A similar note is struck by some of the studies the Italian scholar Sergio Rossi has devoted to the subject. An excellent literary critic, and a student of early modern English letters who has given some important contributions to the field, Rossi seems less at ease when analysing the Lancastrian era, and cannot escape a few clichés. In particular, analysing the much-discussed episode of Poggio Bracciolini's arrival in England, Rossi sees in his subsequent disappointment and in the partial failure of this first cultural contact the proof of an irredeemable chasm between England and Italy. In a 1969 essay he makes the basic assumption that Lancastrian England was still barbarian, completely passive and incapable of amelioration from the point of view of cultural development:

> Il primo Quattrocento dunque, avvolto ancora in una atmosfera feudale e legato a una concezione aristocratica e ritualistica della vita, dimostra come il mondo inglese conservi qualcosa di 'barbaro', termine

---

Mitteilungen 71: 1970, 146–57), warns the readers against this attitude, rightly noting the fundamental differences between the literary scenes of the various centuries.

[56] Simonini, p. 2.

che sottintende tuttavia una latente vitalità [. . .] Queste premesse
giustificano il comportamento dei primi umanisti italiani, i quali, giunti
in Inghilterra, non seppero, o non vollero fare scuola in un ambiente
ancora privo di una moderna vita culturale. Il maggiore di essi, Poggio
Bracciolini, lasciò poche tracce in questo paese ove soggiornò dal 1419,
quando vi giunse al seguito del cardinale Henry Beaufort incontrato
al Concilio di Costanza, fino al 1422. Egli era umanista troppo com-
pleto per pensare di formare scolari e coltivare amicizie in una terra
che considerava di esilio.[57]

The assumption that a 'complete' humanist may recoil in horror at
the idea of cultivating friendship in an alien, barbaric land, may
sound rather laughable today. But what I believe to be Rossi's greater
mistake in this analysis is his belief that history in fifteenth-century
England had still stopped at a feudal, if "vital" stage, and that this
in itself was the greatest hindrance to the development of culture.
In a word, Rossi still keeps faithful to that distinction between barbaric Middle Ages and civilised humanism that confuses, more than
anything, our understanding of the latter, since it stops us from seeing the intellectual progress of the late Middle Ages as the natural
prologue to the development of humanism—a particularly surprising fallacy in a critic who was, after all, very well acquainted at least
with fourteenth- and fifteenth-century literature in England, if not
with its intellectual history, and who had made a specific study of
the poetic production of Scottish humanism. If, in short, Rossi's article contributes little to our identification of the events that coincided
with the birth of humanism in England, it allows us to understand
the difficulty of the modern scholars in their attempts to grapple
with the problem of English humanism.

Even more disappointing are the results in the case of surveys of
late-medieval English literature that were written in the years imme-

---

[57] "The early fifteenth century then, still belonging to a feudal world and bound
to an aristocratic and ritualistic conception of life, demonstrates how the English
world still maintains something barbaric about it, though the adjective implies a
latent vitality [. . .] These assumptions justify the behaviour of the first Italian humanists, who, once landed in England, could not or would not form a school of thought
where there was still no modern cultural life. The greatest among them, Poggio
Bracciolini, left few traces in the country in which he lived from 1419, when he
arrived there following Henry Beaufort, whom he met at the Council of Constance,
to 1422. He was too complete a humanist to find pupils or friends in what he considered a land of exile". Sergio Rossi, "Enrico V dalla cronaca alla poesia", in
Ricerche sull'Umanesimo e sul Rinascimento in Inghilterra, ed. by S. Rossi, Milano: Società
Editrice Vita e Pensiero, 1969: 1–25, pp. 6–7.

diately following the publication of Weiss's book. In most cases, there seems to be little, if any, awareness of the links between the "Italian" activity of the Duke of Gloucester—his correspondence with Italian humanists, his acquisition of manuscripts from Northern Italy to furnish the depleted Oxford chests—and his "English" patronage, whose existence and continuity is demonstrated by the numerous dedications and allusions of contemporary poets. It is the case, for instance, of H.S. Bennett's *Chaucer and the Fifteenth Century*, which was a part of *The Oxford History of English Literature*.[58] To deal with the eternal problem of the literary barrenness of the English fifteenth century, Bennett finds no better solution than to go back to the Hegelian idea of *Zeitgeist*, however tentatively put, as in the opening section of his chapter on fifteenth-century verse: "we must not hope to explain the weakness of Lydgate and others solely in terms of the 'spirit of the age', but, on the other hand, we are not entitled to ignore it".[59] The chapter includes allusions to Duke Humphrey and to the role he played to further the poetic activity of John Lydgate and contemporary writers, but according to Bennett what is expressed in the various prologues or dedications alluding to Humphrey is simply a demonstration of "how widespread the canker of servile imitation is".[60]

Bennett adopts a widely different attitude in a later book, *Six Medieval Men and Women*.[61] It is a gallery of portraits, mainly belonging to the fifteenth-century, and the tone tends to be discursive, since the book is meant for the general reader rather than for the student or scholar of medieval literature. But in writing his portrait of the Duke of Gloucester, the first of the series, Bennett brought to his writing the unifying vision that he had lost in the more specialised pages of literary criticism, and enabled the reader to see this figure in its complexity: a questionable politician and a man of dubious morals, but also a lover of letters who could bring his patronage to influence both the diffusion of Italian humanism in England and the development of literature in the vernacular. The very nature of the

---

[58] Oxford: Clarendon Press, 1947.

[59] Bennett, *Chaucer and the Fifteenth Century*, p. 97.

[60] Bennett, *Chaucer and the Fifteenth Century*, p. 126. In this perspective, this study presents some serious drawbacks if compared with the much earlier anthology compiled by E.P. Hammond, *English Verse between Chaucer and Surrey*, discussed above.

[61] H.S. Bennett, *Six Medieval Men and Women*, Cambridge: Cambridge University Press, 1955.

book, however, prevents Bennett from any in-depth analysis of the
question of English humanism.

The gap between literary criticism and intellectual history has not
been bridged as far as the early fifteenth century is concerned.
However, more recent studies of individual poets who have been
associated with Duke Humphrey, such as John Lydgate or Thomas
Hoccleve, show a somewhat heightened awareness of the issue—at
least, of the importance of patronage, if not of the importance of
humanism. This is the case, for instance, with the study Alain Renoir
wrote on Lydgate's poetry.[62] John Norton-Smith gives the reader a
useful analysis of the sense of contemporary history in Lydgate's writings, but when dealing with the relation between the poet and the
Duke of Gloucester, he seems mainly anxious to underline the avarice
of the latter,[63] while Derek Pearsall on the same subject has been
much more dismissive, reducing Humphrey to the rank of "an erratic,
unprincipled and attractively unsuccessful politician who dabbled in
letters partly because he saw in them a way to prestige and profit,"
adding that his claim as a humanist patron "only looks strong for
lack of contenders."[64] Pearsall's evaluation, besides being reductive,
sounds extraordinarily unfair: hundreds of manuscripts sought, received,
bought and donated can hardly be classified as "dabbling", while
the accusation of being unprincipled could equally well be levelled
against a Federico da Montefeltro or a Filippo Maria Visconti—and
it has very little to do with their status as humanist patrons. Work
on Thomas Hoccleve is unfortunately scantier, and concerned mostly
with his relationship with Geoffrey Chaucer, but some attention has
also been devoted to the question of patronage, probably thanks to
the poet's autobiographical outbursts. Some work has been done on
the relationship Hoccleve had with his royal patrons, especially as
concerns texts such as *The Regement of Princes*.[65] The most important
work in this field, however, has been undertaken by J.A. Burrow,

---

[62] Alain Renoir, *The Poetry of John Lydgate*, London: Routledge & Kegan Paul, 1967.
[63] *John Lydgate. Poems*, ed. by J. Norton-Smith, Oxford: Clarendon Press, 1966,
pp. xii–v.
[64] Derek Pearsall, *John Lydgate*, London: Routledge and Kegan Paul, 1970, p. 224.
[65] On this text in particular see Larry Scanlon, "The King's Two Voices: Narrative
and Power in Hoccleve's *Regement of Princes*", in *Literary Practice and Social Change in
Britain, 1380–1530*, ed. by L. Patterson, Berkeley: University of California Press,
1990: 216–47, and Derek Pearsall, "Hoccleve's *Regement of Princes*: The Poetics of
Royal Self-Representation", *Speculum* 69: 1994, 386–410.

both in a series of critical contributions and in his edition of Hoccleve's *Series*.[66] Analysing this text Burrow correctly identifies a series of references to Duke Humphrey, and gives the historian precious material towards a fuller understanding of the Duke's patronage, even if he does not attempt a full interpretation of the material at his disposal. A recent contribution to the study of the relation between the two poets and the Lancastrian court, including "the mercurial Gloucester," is offered by Paul Strohm in his contribution to *The Cambridge History of Medieval English Literature*.[67] Again, however, little connection is made between this and the rise of humanism. On the other hand, little or no critical attention has been paid to other English writers associated with Duke Humphrey, such as George Ashby, John Russell, or the anonymous Palladius translator. John Capgrave has received a preferential treatment, mainly thanks to Peter J. Lucas's studies on the subject;[68] in the case of Capgrave, however, if there is no doubt on his attempts to acquire Gloucester's protection, there is some doubt as to how these attempts were received, and particularly how close Capgrave was to the new, humanistic attitude towards learning that the Italian scholars were importing in England.[69]

---

[66] "Autobiographical Poetry in the Middle Ages: The Case of Thomas Hoccleve", in *Middle English Literature. British Academy Gollancz Lectures*, ed. by J.A. Burrow, Oxford: Oxford University Press, 1989: 223–46; *Thomas Hoccleve*, Authors of the Middle Ages, Aldershot: Variorum, 1994; *Thomas Hoccleve's Complaint and Dialogue*, ed. by J.A. Burrow, Early English Text Society, New York: Oxford University Press, 1999; there are references to Hoccleve's poetry also in Burrow's *Medieval Writers and Their Work. Middle English Literature and its Background 1100–1500*, Oxford: Oxford University Press, 1982.

[67] Paul Strohm, "Hoccleve, Lydgate and the Lancastrian Court", in *The Cambridge History of Medieval Literature*, Cambridge: Cambridge University Press, 1999: 640–61.

[68] "John Capgrave, O.S.A. (1393–1464), Scribe and 'Publisher'", *Transactions of the Cambridge Bibliographical Society* 5: 1969, 1–35; "John Capgrave and the *Nova Legenda Angliae*: A Survey", *The Library* 5th series, 25: 1970, 1–10; "The Growth and Development of English Literary Patronage in the Later Middle Ages and Early Renaissance", *The Library* 6th series, 4: 1982, 219–48; "An Author as Copyist of his own Work: John Capgrave OSA (1393–1464)", in *New Science out of Old Books: Studies in Manuscripts and Early Printed Books in Honour of A.I. Doyle*, ed. by R. Beadle and A.J. Piper, London: Scolar Press, 1995: 227–48; *From Author to Audience: John Capgrave and Medieval Publication*, The Library, Dublin: University College Dublin Press, 1997. With the collaboration of Rita Dalton, Lucas has also written "Capgrave's Preface Dedicating his Commentary *In Exodum* to Humfrey Duke of Gloucester", *The Bodleian Library Record* 11: 1982, 20–5.

[69] The impact of humanism on English writers will be discussed more in detail in chapter 5.

We should not omit to mention a very singular contribution to the study of Humphrey's patronage of English poets, that is, Ethel Seaton's book *Sir Richard Roos*.[70] Apart from a brief and scathing mention in Everest-Phillips's thesis (see below), Seaton's work has been pointedly ignored by later scholars. It is a literary biography of Richard Roos, a Lancastrian knight to whom has generally been attributed the English version of Alain Chartier's *La Belle Dame sans Merci*,[71] and whose family was somewhat distantly connected to that of Eleanor Cobham, Duke Humphrey's second wife (she was step-cousin of Sir Richard on his mother's side). Two of the surviving manuscripts from Duke Humphrey's library seem to have previously belonged to Robert Roos, Richard's father. On this basis, and with the help of an analysis based on hidden anagrams, Seaton attributes to Roos an amazing quantity of poetry—from Chaucer's *Anelida and Arcite* and *The Legend of Good Women* to some of Wyatt's poems, not omitting almost all the courtly poems generally attributed to Lydgate—and hypothesises an intellectual relationship with Humphrey and his circle that has little basis beyond the recurring reference to "Pleasaunce". It is true that there has been a tendency on the part of some anti-quarians (rather than scholars) to dump on Lydgate any unattrib-uted fifteenth-century poem, and it is true that Humphrey's manor in Greenwich, where his library was housed, was called Plesaunce; but very often Seaton quite frankly seems to build upon nothing but her own conviction.

As for the contributions of recent critical trends, one would have hoped new historicism could find something of interest in the par-ticular situation of English early humanism: but the only, extremely slender contribution I have been able to find simplistically refers to both Henry V and Lydgate as "typically, even reassuringly, medieval",[72] quoting as its support extremely dated secondary sources.

At least one attempt to consider the question of patronage in a context that would combine historical investigation with literary analy-

---

[70] Ethel Seaton, *Sir Richard Roos (c. 1410–1482), Lancastrian Poet*, London: Hart-Davis, 1961.
[71] London, British Library, Harley 372.
[72] Lee Patterson, "Making Identities in Fifteenth-Century England: Henry V and John Lydgate", in *New Historical Literary Study: Essays on Reproducing Texts, Representing History*, ed. by J.N. Cox and L.J. Reynolds, Princeton: Princeton University Press, 1993: 69–107, p. 73.

sis was made by Richard Firth Green in his *Poets and Princepleasers*.[73] In his introduction Green accurately pinpoints the greatest obstacle to a fuller understanding of the question of patronage in fifteenth-century England—namely, the fact that we have surprisingly little information on the day-to-day activities of the perspective patrons of the day; a deficiency that is particularly felt if we compare it with what we know of, for instance, French or Burgundian potentates of the same period.[74] What evidence there is, however, could be profitably compared with what we know of French or Burgundian courtly *mores*, since

> if Latin provided the medieval scholar, churchman, and diplomat with a universal language, it might be said that French, the language of the heraldic motto and the love-token, performed much the same function for the courtier.[75]

From this assessment of the material at his disposal, Green proceeds to a definition of the *familia regis*—a composite household of servants, administrators and counsellors that served as a mirror for every other noble household in the realm. It is within this circle (or within the inner circle Green calls the *camera regis*) that a writer could find his place, in the section of the household that was devoted to the king's, or the nobleman's, entertainment and amusements, an instance of which could be the public reading of poetry. Green's analysis, drawing upon a wide range of material (not last the very poems that thus constituted part of the king's solace), makes for very interesting reading, though he prefers to explore the sociological side of the noble patronage rather than its intellectual implications. Thus, in the case of Duke Humphrey, the writer refers to the fact that "book-collecting [. . .] had become fashionable, and richly-decorated volumes were an established part of the ostentatious fabric of court life",[76] temporarily forgetting that Humphrey's library differed from fashion in that in some cases it seemed to follow different criteria for the choice of books than their bindings or decorations. Green's survey of Humphrey's relations with both Italian and English writers is accurate, if occasionally sketchy.

---

[73] Richard Firth Green, *Poets and Princepleasers: Literature and the English Court in the Late Middle Ages*, Toronto: University of Toronto Press, 1980.
[74] Green, p. 8.
[75] Green, p. 11.
[76] Green, p. 91.

While studies specifically concerned with English humanism, few as they were, did for a time little more than retrace Weiss's steps, and literary criticism did not seem to take into account the possibility that early humanism in England might have influenced contemporary literature, progress was made in adjacent fields—specifically, in philosophical history with a more determined focus upon the definition of humanism in European terms, and in the history of the book, particularly as far as England was concerned. For the former instance it is necessary to cite at least Paul Oskar Kristeller's fundamental essay "Humanism and Scholasticism in the Italian Renaissance", already mentioned in my discussion of Weiss's works. Kristeller's main interest lay in the definition of Italian humanism, and in its eventual repercussions in the rest of Western Europe—a theme that is pursued in a great part of his work.[77] Yet this essay is pivotal also for the present study because it comes back to the original meaning of the word *umanista*, and thus forces the reader to reconsider the movement—if such it was—not from the point of view of its accomplishment (humanism thus becoming *ipso facto* identified with "the rise of classical scholarship")[78] but as the development of the professional career of secretaries or teachers of rhetoric rather than free-lance writers, who "did not invent a new field of learning or a new professional activity, but [. . .] introduced a new, classicist style into the traditions of medieval Italian rhetoric."[79] As I have pointed out above, Kristeller is in no way interested in the English situation, but his definition is surprisingly apt in our case, since it redefines adventures such as Poggio Bracciolini's arrival in England more as a job opportunity for temporarily unemployed secretary than as a humanist's search for undiscovered classical texts; this point of view helps us to understand, at least, that the latter might have been Bracciolini's personal purpose, but the former was at least his avowed one. It also helps the modern historian to obtain a better perspective as far as the work of English scholars is concerned, particularly in the early fifteenth century (since certainly a scholar such as John

---

[77] See also his "The European Diffusion of Italian Humanism", *Italica* 39: 1962, 1–20.
[78] Kristeller, p. 90. For a definition of humanism in European scholarship in the 1940s, see also Augusto Campana, "The Origin of the Word 'Humanist'", *Journal of the Warburg and Courtauld Institutes* 9: 1946, 60–73.
[79] Kristeller, p. 93.

Tiptoft had a clearer consciousness of his purpose when he went to study in Padua, as well as having the advantage of independent financial means), and to see in the presence of a patron such as Duke Humphrey a *conditio sine qua non* for the establishment of even a tentative form of humanism.

Kristeller's work gave a fundamental contribution to a redefinition of European humanism; at the same time, studies more specifically concerned with England explored the history of books and libraries, a key-element to follow the passage from the Middle Ages to the Renaissance in terms of the history of ideas. In this context, much of the groundwork has been done by N.R. Ker. His *Medieval Libraries of Great Britain*,[80] first published in 1941, is still the indispensable guide to medieval books and book-catalogues, as well as to the modern catalogues in which they are described. Together with the volumes and essays that followed,[81] this book remains a necessary compass for the scholar lost in the complicated history of the medieval book. More specifically, Ker's work helps us to understand the situation of the University of Oxford and of the various colleges prior to Duke Humphrey's donations, the short- and long-term consequences these donations had on the life of the University, and the cultural and political significance of Humphrey's activity.

Ker's work applies to the general state of medieval libraries in Britain and to Oxford colleges in particular. On Duke Humphrey's library in particular, and on his donations to the University library of Oxford, there have been a number of specific studies throughout the decades: Vern L. Bullough analysed the section of the library devoted to medical books,[82] while Berthold Ullman, updating an

---

[80] N.R. Ker, *Medieval Libraries of Great Britain*, London: Offices of the Royal Historical Society, 1941. A second, slightly revised edition was published in 1964.

[81] Of particular interest for our field of investigations are the following works: "The Chaining, Labelling, and Inventory Numbers of Manuscripts Belonging to the Old University Library", *The Bodleian Library Record* 5: 1955, 176–80; "Oxford College Libraries before 1500", in *The Universities in the Later Middle Ages*, ed. by J. Ijsewijn and J. Paquet, Louvain: Louvain University Press, 1978: 293–311; and the multivolume *Medieval Manuscripts in British Libraries*, Oxford: Clarendon Press, 1969–92 (the last volume, posthumously published, was prepared with the collaboration of A.J. Piper). Ker's contribution is also present in M. Parkes, "The Provision of Books", in *History of the University of Oxford, vol. 2: Late Medieval Oxford*, ed. by J.J. Catto and R. Evans. Oxford: Clarendon Press, 1992: 407–83.

[82] Vern L. Bullough, "Duke Humphrey and his Medical Collections", *Renaissance News* 14: 1961, 87–91.

earlier attempt by Vickers,[83] proposed a first assessment of still extant manuscript that had once belonged to Duke Humphrey.[84] But up to the present day the most important contribution on the role of Duke Humphrey as a bibliophile, on his donations and on the extent of his library certainly is Alfonso Sammut's *Unfredo duca di Gloucester e gli umanisti italiani*.[85] The book is the result of an extremely rigorous search: it offers us what might well be the definitive account of Duke Humphrey's repeated donations of books to the University of Oxford, as well as a survey of the Duke's relations with Italian humanists. We also have the list of books belonging to King's College, Cambridge, in the years immediately following Humphrey's death, and the list of surviving manuscripts. This work is as far as we can get to the reconstruction of Duke Humphrey's library,[86] and enlightens us on his activity as a buyer and commissioner of books. Sammut draws very few, if any, conclusions; but his work is possibly the most precious instrument we have if we mean to analyse Humphrey's contribution to the development of English humanism.

Along with Sammut's contribution it is also important to cite the research undertaken by A.C. De la Mare, on an equally impressive if perhaps less systematic scale. Among the most important results of this work are the catalogues of two Bodleian Library exhibitions, the former specifically concerned with Duke Humphrey and English Humanism, in 1970, the latter on Duke Humfrey's library and the Divinity School, in 1988.[87] The 1970 exhibition brought together the surviving manuscripts that had once formed part of Duke Humphrey's donation to the Oxford library (a collection including twenty-three manuscripts), extending to Italian books brought to England in the

---

[83] Vickers, pp. 426–38.

[84] Berthold L. Ullman, "Manuscripts of Duke Humphrey of Gloucester", in *Studies in the Italian Renaissance*, Roma: Edizioni di Storia e Letteratura, 1955: 345–55.

[85] Padova: Antenore, 1980.

[86] We shall discuss later, however, the sort of a perspective we can have upon a library from the list of books taken *from* that library and given elsewhere.

[87] *Duke Humfrey and English Humanism in the Fifteenth Century. Catalogue of an Exhibition Held in the Bodleian Library Oxford*, Oxford: Bodleian Library, 1970. *Duke Humfrey's Library and the Divinity School 1488–1988. An Exhibition at the Bodleian Library June–August 1988*, Oxford: Bodleian Library, 1988. Both catalogues have no indication of either author or editor, but a preface in the earlier volume indicates that if the catalogue was the joint work of De la Mare and Richard Hunt, the preparation of the Exhibition had been mostly De la Mare's work. The second catalogue was the result of the cooperation between De la Mare and Stanley Gillam.

early fifteenth century. Thus it offered an overview of the Italian contribution to English humanism, and perhaps helped define the boundaries of humanism as it was intended in England at the time. The second catalogue provides the reader with a history of the University library (concerning both the building and its contents) "from its known beginnings up to the 1550's,"[88] a history accurately reconstructed on the basis of extremely fragmentary evidence, and which incidentally retraced, as far as possible, the destiny of all the surviving manuscripts from Duke Humphrey's donations. Together with the catalogues, De la Mare also wrote a number of articles variously concerned with Humphrey's patronage;[89] besides, we owe her an excellent description of the so-called Fitzwilliam Manuscript (now Duke Humfrey d.2, in the Bodleian Library) containing the complete text of the fifteenth-century translation of Palladius's *De Agricultura*, a translation undertaken at the Duke's request.

More recently, an important contribution to the field, though conceived in more general terms, is the third volume (dealing with the years 1400–1557) of *The Cambridge History of the Book in Britain*,[90] which sets the development of the book and of the various activities associated with it, such as copying, printing, or illuminating, within a wider historical context in which the activities of patronage and commission are also examined. Some attention is paid to Humphrey's relation with Italian humanists, as well as to his support of the University of Oxford, and to the important role he played for the advancement of English letters. Humphrey's intellectual project is briefly delineated, if not investigated in depth:

> The history of the humanist book in Britain [...] may properly be said to begin with the patronage—and, perhaps, the reading—of Duke Humfrey, youngest brother of Henry V. Humfrey seems to have conceived the idea of modelling his household on a contemporary Italian princely court. Why, and on whose advice, is not clear.[91]

---

[88] *Duke Humfrey's Library*, p. 1.

[89] The most important being A.C. De la Mare, "Manuscripts Given to the University of Oxford by Humfrey, Duke of Gloucester", *The Bodleian Library Record* 13: 1988, 30–51, 112–21. The list compiled by De la Mare was, however, left in an incomplete form.

[90] *The Cambridge History of the Book in Britain, vol. 3: 1400–1557*, ed. by L. Hellinga and J.B. Trapp, Cambridge: Cambridge University Press, 1999.

[91] *The Cambridge History of the Book in Britain*, p. 293. On the humanist book in Britain in the fifteenth century, see also J.B. Trapp, "Il libro umanistico tra Italia e Inghilterra dal '400 al primo '500", *Scrittura e civiltà* 22: 1998, 319–37.

Another, widely different approach to the development of the literary fifteenth century has been from the point of view of linguistic
changes. In this case, there is very little that refers explicitly to
humanism. Yet the focus on the progressive affirmation of the vernacular, first as the language of common speech, then of a popular
kind of literature, and gradually of public affairs, law and politics,
till it became in the fifteenth century the official language of Chancery,
throws new light on the very particular nature of English humanism, especially as far as Duke Humphrey's activity is concerned.
Studies in this field, as opposed to general studies on the evolution
of the English language, are not very numerous but in some case
extremely significant. We should take into account, among the early
studies, John Taylor's article,[92] noting the diffusion of the vernacular in writings by members of the religious orders between the fourteenth and the sixteenth centuries. But the most important contribution
is a series of articles written by John Fisher, which have been subsequently united in a book.[93] Fisher analyses how the language of
Chancery, standardised during the reign of Henry V after centuries
that had seen the exclusive use of French and Latin, was at the root
of the emergence of English as the official written language of the
nation during the fifteenth century.[94] By underlining the relation
between political decisions and linguistic evolution, Fisher highlighted
also the corresponding evolution in the production and diffusion of
a literature in English, examining also what data we have concerning manuscripts in English in private libraries, as opposed to what
we know of literary production in English:

> It is the politics of the movement of the written language from Latin
> and French to English that concerns me here. We are not now talk-
> ing about when secular poetry began to be *composed* in English. From
> 1300 on, and particularly after 1350, more and more literature was
> composed in English, but clearly there was no audience that caused
> these English writings to be copied and disseminated. All the manu-

---

[92] J. Taylor, "Notes on the Rise of Written English in the Late Middle Ages",
Proceedings of the Leeds Philosophical Society 8: 1956, 128–36.
[93] John H. Fisher, *The Emergence of Standard English*, Lexington: University Press
of Kentucky, 1996.
[94] As far as Henry V's role is concerned, an important contribution on the field
is to be found in Malcolm Richardson, "Henry V, the English Chancery, and
Chancery English", *Speculum* 55: 1980, 726–50.

scripts of Geoffrey Chaucer, John Mandeville, John Trevisa, John Barbour, Laurence Minot, and other fourteenth century secular English authors date from after 1400.[95]

As for Duke Humphrey of Gloucester, he appears first in connection with John Lydgate; of the latter's relentless search for influential patrons it is said that "the list of Lydgate's patrons reads like a *Who's Who* of both the courtly and the commercial circles in England, suggesting influential support stemming from the Lancastrian affinity for the cultivation of English."[96] Thus Fisher establishes a first link between a politically-determined linguistic change and literary patronage: part of the Lancastrian policy in their effort "to elevate the prestige of English"[97] is a conscious support of poetry, or at any rate of literature, in the new national language. Though, therefore, the Duke of Gloucester is not made the subject of particular discussion, nor is the development of humanism mentioned, Fisher's study is extremely useful in highlighting the role of "Chancery Standard" in the evolution of the language, and by implication the role political propaganda played in linguistic and literary choices.

In recent years literary critics specifically concerned with the English fifteenth century have started taking into account the relations between some members of the English aristocracy and Italian humanists, and to see if this activity could have any bearing on the state of English letters. Among these scholars we must certainly cite V.J. Scattergood. In his *Politics and Poetry in the Fifteenth Century* (1971) he analyses what is still an obscure corner of English literary production, that is, the mass of fifteenth-century writings on political or social subjects, thus investigating a kind of literature that more than any other was dependent on contingent events, contemporary affairs, and the fluctuations of power. He therefore continues, in some way, C.L. Kingsford's pioneering work (though limiting his attention to poetic production), with a heightened consciousness of the relationship between writing and political power. Thus a section of his book is devoted to "domestic affairs", and in this section Humphrey of Gloucester finds a place both as one of the political potentates and as a patron. Scattergood notes how the Duke received "enormous attention in contemporary

---

[95] Fisher, p. 19.
[96] Fisher, p. 32.
[97] Fisher, p. 32.

poetry"[98] and attributes this partly to his personality and public image, but also to his "generous literary patronage". Though concentrating his attention on Humphrey's patronage of English poets, the critic correctly links this with a notion imported from Italian humanists: "it was a frequent claim of humanist authors that their art could confer immediate glory and lasting reputation on their patrons."[99] Thus Scattergood takes up Weiss's idea that Humphrey was in part seeking personal aggrandisement in his patronage—though he also notes that much literary output connected with the Duke was not commissioned by him.

On the other hand, even very recent work shows a very limited awareness of the issue: in a 1992 essay, for instance, David Starkey rightly underlines the existence of a medieval element in fifteenth-century literature, but as far as the relation with contemporary European culture is concerned, he upholds a rather vague concept of "complacent insularity" on the part of England and adds that "it is important to remember that early fifteenth-century Italians were at least as likely to be influenced by England as the other way around",[100] a statement which does not seem to be really supported by the evidence we possess.

Only in later years has a real interest in English humanism and its implication re-awakened, producing studies of considerable magnitude in some cases. Denis Hay's essay published in *Itinerarium Italicum*[101] in 1975 deserves a mention, first of all, for its accurate criticism of Weiss's theoretical position. Hay highlights Weiss's fundamental contradiction when the latter attempts a vague definition of humanism as a cultural movement marked by its "advantages over scholasticism"—not advantages in didactic terms, but in a rather blurred relaunch of the concept of *Zeitgeist*. Hay's quotation from Weiss's *Humanism in England* is particularly apt, and is repeated here:

---

[98] V.J. Scattergood, *Politics and Poetry in the Fifteenth Century*, London: Blandford Press, 1971, p. 142.

[99] Scattergood, p. 143.

[100] David Starkey, "England", in *The Renaissance in National Context*, ed. by M. Teich and R. Porter, Cambridge: Cambridge University Press, 1992: 149–63, p. 149.

[101] Denys Hay, "England and the Humanities in the Fifteenth Century", in *Itinerarium Italicum*, ed. by H.A. Oberman and T.A. Brady, Leiden: Brill, 1975: 305–67, reprinted in *Renaissance Essays*, ed. by D. Hay, London: The Hambledon Press, 1988: 169–231.

In its attempts to unify all knowledge within a system of knowledge, scholasticism lacked flexibility and powers of adaptation, was difficult of application in particular instances, and left no room for romanticism. Humanism on the other hand with its leanings towards Platonism displayed a wider scope, greater elasticity, and less dogmatism and adherence to formulae.[102]

What Hay proposes, on the other hand, is a comparison between the social and cultural context in Italy and England (analysing also the cultural contacts between the two countries at the time), keeping in mind parallel developments in the rest of Europe. While the picture he thus draws is exhaustive and occasionally revealing, his conclusions seem to concentrate mainly on what he terms the English Renaissance, that is, the Tudor rather than the Lancastrian period. Some points may, however, be underlined: Hay's awareness of the important role France played in the early stages of English humanism, and the close connection between the first signs of humanist activity and the book transactions in the two great English universities.

Apart from Hay's essay, in the 1970s and 1980s the scholarly production on the subject was mainly limited to doctoral dissertations. Two of them deserve special mention—D.R. Howlett's work on John Whethamstede,[103] and L.C.Y. Everest-Phillip's study on the patronage of Humphrey.[104] Howlett's study is of impressive magnitude and covers every conceivable aspect of Whethamstede's cultural activity, though his conclusions may be occasionally controversial, as when he argues that the abbot of St Albans was at one point a patron of the composer John Dunstable—a hypothesis that is based on really scanty evidence. Howlett, however, is on surer ground when he discusses Whethamstede's patronage of poets such as John Lydgate, and Thomas Norton, whom the critic believes to be the author of the Middle English translation of Palladius's *De Agricultura*. In this case, the argument is more convincing, and the analysis of the translation and of a number of hitherto unnoticed characteristics of the so-called Fitzwilliam manuscript (that is, the presentation copy, dedicated to Duke Humphrey who commissioned the translation) is extremely

---

[102] Weiss, *Humanism in England*, p. 2. See Hay, pp. 170–1.
[103] D.R. Howlett, "Studies in the Work of John Whethamstede", D.Phil, Oxford, 1975.
[104] L.C.Y. Everest-Phillips, "The Patronage of Humphrey, Duke of Gloucester. A Re-evaluation", Ph.D., York, 1983.

revealing, throwing light on one of the very few material proofs that
we have of Humphrey's patronage of English writers, and particularly, of his attention for the rise of the vernacular.

In her 1983 thesis, Everest-Phillips proposes a re-evaluation of the
patronage of Duke Humphrey, observing how the twentieth-century
critical perspective may be vitiated by nineteenth-century antiquarian enthusiasm, and attempting instead to go back to the late-medieval
idea of patronage, though her assumptions in this case owe perhaps
too much to Holzknecht's study on the subject,[105] frequently quoted
throughout the thesis. Decidedly reducing the exceptional position
later scholarship has assigned to Gloucester, she notes how

> outside the sphere of Duke Humphrey's direct influence—that is, those
> writings which were clearly executed under his auspices—one looks in
> vain for contemporary references to the Duke's interest in the Arts.
> The Duke's leanings towards literature and scholarship were evidently
> not the predominant attribute which contemporary chroniclers felt
> obliged to comment on when referring to the Duke.[106]

This is not entirely true; apart from the fulsome dedications of the
poets, which might for the greatest part (but not entirely) be ascribed
to convention, it is sufficient to glance at the collection *Epistolae Academicae Oxonienses*[107] to see how the University relied on Duke Humphrey
as a patron, an advisor, and a donor of books, on quite a different
scale from, let us say, the Bishop of Winchester, the King, or even
the Duke of Bedford. Everest-Phillips's work is unusual in that it
concentrates on Humphrey's patronage of English poets, and obtains
its best results in this field. Her detailed analysis of the Palladius
translation, with the analogies she draws between this poem and a
fifteenth-century Vegetius translation, *Knyghthode and Bataile*, is original and extremely convincing; indeed, in the current dearth of studies on this fascinating text, it deserves to be better known. Equally
relevant are her observations on Lydgate and Hoccleve, while other
fifteenth-century poets are introduced with some straining. When she
turns her attention to the relation between Humphrey and the Italian
humanists, on the other hand, she appears occasionally out of her

---

[105] K.J. Holzknecht, *Literary Patronage in the Middle Ages*, referred to and described
above.
[106] Everest-Phillips, p. 12.
[107] *Epistolae Academicae Oxonienses*, ed. by H. Anstey, Oxford: Clarendon Press, 1898.

depth, and has to rely (sometimes heavily) on secondary sources. Yet altogether this study offers an extremely valuable contribution to our knowledge of patronage in fifteenth-century England, and throws new light on the English side of Duke Humphrey, allowing a new assessment also of his patronage towards the University of Oxford. An added bonus of the volume is that it includes the first (and hitherto the only) complete edition of Tito Livio Frulovisi's *Hunfroidos*, a Latin poem composed in praise of the Duke's military exploits, and a very important document to understand the nature of Humphrey's patronage.[108]

One of the most interesting recent contributions to the study of English humanism, and perhaps the most organised attempt to undermine some of the basic assumptions transmitted by Weiss's occasionally cumbersome heritage, comes from the work of the Oxford scholar David Rundle. His already quoted paper "On the Difference between Virtue and Weiss", published in 1996, clearly shows its polemical intent in its title: Rundle means to challenge Weiss on the seminal ground of the definition of humanism, and by limiting his observations to English intellectual history in the early fifteenth century, he invites the reader to a fundamental revision of the role of both Italian and English humanists:

> There is much more intelligent activity than is usually credited. I would agree that the traditional interpretation not only underrates the English; it also misconstrues the humanists.[109]

The revision is based not only on a reconstruction of Poggio's activity as a book hunter in English libraries, but also on a discussion of the role of Duke Humphrey of Gloucester as a patron and promoter of cultural activity—a role which Rundle sees as compensating for Duke Humphrey's failure as a politician, therefore mainly limited to personal propaganda:

---

[108] This text survives in one manuscript, now in the Biblioteca Colombina in Seville (7.2.23, ff. 62r–84r). In his "Humphrey Duke of Gloucester and Tito Livio Frulovisi", referred to above in this chapter, Roberto Weiss described the manuscript and underlined the importance of this text in historical rather than literary terms; he also published, in the same article, some fifty lines from the poem. Some of Weiss's unpublished papers, now preserved in the library of the Warburg Institute, London, give us some indications that he was working on an edition of the text; if this was so, however, the task was never completed.

[109] Rundle, "On the Difference between Virtue and Weiss", p. 183.

Undeniably, Humphrey was the pre-eminent—though, as I have suggested, by no means the only—patron of humanist texts and their
authors in the 1430's and 40's. However, while scholars might dedicate their writings to this *illustrissimus princeps*, he rarely returned the
compliment and dedicated his attention to them. Indeed, some of the
humanists who knew Humphrey well gravely doubted their patron's
desire or ability to appreciate their works.[110]

Yet Rundle continues his paper acknowledging Duke Humphrey's
contribution to English humanism, even if Humphrey's motives may
have been far from disinterested, and his cultural policy far from
systematic.

More complete and detailed, as well as less polemical in its intent,
is Rundle's D.Phil. thesis, "Of Republics and Tyrants," completed
the following year.[111] The work is concerned with a larger perspective, since Rundle is analysing the reception of humanist writing in
England, rather than a single patron; one of the important results
of this point of view is the highlighting of the fact that Duke Humphrey
may have been a point of reference, but his certainly was not an
isolated attempt at establishing a contact with Italian humanists in
the early fifteenth century. Another element Rundle underlines is
that in the representation of humanism in England there have been
not a few misconceptions and stereotypes. Thus the Duke of Gloucester,
far from being an exceptional instance, was also motivated by political rather than personal interest:

Humphrey, duke of Gloucester had little choice but to appear interested
in books; he inhabited a culture where political power and learned wisdom were perceived as necessary partners. The philosopher-king was
a well-known ideal, formulated by Boethius as if it were a tenth beati-
tude: *beatas fore res publicas si eas vel studiosi sapientiae regerent vel earum rec-
tores studere sapientiae contigisset.* This medieval commonplace was one which
humanists, with their knowledge of its Platonic source, perpetuated.[112]

Rundle's contention is that Humphrey, politically dwarfed by Henry
V's memory (and owing to his brother his position as a Protector
of England), emulated the dead King even in his patronage, sup-

---

[110] Rundle, "On the Difference between Virtue and Weiss", p. 194.
[111] David Rundle, "Of Republics and Tyrants: Aspects of Quattrocento Humanist
Writing and their Reception in England, c. 1400–c. 1460", D.Phil., Oxford, 1997.
[112] Rundle, "Of Republics and Tyrants", p. 102 (for the Latin quotation, see
Boethius *Cons.* I pr. iv; Plato *Republic* 473c).

porting the same poets (John Lydgate and Thomas Hoccleve), and asserting his intellectual independence only at a later stage of his life, when his political role did not interfere with the extent of his cultural activity. On the other hand, Italian humanists would come to England, accepting the Duke's invitation, possibly as a result of mutual misapprehension:

> humanists went to the length of contacting Humphrey not just because of his assumed largesse but, equally, because of his (unwitting) assistance to their pedagogic pretensions [. . .] Humanists needed princes like Humphrey—or, rather, like the man they could make Humphrey out to be. For, in the end, what mattered was not that the prince responded to the teaching but that he could be characterized as so doing. Ironically, then, at a certain level, the patron himself is unimportant [. . .] The philosopher-king is curiously underused; the authors appear to have preferred to tax their ingenuity in concocting a description of how their duke expressed his love of learning.[113]

The point is well taken, though it fails in a productive confrontation between the two sides of Humphrey's activity; in certain instances, besides, the critic appears rather to strain facts to fit his theory, as in the passage quoted above concerning Humphrey's "real" cultural interests, which find a political explanation in the early part of Humphrey's life, but no explanation at all for the last years. As for the Duke's activity as a book-collector, Rundle claims that "in large part, this was a collection not of Humphrey's making: many of the books in his collection were gifts, not purchases".[114] Once again we are presented with a theory rather than with facts concurring to an explanation: what is left of the Duke's library, and what we know of the many manuscripts that are no longer surviving, shows that a considerable percentage was constituted by books which were not embellished presentation copies, or precious gifts. We also know that in some cases Humphrey actively sought a book, as in the case of the Acts of the Council of Constance, which he bought from the heirs of Thomas Polton, Bishop of Worcester.[115] Although some of the points are extremely well taken, and Rundle shows a heightened awareness of the relationship between politics and patronage, there are still many sides of Humphrey's activity which are left unexplained.

---

[113] Rundle, "Of Republics and Tyrants", pp. 134–5.
[114] Rundle, "Of Republics and Tyrants", p. 150.
[115] See Sammut, p. 108.

In a more recent essay the scholar challenges the traditional interpretation of the relations between noble patronage and humanist
interests in England, maintaining that the overestimation of the
role played by magnates such as Humphrey or John Tiptoft diminishes the vital role of English humanist interests. Thus apparently
minor characters such as Adam de Moleyns are sacrificed to the
brighter light of princes and noble patrons.[116] This reassessment,
mainly based on negative evidence, goes hand in hand with a discussion of the role of Italian humanists in England that takes sometimes polemical tones: these "self-congratulatory intellectual coteries"
are described as taking upon themselves "the wise man's burden of
bringing civilization to the unlettered",[117] while it may be argued
that the status Italian humanists were forging for themselves as professional intellectuals made such solicitations of the favours of foreign potentates inevitable, and that the discussion of whether or not
a patronising attitude was intended adds little to our understanding
of the movement and of its implications. It is also true, besides, that
Duke Humphrey was not the one Englishman to whom Italian
humanists applied for patronage; it is true, on the other hand, that
he was the only one whose response had such an impact. It goes
without saying, however, that Rundle's urging towards a re-evaluation of the role of English humanists underlines a real need in
fifteenth-century cultural studies.

The distance between Weiss's achievement and Rundle's can be
measured in terms of the manuscript discoveries[118] and of the more
accurate historical research that has taken place in the intervening
decades—thus, if in the case of Rundle's work we do miss the breadth
of vision that was, and is, such a fascinating characteristic of Weiss's
book, it is indispensable now to take into account a quantity of historical and scholarly updating, even if this forces us to narrow our
perspective—one wonders, indeed, whether it would be possible today
to write a book with Weiss's sheer daring. This is possibly what

---

[116] David Rundle, "Humanism before the Tudors: On Nobility and the Reception
of *studia humanitatis* in Fifteenth-Century England", in *Reassessing Tudor Humanism*, ed.
by J. Woolfson, Basingstoke: Palgrave Macmillan, 2002: 22–42.

[117] Rundle, "Humanism before the Tudors", p. 24.

[118] Another important contribution in this sense is David Rundle, "Two Unnoticed
Manuscripts from the Collection of Humfrey, Duke of Gloucester", *The Bodleian
Library Record* 16: 1998, 211–24, 299–313.

Susanne Saygin has attempted in a recent volume,[119] though in her case the analysis is confined to the activity of Duke Humphrey, and does not embrace the whole century as in the case of Weiss's book. Once again, Saygin prefers to concentrate her attention on the Italian side of Humphrey's activity, but she does not forget possible repercussions of this activity as far as English writers were concerned, trying to unify the perspectives on Humphrey as a politician, a book-collector and a patron; she even sees a definite link between these different sides in Humphrey's attempt to import into England the attitude of humanist political writing (its didactic purpose in particular), which she maintains was put into practice, for instance, in one of Lydgate's works, *The Serpent of Division* (it should be added, however, that there is no positive proof that *The Serpent of Division* was written at Duke Humphrey's commission, or even that the date suggested by Saygin for the composition of the poem is correct—what evidence we have points in a different direction). There is thus, according to Saygin, an explicit design behind Humphrey's patronage: the scholar's enquiry aims, as she writes in her Introduction, at showing "the full patron/broker/client network in action".[120] Saygin's fundamental theory is that Humphrey's cultural activity was mostly aimed at the education of the young King, and to a Lancastrian propaganda that did not have in mind, like most Lancastrian propaganda, a popular audience, but the same court in which so much was made to undermine Humphrey's own power. In itself, the theory appears tenable, and certainly deserves further consideration, yet it might be argued that Saygin is proposing her theory before she has collected her facts, and this attitude vitiates what is otherwise an extremely accurate analysis of all the documents at our disposal—there is no doubt, for instance, that she is forced not only to give a re-reading of a series of historical facts, such as Gloucester's position after Henry V's death, but to base such re-readings on insufficient evidence.[121] Besides, we really do not know that Humphrey's influence over the young King would justify his thinking of such a project as

---

[119] Susanne Saygin, *Humphrey, Duke of Gloucester (1390–1447) and the Italian Humanists*, Leiden: Brill, 2002.

[120] Saygin, p. 3.

[121] See, for example, her hypothesis that Gloucester's claim to the regency after Henry V's death was effectively opposed thanks to the direct intervention of the Duke of Bedford (Saygin, pp. 26–29).

feasible. His protectorate lasted only until Henry of Windsor was crowned king, and this happened at an extremely early stage, when the King was nine years old. Presumably, Humphrey would not expect him to read Latin treatises on politics or English poems of the mirror of princes tradition much before that age; on the other hand, Henry's coronation meant that Humphrey's rank was reduced to that of chief councillor, and would not be directly and officially concerned with Henry's education, if ever he had been so.[122]

Saygin's hypotheses are therefore fascinating but too often unsupported; unfortunately, she builds supposition over supposition. The book undoubtedly points in the right direction when it suggests a more comprehensive view of Duke Humphrey's activity and interests; it must be added that too often historical or even literary evidence of the Duke's patronage is frustratingly elusive. It is true that studies on English humanism have too often been conditioned by the conviction, inherited from Jacob Burckhardt, of the inherent superiority of Italian humanism over the rest of Europe (a conviction that seems to have been, at any rate, shared by Humphrey himself); on the other hand, it is increasingly clear that humanism in England still needs thorough research.

---

[122] A careful reading of Henry V's will shows that Thomas, Duke of Exeter, rather than Humphrey, was entrusted with young Henry's education.

CHAPTER TWO

THE BEGINNING OF HUMANISM IN ENGLAND

The possible date at which we can start speaking of humanism in England is still a matter for debate. This is in part a common problem to any such classification: the same issue, only possibly made more complex by the wealth of literary production available, appears in the case of Italian humanism, if, for instance, on the one hand we can see in Francesco Petrarca the first humanist, and on the other talk of a medieval Boccaccio. England, however, may benefit from a clearer chronological division than Italy thanks to the fact that national history, already centring upon the concept of England as one individual state by the fifteenth century, would provide for events that had a resonance in all English centres of culture, thus marking a substantial difference from the fragmented and well-nigh chaotic political situation in Italy; besides, by this time intellectual activity in England tended to concentrate in few locations—one might almost say, in few noble or ecclesiastical households. An intellectual seeking employment would look first of all at the royal court, or at the minor courts set up by nobles such as Duke Humphrey, and then at the great bishops' houses and monasteries; but in any case he would have to be informed about national politics and the struggle for power at court, which would have been a point of reference to determine, very prosaically, which way the wind was blowing.

Thus it is tempting to look for a single event that would have triggered the scholarly and didactic activity we call humanism, and part of the critical discussion on the subject has centred upon this point. A number of events have been chosen by critics as landmarks in this case: one such, for instance, is the death of Henry V, in 1422.[1] It was an event that had immense consequences both in England and abroad, since it shaped relations between England and France for decades to come and effectively marked the onset of the

---

[1] See, for instance, A.G. Rigg, *A History of Anglo-Latin Literature 1066–1422*, Cambridge: Cambridge University Press, 1992, p. 241.

decline of the Lancastrian supremacy, but particularly because it
determined a long interregnum, during Henry VI's minority, in which
there was no central figure to whom both politics and poetry might
refer: as V.J. Scattergood correctly notes,

> Henry VI (partly because of his youth and partly through natural
> diffidence) played a comparatively unimportant role. His accession,
> coronation and marriage to Margaret of Anjou were perfunctorily cel-
> ebrated by contemporary poets, but their main attention in these years
> was focused upon the leading men of the Council—Cardinal Henry
> Beaufort, Humphrey, Duke of Gloucester, William de la Pole, Duke
> of Suffolk, and Richard, Duke of York.[2]

It is perhaps a proof of the stability of the English monarchy that
it held firm, in spite of much inner conflict, even during the long
years of Henry VI's minority.[3] In this anomalous situation, however,
the wielding of power seemed to need cultural patronage as one of
its tools; English humanism, in this perspective, appears almost to
answer a precise requirement on the part of the temporary rulers,
who would call Italian scholars so that they could work as secretaries in English households, or would ask these scholars to write
and dedicate to them Latin translations of Greek classics in the
attempt to acquire international status, perhaps to influence the young
King's education, or to determine the intellectual development of a
nation. It is difficult to assess the political value that noblemen would
consciously attach to their patronage, or to trace the boundary
between political calculation and a real, personal interest in books
and in the extraordinary new movement whose echoes reached
England thanks to the migrating Italian humanists. There is little
doubt, however, that Henry V's untimely death triggered a series of
reactions that went beyond the possible survival of the reigning
dynasty. Once again, the unique characteristics of English humanism owe much to unique political circumstances.

More often, however, the critics' attention has focused on events
that were both more relevant to the question of humanism and more
restricted in scope than Henry V's death: in particular, an authoritative voice such as Roberto Weiss's chose as the most significant

---

[2] V.J. Scattergood, *Politics and Poetry in the Fifteenth Century*, London: Blandford
Press, 1971, p. 137.
[3] On this point see Bertram Wolffe, *Henry VI*, London: Eyre Methuen, 1981,
chapter 1.

intellectual landmark the visit of the humanist Poggio Bracciolini to England, going so far as to state that "before Poggio came to England in 1418, it is quite impossible to find [. . .] any humanistic manifestations in this country".[4] The date of Bracciolini's arrival, however, is still a matter of controversy, though it can be assumed that it took place at some stage between 1419 and 1423.[5] In 1414–17 the Council of Constance had drawn together a number of humanists, including Poggio. The Council was not only a political and religious occasion, but also a moment of international cultural exchange, and "a large and thriving book-market".[6] There the Italian humanist had met the Bishop of Winchester, Henry Beaufort, who would later become one of Duke Humphrey's staunchest political opponents, but seemed content at this stage to be his rival in patronage—or rather, to anticipate Humphrey's future activity. Beaufort offered Poggio employment in his household, asking the humanist to follow him in his return trip to England.

Poggio therefore started his service at the Bishop's household in Mantua, going to Normandy first and then to England as a member of Henry Beaufort's retinue. He spent four years in this country, mainly in London but temporarily moving to Salisbury in the summer of 1420, being duly disillusioned from what he saw, and bitterly reporting on the lack of scholarship or of rewarding libraries, as this extract from a letter to Niccolò Niccoli shows:

---

[4] Roberto Weiss, *Humanism in England During the Fifteenth Century*, Oxford: Blackwell, 1941 (3rd ed. 1967), p. 7.

[5] In his *Humanism in England* (p. 4), Weiss dates the episode in 1418; in a more recent study, however, Martin Davies proposes a more accurate estimate, focusing on the years between 1419 and 1423, fixing on the earlier as the most probable. See Martin C. Davies, "Friends and Enemies of Poggio: Studies in Quattrocento Humanist Literature", D.Phil., Oxford, 1986. Weiss also proposes 1485, with the accession of Henry VII to the throne, as the year in which humanism saw its conclusion in England—again, a point that might be well challenged, though for different reasons. On Poggio's visit, see also J.B. Trapp, "The Humanist Book", in *The Cambridge History of the Book in Britain*, vol. 3: *1400–1557*, ed. by L. Hellinga and J.B. Trapp, Cambridge: Cambridge University Press, 1999: 285–315, pp. 292–3. In the same essay Trapp writes that "the history of the humanist book in Britain [. . .] may properly be said to begin with the patronage—and, perhaps, the reading—of Duke Humfrey, youngest brother of Henry V" (p. 293).

[6] Margaret Harvey, *England, Rome and the Papacy 1417–64. The Study of a Relationship*, Manchester: Manchester University Press, 1993, p. 40. Harvey also notes that the Council of Constance had other repercussions for English humanism: "At it also Robert Hallum and Nicholas Bubwith received dedication of a copy of Serravalle's commentary on Dante's *Commedia*, which John Whethamstede, abbot of St Albans, later used from Duke Humfrey's library" (*ibidem*).

Equidem, ut scripsi ad te alias, cum hic esset ingens pestis, peregri-
natus sum cum domino; sed hec peregrinatio nihil habuit iocunditatis
tum propter multa, tum vero quia nihil librorum repperi. Monasteria
sunt hic opulentissima sed nove fundationis; sunt enim constructa a
regibus ut plurimum citra quadrigentesimum annum. Quod si qua sunt
antiquiora, ea carent libris gentilibus, referta novis doctoris et maxime
ecclesisiaticis [*sic*]. Vidi pretera inventaria diligenter facta, in quibus
nihil erat dignum studiis humanitatis. Nec, mehercule, mirum.[7]

Bracciolini, as we can see, is extremely explicit on this point. Yet
his reaction, as shown in this and other letters to Niccoli, has given
rise to some controversy. We turn, once again, to Weiss for a first
assessment:

Poggio's visit to England is interesting as showing how he reacted to
the English environment and to the various Englishmen he met. His
employer does not appear to have taken much interest in Poggio's
studies once he had landed in England. During the early period of his
stay in Beaufort's household he was often left behind in London while
the Bishop was travelling. Later, however, he is known to have accompanied his master occasionally on journeys through England, and in
spite of Poggio's complaints it is possible to perceive that Beaufort was
anxious to retain him in his service, and was trying to meet his wishes.
On the other hand it is not surprising that Beaufort showed few inclinations for Italian culture. When one's interests are centred around a
single object, one seldom finds sufficient leisure for other pursuits, and
as Beaufort's energies were absorbed by politics, both English and
Papal, he could hardly spare time for the patronage of letters.[8]

It would thus seem that, in the case of the Bishop of Winchester at
least, the employing of humanists—more specifically, of Italian humanists who had already acquired some fame in Europe—was more a
matter of status than of real cultural interest. Yet other factors concurred to make this first visit of a humanist in England a failure.
What has too little been taken into account is that Poggio had the

---

[7] "Indeed, as I wrote to you elsewhere, as the plague had arrived here, I began
travelling with my lord; but there was no great pleasure in this travelling, since I
could find no books. Monasteries here are very rich but of new foundation; they
have been built by kings no more than four hundred years ago. If older ones survive, they have no secular books, but are full of the most recent works of the
Doctors of the Church and especially of ecclesiastics. I also saw very carefully compiled inventories, in which there was nothing worth of humanist studies. And nothing
interesting, indeed!" (*Poggio Bracciolini. Lettere. I: Lettere a Niccolò Niccoli*, ed. by H. Harth,
Istituto Nazionale di Studi sul Rinascimento, Firenze: Olschki, 1984, pp. 34–5).
[8] Weiss, *Humanism in England*, p. 18.

misfortune of entering the Bishop's service at a time in which the latter's fortunes were rather at a low ebb: Henry V, wary of the numerous honours Pope Martin V had bestowed upon Henry Beaufort in the previous years,[9] was afraid of papal interference into English affairs, and the Bishop had to work hard to regain the King's trust. Besides, there seems to have been little in the Bishop's manners or taste to attract Bracciolini's interest. Henry Beaufort did not appear to have a real need for a Latin secretary, since his affairs were mainly concerned with his own country, and we have little evidence of his promoting the advancement of learning among his countrymen. It is interesting to see, on the other hand, how this pioneer among humanists reacted to England. Bracciolini may have seen in the Bishop of Winchester's invitation the means of gaining an international reputation, a permanent job, and perhaps everlasting glory with the discovery of some manuscripts which had so far escaped the attention of the less well equipped English scholars. If this was so, he was bound to be disappointed on almost all counts—already in 1421 he had started petitioning the Bishop so that his service could be ended, though we know he was back in Rome only in February 1423.[10] In his study on Poggio's activity, Davies comments on his English sojourn with these words:

> Poggio's stay in England from 1419 onwards was a gloomy time. He did not take to the climate or the people, and above all the Bishop proved a disappointment, being niggardly and without any great regard for learning. The monasteries of England were largely bare of the classical works he had hoped to turn up and he was obliged to turn to patristic and scholastic authors for reading matter.[11]

If there is one doubtful point in Davies's account, it is probably the word "obliged". There is nothing to show us that Bracciolini was not indeed interested in the patristic and scholastic authors he had occasion to read in the English monastery libraries, bar a certain propensity on the part of twentieth-century criticism to keep ecclesiastical literature and humanist interests carefully separated. After

---

[9] In 1417 the Pope had named him for the cardinalate, besides making him legate *a latere* and giving him the seat of Winchester. See G.L. Harriss, *Cardinal Beaufort: A Study of Lancastrian Ascendancy and Decline*, Oxford: Clarendon Press, 1988, pp. 94–6.

[10] See Harriss, *Cardinal Beaufort*, pp. 100–1.

[11] Davies, p. 6.

all, Poggio's meeting with Henry Beaufort had taken place in an
ecclesiastical milieu—ecclesiastical councils, and the Council of
Constance in particular, had been the occasion for cultural exchanges
on a widely international scale. On the other hand, Poggio's English
employment may have stood him in good stead when, after his return
to Italy, he was appointed papal secretary.[12] We shall see as we
progress in our study how English humanism is strongly characterised
in religious terms; we may perhaps come to question, even in the
case of Italy, to what an extent the definition of *humanae litterae* meant
an exclusion of the *divinae*.

Our account of Bracciolini's meeting with Henry Beaufort, however, together with our first glimpses of the consequences it had,
gives us a first idea of how the political structure of a country can
affect the development of intellectual thought. Italy's looser political
structure at the time, its division into minimal units, whether they
were small states or simply individual cities, seems to have favoured
a form of cultural patronage that England was incapable of producing. On the other hand, England's relative isolation, and its
equally relative marginality in medieval European history, may constitute some of the reasons why the country offered such a meagre
reward to Bracciolini's detective efforts, but may also explain other
phenomena we connect with English humanism. This demonstrates
once more the impossibility of setting up a comparison between two
forms of humanism which experienced a completely different progress.
Even setting personal attitudes apart, Duke Humphrey could never
have become another Lorenzo il Magnifico, but then, one might
add, he might have wanted to reach a much higher status in the
first place. Besides, Poggio's visit, if it had any effect, delayed rather
than promoting the arrival of Italian humanists to England, since,
after Bracciolini's mainly negative experience, it would have been
difficult for English patrons to call to their court humanists of the
calibre of Leonardo Bruni, as Humphrey attempted to do a few
years later.[13]

However, it is possible to see the question of Poggio's attitude
towards England under a new light, aside from his controversial reac-

---

[12] Susanne Saygin, *Humphrey, Duke of Gloucester (1390–1447) and the Italian Humanists*,
Leiden: Brill, 2002, pp. 238–54.
[13] We know that the Duke of Gloucester invited Bruni in Inghilterra, but the
latter refused, as is shown in a letter dated 1434. See Sammut, pp. 146–8.

tions to the country as they are expressed in his letters. One of the results of his English sojourn was the interest Bracciolini showed in recent English history, and particularly in Henry V. This is shown by two pieces written by the humanist, though not appearing in the published *Opera Omnia*,[14] the second of which may be of particular interest. It is *Vitae Pontificum*, probably written in "his very last days in 1459",[15] a fragment of a historiographical undertaking, never completed because of his death, as it is demonstrated that the last pages deal with events that took place in the last year of Bracciolini's life.[16] Editing these fragments, Martin Davies conjectures that they might have been written in preparation for a larger work:

> There are signs that those notes were in the course of elaboration into a full-blown history which would have paralleled and balanced the recently finished *Historiae Florentini populi*: the direct speech given to Henry V before Agincourt (v. 220ff.) is a device typical of classical and humanist historiography which contrasts with the dry recital of events elsewhere.[17]

As we can see from the quotation above, one of the fragments[18] concerns Henry V, whom Bracciolini claims to have met at Rouen, after the fall of the city, in 1419. We shall see in the case of Tito Livio Frulovisi how Henry V's life seems to have attracted the attention of a number of humanists, and to have been considered, for different reasons, an excellent instance of the exemplary life that could become the humanist historian's chosen topic. The fragment is too brief to allow us a comprehensive view of Bracciolini's attitude towards the English King; however, his wisdom is stressed, and his moral qualities are given greater prominence than his military ability:

> Rex fuit magni animi, non minoris consilii, promissa et datam fidem constanter servavit, adeo ut suis verbis staretur que nunquam fuerunt

---

[14] *Poggius Bracciolini. Opera Omnia*, ed. by R. Fubini, Torino: Bottega d'Erasmo, 1969. The two unpublished pieces have been edited by Martin C. Davies and appear in his "Friends and Enemies of Poggio".

[15] Davies, p. 28.

[16] "One can also point to the existence of doublets—alternative phrases whose final form had not been settled—and lacunae in the text where research never completed was intended to reveal a name or a fact" (Davies, p. 45).

[17] Davies, p. 47.

[18] Davies, pp. 57–8, ll. 209–67. Further references and quotations from Bracciolini's fragment are taken from this edition, and indicated by line number.

irrita [. . .]. Vigilantissimus fuit ac diligentissimus ut qui pauca per alios
ageret: ipse et belli et pacis munera obibat.[19]

Besides, his careful activity as a writer is underlined: "nullas litteras
scripsit quas non prius legerat, multa addens, demens nonnulla. Paucis
verbis utebatur et iis sententiis gravibus refertis"[20]—a peculiarly interesting homage for a king whose testament, opened and read probably while Bracciolini was still in the retinue of Henry Beaufort, had
caused so much controversy in the King's Council. The rest of the
fragment is mainly concerned with Henry V's French campaigns,
and concludes with an optimistic "ita universo regno pax est red-
dita".[21] If the fragment was written in 1459, Bracciolini probably
knew that Henry's peace had been uncertain, and of very short duration; yet, as far as it is possible to infer from the short fragment,
the humanist does not intend to detract anything from Henry's stature
as a statesman.

Thus from the start English humanism, even in this very idio-
syncratic form, appears peculiarly concerned with the writing of history, and particularly with history as a description of recent events
proposed in the form of *exempla*. This is particularly significant since
not only there is a wealth of half-forgotten historical literature in the
English fifteenth century, but patrons such as Humphrey of Gloucester
seemed particularly interested in the writing and rewriting of recent
history as one of the most convincing vehicles for political propaganda. It must be added that this new interest coincided with a
widening of the scope of patronage: as Bennett correctly notes, the
production of literature was influenced by the presence of a wider
public in the fifteenth century,[22] and whether this public was secular
or religious, interested in works in Latin or in the vernacular, the
phenomenon is interesting because it highlights two factors: a heightened interest in writing meant that it was easier to conceive of lit-

---

[19] Lines 209–15. "He was a magnanimous king, of no little wisdom, who always
kept his word, and who always acted so that his words would never be empty. He
was very careful to let as few people as possible do things in his name: he himself
received the gifts of peace and war".

[20] Lines 216–6. "He wrote nothing without reading it first, adding many things,
subtracting a few. He used few words, and those few often interspersed with wise
maxims".

[21] "Thus peace has come back to the whole kingdom".

[22] Bennett, H.S., "The Production and Dissemination of Vernacular Manuscripts
in the Fifteenth Century," *The Library* 5th series, 1: 1947, 167–78, p. 167.

erature as a means of political communication or even persuasion; an increased number of patrons would also exercise a greater pressure on writers; thus what was being written was strictly connected with the historical and social background against which it was conceived; a phenomenon that had concerned historiography in England since the twelfth century, but that finds new strength in the fifteenth. Thus we begin to see Humphrey's activity not as an isolated and ultimately failed attempt to imitate Italian patronage and Italian humanism, but as the foremost example of an attitude that was taking roots in England.

To move the question to a strictly literary ground, there are perhaps other factors that might be taken into consideration if we wish to determine upon an event or a period of time for the rise and spread of humanism in England. Book production, for instance, saw a significant rise in the early fifteenth century, accompanying a renovated commercial interest in English vernacular literature.[23] However, the most significant event is probably the development of an analogous movement in Scotland, which took place roughly in the same years and, from a literary point of view, had extraordinary results. Though the label of "Scottish Chaucerians" that has been attached to them in modern criticism may sound, and possibly is, rather dismissive, the poets we group under this label achieved a distinction unparalleled by contemporary writers in England, with whom they shared an interest in the classical tradition (evident, for instance, in Robert Henryson's poetry, or in Gavin Douglas's translation of the *Aeneid*), but from whom they were distinguished by a more original voice. It might seem easier to speak of Scottish fifteenth-century humanism altogether, especially because the approach of these poets and scholars to the classics seems to need little mediation or outside intervention. It is easy to imagine a close exchange of ideas or even

---

[23] I owe this observation to A.S.G. Edwards and Derek Pearsall, who add: "Even the most cursory comparison of the seventy-five years periods on either side of 1400 reveals a spectacular transformation: in broad figures, one is speaking of the difference between a rate of production that leaves extant about thirty manuscripts and one that leaves extant about six hundred. Prior to 1400, with some notable exceptions, production of books of vernacular writing is largely devoted to religious material, and was probably dominated by the religious establishment" ("The Manuscripts of the Major English Poetic Texts," in *Book Production and Publishing in Britain 1375–1475*, ed. by J. Griffiths and D. Pearsall, Cambridge: Cambridge University Press, 1989: 257–78, p. 257.

of books between Scotland and England at all times (certainly easier than a slow and perilous exchange between Italy and England),
but in this case we even have a poet-king who represents, both with
his life and his writings, the closeness of this connection: James I of
Scotland, believed to be the author of *The Kingis Quair*, and for eighteen years a prisoner of the English crown—a condition he shared
with another nobly-born poet, Charles, Duke of Orléans. Given the
status of the two prisoners and the length of their stay, they were
allowed leisure and the means of reading and writing, and received,
at least in the case of James, who was captured when he was barely
twelve, a gentleman's education. The future King of Scotland thus
in his poem showed the influence of the Boethian and Chaucerian
tradition as well as an affinity with European poetic voices that were
just being imported into England, such as Dante Alighieri, or Guillaume
de Deguileville.[24] It is no wonder that at the end of his poem, generally recognised as distinctly autobiographical in tone, he saw fit to
thank not a Scottish bard, but two English poets who endowed him
with his true literary inheritance:

> Vnto th'inpnis of my maisteris dere,
> Gowere and Chaucere, that on the steppis satt
> Of rethorike quhill thai were lyvand here,
> Superlatiue as poetis laureate
> In moralitee and eloquence ornate,
> I recommend my buk in lynis sevin—
> And eke thair saulis vnto the blisse of hevin[25]

thus acknowledging a debt to English rather than Scottish literature.

This excursus into the flourishing of Scottish poetry in the fifteenth
century has perhaps shown the reader a few things. Humanism was
not simply a phenomenon imported from continental Europe thanks
to a handful of Italian adventurers, but was establishing firm roots
in the country also by means of native scholars and poets. There is
at least one Italian humanist visiting Scotland at the time, Aeneas

---

[24] See Alessandra Petrina, *The Kingis Quair of James I of Scotland*, Padova: Unipress,
1997. On James's reading of Dante, see "Courtly Ladies and *Donne Gentili*: A Comparison between Dante's Beatrice and the Lady of the *Kingis Quair*", forthcoming
in *Older Scots Literature*, ed. by S. Mapstone.
[25] *James I of Scotland. The Kingis Quair*, ed. by J. Norton-Smith. Leiden: Brill, 1981,
lines 1373–79.

Silvius Piccolomini, who appears favourably impressed with this poet-king, as his portrait in *De viris illustribus* shows.[26] As in the case of the humanistic Petrarch and the medieval Boccaccio, mentioned above, humanism in England does not start from a single event, and is not imported piecemeal by a single man, or even by the concerted efforts of a patron and his circle, but finds a series of concurrent causes in a number of historical and intellectual events and literary contributions.

Above all, the presence of a contemporary cultural movement in Scotland emphasises the strong continuity between the Middle Ages and the Renaissance, both in Middle English and in Middle Scots literature. The legacy of Chaucer above all, but also the books that were more commonly at the writers' disposal in the fifteenth century, meant that humanism could be intended primarily as a continuation of Medieval traditions, but more importantly as a reassessment of an extremely significant inheritance. The intellectual historian David Starkey has taken this point to show that the Italian contribution has been overestimated; taking as an instance Henry V's commissioning of *The Troy Book* to John Lydgate, and showing how Lydgate's sources tend to be thirteenth-century texts rather than Homer or Virgil, he concludes:

> This complacent insularity is easily understood and, so long as England were winning, there was no need to change it. Indeed, it is important to remember that early fifteenth-century Italians were at least as likely to be influenced by England as the other way around.[27]

Such a statement risks becoming merely a sweeping generalisation, and can be criticised on a number of factual points. The thirteenth-century text Lydgate was using for his poem was Guido delle Colonne's *Historia Destructionis Troiae*; the fact that it came from Italy (and that so many poets of the English fourteenth and fifteenth centuries found their inspiration in Italian texts) rather undermines Starkey's main assumption. Besides, a quick glance at Lydgate's production and at his sources proves that, whatever we may say of this poet, he could

---

[26] *Enee Silvii Piccolominei postea Pii PP.II De viris illustribus*, ed. by A. van Heck, Città del Vaticano: Biblioteca Apostolica Vaticana, 1991, pp. 92–3.

[27] Starkey, David, "England", in *The Renaissance in National Context*, ed. by M. Teich and R. Porter, Cambridge: Cambridge University Press, 1992: 149–63, pp. 148–9.

never be accused of insularity; if anything, he personifies that attitude of eager curiosity towards "continental" literary productions that
is so typical of Middle English literature. Besides, while the Italian
influence over English letters is amply demonstrable, not only thanks
to the poetic production of the time in England, but also because
of the number of manuscripts that were produced in Italy and were
acquired by English bibliophiles, there is no such movement in the
opposite direction: up to this point, English intellectual life may be
said to have made little or no impact on Italian observers and readers. It is true, on the other hand, that the beginning of humanism
in England does not entail the end of the Middle Ages, or rather,
that English humanism maintains and continues a literary tradition
that had found its real turning point a century earlier, with the work
of Geoffrey Chaucer.

On the other hand, it is important to underline the links between
literary production and contemporary history, and between historical and strictly literary writing, as an original characteristic of this
century. Once again it might be worth quoting David Starkey, who
rightly highlights in Humphrey of Gloucester, not only the bibliophile and the literary patron, but also the leader of a strong pro-
war movement:

> Humphrey of Gloucester, the Protector of England, longed to cut a
> figure on the European stage and clearly saw the role of Renaissance
> prince as the most glamorous. His collection of books became the
> nucleus of Oxford university library; he employed successive Italian
> humanists as his secretary, and he commissioned books in Italy and
> England [. . .] What has not been sufficiently emphasized, however, is
> that this literary patronage was intended to bolster the arguments of
> the war party, of which Gloucester was leader. The subjects alone
> make this plain.[28]

We have seen above how Poggio Bracciolini showed interest in the
English nation almost only in terms of its recent history. Duke Humphrey employed an Italian humanist, Tito Livio Frulovisi, and the
most notable result of this cultural relation was Frulovisi's *Vita Henrici
Quinti*, which remained a model for chroniclers in the years that followed, and was even translated into Italian by another humanist,
Pier Candido Decembrio. The following chapters will show how the

---

[28] Starkey, p. 149.

writing and making of history were one of the main preoccupations of Duke Humphrey both as a politician and as a literary patron, how he tried to use historical examples to defend his political choices or make his claims to power, and how poems and "lybels" became a common means of political propaganda in the Lancastrian era. For the moment, it is important to underline that this is one of the characteristics that give English humanism its unique character, and is certainly a characteristic to be taken into consideration, together with the cohabitation in English humanism of *divinae* and *humanae litterae*, which is discussed below.

Divinae and humanae litterae

The discussion on this point should start with a postulate, that nonetheless has a firm basis in history: in the late Middle Ages in Europe secular authority still finds its transcendental justification in the sanction of religious hierarchies. Following the same pattern, secular literature finds its support in religious literature. The only, and very partial, exception to the postulate appears to be Italy—as concerns both secular authority and secular literature. The unique situation of the country, with an extraordinary fragmentation into independent towns and minor states, and with an ongoing friction between some of these states and Papal authority, probably contributed to make this possible. It might be argued that Italian humanists were at their most meritorious once they enfranchised secular literature, rediscovering textual worth and, thanks to their reading of the classics, a new, "humane" sense of history (the most memorable instance of this attitude being Lorenzo Valla), as well as promoting the autonomy of intellectual life and elevating it to the status of a profession, or a liberal art. However, it must not be forgotten that many of them still found or sought employment in the papal Curia, or were themselves in holy orders, so that the link with ecclesiastical authority was very much alive even in Italian humanism. There was, perhaps, a heightened consciousness of its presence, and of the fact that it was possibly ceasing to become inevitable.

It is difficult to maintain that English humanism achieved the same cultural consciousness as the analogous movement in Italy, not only in terms of the enfranchisement of secular literature from religious sanction, but also as concerns the close connection with the hierarchies of both lay and religious power. With the preservation as well as the diffusion of learning still entrusted to monasteries such as Bury St Edmunds, or St Albans; with budding universities such as Oxford or Cambridge hosting well-endowed Benedictine colleges, and still heavily dependent on the munificence of religious orders or of private individuals playing a public role, such as Duke Humphrey, intellectual life in the English fifteenth century structured itself upon an ideology inevitably reproducing relations of power.[29] Three texts in the vernacular can be considered central to the literary landscape of the first half of the century: these three texts were Thomas Hoccleve's *Regement of Princes*, John Lydgate's *Fall of Princes*, and (with some straining of dates) John Gower's *Confessio Amantis*; they were all centrally concerned with kingship. Of these three works, the first two at least were closely connected to the Lancastrian house, were indeed part of the Lancastrian ideological project, as shall be shown in the following chapters. At the same time, the texts found their literary justification in a double *auctoritas*: the writers of the past from which these works drew their inspiration (medieval, rather than classical writers), and the divine authority. The fifteenth-century poet might find himself in a three-tiered relationship: to his patron, to his literary authorities, and to his God. Thus Lydgate, rendering into his English *Fall of Princes* Boccaccio's *De casibus virorum illustrium* via the French version redacted by Laurence de Premierfait, finds it indispensable to acknowledge, in a prologue added to the original text, all his *auctoritates*: the French writer, the Italian one, his master Chaucer, the Duke of Gloucester, and finally Calliope and her sisters. The fact that the prologue extends to over 400 lines bears witness to Lydgate's prolixity (the contemporary Palladius translator manages the same task in little over a hundred lines), but also to the complex situation in which the late medieval author could find himself. This dependence from a divine sanction informs also the new intellectual movement, and the patronage that is being fashioned for it.

The distinction between *divinae* and *humanae litterae*, then, should be subjected to a fresh analysis, which might lead us to a re-definition

---

[29] On this point, see Larry Scanlon, "The King's Two Voices: Narrative and Power in Hoccleve's *Regement of Princes*", in *Literary Practice and Social Change in Britain, 1380–1530*, ed. by L. Patterson, Berkeley: University of California Press, 1990: 216–47, p. 217.

of humanism not only in English but in European terms. Seen in this wider perspective, the fifteenth century saw a general shifting of the centres of cultural power: they were no longer the monastery libraries but the courts, the schools, the new-born universities; in a word, places which might refer to the local centre of political power for support or recognition, and might choose to ignore, or even challenge, the claims of ecclesiastical power. It is also generally assumed that the objects of scholarly investigation changed too: no longer religious texts, ranging from the Bible to the heavy inheritance of patristic and scholastic philosophy, but the newly discovered texts of classical Rome and Greece, now freed from the medieval, Christian-oriented interpretation. This is only partly true. A pattern of continuation and development rather than an abrupt break with the past is discernible in the humanistic movement, while the direct challenges against ecclesiastical power, of which a notable instance was, as we noted above, Lorenzo Valla's *De Falsa et Ementita Donatione Constantini*, were the exception rather than the rule. Just as ecclesiastical libraries continued to supply the humanists with books (and while some of the high ecclesiastics themselves may have still supplied humanists with the means of living), Latin texts continued to be read, fresh knowledge being added in the scholars' approach to the manuscripts. The acquired competence of the Greek language (though by no means belonging to the majority of humanists) certainly improved the readers' acquaintance with Greek texts, and allowed the translation of a number of these works into Latin, thus making them accessible to a yet wider audience. Monastery libraries remained precious resources, but the range of the cultural debate was widened and diversified by the contribution of new, lay centres of learning, such as the universities. At the same time, the ecclesiastical hierarchies maintained a powerful control over learning and the transmission of culture.

Once again, a partial exception may be made for Italy, whose very peculiar political situation allowed for a diversified organisation of education. Besides, Italian humanists in many cases deliberately sought a new, original approach to the same classical texts their medieval ancestors had read and translated; and the reaction against, for instance, the thirteenth-century *Aristoteles latinus* that was still in use in European universities in the fifteenth century could be not only in terms of a more elegant Latin prose, or a clearest understanding of the intricacies of Greek grammar; it could also imply the humanist's belief in his own deeper understanding of the texts. There is little doubt that humanism remains, above all, a philological and educational programme, rather than a philosophical one; but we can reasonably assume that for many humanists philology could be an interpretative key that would allow the re-discovery of the "truth" of classical texts. Thus, Leonardo Bruni complains of his predecessors, when confronted with the task of translating Aristotle, in purely linguistic terms:

> Aristotelis *Ethicorum* libros facere Latinos nuper institui, non quia prius traducti non essent, sed quia sic traducti erant, ut barbari magis quam Latini effecti viderentur. Constat enim illius traductionis auctorem (quicumque tandem is fuerit, quem tamen ordinis praedicatorum fuisse manifestum est) neque Graecas neque Latinas litteras satis scivisse.[30]

Bruni's target in this case is the medieval translator William of Moerbecke, and his supposed ignorance of Greek (and perhaps even of Latin). But, as he then explains in an essay following the previously quoted text, he is not concerned simply with the possibility of an inelegant, "barbarian" translation:

> Denique interpretis vitia sunt: si aut male capit, quod transferendum est, aut male reddit; aut si id, quod apte concinneque dictum sit a primo auctore, ipse ita convertat, ut ineptum et inconcinnum et dissipatum efficiatur.[31]

And here the humanist clearly shows how, underlying the search for accurate reproduction, there is the conviction that this implies an introduction to the authentic text, free of the medieval linguistic (and perhaps ideological) misinterpretations.

Yet this attitude concerned only a minority of intellectuals, and tended to be fairly localised. In the case of England, by the begin-

---

[30] "Lately I set out to translate into Latin Aristotle's *Ethics*, not because it had not been translated before, but because it was translated in such a way that it seemed in a barbarian tongue rather than in Latin. Actually the author of that translation (whoever he was, and it seems evident that he was a preaching friar) knew neither enough Greek, nor enough Latin". See "Praemissio quaedam ad evidentiam novae translationis Ethicorum Aristotelis", in *Leonardo Bruni Aretino. Humanistisch-philosophische Schriften mit einer Chronologie seiner Werke und Briefe*, ed. by H. Baron, Leipzig: Teubner, 1928, pp. 76–7.

[31] "In short, these are the faults of the translator: he either understands imperfectly what must be translated, or translates imperfectly; or if the author wrote something aptly and elegantly, his translation is inept, inelegant, inadequate". *De interpretatione recta*, in *Opere letterarie e politiche di Leonardo Bruni*, ed. by P. Viti, Torino: UTET, 1996: 145–93, p. 158.

ning of the fifteenth century culture still seemed firmly in the hands of the ecclesiastical power—it must be noted that England maintained a structure of power in which religion, particularly as represented by the high ecclesiastical hierarchies, played an essential role in the organisation of national and local government. Besides, a scholar would have had very few possible alternatives to monastery libraries as his fields of activity, as even the possession of books was far from becoming common, and books were often *de facto* identified with religious books:

> The better endowed clergy, the bishops, cathedral clergy and members of collegiate churches, and university teachers, formed almost the only class of the population who, occasionally before 1400, and frequently after, possessed small libraries of their own. The only other possessors of libraries are seen to have been certain members of the regular orders, great nobles, and lawyers [. . .] Few except bibliophiles actually possessed romances or vernacular chronicles, though a popular knowledge of romances was widespread through singing or recitation.[32]

What fruit humanism did yield in England, therefore, owed its nature and existence to an uneasy balance between political and ecclesiastical power, and was determined by a religion that still and pervasively played a major role not only in the ordinary citizen's everyday life, but also in the higher political and social spheres, and heavily influenced patronage and the construction of culture. It is possible that our perspective of Italian humanism is rather too biased towards *humanae litterae*, and still owes something to an ideological dichotomy between Middle Ages and Renaissance which studies such as Huizinga's have not completely dispelled. What is certain is that we constantly tend to underestimate the central relevance of patristic authors, and above all of the medieval scholastic inheritance, when considering the efforts and achievements of the Italian Quattrocento. In England the influence was even more marked, not only because, as Sammut observes, "as it happened in the rest of Europe, in England humanism originated and developed thanks to the contacts with the Roman Curia",[33] but also because the relationship between church and king

---

[32] Margaret Deanesly, "Vernacular Books in England in the Fourteenth and Fifteenth Centuries", *Modern Language Review* 15: 1920, pp. 349–58, this quotation p. 350.
[33] Sammut, pp. 5–6 (my translation).

is part of that conflict for power in which men like Humphrey of Gloucester tried to weigh in with a cultural, and not only a political, contribution.

The influence of ecclesiastical hierarchies over literary production in fifteenth-century England might be also seen against the background of the interplay between religious and secular power, then extremely strong in the country. Matters like the appointment of new bishops could be of advantage to both king and pope;[34] the early history of Cardinal Beaufort and of his double allegiance to King Henry V and Pope Martin V—an allegiance, as we have seen, whose precarious balance the Cardinal could manage only with extreme difficulty—shows that ecclesiastical power might always trigger the problem of the interference of the papal Curia into national politics, but at the same time was strictly connected with lay power. It may perhaps be added, then, that the distinction between *humanae* and *divinae literae* is at worst a fictitious one, and at best a concern of intellectuals rather than patrons, or that an issue that was extremely present in Italian humanism has been rather arbitrarily exported by later critics and historians into the widely different English context.

When taking into consideration the situation of fifteenth-century England, thus, we might be wary of generalisations such as Roberto Weiss's statement that "English learning during the fifteenth century was practically the monopoly of ecclesiastics",[35] but we should not at the same time underestimate the importance of the role the Church played in intellectual life. Quite simply, the interplay is far more complex than the early scholars of English humanism could imagine. Some instances may be illuminating: before 1500, the University of Oxford included not only ten secular colleges that have survived to the present day, but three Benedictine colleges, an Augustinian abbey and priory, a Cistercian abbey and college, and Dominican, Franciscan, Carmelite and Austin friaries; all these houses hosted their own, often well-endowed, libraries.[36] This does not mean, as

---

[34] "Vacancies afforded opportunities for gain to pope and king: the pope especially by translations which multiplied vacancies and the services and annates which accrued from the subsequent provisions; the king by exploiting his regalian right and drawing income from the temporalities of an empty bishopric". See Margaret Harvey, *England, Rome and the Papacy 1417–64. The Study of a Relationship*, Manchester: Manchester University Press, 1993, pp. 289–90.

[35] Weiss, *Humanism in England*, p. 179.

[36] N.R. Ker, "Oxford College Libraries before 1500", in *The Universities in the Late*

Weiss writes, that "ecclesiastics ruled the Universities",[37] but their presence was certainly felt, as it was felt in administration and civil service. Events such as the Council of Constance and, a few years later, the Council of Basel show how relevant ecclesiastical assemblies could be, and how influential for international diplomacy, as well as for the exchange of manuscripts and ideas, and for the transmission of learning in Europe. What is even more important, everyday life demanded education, and by implication what we have called the transmission of learning at a local level, mainly to ecclesiastics: outside ecclesiastical circles, the pursuit of culture could be the privileged domain of the rich aristocracy, but it was far from being the habitual employment of the middle classes, though recent religious and social movements such as Lollardy demonstrate that this order of things was far from being accepted at all levels of the community.

It is indeed in these movements that we see a sign of restlessness, an indication of the onset of those changes that in countries such as Italy are, almost without discussion, subsumed under the name of humanism. While, at the level of official ecclesiastical culture, texts in English still found a place with much difficulty, and while aristocratic bibliophiles such as Humphrey of Gloucester collected manuscripts almost solely in Latin and French, a religious literature in English was flourishing at the time, though it was almost all of a "non-official" nature, and would become the target of the anti-Lollard repression typified in Arundel's *Constitutions*, composed between 1407 and 1409 but come into full effect only after the Oldcastle rebellion in 1414. A recent, very interesting study by Nicholas Watson has established a precise link between the enforcement of the *Constitutions* and a sharp decline in the diffusion of vernacular manuscripts:

> The Constitutions were notorious for well over a century, taking a prominent role in Sir Thomas More's *Dialogue Concerning Heresies* (written in the 1520's), where they are still assumed to be one of the causes of the rarity of vernacular Bibles and of the reluctance on the clergy's part to disseminate biblical learning.[38]

Middle Ages, ed. by J. Ijsewijn and J. Paquet, Louvain: Louvain University Press, 1978: 293–311, reprinted in *Books, Collectors and Libraries. Studies in the Medieval Heritage*, London: The Hambledon Press, 1985, pp. 301–20, p. 301.

[37] Weiss, p. 179.

[38] Nicholas Watson, "Censorship and Cultural Change in Late Medieval England: Vernacular Theology, the Oxford Translation Debate, and Arundel's Constitutions of 1409", *Speculum* 70: 1995, 822–64, p. 830.

We may take the same analysis to demonstrate not only the undoubted efficacy of the anti-Lollard repression, but also the strength non-official religious literature had in spite of every attempt to dissuade the laity from reading and transmitting it. It has been noted that, in spite of every attempt at repression, more than 250 manuscripts of the Bible in the vernacular are still extant, against 117 copies of *Ayenbite of Inwit*, and sixty-four of *The Canterbury Tales*.[39] Such a number, indeed astonishing, is once again revelatory of the force of the movement, and of the sheer need for texts in the vernacular. On the one hand, then, we have scholars and book-collectors reading and translating from Latin and French; on the other, the late fourteenth and fifteenth century in England see a flourishing of religious literature in the vernacular—the most obvious instance being the literature produced by the mystics. The audience for the latter type of texts has been identified in its general traits by Anne Hudson and H.L. Spencer in the following passage:

> that largely hidden world of which the Lollard knights are but one manifestation, a world of financially and socially secure laypeople, of increasing education, sincerely devout but because of that sincerity aware of the discrepancy between gospel precept and ecclesiastical actuality, anxious for religious reform but not for social revolution.[40]

Its main characteristics, as described here, mark its distance from the proto-humanistic audience of which Humphrey is such a prominent example. Often anti-Lollard repression, and the censorship upon reading that was its inevitable consequence, took the traits of an embryonic class struggle; writing of Arundel's *Constitutions*, Watson notes that "the legislation was repeatedly used to identify lower-class owners and readers of non-Lollards works as heretics".[41]

The issue of the diffusion of non-orthodox theological texts, however, raises an inevitable question, that is, what influence could this non-official religious literature exercise upon lay literature, and more important, what role it could play on the development of a form of humanism that was, as we have seen, mainly in the hands of aris-

---

[39] Christina von Nolcken, "Lay Literacy, the Democratization of God's Law, and the Lollards", in *The Bible as Book: The Manuscript Tradition*, ed. by J.L. Sharpe and K.V. Kampen, London: The British Library, 1998: 177–95, p. 179.

[40] Anne Hudson and H.L. Spencer, "Old Author, New Work: The Sermons of MS Longleat 4", *Medium Aevum* 53: 1984, 220–38, p. 233.

[41] Watson, p. 831.

tocratic patrons or high ecclesiastics. It is difficult to imagine Humphrey of Gloucester, or even one of the English writers he protected and encouraged, studying Margery Kempe's work. It is thus tempting to envisage in fifteenth-century England two cultures, two forms of literary production running parallel but never actually touching each other: an official culture, mainly in the hand of noblemen and high ecclesiastics, patronising poets, such as John Lydgate, who would in the main content themselves with being servile imitators of classical models; and a culture of the middle classes, and in particular of that portion of the middle classes which was acutely aware of religious dissent and restlessness, and which sought, even in defiance of the dictates of the Church, an autonomous mode of expression. This dichotomy, straightforward as it may seem, is yet crossed by another, centring on the difference between reading for entertainment and reading for instruction, or for devotional purposes. Especially in the case of a private owner of books who did not have at his or her disposal the ample financial means that were available to Duke Humphrey, the acquisition of a book could be undertaken only with some deliberation, and such an expense could be more justified if the book had a moral or didactic purpose, was meant to help the reader's soul and not only to divert and engage his/her mind.

On the other hand, the co-existence of the most virulent phase of Lollard repression with the beginning of humanism in England may have had some interesting side-effects. Anti-Lollard investigation centred with particular attention upon the possession or use of books; and if the main target was obviously the ownership of religious books in the vernacular, by extension it also concerned books in general and the ability to read them. The diffusion of Lollardy had created a good market for books and had attracted around itself many of the activities concurring to book production: among the Lollards were parchemyners and scribes, and even if most Lollards belonged to the low classes, they obviously attributed a great value to literacy. Conversely, the production of Lollard books attracted the attention of non-Lollard buyers, and this could take place even outside the activity of censorship: among the owners of the Wycliffite Bible were even people who were by definition orthodox, such as Henry VI.[42] Thus the private ownership of books in the vernacular,

---

[42] On this point see Anne Hudson, "Some Aspects of Lollard Book Production",

or a close concern with the activity of book production, became *ipso facto* a reason of concern for the censor: Watson notes that in the *Constitutions*, unlike what happens in the earlier *De heretico comburendo* (enacted in 1401), there is no distinction between Lollard texts and other theological texts in the vernacular, which means that all vernacular religious texts, or simply all vernacular texts dealing in some way with religion and making use of Scriptures, could be banned.[43] Inevitably, this form of censorship would strike a private owner or reader of no high social standing rather than a nobleman or a high ecclesiastic; but the equation between heresy and literacy increased the fear of the power of the book:

> The combination of anxiety that heresy would result from unauthorized access to the scriptures with nervousness of the magical properties associated with books and their use is nowadays seen to be connected with restricted literacy, and particularly with the desire to sustain the restriction.[44]

The curiosity, or even the longing for the possession of books; the activity of book-collection; the discovery of hitherto unknown texts; all these characteristics of humanism in its broader definition were then liable to incur the suspicion of a religious censure that, in the first decade of the fifteenth century, had enormously widened its scope. Even privileged book-collectors and patrons such as Duke Humphrey knew that control was being exercised, and, even if their social status allowed them free possession of otherwise illegal books, they were aware that such a possession could become a weapon in the hands of political enemies (and indeed, this seems to have been partly the case in the years of the downfall of Duke Humphrey and of his second wife, Eleanor Cobham).

Thus humanism and religious restlessness concur in urging a redefinition of the concepts of book, literacy, and literature. It may be true, as Weiss states, that "in the history of English classical studies during the fifteenth century Humphrey of Gloucester and Tiptoft

---

in *Schism, Heresy, and Religious Protest. Papers Read at the Tenth Summer Meeting and the Eleventh Winter Meeting of the Ecclesiastical History Society*, ed. by D. Baker, Cambridge: Cambridge University Press, 1972: 147–57, p. 148.

[43] Watson, p. 829.

[44] R.I. Moore, "Literacy and the Making of Heresy *c.* 1000–*c.* 1150", in *Heresy and Literacy, 1000–1530*, ed. by P. Biller and A. Hudson, Cambridge: Cambridge University Press, 1994: 19–37, p. 22.

typified a small minority";[45] the concern the former expressed for the transmission of these studies in England, and his effort to give literary dignity to scientific texts or works in the vernacular, while at the same time proclaiming a ferocious orthodoxy in his activity against the Lollards, show that he was aware of the necessity for a redefinition, and meant to participate in the cultural debate with a contribution that found its roots in ideology, while steering resolutely away from religious disputes. The complex relation between religious and lay power in fifteenth-century England, the presence of a strong religious movement that put itself in direct opposition to ecclesiastical hierarchies, and consequentially the complex relation between *divinae* and *humanae litterae*, highlight all the different connotations humanism acquired when it passed, or was transmitted, from Italy to England; and if we can agree with Weiss when he states that humanism in England was little else but the continuation of medieval attitudes,[46] we should not read this statement with the same patronising attitude with which Weiss seems to have written it. In this situation, as I wrote above, the Duke of Gloucester intervened without interfering directly in the religious debate, at least as concerns his activity as a book-collector and patron. Humphrey appeared mainly concerned with giving the English language a new role in literature that could equal its new role in politics and administration, since in the same decades in which he was culturally active English was emerging as a national language, posing new issues (the use of language as a marker of one's nationality) that would inevitably find an echo in contemporary literary production.

The establishment of English as the language of policy and administration

The question of the enfranchisement of English from its dependence on Anglo-Norman between the fourteenth and the fifteenth century has been much debated, and scholars have often arrived at surprisingly contrasting results. Rather than focus upon this amply discussed topic, however, I should prefer to concentrate here on the Lancastrian contribution to the rise of the vernacular, putting it into relation with

---

[45] Weiss, *Humanism in England*, p. 179.
[46] Weiss, *Humanism in England*, p. 182.

the influence early humanism might have had on the phenomenon.

By the beginning of the fifteenth century, the hitherto little challenged co-existence of three languages in England—Latin in ecclesiastical and academic circles, French at court and in the centres of
administration and power, English as the language commonly spoken by the King's subjects—was meeting a number of challenges.
There is evidence to the point even in the previous century: we find
a mention of "the king's English" in Geoffrey Chaucer's *Treatise of the
Astrolabe*, in the introductory section addressed to "Lowys my sone":

> And Lowys, yf so be that I shewe the in my lighte Englissh as trewe
> conclusions touching this mater, and not oonly as trewe but as many
> and as subtile conclusiouns, as ben shewid in Latyn in eny commune
> tretys of the Astrelabie, konne me the more thank. And preie God
> save the king, that is lord of this langage, and alle that him feith berith
> and obeieth, everich in his degre, the more and the lasse.[47]

Latin had stopped being the sole language used by the church already
by the end of the fourteenth century: works emanating from members of religious orders, but written for a lay audience, would be
written in one of the two vernaculars, and if until the fourteenth
century religious works in French were meant almost exclusively for
an aristocratic readership, and thus had a very specific, audience-
oriented focus, the increase of devotional works in English between
the second half of the fourteenth century and the beginning of the
fifteenth also meant a widening of their perspective: "unlike their
French compositions, English works by members of the Religious
Orders appealed to the widest possible medieval audience consisting
of the lower clergy, and the laity both literate and 'lewede'".[48] The
phenomenon concerned particularly orders such as the Benedictines,
and met in many instances the interest of the newly-risen Lollard
groups: we sometimes find annotations in Lollard hands in the manu-

---

[47] Geoffrey Chaucer, *A Treatise on the Astrolabe*, in *The Riverside Chaucer*, ed. by L.D.
Benson, Oxford: Oxford University Press, 1987: 661–83, p. 662. The 1387 *Dialogue
Between the Lord and the Clerk on Translation* by John Trevisa is a good example of the
ideological weight of this issue (an extract from the *Dialogue* is published, with an
interesting commentary, in *The Idea of the Vernacular: An Anthology of Middle English
Literary Theory, 1280–1520*, ed. by J. Wogan-Browne, N. Watson, et al., Exeter:
University of Exeter Press, 1999, pp. 130–8).
[48] On this point, see John Taylor's article, somewhat dated now but still extremely
useful: "Notes on the Rise of Written English in the Late Middle Ages", *Proceedings
of the Leeds Philosophical Society* 8: 1956, 128–36, p. 128.

scripts of these devotional works in English.[49] Once again, as in our previous discussion on *divinae* and *humanae litterae*, we find that the historian dealing with the rise of humanism in England against its historical background must reckon with this movement. The early fifteenth century thus seems to express its renewed interest in books in two forms: at the level of the aristocracy, it takes the form of book-collecting and of a more or less conscious imitation of the models of patronage arriving from Italy; on the other hand, the middle classes seem to use this new interest in books as an answer to Arundel's *Constitutions*. In both cases the book becomes an instrument of ideology; in both cases, even if this is far more evident in the case of Lollardy, the ideological manipulation of culture meets the need of a language that can be identified with the nation itself, that can mark a distance both from the former conquerors, now newly if only partially subjected in their turn, and from a model of learning and culture that is still used but no longer passively accepted to the exclusion of autonomous contributions. It is significant that Henry V's switch from French to English in his correspondence occurs in 1417, that is, the year of his second invasion of France;[50] it seems to show that the turning point in the English linguistic policy took place at exactly the same moment in which the French adventure appeared to concretise itself into an acquisition of permanent dominions. Henceforward Henry would write in English in his correspondence with the Privy Council, or with his brother John, Duke of Bedford, who was looking after Henry's interests in England; therefore he established the possibility, and began the use, of English for officialdom; his was of course not the first instance of such an ideological choice, but certainly his use of language as a political weapon had a decisive meaning and showed this king's awareness of the propaganda value of language. This is also shown, as Malcolm Richardson demonstrates, in the King's foreign policy:

---

[49] Taylor, p. 130. See also Nicholas Watson, "Conceptions of the Word: The Mother Tongue and the Incarnation of God", in *New Medieval Literatures 1*, ed. by W. Scase, R. Copeland and D. Lawton, Oxford, Clarendon Press, 1997: 85–124.

[50] See Malcolm Richardson, "Henry V, the English Chancery, and Chancery English", *Speculum* 55: 1980, 726–50. Analysing Henry's correspondence, Richardson arrives at the conclusion that, until 1417, "all of his correspondence was apparently in French or Latin; afterward he corresponded with his countrymen mostly in English" (p. 727).

An interesting excerpt from an argument at the Council of Trent over
the composition of the various 'nations' at church councils throws some
light on the English attitude toward language at that time. Henry's
ambassadors demanded to know "whether nation be understood as a
people marked off from other by blood-relationships and habit of unity
or by peculiarities of language (the most sure and positive sign and
essence of a nation in divine and human law)" [. . .] Shrewdly mea-
suring the rise of English nationalism, Henry always took pains to balance his international ambitions with patriotic flourishes toward his
own people. His use of English was only a part of a larger plan.[51]

After his early death, his brothers, probably implicitly, undertook the
charge of continuing the same policy.

At the same time, the diffusion of English could be seen, more
slowly if more pervasively, in private correspondence and in the
official records of the central government, of boroughs and guilds.
The impulse thus comes both from above, with the adoption of a
new linguistic policy on the part of the King, and from below, with
the increasingly felt need to make of the commonly spoken language
also the normal means of written communication. The parallel development of English as a literary language, especially marked by the
flourishing of translations of Latin classical treatises (one obvious
instance is the first English translation, dated 1408, of a very famous
treatise on warfare, Vegetius's *De re Militari*, while the activity of
John Lydgate marks perhaps the climax of this movement), can be
seen as a consequence of this double impulse. As has been noted,
moreover, this development coincides with the increase of literacy
among the laymen and the emergence of a new social group, the
laici literati: both literate and lettered laymen, whose skill coupled
with their social position granted them work among the better-off
members of the middle class, who might find themselves in need of
a clerk to assist them in their trading or other activities.[52] At the
same time, clerks found they were no longer the sole possessors of
this skill: while their position was steadily rising and offering an alternative to the lettered skills of monks, literacy was also spreading
among the upper and middle classes. Literacy is to be meant here
in its modern sense, as the ability to read and write in one's native

---

[51] Richardson, p. 741.
[52] A point made by Rolf Berndt in his "The Period of the Final Decline of
French in Medieval England (Fourteenth and Early Fifteenth Centuries)", *Zeitschrift
für Anglistik und Amerikanistik* 20: 1972, 341–69. See, in particular, p. 344.

language, rather than the knowledge of classical tongues and/or texts: it is obvious that, with the rise and diffusion of literacy expressing itself mainly for practical purposes, the need for a sole, unifying language, coinciding with the commonly spoken language, became ever greater.

It goes greatly to the Lancastrian kings' credit that they met this need and combined it with their own propaganda purposes. In doing so, they showed intuition and the same ability to understand sociological and intellectual changes that we can find, to a certain extent, in the policy of Duke Humphrey of Gloucester. It is only recently that the role of the Lancastrian kings has been studied with a systematic approach,[53] and examined in perspective with the concomitant rise of English as the language of Chancery. The use of French as the language of officialdom and administration since the Norman Conquest had not been the result of legislation, or of a specific policy: very simply, it was the language spoken by the class that was holding power and controlling the administrative centres of the country. This meant that by the fourteenth century the coexistence of the two languages (with the addition of Latin) had reached almost a paradoxical point, since English was acquiring a higher status by means of the rising middle class. John H. Fisher presents a precise picture of the situation:

> by the 1360's most oral exchange in commerce and government must have been carried on in English, but the records were still kept in Latin and French. Formal education was in Latin, and the writing masters who taught English clerks the secretarial skills of *ars dictaminis* taught them in Latin and French. Virtually all religious and cultural writings intended for any kind of circulation were in Latin and French.[54]

It is true that we have secular poetry written even before this date, but a correct estimation of the diffusion of written English can be made by taking into account the production and spreading of manuscripts in the vernacular and the use of the vernacular in an official,

---

[53] See John H. Fisher, *The Emergence of Standard English*, Lexington: University Press of Kentucky, 1996. Even Fisher, however, concentrates on Henry V on the one side, and Caxton on the other, leaving much unsaid as concerns the protectorate and the reign of Henry VI. For a more recent if limited assessment, see Tim William Machan, "Politics and the Middle English Language", *Studies in the Age of Chaucer* 24: 2002, 317–24.

[54] Fisher, p. 19.

non-literary context, rather than examining individual examples of poets that found English their most obvious mode of expression. N.F. Blake rightly observes that, whatever its literary shortcomings, "to the historians [. . .] the fifteenth century [is] morally, intellectually and materially an age not of stagnation, but of ferment".[55] It is indeed reductive to evaluate the intellectual development of a community solely by taking into consideration its literary production, and by linking to this one factor the evolution of the language. We shall, in the following chapters, analyse the role patronage played in the production of literature, and see whether intellectual history offers any explanation to the mystery of the "dull century"; what is more interesting here is to take into consideration the establishment of the vernacular in non-literary texts, texts that had primarily a practical use and were not the result of individual poetic utterance.

Coming back to the political and social context in the late fourteenth and early fifteenth centuries, thus, what we see is the paradox of the co-existence of three languages being used in one society slowly coming to a crisis; and, already during the reign of Henry IV, we can witness instances of the use of English in official contexts. This may be the result of this King's policy in order to secure the support of the commons, since the aristocracy could and did represent a source of social unrest;[56] if this be the case, the consequence is a rise in the diffusion of the English vernacular, coinciding with the rise of the commons, or rather of the attention the Lancastrian kings paid to this particular social group. As the commons become a force to be reckoned with, there is an increase in the writings meant for them: religious sermons and tracts, political pamphlets, songs and ballads (we shall see in chapter 3 how some of them were crucial to the Lancastrian policy during Humphrey of Gloucester's protectorate and later, during Henry VI's reign), but also writings referring to everyday business, administration, legal matters. It is on these last points that the new needs of this rising group

---

[55] N.F. Blake, "The Fifteenth Century Reconsidered", *Neuphilologische Mitteilungen* 71: 1970, 146–57, pp. 146–47.

[56] Fisher, pp. 20–21. The reference is to entries in the Rolls of Parliament concerning Richard II's deposition and Henry IV's claim to the throne: "the only conceivable reason for these entries to be recorded in English at a time when the official entries in the Rolls were still uniformly in Latin and French was that they were meant to appeal to the commons".

clash with a usage established since the eleventh century, and it is here that the crown can more directly intervene. The ascension to the throne of Henry V, and the renewed interest in the now successful war with France, created yet another link, between the use of English and the definition of England as a nation, finding a new unity in the opposition to the erstwhile invader. The use of English then (Henry V issued in 1416 five proclamations in English to the citizens of London, requiring their material and financial support in his military campaigns) found not only a political but a nationalistic *raison d'être*.

John Fisher links this activity in the early Lancastrian era with the existence of a literary circle centring upon Thomas Chaucer, the son of Philippa Chaucer and first cousin to the Beauforts.[57] His connections and social position made him an intermediary between the commons and the King, while his literary interest can be seen in his patronage of John Lydgate; this patronage was also based on friendship and on a collaboration that might have culminated in the issuing of the Ellesmere manuscript of *The Canterbury Tales*. This activity, together with the attempt to enhance the status of the English language through the glorification of the one poet, Geoffrey Chaucer, whose English was deemed worthy of standing beside French, find a counterpart a few decades later in the activity of Henry V's brother and self-appointed intellectual heir, Humphrey of Gloucester. Significantly, one of the poets most constantly patronised by Humphrey was the same John Lydgate we see, in 1412, acknowledging Henry V's role in the advancement of English, in the Prologue of his *Troy Book*, commissioned by this prince and mentioned above in this chapter. Henry, Lydgate writes

> hath desire, sothly for to seyn,
> Of verray knythod to remembre ageyn
> The worthynes[58]

In order that this *worthynes* may be of example to the present times; and he has ordered Lydgate

---

[57] Fisher, pp. 25–26. Fisher's position has been recently discussed and partly challenged: see, for instance, Jeremy J. Smith, "Chaucer and the Invention of English", *Studies in the Age of Chaucer* 24: 2002, 335–46.

[58] Prologue, ll. 74–6. See John Lydgate, *Troy Book*, ed. by H. Bergen, Early English Text Society, London: Kegan Paul, Trench, Trübner, 1906.

Of hem of Troye in englysche to translate,
The sege also and the destruccioun,
Lyche as the latyn maketh mencioun,
For to compyle, and after Guydo make,
So as I coude, and write it for his sake,
Bycause he wolde that to hyghe and lowe
The noble story openly wer knowe
In oure tonge, aboute in euery age,
And y-writen as wel in oure langage,
As in latyn and in frensche it is;
That of the story þe trouth[e] we nat mys,
No more than doth eche other nacioun.[59]

Lydgate's literary production, for the moment setting aside its literary merits, is an invaluable source to understand the intellectual history of his time: in defining the poet a "public relations agent," Fisher appropriately notes: "the list of Lydgate's patrons reads like a *Who's Who* of both the courtly and commercial circles in England."[60] But a like support to the advancement of English in administrative as well as literary circles is given by Thomas Hoccleve, another poet who benefited from the Lancastrian patronage. It is in the activity of poets who were closely linked to the court, or that worked in public administration, that we can see the link between the advancement of English as an official and as a literary language.

It must also be noted that the elevation of English to the role of national language coincides with its standardisation, and this may be, in literary terms, a loss. In the passage from the literature in the vernacular of the fourteenth century to that of the fifteenth we lose not only a number of characteristics harking back to the alliterative revival tradition, but also the variety given by the many dialects used, and by the many centres of literary expression in which these dialects were employed.[61] The recognition of English as a standard language for written expression goes hand in hand with the acknowl-

---

[59] Prologue, ll. 106–17. "Guydo" is Guido delle Colonne.

[60] Fisher, p. 32. On the relation between poet and patron in the composition of the *Troy Book*, see also Christopher Baswell, "*Troy Book*: How Lydgate Translates Chaucer into Latin", in *Translation Theory and Practice in the Middle Ages*, ed. by J. Beer, Kalamazoo: Western Michigan University, 1997: 215–37.

[61] See Blake, pp. 147–8. In the same article Blake correctly notes, however, that though the fifteenth century did not seem particularly interested in pre-Chaucerian poetry in English, "many fifteenth-century poets use alliteration more frequently than Chaucer did" (p. 154).

edgment of Chaucer as the father of that language; the same writers, such as Lydgate or Hoccleve, who recognise the crown as their reference and common patron recognise also Chaucer as their literary, and by implication linguistic, father. The influence of other literatures outside England, and the arrival of the Italian humanists, may change literary attitudes and reading habits, but have at this point a more limited influence on the development of the language.

Our brief foray into the development of English as the language of policy and administration has thus brought us back to literature. Though it is undoubtedly a mistake to measure the progress of a language only by the standards of its literary production, in the case of the English fifteenth century there is often an interesting coincidence of purpose between the language of literature, the language of state, and the language of policy; and if the Lollard movement used English as a means to claim a new approach to religion and to the social issues connected to it, the rulers of the country used English as a means to state a new alliance between themselves and their subject; the fact that a number of writers of the period were connected to political authority, either by their social situation or by patronage, further complicates this relation. This does not help understand the mystery of the "dull century": how a time so ideologically and socially complex could prove so disappointing in its literary output. But it suggests a new perspective for our analysis of fifteenth-century literature: setting aesthetic considerations apart, we would do well to look at the literature of this time as a mirror of extraordinary political changes, not only at a national but at a European level. The development of English as a national language, a development aided by the literature that accompanied it, is even more significant in a historical and literary context in which the language to be used in writing was determined by the literary genre or the practical purpose of the text rather than by the nationality of the writer.[62] In examining the issue of national language, we should not forget that the late Middle Ages share a concept of linguistic consciousness widely different from ours. To prove this point, Leonard Forster in a 1970 essay mentions a fifteenth-century manuscript now in Cambridge University Library that contains a poem alternating

---

[62] On this point, see H.J. Chaytor, *From Script to Print*, Cambridge: Cambridge University Press, 1945, chapter 3.

lines in English, Anglo-Norman and Latin, or, as the critic calls it, "a charming polyglot poem",[63] and correctly notes: "this is not merely a *tour de force* by a talented linguist; it presupposes a polyglot audience in England capable of appreciating it".[64] The poem is intended for an English audience, but the same audience is expected to understand the passages in languages other than English, or at least their significance, without associating with a nation different from their own, but at the most from a social class or community different from their own. Forster's notes on language consciousness, concluding his analysis of the poem, are equally interesting:

> It is clear that people in earlier centuries had a much less developed sense of what linguists have come to call 'language loyalty' than most of us have today. This is apparent even in situations which we would nowadays consider extreme. In the fifteenth century the French general Charles d'Orléans was captured by the hated English and spent twenty-five years in an English prison. He was a reputable poet in French and passed the time of his long imprisonment in learning English and even writing a number of delightful poems in English, which are still preserved. English was the language of the enemy. The difference in attitude becomes apparent if we try to envisage a parallel case in our own day, for instance a German general in Russian captivity.[65]

It is in this context that the Lancastrian attempt marks a novelty not only in linguistic terms, but in terms of social consciousness: their organised propaganda, the use (inaugurated by Henry V) of English first as a distinctive trait for a nation that was at the moment engaged in the war against France, and then for a privileged communication between the King (or, in the years of the protectorate, the King's Council) and the commons, develop, at least in England, an identification between the idea of a language and the idea of a nation.

---

[63] Leonard Forster, *The Poet's Tongues: Multilingualism in Literature. The de Carle Lectures at the University of Otago 1968*, London: Cambridge University Press, 1970, p. 16.
[64] Forster, p. 17.
[65] Forster, p. 19.

CHAPTER THREE

A SENSE OF HISTORY: DUKE HUMPHREY LIVING AND WRITING HIS OWN TIMES

Political history plays a very prominent role in the vicissitudes of this active, impetuous, often blundering prince. On the one hand, the events of contemporary England placed him in a position that made even his literary patronage impossible to evaluate outside the consideration of his public role. On the other, Duke Humphrey understood, and perhaps exaggerated, the role of political writing and of historiography, and, led by a belief in the power of the written word, often sought or commissioned books, and possibly other types of texts, with a close relevance to his own and his country's fortunes. Thus the investigation of the relation between politics and patronage might shed light upon both. It may be argued that in the case of the Duke of Gloucester, patronage, or an intense cultural activity that attempted to keep pace with contemporary European intellectual movements, was a form of compensation for an unrewarding role on the English political scene, and for the inevitable frustration he experienced in his constant clashes with the King's Council. Humanists, particularly in Italy, had stressed the importance of their craft in the service of potentates, partly because they were obviously motivated by self-interest, but also because both the humanists and their patrons seemed to have a Platonic faith in the power of thought, or in any case of political and historical writing. There is no doubt that, however unfortunate the political career of Duke Humphrey, his cultural efforts earned him a fame possibly superior to his political merits. There is also little doubt that, besides his popularity within an intellectual circle he had contributed to create, he also enjoyed a less easily explicable popularity with the common people. V.J. Scattergood is undoubtedly right when he observes:

> The personality and achievements of Humphrey of Gloucester received enormous attention in contemporary poetry. There are a number of possible reasons for this. His affable personality and forthright nationalistic policies apparently endeared him to many, in particular the common people of the capital. His exploits tended to be of the sensational

Fig. 1. Humphrey de Gloucester.

kind. But he also undoubtedly profited from his generous literary patronage. That his interest in learning and literature was genuine is beyond doubt. His encouragement of Italian scholars and his assiduous collecting of books make him one of the most important figures in the spread of humanistic learning in England. This, and his generosity to English authors won for him fulsome tributes.[1]

Whether he was fully aware of it or not, Humphrey thus created a completely new role in English political life, a role that was partly suggested by the very peculiar situation in which the English crown found itself after the death of Henry V. It was a monarchy that was holding sway over a territory of unprecedented width and was at the same time lacking a *de facto* king; a monarchy with an invested Protector in the Duke of Gloucester, who had received the title thanks to his brother's will, but whose power was continually countermanded by a Council that felt, perhaps rightly, that the Protector would undoubtedly claim all the rights his title entailed, but might lack the necessary energy and constancy to pursue all its duties. In this very insecure position, Humphrey reacted with the arrogance and bluster of a true brother of Henry V, but at the same time he had enough intelligence and sensitivity to realise that even Henry V's glorious model would not have adapted itself perfectly to the new requirements of changed times and conditions.

The nearly impossible situation in which Humphrey found himself from 1422 to his death, in a kingdom that was itself "curiously compacted of old and new,"[2] and his innovative if not always successful reaction, have made him something of an enigma for historians and scholars of humanism, and have prompted widely different evaluations on the part of modern readers of political and intellectual history. The most important work on Duke Humphrey to date, Kenneth Vickers's biography, reflects this dilemma in that, while condemning the prince and Protector, it has nothing but praise for him as a patron, even if the historian is perfectly aware that these two sides of the Duke's personality remained closely connected. The solution Vickers finds is that Humphrey found in patronage an

---

[1] V.J. Scattergood, *Politics and Poetry in the Fifteenth Century*, London: Blandford Press, 1971, p. 142.

[2] E.F. Jacob, *The Fifteenth Century, 1399–1485*, Oxford History of England, Oxford: Clarendon Press, 1961, p. 317.

outlet for frustrated energies, and could apply there his considerable intelligence:

> Humphrey felt the full force of this movement; his life was moulded thereby. His activity and many-sided energy found their origin in this new spirit. His fervid imagination, which led him into impossible projects, his love of display, above all, his desire to stamp his individuality on the politics of his country, all sprang from the new realisation which was vouchsafed to him—the realisation of his own individuality.[3]

The principle on which Vickers bases his analysis is undoubtedly sound, though phrases such as "the realisation of his own individuality" sound vague, romantic and improbable; there is no doubt, however, that the historian has correctly pinpointed some of the leading characteristics of the Duke's personality, especially as concerns the desire to impress the mark of his personality on contemporary events. We can quote the portrait given of him in the *Dictionary of National Biography* as an apt epitome of the modern historian's attitude: "Gloucester was a man of great and restless energy, hot-tempered and impulsive, of gracious and popular manners, eloquent, plausible, and affable."

The youngest child of Henry IV, Humphrey seems to have spent a surprisingly sheltered childhood and youth, and proved himself initially during Henry V's first French campaign. There is no way of saying whether this experience determined his subsequent attitude towards politics and, in particular, towards the French war; but there is little doubt that thenceforward, consciously or unconsciously, he attempted to model his own actions on those of his heroic brother, and perhaps, to hope that the young Henry of Windsor would follow his father's footsteps one day. Unfortunate military campaigns and a consistent reduction of his power in England doomed these attempts to failure; but his cultural activity must be read in the light of this constant straining towards a role he could not acceptably impersonate.

On the other hand, much has been made of the Lancastrian passion for books, to the point of attempting to deprive Humphrey's activity of any originality, or of its exceptional quality, in the name of a cultural concern that was common in the family, and perhaps

---

[3] Kenneth H. Vickers, *Humphrey Duke of Gloucester. A Biography*, London: Constable, 1907, p. 341.

among the English nobility in general. There is no doubt that many members of the Lancastrian family, including the three kings, were intellectually alert, and shared a bibliophilia that is most especially marked in the case of Henry IV's two youngest sons, John, Duke of Bedford, and Humphrey. They all received a gentleman's education, and knew, or at least studied, Latin, as well as English and French. Patronage was a common practice also in the Bohun side of the family (Henry IV's wife was Mary Bohun): in the fourteenth century they had been both patrons and collectors, particularly in the case of Humphrey Bohun.[4] In particular, "there is some evidence to suggest that Bedford had literary tastes, which, under different political and military circumstances, he could well have cultivated more deeply."[5] Comparisons have been attempted between the two youngest sons of Henry IV, John and Humphrey, in terms of their cultural activity, and at a superficial glance it might seem that Humphrey did not achieve anything more important, or more spectacular, than his brother: after all, the Duke of Bedford had acquired the renowned library of the Louvre in the early 1420s, and his order to have a new inventory made of the contents of this library prior to its acquisition suggests that he took an active interest in it.[6] The fact that he was conscious of his younger brother's taste in reading is demonstrated by the fact that in 1427 he sent Humphrey, among other volumes, a beautifully decorated manuscript with a French translation (by Pierre Bersuire) of Livy's *Histories*; in a letter to the King of Naples, dated 1445, Duke Humphrey describes himself while reading this book.[7] The Lancastrian passion for books takes,

[4] See L.C.Y. Everest-Phillips, "The Patronage of Humphrey, Duke of Gloucester", Ph.D., University of York, 1983, pp. 35–42. See also Lucy Freeman Sandler, "The Illustration of the Psalms in Fourteenth-Century English Manuscripts: Three Psalters of the Bohun Family", in *Reading Texts and Images. Essays on Medieval and Renaissance Art and Patronage*, ed. by B.J. Muir, Exeter: University of Exeter Press, 2002: 123–51.

[5] Jenny Stratford, "The Manuscripts of John, Duke of Bedford: Library and Chapel", in *England in the Fifteenth Century: Proceedings of the 1986 Harlaxton Symposium*, ed. by D. Williams, Woodbridge: Boydell, 1987: 329–50, p. 347.

[6] The most complete information on the books owned by the Duke of Bedford at the time of his death can be found in Jenny Stratford, *The Bedford Inventories. The Worldy Goods of John, Duke of Bedford, Regent of France (1389–1435)*, London: Society of Antiquaries, 1993.

[7] The manuscript is among the books belonging to Humphrey that have survived, and is now in Paris (Bibliothèque de Sainte Geneviève, franç. 777). See Alfonso Sammut, *Unfredo duca di Gloucester e gli umanisti italiani*, Padova: Antenore, 1980, p. 122. For the letter to the King of Naples (to whom Humphrey subsequently sent the book, possibly in the same manuscript), see Sammut, pp. 215–6.

however, different forms. In the case of Bedford, as far as we can
understand from the very little that has survived of his library, such
passion was directed mainly towards devotional books, and he seemed
equally, if not more, interested in the beauty of the rubrics and of
the illuminations: thus much is shown by the Bedford Psalter and
Hours, beautiful presentation copies, but which tell us very little of
the Duke's intellectual interests. Another group of surviving manuscripts seems to indicate that he shared his brother's interest in popular science, astronomy and medicine; unlike what happens in the
case of Humphrey, however, we only have indications as to his possessing the books, and we know nothing about their intended use.

The real difficulty if we attempt any comparison between John
and Humphrey in terms of cultural patronage is that events, per-
versely so favourable in the case of Humphrey (since his very failure in politics turned out to be one further reason to enhance his
heightened interest in the transmission of culture), did not allow John
to express his intellectual projects in any durable form. The inventory of the royal library in the Louvre, ordered in 1423 (he subsequently bought the contents of this library at a very good price),
suggests that he wanted to make use of this extraordinary resource,
whether by organising his own library or by endowing a university
or monastery; but his involvement in the French wars first, and then
his untimely death, prevented him from putting this desire into practice. There is also reason to believe that, at various stages, he
attempted to patronise the universities of Paris, Oxford and Caen;
once more, however, he was destined to be disappointed. Commenting
on these various, fruitless attempts, M.J. Barber rightly concludes
that "the evidence we have reviewed cannot be stretched to make
any special case for John, Duke of Bedford, as a man of letters or
even as a bibliophile".[8] Likewise, the collection of the *Epistolae Academicae
Oxonienses* shows us that the University would appeal not only to
Duke Humphrey's generosity, but also, and at one stage considerably often, to the Duke of Bedford.[9] More specifically, in 1433 he
was asked to carry into execution his project of founding lectures in

---

[8] M.J. Barber, "The Books and Patronage of a Fifteenth-Century Prince", *The
Book Collector* 12: 1963, 308–15, p. 315.
[9] *Epistolae Academicae Oxonienses*, ed. by H. Anstey, Oxford: Clarendon Press, 1898.
See, in particular, the letters dated 1433 (pp. 81–2, 94–5, 105).

the seven liberal arts and the three philosophies (an identical letter being sent to Duke Humphrey on the same date),[10] but in the case of Bedford the absence of a letter of thanks on the part of the University seems to show that nothing came of it.

There is no way of knowing whether this failure to concern himself with intellectual activity in Oxford was due to a lack of real interest on the part of the Duke, or to his pressing engagements in France. But in spite of being the regent of a territory that was, at the time, culturally more advanced than England, the Duke of Bedford left few if any traces of his intellectual interests, and certainly did not play, whether in England or in France, a role comparable to that of his brother Humphrey in terms of patronage. It is possible that Humphrey's importance has been exaggerated by nineteenth-century antiquarians, as Everest-Phillips contends;[11] yet there is little doubt that no nobleman or potentate in England equalled his activity during the reign of Henry VI, as was frequently acknowledged by his contemporaries—and not only by those who benefited from his patronage. The judgements of fifteenth- and sixteenth-century chroniclers on the political activity of the Duke of Gloucester are often contrasting, and owe much to the current propaganda: thus Yorkist historians would exalt the "good duke" to underline the weakness of Henry VI, or the instability of the Lancastrian rule; however, his patronage, whenever mentioned, is generally recognised as exceptional: we see this in the case of Aeneas Silvius Piccolomini, who wrote in 1444 (when Humphrey's power was already steadily declining) of the Duke of Gloucester "qui studia humanitatis summo studio in regnum vestrum recepit, qui, sicut mihi relatum est, et poetas mirifice colit et oratores magnopere veneratur",[12] as well as in the case of the sixteenth-century chronicler Richard Grafton, who even attributes to the Duke the building of the Divinity School

---

[10] *Epistolae Academicae Oxonienses*, pp. 106–8.

[11] Everest-Phillips, pp. 20ff.

[12] "He who has welcomed humanist studies in your country with the greatest interest, and, as I have been told, greatly reveres poets and orators". *Der Briefwechsel des Eneas Silvius Piccolomini*, ed. by R. Wolkan, Wien: Alfred Holder, 1909, p. 325. For an interesting comment on Piccolomini's praise, see David Rundle, "Humanism before the Tudors: On Nobility and the Reception of *studia humanitatis* in Fifteenth-Century England", in *Reassessing Tudor Humanism*, ed. by J. Woolfson, Basingstoke: Palgrave Macmillan, 2002: 22–42.

in Oxford.[13] Besides, there is at least one very visible trace of Humphrey's patronage in the extraordinary endowment of books to the University of Oxford—in the following chapter I shall discuss the relationship between the various donations and contemporary political events, or moments of Humphrey's personal life.

Duke Humphrey's failure as a politician

In the introductory section to this chapter Kenneth Vickers has been quoted as highlighting a fundamental dichotomy between Duke Humphrey's two roles—the prince and the patron. The dichotomy has been frequently underlined: already in 1879 the Italian scholar Attilio Hortis could write "Tra' principi d'Inghilterra il più dotto e in una il più allegro e il più popolare era certamente Umfredo duca di Gloucester" and shortly afterwards add that "il duca era stato per l'Inghilterra una disgrazia, per il rinascimento della letteratura un beneficio."[14] Thus the Duke continues to present a puzzle to any historian who might wish to reconcile the two sides of his personality, though possibly the puzzle is more in the widely divergent effects his double activity had than in the cultural and ideological perspective with which he started.

As has already been underlined in chapter 1, Kenneth Vickers has already written an excellent (if now relatively dated) biography of the Duke of Gloucester, and the present writer does not attempt a similar historical reconstruction. But it is important nonetheless to underline some of the main events of the Duke's life, especially prior to his commitment to cultural patronage, to throw some light on the relation between the politician and the intellectual patron. Gloucester's first public role was during Henry V's first French campaign, and he distinguished himself at the siege of Harfleur (he was then in his early twenties, that is, relatively late for a fifteenth-century

---

[13] *Grafton's Chronicle; or History of England*, London: Johnson, Rivington, et al., 1809 (a facsimile of the 1569 edition), I, p. 631.

[14] "Among the princes of England, Humphrey duke of Gloucester certainly was the most learned, and at the same time the merriest;" "the duke was a catastrophe for England, a blessing for the renaissance of literature." Hortis, Attilio, *Studj sulle opere latine del Boccaccio con particolare riguardo alla storia della erudizione nel Medio Evo e alle letterature straniere*, Trieste: Julius Dase, 1879, pp. 642, 643.

English nobleman). Both there and at Agincourt, in 1415, he showed courage and a disregard for personal safety that might have led him to real danger in the battle, had his elder brother not been there to defend his life; at various stages of the campaign he was, besides, universally praised for his management of siege tactics. Scholars such as H.S. Bennett see in Humphrey's good reputation as a director of siege artillery the result of a careful study of the medieval treatises on the subject.[15] It is true that the list of manuscripts donated to Oxford University library in 1444 (the last, and most important donation of which there survives a detailed record) included Vegetius's treatise *De re militari*,[16] and that Nicholas Upton dedicated to him his *De studio militari*;[17] the name of Humphrey, besides, has been often curiously associated with Vegetius's treatise by contemporary writers; an interesting instance is to be found in Thomas Hoccleve's *Dialogue*. The poet/narrator, talking with a friend while recovering from a bout of illness, is reminded of a book he was to write for the Duke of Gloucester, and says:

> For him I thoghte han translated Vegece
> Which tretith of the art of chiualrie;
> But I see his knyghthode so encrece
> þat no thyng my labour sholde edifie,
> For he þat art/wel can for the maistrie.[18]

The allusion is clear: Humphrey is considered well conversant with the treatise, or at any rate with military art, so that he does not need a translation of Vegetius. What is less clear is the date of Hoccleve's text, and therefore of the allusion—scholars believe it refers either to 1419 or 1422, but in any case, a few years after the Agincourt campaign.[19] On the other hand, Upton's treatise was, in all probability, written as late as the 1440s, and to infer from this that Humphrey's military prowess at the age of twenty-five was linked to his erudite interest in military treatises is, perhaps, an unfounded

---

[15] H.S. Bennett, *Six Medieval Men and Women*, Cambridge: Cambridge University Press, 1955, pp. 4–5.

[16] Sammut, p. 80.

[17] *Nicolai Vptoni De Studio Militari, Libri quatuor. Johan de Badoaureo, Tractatus de armis. Henrici Spelmanni Aspilogia*, ed. by E. Bysshe, Londinii: Typis Rogeri Norton, 1654.

[18] *Thomas Hoccleve's Complaint and Dialogue*, ed. by J.A. Burrow, Early English Text Society, Oxford: Oxford University Press, 1999, p. 63, ll. 561–65.

[19] For a brief discussion on this point, see Burrow's Introduction to his edition of Hoccleve's text, quoted above, pp. lvii–lix.

assumption. Thanks to this first successful assay, the Duke of Gloucester did maintain his reputation for an excellent organisation of sieges even when he was found less successful as a campaigner or a strategist, in later years.

Both Humphrey's promptness at the Harfleur siege and his reckless behaviour at Agincourt were fundamental to determine one side of the reputation he acquired with contemporary and later chroniclers—the reputation of "unsustained impetuosity"[20] to which historians have frequently returned. Among so many contrasting evaluations, this characteristic seems to be acknowledged by friends and foes alike, and is a constant whether we consider the Duke's military exploits, his decisions in national or international activities, or his cultural patronage. The overall impression is of a man that did not have the patience to sustain a prolonged effort, but who had sudden and burning enthusiasms, on the spur of which he would immediately act; a man who understood in advance of his time what was changing, and who would react to it, even if he found himself powerless to direct men and events towards these changes. Both his readiness to accept new military methods[21] and his surprising and lasting understanding with the middle classes, which had won him the support of the London citizens since as early as 1419, demonstrate his profound acceptance of the necessity of renovation in politics. The almost constant support he received from the middle classes could have been greatly to his advantage if he had been able to make use of it.[22] It can be also read as an instance of statesmanship on Gloucester's part, or at least of his ability to see farther than many noblemen of his time. On the other hand, it might also be the almost inevitable bonus for a member of the royal family that so often, and so evidently, found himself in violent opposition with the King's Council and some of the most powerful men of the realm, such as Henry Beaufort first, and William de la Pole, Duke of Suffolk, in the last years of his life. Vickers sees in this attitude an instance of Humphrey's wisdom and foresight, and at the same time a form of contempt for the "effete nobles;"[23] it does seem, however, that at

---

[20] Vickers, p. 49.
[21] Vickers, p. 49.
[22] Vickers, p. 84.
[23] Vickers, p. 85.

this point Vickers is simply attempting to salvage something from an almost unanimously negative evaluation of Duke Humphrey as a politician. The very lack of consistency the Duke showed in all his enterprises plays against any attempt to praise his statesmanship; his ambition, though constantly ruled by his devotion to the royal family and the person of the King, never found real scope in the pursuit of one desire. Once again, Vickers has summed up very neatly this trait of the Duke of Gloucester's personality: "His ruling passion was ambition, but he did not know how to satisfy it. Thus his future life will be found to be consistent in so far as it is governed by one overwhelming desire, but totally inconsistent in detail."[24]

A reading of Gloucester's understanding with the middle classes as a sign of his modernity is revealed as essentially misleading if we compare it with other traits of his political attitude and especially with his position as concerns the religious dissent that spread in England at the time: apart from politics and patronage, his main interest seemed to be "the upholding of orthodoxy against the Lollards,"[25] an activity for which he is also praised in the dedicatory prefaces of some of the works he commissioned. This is demonstrated, for instance, both by the Prohemium to the translation of Palladius's *De Agricultura*, in which a precise reference is made to heretics' trials in which the Duke had played a role,[26] and by John Lydgate in his *Fall of Princes*, in which it is declared that the Duke is such a staunch supporter of the true church "that in this land no Lollard dar abide."[27] It is therefore evident, since both poets were writing at Humphrey's request, that the Duke rather prided himself on his activity against heresy, though a Lancastrian prince, knowing that the Lancaster claim to the throne had somewhat dubious foundations, would probably insist on his defence of orthodoxy as a mark of the righteousness and legitimacy of his cause.

The often ferocious defence of orthodoxy that is attested by these poems and a number of other texts sorts ill with Humphrey's supposed modernity in the matter of his alliance with the middle classes;

---

[24] Vickers, p. 124.

[25] Roberto Weiss, "Portrait of a Bibliophile XI: Humphrey, Duke of Gloucester, d.1447", *The Book Collector* 13: 1964, 161–70, p. 162.

[26] *The Middle-English Translation of Palladius De Re Rustica*, ed. by Mark Liddell, Berlin: E. Ebering, 1896, ll. 50–3.

[27] *Lydgate's Fall of Princes*, ed. by H. Bergen, Early English Text Society, Oxford: Oxford University Press, 1923–27, vol. 1, p. 12.

on the other hand, it is perfectly consistent with the role Humphrey attempted to uphold all his life: that of the righteous, occasionally harsh but just ruler, preparing a well-ordered and prosperous realm to hand over to the future King, his nephew. In this perspective, Humphrey's activity against the Lollards loses much of its ferocity: the well-ordering of the kingdom entailed also a relentless defence of orthodoxy, and whatever may have been written of his human-istic attitude, there is no doubt that he never underestimated the role of the ecclesiastical hierarchies in the control of political power in England, and the importance of religious orthodoxy for a rela-tively untroubled maintenance of social order. It must also be remem-bered that the activity for the suppression of Lollardy was also an integral part of Lancastrian politics.[28] The resulting portrait of Duke Humphrey reveals him as a man genuinely concerned with the preser-vation of the political *status quo*, and intent on defending the Lancastrian rule in extremely insecure times, occasionally attempting to look at the example of the Italian potentates, or at the instruction offered by classical and medieval authors, as to the ways in which this goal was to be reached.

The historians' judgement on Duke Humphrey varies but little with time: "tenacious and aggressive"[29] are among the most recur-ring adjectives to describe his personality. A personality that made him plenty of enemies among the King's Councillors, but endeared him to the common people and particularly to the London middle classes, whatever he may have thought of or done with their sup-port. This support, intermittent and often ineffectual as it was, may be at the root of Humphrey's posthumous fame as "the good duke," and in part may have constituted the response of the middle-class townsmen to Humphrey's equally intermittent interest in their behalf.[30] But one important reason for this support might also have been merely the "dash and flamboyance" Humphrey so often displayed,

---

[28] On this point see Paul Strohm, "Counterfeiters, Lollards, and Lancastrian Unease", in *New Medieval Literatures 1*, ed. by W. Scase, R. Copeland and D. Lawton, Oxford: Clarendon Press, 1997: 31–58.

[29] B. Wilkinson, *The Later Middle Ages in England 1216–1485*, London: Longmans, 1969, p. 259.

[30] H.S. Bennett in particular often returns on this point: see his *Six Medieval Men and Women*, p. 9.

particularly in his relations with the King's Council.[31] What historians often forget in their evaluation of the Duke of Gloucester, or
indeed, of many of the noblemen surrounding young Henry of
Windsor, is the extremely delicate and complex political situation
with which they were dealing. Henry V may have died in a halo
of glory, but he left a kingdom of extremely difficult management:
he had had no time to consolidate his conquests in France, or to
solve the impasse in which the crown found itself, even after Henry's
marriage with Catherine of Valois. He had paid insufficient attention to the political and social divisions at home—"to busy giddy
minds with foreign quarrels" may have been an effective policy for
the time being, but could not be a reasonably successful long-term
one. Above all, the crown, now in the hands of a dynasty that had
had no time to assert itself with stability, was destined to Henry's
son, then less than a year old; without the possibility of forming any
precise expectations on the political ability of the future Henry VI,
the King's Council and the Parliament knew that they were facing
a very long interregnum of instability, and possibly of internal conflict.
It is indeed surprising that, setting aside momentarily personal con-
flicts and even the occasional flare-up of the enmity between Gloucester and Beaufort, to name only the most apparent motive of
discord within the King's Council, this organism was able to give
Henry VI, when the latter was crowned, a relatively well-ordered
kingdom, safe at home and determined to defend its conquests abroad.
It was a very precarious stability, destined to collapse in the following decades under the joint forces of Henry VI's weakness and
of Queen Margaret's determination, as well as under the pressure
of an ultimately disastrous French war; but it shows the maturity of
the Council and of the Parliament at the time. It is then possible
to subscribe to John Watts's evaluation of the King's Council during the Protectorate:

> the great lords of Henry's reign—Bedford, Gloucester, Beaufort, Suffolk,
> York, Somerset and the queen—were [. . .] neither fools nor knaves,
> nor, for that matter, were they heroes: they were victims, driven by
> the hideous logic of a dysfunctional system to the fruitless creation and
> defence of an authority which could not be exercised. The crisis of

---

[31] See Peter Heath, *Church and Realm, 1272–1461: Conflict and Collaboration in an Age of Crisis*, Fontana History of England, Glasgow: Fontana Press, 1988, pp. 298–9.

> Henry VI's reign was not brought about by overmighty subjects, by
> the misapplication of patronage, by defeat in war, by dynastic strug-
> gle, or by financial insolvency. Its fundamental course was truly con-
> stitutional: the inability of monarchy, a means for the satisfaction of
> the public interest in the body of a single man, the adjust to one of
> the possible extremes of human frailty.[32]

It may also be added that the anomaly of the situation was not
confined to the internal structure of government, but also related to
the duality of a crown that could never, even in the years of Henry
V's reign, become one. The historian A.R. Myers sees in "the strength
of the monarchy at a comparatively early date" the most important
characteristic of political England in the Middle Ages.[33] There is no
doubt that this was an extremely valuable asset. The difficulty of
controlling both reigns, even once it was clear that the perhaps abler
John of Bedford was destined to be regent of France, never appeared
to have been overcome, and the possibility of a renewed war with
a hardly subdued enemy was ever present. It is perhaps on this issue
that the historian David Starkey has recently based his interpretation of the role of Duke Humphrey, considering his activity in the
context of a permanent state of national emergency, and seeing the
King's Council as split on this issue. This was indeed a vital point
in the activity of both Council and Parliament, and an issue that
was also to influence Humphrey's activity as a literary patron, as
shall be seen later in this volume; it certainly co-existed with and
was made more urgent by the instability of the throne, and the
incongruity of the existing structure of power. Starkey errs, I believe,
when he makes the war with France the prime mover of the political situation in fifteenth-century England as a whole, and extends
its influence to the development of intellectual activity, as he writes
in the conclusions of his 1992 essay:

> Now on the defensive, the English were more susceptible to foreign
> ideas and the proponents of both policy options in turn drew on the
> Renaissance. First, and for long uniquely, was the war party. In part
> this was an accident of those very Renaissance things, personality and
> patronage. Humphrey of Gloucester, the Protector of England, longed

---

[32] John Watts, *Henry VI and the Politics of Kingship*, Cambridge: Cambridge University
Press, 1996, pp. 365–6.

[33] A.R. Myers, *England in the Late Middle Ages*, Harmondsworth: Penguin, 1952,
8th edition 1971, p. 15.

to cut a figure on the European stage and clearly saw the role of Renaissance prince as the most glamorous. His collection of books became the nucleus of Oxford university library; he employed successive Italian humanists as his secretary, and he commissioned books in Italy and England [. . .] What has not been sufficiently emphasized, however, is that this literary patronage was intended to bolster the arguments of the war party, of which Gloucester was leader. The subjects alone make this plain.[34]

The subjects of the works commissioned by Humphrey, or even of the books acquired, or donated by him, are of so various a nature that it is extremely difficult to infer from them the existence of an ideological project, as both Starkey and, with a more articulated approach, Susanne Saygin have attempted to demonstrate.[35] There is no doubt that in Duke Humphrey's life the two roles, politician and patron, are in a continuous interplay, and that his patronage in particular is influenced by a number of contemporary events, as well as by the Duke's own complex role in the history of fifteenth-century England. I venture to suggest that the exploration of this relation between politics and patronage may give less straightforward results than what has been suggested by the historians mentioned above, and that the root of Humphrey's unique position in English political and intellectual history is to be sought first of all in the uniquely odd and uncomfortable role that was assigned to him during Henry of Windsor's minority.

Protector of England

From the beginning of his political career, which can be said to have started in actual fact only with Henry V's death, Duke Humphrey of Gloucester was placed in a rather peculiar position. To begin with, his public role started rather late, perhaps because as the youngest brother there was no real need for him to take an active

---

[34] David Starkey, "England", in *The Renaissance in National Context*, ed. by M. Teich and R. Porter, Cambridge: Cambridge University Press, 1992: 149–63, p. 149.

[35] See Susanne Saygin, *Humphrey, Duke of Gloucester (1390–1447) and the Italian Humanists*, Leiden: Brill, 2002. A full discussion of the many points raised by this book as regards Duke Humphrey's ideology is presented in chapter 1 of the present volume.

part in English politics. He had been knighted, it is true, in 1399, the day before his father's coronation, but was made Earl of Pembroke and Duke of Gloucester only on May 16, 1414, when he was twenty-four yeas old—not too precociously for a younger son of Henry IV; it must be noted that until this date he had given but little proof of his ability as either a soldier or a statesman, and that as long as Henry V was alive Humphrey did little more than follow his brother's instructions.

The relation between Humphrey and his eldest brother, the King, gives us a number of interesting clues in our attempt to understand the Duke's personality. While separated from his father during the latter's exile in the 1390s, Humphrey had never been long separated from his brother, and had followed him in his rapid ascent and in his dazzling military exploits. For the first time, he had made a name for himself following Henry in his French campaigns, though no real, permanent responsibility was involved—he did, however, have the command of one of the three divisions into which the English army was divided. One episode seems to throw particular light on the close relationship between the two: Humphrey, then twenty-five, took part in the battle of Agincourt; there he was dangerously wounded while struggling against the Duke of Alençon, and was saved only by his brother Henry's providential intervention, while his own sol-diers would have left him for dead. The episode in itself may be of little relevance; but, first of all, it gives us an idea of Humphrey's reckless courage—something that contemporary poets or ballad-writ-ers noted, too, when describing the battle of Agincourt:

> The duke of Glowcestre also that tyde
> Manfully, with his mayné,
> Wondes he wrought ther wondere wyde.[36]

What is more important, the episode became significant (more, per-haps, than its actual relevance was at the moment) in later chroni-cles; the King's providential intervention was afterwards described and given great relevance in Tito Livio Frulovisi's *Vita Henrici Quinti*, a work commissioned by Duke Humphrey and probably benefiting

---

[36] "On the Battle of Azincourt", in *Political Poems and Songs Relating to English History, Composed during the Period from the Accession of Edw. III. to the Reign of Ric. III.*, ed. by T. Wright, Rolls Series, London: Longman, Green, Longman and Roberts, 1859–61: 123–7 (the lines quoted here are to be found on p. 125).

from the Duke's direct reminiscences and suggestions.[37] Even later accounts of the episode written by English chroniclers seem all to be drawing on Frulovisi's vivid rendition—the Italian humanist appears to anticipate Polydore Vergil in passages such as this:

> Ecce dum impetu valido regis frater serenissimus Humfredus Gloucestriae dux incautius forte pugnaret, in illis mucrone transfixus, semianimis ad terram prosternitur: ipse vero rex frater Humfredi cruribus intra suos pedes repositis. Ceciderat namque dux inclitus ad suos obverso capite, sed pedibus ad hostes, ubi rex diu fortissime pugnans frater fratrem ab hostibus tutatus inter suos reportari fecit.[38]

It should be noted how Humphrey's valour is in no way diminished by his misfortune—he may have been incautious, but the writer highlights his falling "obverso capite, sed pedibus ad hostes", facing the enemy; Henry's intervention takes an almost epic quality in the image of the brother saving the brother, "fortissime pugnans." For the rest of his life, whether acting as a soldier or as a politician, Humphrey seems always to refer to this specular image, to the better mirror of himself that was Henry V. In this perspective, Frulovisi's *Vita Henrici Quinti*, whose contents and tone are strongly determined by Frulovisi's patron and employer, can be seen as a mirror with an active role, "the means by which the ideal is seen in a transient image";[39] a function that was often present in late-medieval writings in England.

---

[37] Even if, as David Rundle rightly notes, in the preface to the *Vita* Frulovisi underlines that Humphrey's commission was given "rogatu supplicationibusque meis" ("Humanism before the Tudors: On Nobility and the Reception of *studia humanitatis* in Fifteenth-Century England", p. 27).

[38] "While Humphrey of Gloucester, the valiant brother of the king, was fighting with great enthusiasm but little caution, wounded by a spear, he fell almost inanimate to the ground; then the king had his feet between his brother's legs. The Duke had fallen with his head towards his army, but his feet towards his enemies, so that the king fighting most bravely protected his brother from his enemies, and had him brought safely among his own". *Titi Livii Forojuliensis Vita Henrici Quinti Regis Angliae*, ed. by T. Hearne, Oxonii: E Theatro Sheldoniano, 1716, p. 20.

[39] Anna Torti, *The Glass of Form. Mirroring Structures from Chaucer to Skelton*, Cambridge: D.S. Brewer, 1991, p. 2. What Weiss writes on Frulovisi's *Vita* also deserves mention: "A biography of Humphrey's brother, King Henry V, it was in no less degree a characterization, almost a dramatization, of the French war, and one on which Humphrey was well cast if not without justification. The better to serve the ends of his patron who at the moment of its composition was clamouring for war, this time against Burgundy, Frulovisi relegated events in England to the background, so as to focus attention on the heroic appeal of the campaigns" (Roberto Weiss, *Humanism in England During the Fifteenth Century*, Oxford: Blackwell, 1941, pp. 42–3).

Henry V is often invoked, often referred to; always, when contrasting the wishes of the King's Council, or even of his own brother Bedford, Humphrey claims to be acting according to the dead King's wishes. It may be in part a rather obvious political manoeuvre, but Henry V seems to have been, even more than his father, the most influential person in Humphrey's life and in his political activity. Besides, the undoubted charismatic value of the dead King's memory could help to make some of Duke Humphrey's moves acceptable even to those who opposed his policy. After leaving Gloucester's employment, Frulovisi presented John Stafford, Bishop of Bath and Wells, with a copy of the same work; since Stafford was anything but favourable to Humphrey, it may be said that the testimonial value of the *Vita* could surpass its role as propaganda writing: "such a biography was a homage to a king who all could agree had presided over English greatness".[40]

Henry V's French campaign gave Humphrey further opportunities to distinguish himself. After the Agincourt episode, he gave a more certain proof of his military ability in the siege of Cherbourg (March 1418), which he successfully led, this time without the direct assistance of his brother. It was the first time in which he assumed complete responsibility for a decisive stage of the French campaign, and the enterprise involved some risk—Cherbourg was almost impregnable and well garrisoned. The same characteristics of impetuosity and obstinacy that marked Duke Humphrey throughout his life and that have been so often lamented by historians served him well on this occasion: with surprising quickness and energy he overcame both natural and human obstacles; Cherbourg was surrendered on August 23 of the same year, and he could hand the conquered town almost intact to the English King.[41]

Whatever the political implications of this episode, it made great impression, and contributed much to the popularity of the Duke of Gloucester, associating him in the popular imagination with the war party even during the years of Henry VI's reign. Thenceforward, and probably thanks to this first, successful exploit, Duke Humphrey's

---

What Weiss writes is undoubtedly right; yet he possibly overestimates the role of Humphrey as one of the characters of Frulovisi's biography.

[40] David Rundle, "Humanism before the Tudors: On Nobility and the Reception of the *studia humanitatis* in Fifteenth-Century England", p. 27.

[41] For a detailed account of the siege, see Vickers, pp. 60–70.

military activity was to be connected mainly with siege tactics—
shortly after Cherbourg, he took part in the siege of Rouen, and
though his role here was decidedly secondary, anonymous fifteenth-
century poems such as *The Siege of Rouen* stress his bravery and good-
ness in this occasion.[42] In later years, the siege of Calais, undertaken
in 1436, was another moment in which English hopes seem to be
concentrated upon Humphrey. However, Vickers is probably right
when he writes, after his analysis of the siege of Cherbourg, that
"Gloucester was an able man and a brave soldier, but he could
never have become even a passable commander".[43] Humphrey lacked
his brother Henry's ability for political calculation, his far-seeing attitude as a strategist, and possibly even his extraordinary qualities as
a leader of men. He could not sustain any campaign for a long time
(this, actually, seems to be true of every side of his activity), nor
could he maintain the unstinted devotion of his soldiers for so long,
and he would often abandon a military project that had reasonable
chances of success out of sheer weariness. On the other hand, he
could learn much from his brother, and possibly, as was evident in
the Cherbourg episode, elaborate a pattern of siege tactics that owed
something not only to Henry V's example, but also to his own knowledge of military theory.[44]

Before his elder brother died, Humphrey was temporarily *custos
Anglie*: he had been made captain of Rouen after its successful siege
and conquest, in January 1419, and on December 30, 1419, he
received a commission to be guardian and lieutenant of England in
the place of the Duke of Bedford,[45] who was conducting peace negotiations in France. This meant that temporarily he held the executive power in his own country and presided over Parliament and
Council, though the Council's assent was indispensable if he was to
carry into execution any deliberation. While the captaincy of Rouen
had been simply an emergency measure in times of war, the regency
of England, though temporary, carried very real power with it. It

---

[42] The poem is published at the end of *The Historical Collections of a Citizen of
London in the Fifteenth Century*, ed. by James Gairdner, Camden Society, London:
Nichols, 1876.

[43] Vickers, p. 69.

[44] Vickers's comment on the siege of Cherbourg is: "Again and again we find
traces of Henry's tactics adapted with great skill to the needs of the present case
with some slight elaboration" (p. 69).

[45] Vickers, p. 81.

must be understood, however, that in this case his position was very
different from the one he held after Henry V's death. Besides, in
1419 Henry V was still very young and expected to live, so that the
throne of England appeared then to be in very secure hands, and
Humphrey could pose no real threat of supremacy to the King's
Council.

Thus the first stage of Duke Humphrey's involvement with France
was over by 1419. After taking part in the siege of Rouen, and wit-
nessing the capture of Ivry and other castles in the north, he was
sent back to England, as we have seen before, to replace Bedford
as temporary Regent of England, while his brother accompanied
Queen Catherine to Paris in May 1422. This replacement seems to
have been the prelude to Humphrey's life-long concern with the welfare of the English crown, while after the death of Henry V the
Duke of Bedford was destined to reign, in his nephew's name, over
the French territories now annexed to the English crown. The reasons of this double assignation on the part of Henry V are not
entirely clear, though the connection between this and his last will
is clear; it is possible that Henry, recognising superior political abilities in his brother John, preferred him for the freshly-conquered
and still uncertain possessions in France, in particular as concerned
the duchy of Normandy, while his other brother, Thomas, Duke of
Clarence, was equally employed in Anjou; the King was counting
on the Council as well as on Humphrey for the management of
affairs in England. However, Gloucester was in England by December
1419, awaiting the King's return, which took place in 1420 (even if,
as it turned out, Henry's stay in England on that occasion was of
extremely short duration).

Henry V's death, in 1422, was certainly an unwelcome surprise
for his followers and for the King's Council: the King was then
thirty-five, he had come back to France to make sure of conquests
that had become rather uncertain after his brother the Duke of
Clarence had been killed in a skirmish at Baugé, in 1421; he had
recently visited England to celebrate his marriage, but so short had
been his sojourn that he had had no occasion even to see his new-
born son, the future King of England. There is little doubt that both
he and his Council were counting on many more years of reign,
and that his untimely death might have thrown the realm into utter
confusion. As for Henry's French possessions, they were but newly
acquired: obeying to a political principle that was based upon a total

commitment to war,[46] Henry had been almost completely devoted to his campaigns, concentrating on his aggressive policy in the continent and possibly reserving the consolidation of his now double crown to a later stage.

The years that followed Henry V's death were the years of most direct political activity for Humphrey of Gloucester, and also the years in which the Council, and by implication the throne, underwent and passed their most difficult test, maintaining a united front and striving to give power and strength to a newly-moulded kingdom, in order to hand it intact to the new King. The strain that this effort implied is evident, for instance, in the very early coronation of Henry of Windsor, who became King Henry VI at the extremely tender age of nine, but also in the frequent contrasts between prominent men such as the Duke of Gloucester and the Bishop of Winchester, in the urgently requested interventions of the Duke of Bedford once these contrasts reached a point of no return, and in the occasionally autocratic attitude Henry VI had to show in the first years of his reign (for instance, when dealing with the role of the Duke of Gloucester himself, and later, when determining his ultimate downfall).

Before his death, Henry had amply disposed for the management of affairs in France: the regency was firmly in the hand of John, certainly the most capable among his brothers, and subsequent events demonstrate that both the power and the responsibility of the Duke of Bedford in the newly acquired territories were never seriously under discussion. Humphrey's position was far less secure, as we shall see. Henry V had written his last will at Dover on 10 June 1421, before sailing to France for what would be his last campaign. In this will there were no specific dispositions for the regency of France, even if this issue could then be considered the most pressing problem; equally nothing was said as concerned the management of affairs in England. The full dispositions for Henry's English inheritance (and we shall presently see how ambiguous the term is) were not contained in this will, but in a codicil written on 26 August 1422 at the castle of Bois de Vincennes, when the King was already struck by dysentery and was evidently conscious of impending death.

---

[46] On Henry's war politics, see C.T. Allmand, "Henry V the Soldier, and the War in France", in *Henry V. The Practice of Kingship*, ed. by G.L. Harriss, Oxford: Oxford University Press, 1985: 117–35.

The story of both will and codicil from their drafting to their final rediscovery in the twentieth century is curious.[47] They were certainly known to the surviving members of the royal family, and by implication to the future King, and formed the basis of the discussion on the division of power in England in 1422. As was probably expected of him, Henry V had written a number of wills in his life; the first, dated 24 July 1415, just before the first French campaign, shows that the King was perfectly aware of the danger such campaigns might entail, and of the necessity of leaving adequate dispositions for the welfare of the realm, as well as of his own household, in the case of his death. The testament written in 1421 was the third of a series, all three having been written on the eve of a campaign. The codicil, or codicils,[48] must have been added to this last will in a hurry, but there is no doubt that they constituted a clear expression of Henry V's intentions, as expressed before authoritative witnesses,[49] and that they bound the King's Council, as well as the surviving relatives, to a definite line of conduct. After going through various hands, both will and codicil disappeared some time before 1445. A copy reappeared in 1978, during work on uncatalogued archival material in Eton College.[50] Though there has been found no specific reason for the ownership of the copy on the part of Eton, the connection between Henry V's will and the college can be easily established: since Henry VI was the founder of the college in the early 1440s, he might have decided to entrust the college a copy for safe-keeping—the intermediary in this case might have been William Alnwick, keeper of the Privy Seal in 1426 and Bishop of Lincoln (a

---

[47] Both texts are now printed in Patrick and Felicity Strong, "The Last Will and Codicils of Henry V", *The English Historical Review* 96: 1981, 79–102. The article also includes a full discussion of the two texts and of their political implications. For a detailed discussion on Henry V's will and of the relevant codicil, see also the first chapter of Bertram Wolffe, *Henry VI*, London: Eyre Methuen, 1981.

[48] There is some uncertainty on this point, since only one codicil has been recovered, together with the will, but some contemporary documents seem to allude to *codicils* in the plural. See Strong, pp. 81–9.

[49] According to Strong (p. 81), the codicils of August 1422 were brought back from France together with the body of the King, possibly by Thomas Duke of Exeter. They were shown, together with the will, before the Archbishop of Canterbury, the Bishop of Winchester, the Duke of Gloucester and the Duke of Exeter in November 1422.

[50] Thomas Martin, an antiquary, had made an allusion to the same document in the Eton archives in 1724, but the reference has been inexplicably glossed over by later historians.

diocese which included Eton) from 1436 to 1449. However, the dis-
appearance of the will in the following centuries has rather clouded
the matter of Humphrey of Gloucester's role for modern historians:
he is often, and inappropriately, called Regent of England (for instance,
by Vickers himself, but also by more recent historians), while in
actual fact he had no such title. For the same reasons, on this issue
the reports of the York and Tudor chroniclers carry very little authority, and do not allow us to establish the extent of the Duke of
Gloucester's authority and responsibility, or the limitations imposed
on him by the Council.

The 1421 will made provisions for Henry's personal possessions
and for the belongings of his household: his own body first, then his
French prisoners (and it is interesting to note at this point that, while
the other prisoners were to be offered for ransom, the Duke of
Orléans and the Earl of Eu were to remain "in custodia heredis seu
successoris nostri", a phrase implying Henry's own uncertainty on
the matter of his succession),[51] his churches and finally his household goods are carefully distributed. Accurate provisions are also
made for the welfare of his own soul, and the numerous members
of an extended family are named almost one by one. Little or no
mention is made of the yet unborn son, apart from generic references to an heir or successor, as in the case of the dispositions made
for the French prisoners quoted above; even if Henry at this point
surely knew that Queen Catherine was pregnant, he obviously had
no idea of the successful outcome of the pregnancy, or of the fact
that the baby was male. The Queen herself was adequately provided
for, as was the whole royal household. On the other hand, no mention was made of political affairs, and of how the double crown was
to be managed. Several explanations can be found for this silence,
though none is completely satisfactory. In writing a will in 1421, as
he had done in the two previous cases, Henry had every reasonable
expectation to live; besides, it may be argued that testamentary dispositions may only concern one's personal property—it is difficult to
maintain that a kingdom may be regarded as the King's property,
and disposed of as such. Furthermore, at this point the King was
still very much uncertain with regards to his heirs.

---

[51] "In the custody of our heir or successor". Strong, p. 92.

The codicil was evidently written in a different spirit. Dated just five days before the King's death, it was obviously dictated by real urgency, and by an awareness of the extremely precarious position in which the King's premature death left his son, now newly-born, as well as the kingdom as a whole. The codicil is clearly *infra testamentum*, and thus to be read as part of the previous document, but it dispenses with many of its legal and formal niceties, concentrating on very few legatees: the Queen, explicitly named *regina Anglie*, and the young prince (here called *princeps Wallie*), together with a small number of churches. Once again, no explicit reference is made to the crown; but in the legacy young Henry is evidently treated as the successor, and accurate dispositions are made for his safekeeping and wellbeing during his minority.

It is on these lines, referring to the care of the person of Henry V's son, that Duke Humphrey based all his claims to power in the long interregnum that took place between Henry V's death and the coronation of Henry VI. They are worth quoting extensively:

> Volu[mus] etiam quod carissimus frater noster Humfridus dux Gloucestr' habeat tutelam et defensionem nostri carissimi filii principales. Et quod avunculus noster dux Exon' habeat persone sue regimen et gubernationem ac servitorum suorum circa personam suam electionem et assumptionem. Volumus etiam quod circa personam suam et in hospitio suo assistant sibi dilecti nobis et fideles Henricus Fitz Hugh, camerarius noster, et Walterus Hungerford, senescallus hospitii nostri, quorum alterum semper cum ipso esse volumus.[52]

As we can see, neither the regency of France nor the regency of England are mentioned, whatever dispositions Henry might have given orally.[53] Henry Beaufort, Bishop of Winchester and one of the most powerful men of the realm, goes equally unmentioned (if not,

---

[52] "We wish our dear brother Humphrey, Duke of Gloucester, to be in charge of the protection and defence of our very dear son. And let our uncle of Exeter have the care and governance of his person, and the choice of the servants who are to be around him. We also wish our faithful and dear *camerarius* Henry Fitz Hugh and our *senescalcus* Walter Hungerford to help him and assist him in his house, so that one or the other of them may be always with him". See Strong, pp. 99–100. It is perhaps ironical that this crucial passage is among the most damaged by damp and rodents in the original manuscript. Thus the word *regimen*, for instance, is in part the editor's conjecture.

[53] As seems to be implied in some of the later chronicles: see, for instance, *The Brut or the Chronicles of England*, ed. by F.W.D. Brie, Early English Text Society, London: Kegan Paul, Trench, Trübner, 1906–8, II, p. 429.

in the 1421 will, as merely one of the many executors), which might go to demonstrate the personal nature of the testamentary provisions contained in both will and codicil. The existence of a *de facto* regency in France, however, solved, at least in part, the problem of the continuity of power. Humphrey was possibly hoping that by analogy with what was happening in France, the words *tutela* and *defensio* might be read as investing him with the power of regency, and that this arrangement could be considered valid until the child became of age. Both Humphrey and a number of later critics and historians seem to have overlooked the fact that Henry V had mentioned other people as responsible for the upbringing of Henry of Windsor: if Humphrey was to be the principal defender and protector, Thomas Beaufort, Duke of Exeter, had the governance of the child's person, as well as the responsibility for the prince's retinue; both Exeter and Gloucester were to be assisted by FitzHugh and Hungerford in their task. Susanne Saygin, to quote a very recent instance of misreading of the codicil, argues that on the strength of this document Humphrey decided on a project of humanistic education of the young prince, and sees the commissioned translations of Aristotelian and Platonic texts as stages of this didactic programme. Much could be argued about the practical utility of these texts for the future King of England, or about the actual ideological achievements on the part of Gloucester; but what is more important is that Saygin's premises are erroneous, in that the codicil expressly stated that the Duke of Exeter, rather than Gloucester, was to be given *regimen et gubernationem* of the royal child. Even the twentieth-century editors of the will and codicil are somewhat generous towards Duke Humphrey in their reading of the text, since they extend the reference to the person of the prince expressed in *nostri carissimi filii* to cover "the prince's inheritance".[54]

The interpretation of the codicil as Humphrey wanted it was met with strong opposition on the part of Henry V's old councillors, and by 5 December 1422 it had been agreed that the Duke of Gloucester would accept simply the title of "Protector and Defender". If both position and salary were excellent (he received eight thousand marks a year), the real executive power remained with the Council. Humphrey thus was not to be guardian of the prince, as he had earlier hoped, but was left with the lesser role of protector, a role that was to be

---

[54] Strong, p. 85.

ceded to his brother John whenever the latter was in England. Such
modifications may have been rendered necessary by the fact that the
Council did not share the dead King's high esteem of his brothers,
and particularly of Humphrey; but it must also be said that the ter-
minology of the text on this particular point was open to different
possible readings. Appropriately, Patrick and Felicity Strong gloss the
expression *tutelam et defensionem nostri carissimi filii principales* with a rather
sardonic "whatever the phrase may have meant".[55] It is immediately
evident that the most pressing problem of interpretation rested with
the term *tutela*. It was the term used under Roman law for the
guardianship of a male below the age of puberty, and as such
Gloucester read it. In this case it did not necessarily include the
actual care of the child, but the managing of his affairs: "the Roman
'tutor', in fact, was first and foremost the controller of the property
of his ward in the time of the latter's incapacity to administer it
himself".[56] Once "his affairs" were read as including the management of the crown, and of the actual political powers held by a
King in the normal course of his adult governance, *tutela* extended
the authority of Gloucester to that of the actual regent of England.
By analogy, at this point, *defensio* could be associated to the former
term and thus come to be read not as simple protection of the person of the King, but invest the Duke with the responsibility of
defender of the realm, and therefore give him authority also in foreign affairs—or even, paradoxically, invest him with authority over
the French territories.

As we have seen, however, this was far from the Council's reading of the codicil. Already in 1422, after the public reading of both
will and codicils, the Council had expressed its rejection of Humphrey's
reading, or in any case of any reading that would attribute too ample
a power to the Duke of Gloucester. The latter attempted to raise
objections, and a communication of his to the lords during the first
Parliament held in the name of Henry VI (1422) shows his determination.[57] The communication originated from a former petition of

---

[55] Strong, p. 84.
[56] J.S. Roskell, *Parliament and Politics in Late Medieval England*, London: The Hambledon
Press, 1981, p. 206.
[57] The document, preserved in the Public Record Office, is published and discussed in S.B. Chrimes, "The Pretensions of the Duke of Gloucester in 1422", *The
English Historical Review* 45: 1930, 101–3.

the commons, requiring a prompt decision as to who should have the governance of the kingdom. Gloucester probably used the petition of the commons, in part because he believed he could count on the commons' support, in part because during the confrontation with the lords it gave him the opportunity to show that the title of protector and defender would not satisfy the commons', and by implication the country's, need for a strong central authority: "it semeth to my lord that by the word Defensor the peticion of the commune nys nat satisfied", recites the document in its opening paragraph.[58] What is interesting about this communication (which, incidentally, did not help further Gloucester's cause) is that the Duke used thorough historical research in his argument: to find previous instances of his position in English history he goes back to the reign of King Richard, presumably using an example of an enfeebled kingdom, in order to contrast it with what should be done at the present moment: the document argues against the behaviour of the old King's councillors, since "they haue assented for to call my lord Defensor of this Reme and chief counseiller of the kyng natwithstanding that they coude fynde no recordis but of kyng Richardis tyme".[59] He also cites an instance from the reign of Henry III, in which the Earl of Pembroke was called *Rector Regis et regni Angliae*. The attempt on the part of Humphrey is clearly to use the historical precedent as a support for his cause, and certainly, as Chrimes writes, "the document shows that Gloucester was very thorough in the methods he adopted in his bid for power, and that in that cause, at any rate, he excelled his brother lords in his capacity for historical research".[60] If so, the negative outcome of the petition must have shown Humphrey that historical accuracy could be but a poor weapon. In the end, the Duke of Gloucester was to remain Protector and Defender, and take also the title of first Councillor of the King—a title that he was to maintain even after Henry of Windsor was crowned; with the already mentioned proviso, however, that he should resign all these titles to the Duke of Bedford if the latter happened to be in England at any given moment.

In his dispute with the Council Humphrey did not have the Duke of Bedford on his side, since the latter obviously preferred to defend

---

[58] Chrimes, p. 102.
[59] Chrimes, p. 102.
[60] Chrimes, p. 102.

his own greater claim as nearest in blood to the late King and heir presumptive in the event of young Henry's death—a possibility that, in an age of widespread infant mortality, was far from being unlikely. Gloucester's attitude probably helped the Council to reinforce its structure, maintain internal harmony and implement its policies in the attempt to defend itself from the Duke's pretensions; at the same time, Humphrey's attitude gave other members of the Council the opportunity to gain favour with the nobility, and create political alliances that would survive the turmoil following Henry of Windsor's coronation and ultimately would spell defeat for the Duke: "Gloucester's pre-eminence in status and blood combined with his inability to assert a natural leadership in the Council made him a semi-isolated figure, while Beaufort increasingly forged connections among the nobility".[61] The Council seemed particularly afraid of a certain lack of reliability and steadiness on Humphrey's part, as well as of the arrogance and obstinacy he had already shown. However, Humphrey himself seems to have come to accept the attribution of the title of Regent to the Duke of Bedford, if I am interpreting correctly the annotation on an illuminated manuscript of Livy's *Ab urbe condita* in the French translation of Pierre Bersuire, donated by Bedford to Gloucester: "Cest livre fut envoyé des parties de France et donné par mons le regent de royaume, duc de Bedford, a mons le duc de Gloucestre, son beau frère, l'an mil quatre cens vingt sept".[62]

It must be added that one of the main supporters of this reduction of Humphrey's power was that same Henry Beaufort, mentioned in the quotation above, who had been apparently entitled to expect more from King Henry's will than the mere role of testamentary executor. The Bishop of Winchester was the son of John of Gaunt, therefore Humphrey's uncle, and great-uncle to the infant Henry VI; he had been chancellor under both Henry IV and Henry V, and his supporters formed a very strong group in the Council. When discussing the arrival of Poggio Bracciolini in England, as belonging to the retinue of the Bishop of Winchester, we have also seen the latter in a stage of temporary decrease of royal favour and power: it has been argued that the enmity between Beaufort and Gloucester

---

[61] G.L. Harriss, *Cardinal Beaufort. A Study of Lancastrian Ascendancy and Decline*, Oxford: Clarendon Press, 1988, p. 133.
[62] Paris, Bibliothèque de Sainte Geneviève, franç. 777, f. 433v. See Sammut, p. 122.

had started exactly at this point, when Pope Martin V had named the Bishop for the cardinalate (18 December 1417), conferring on him also the title of legate *a latere*, and the seat of Winchester. This meant that at this point Henry Beaufort had received rather more honours than either Henry V or Humphrey had expected; besides, the naming of a legate meant a Papal interference into English affairs, while "Henry had exercised a close, paternalistic control over the church, promoting men who combined spiritual integrity with belief in royal leadership."[63] The Bishop of Winchester was formally restored to the King's favour only in 1421, which means that at the time of Henry V's death, and of the discussion on the will, he was again in the ascendancy, and could use (and, apparently, did use) his influence to persuade the Council to decide against Gloucester's requests.

The hostility between Beaufort and Gloucester is one of the most important and lasting elements of English policy during Henry VI's minority, and might be said to have influenced, to some extent, even Humphrey's indefatigable activity as a patron, especially in his later years. It would be difficult to find two other public characters with such different and contrasting personalities in Lancastrian England. From this clash of wills Gloucester was destined to come out the loser: he lacked Beaufort's tenacity and patience, his ability to make the best of an extremely poor outlook, his slow but never-ceasing work to make himself useful allies in the Council and among the nobility; he also lacked his greed, that made him in more than one occasion an indispensable prop for the vacillating Lancastrian finances. Possibly Gloucester's arrogance prevented him from seeing the usefulness of such manoeuvres—but it might be argued that, even if he had realised how important they were, particularly in the years of the oligarchic regime created *de facto* by the minority of the King, such an effort would have been incompatible with his personality. Humphrey of Gloucester's political decisions and actions, whatever their motivations, were always characterised by flamboyance and love of display; his expenses always seem to have been well above his means; even his intellectual activity bears the same traits, as we shall see in the following chapters. But, both as a politician and as a patron, it seemed impossible for him to persevere in any enterprise, and to wait for the natural outcome of any decision or strategy.

---

[63] Harriss, p. 95.

The much-debated interpretation of Henry V's will and codicils, and the consequential decision of the King's Council as concerned the position of the Duke of Gloucester, together with his enmity with the Bishop of Winchester, form the basis, at least for the greatest part, of Humphrey's often controversial political attitude in the years to come. Twentieth-century historians have commented on this, even when they were basing their considerations on an imperfect knowledge of Henry V's will; thus E.F. Jacob rightly writes that "the course of the duke's life and his whole attitude towards the Council were largely to be determined by the rejection of Henry's plan by the magnates in the first parliament of the new reign".[64] It may also be argued that Humphrey's subsequent career as a patron of English writers and Italian humanists may have been in large measure determined by this disappointing failure in the early years of his political activity. He was not the man to bear with such a disappointment in silence—neither did he have the patience to attempt to improve his position by a long-term policy of alliance with the most influential members of the Council. The following years often see him in direct confrontation or even contention with the most powerful councillors; occasionally, he tried to divert his attention and give new scope to his pent-up energy by means of military campaigns in the continent; none of them, however, was pursued with great constancy, as we shall see presently, so none of them was rewarded with lasting success.

Further noteworthy episodes in Humphrey's career, prior to his most serious involvement with intellectual activities in England, show him with essentially the same characteristics. Shortly after his defeat, in January 1423, he married Jacqueline of Hainault, and this marriage gave rise to a number of contrasting and occasionally violent reactions, both in England and abroad. Humphrey may have seen in this marriage the occasion for a new rise in politics, a chance to conquer a position of eminence even outside the King's Council. After a singularly loveless marriage, Jacqueline had flown from her second husband, John IV of Brabant,[65] in 1421, seeking refuge at the English court; it seems extremely probable that Henry V had

---

[64] E.F. Jacob, *The Fifteenth Century, 1399–1485*, Oxford History of England, Oxford: Clarendon Press, 1961, p. 211.

[65] Jacqueline's first husband, the dauphin John (Charles VII's elder brother), had died soon after their marriage.

looked favourably, if not directly connived, at her flight,[66] since in England she was given a pension, and was godmother to Henry VI. Jacqueline had also petitioned Pope Martin V for an annulment of the marriage, but the Pope (as far as it is known) had taken no definite decision in this sense; there was, however, some form of divorce in 1422, thanks to the intervention of the Spanish antipope Benedict XIII.

Once Gloucester had married her, he may have seen this new alliance as giving him the right to Jacqueline's dominions, and possibly thought that this move meant the possibility of becoming direct ruler in the territories of Hainault, Holland, and Zeeland (since Jacqueline was the only daughter of William IV, count of Hainault, and at her father's death had inherited his sovereignty over this land), thus establishing a strong hold over a territory that did not belong to the English crown, and in which he could then exercise a form of absolute power, unchecked by Parliament or Council. This is the interpretation offered by John Lydgate, whose propaganda poetry is generally tinged with a pacifist bias, in a poem celebrating the marriage, where the poet expresses the hope that this marriage will unify England and Holland in the same way as the marriage between Henry V and Katherine confirmed the unity between England and France. Marital and political alliances thus become ordained by heaven, bringing back a lost cosmic order, since such peaceful unions are part of God's design:

And, as I hope, of hert and menyng truwe
    þe mortal werre ceesse shal and fyne,
Betwene þoo booþe, and pees ageyne renuwe,
    To make loue with cleer beemys shyne,
    By þe meene of hir þat heeght Katheryne,
Ioyned til oon, his deedis can you telle,
Henry þe Fyffte, of knighthoode sours and welle.

And firþerdovne for to specefye,
    þe dewe of grace distille shal and reyne
Pees and acorde for to multeplye,
    In þe boundes here of oure Brettaygne
    To fynde a wey wherby we may atteyne
þat Duchye of Holand by hool affeccoun
May beo allyed with Brutus Albyoun.[67]

---

[66] Harriss, p. 135.
[67] "On Gloucester's Approaching Marriage", ll. 43–56, in *John Lydgate. Minor*

Lydgate may have interpreted the desires of the English citizens rather than of the Duke himself, but there is no doubt that the marriage gave Humphrey, at least momentarily, the illusion that Holland and the rest of the territories connected with Jacqueline could be easily conquered and annexed to the English crown.[68]

It may also be argued that Humphrey saw this marriage as giving him the possibility of gaining the upper hand in his almost life-long confrontation with his brother Bedford. He probably also felt an odd kind of justification and even inevitability in his enterprise in the sanction Henry V had formerly given to Jacqueline's separation from John of Brabant. Whatever the motivations and drives behind his undertaking, he began it with characteristic enthusiasm, only to abandon it with equally characteristic weariness. The difficulty in the recognition of his sovereignty over the territories of Hainault lay in the fact that the Duke of Burgundy (related to both Jacqueline and her former husband) had to assent to it, and the assent was to be gained either by compromise or by a victory over Burgundy. Philip, Duke of Burgundy and the Duke of Gloucester had never been friends; nevertheless, in this case Duke Humphrey did seek a compromise, but when his attempts failed (Gloucester had refused Bedford's and Burgundy's agreements, or what they had tried to stipulate even without his approval), in June 1424, he began to prepare for a campaign in Flanders, landing at Calais on 18 October. He was accompanied in this expedition by Jacqueline herself—it was probably hoped that her presence would win the devotion of the Hainaulters to her own and Gloucester's cause.[69]

Contemporary chroniclers' accounts of this delicate phase of Gloucester's political activity are generally heavily biased in one sense or another, and therefore none too reliable. Had Humphrey's campaign been successful, it would have served the English foreign policy in no uncertain manner, since it would have enlarged and consolidated the English hold on the continent. In a way, Gloucester may have

---

Poems, vol. 2: Secular Poems, ed. by H.N. MacCracken, Early English Text Society, Oxford: Oxford University Press, 1934, pp. 601–8.

[68] On Lydgate's view of the two Lancaster marriages see Scott-Morgan Straker, "Rivalry and Reciprocity in Lydgate's *Troy Book*", in *New Medieval Literatures 3*, ed. by D. Lawton, W. Scase and R. Copeland, Oxford: Oxford University Press, 1999: 119–47, pp. 125–6.

[69] For a detailed account of the Flanders campaign, see Harriss, *Cardinal Beaufort*, pp. 134–49.

been hoping to continue his brother Henry's expansionistic activity, with a rapid and gloriously bloodless (on the part of the English) raid that would equal the surprising and splendid victory at Agincourt. Henry V, after all, had never discounted the possibility of continuing his campaigns and extending his kingdom to reach the Flemish territories, and up to the last stage of his life Humphrey saw himself as the true interpreter and successor of Henry's policy in Europe, as is amply demonstrated by the tenor of Frulovisi's *Vita Henrici Quinti*. Therefore, nominally this new role for the Duke of Gloucester was a very desirable event for both himself and England, but such a conquest would have no possibility of ever becoming permanent and would only give yet more instability to England's already uncertain foreign possessions—a fact both the Bishop of Winchester and the Duke of Bedford seemed to have realised perfectly, even if the latter tried to help his brother's project by requesting the Pope to give his blessing and assent to Gloucester's marriage with Jacqueline. The real enemy in this case was not the weak Duke of Brabant, but the far more powerful Duke of Burgundy, who would obviously oppose such an expansion on the part of the English, and who had claims of his own to these territories. Besides, the Hainaulters, though never offering direct resistance to the Duke's army (Gloucester and his five-thousand-strong army marched through the Burgundian territories in comparatively undisturbed peace), refused to recognise him as their lord, and put him in the uneasy position of having to start slow and laboured negotiations with all the parties involved. This sort of careful weaving of political relations was most contrary to Duke Humphrey's character, and his impatience and lack of steady purpose as much as any external factor determined the ultimate failure of the project. Early success was followed by a slow retreat and discouragement, until Gloucester returned to England on 12 April 1425, ostensibly to prepare for a duel to which Philip of Burgundy had challenged him, as it had seemed a possible way to conclude the stalemate. Once in England, however, the Duke of Gloucester seemed quickly to lose heart, to the point that, having left his wife Jacqueline in Flanders, he started an affair with one of her ladies-in-waiting, Eleanor Cobham. The daughter of lord Cobham of Sterborough, she became Humphrey's second wife probably in 1428, after the Pope had annulled his first marriage in the January of the same year, by declaring Jacqueline still legally the wife of the Duke of Brabant (though Brabant had died in the meantime, the Pope's decree meant that Humphrey's marriage was to all effects illegal). The Flemish expedition had thus abruptly and ingloriously reached its conclusion, and the Duke of Burgundy could easily reconquer the lost territories and even make Jacqueline prisoner, shortly after Gloucester's return to England, and in spite of the five hundred men Gloucester had sent to her help.

If the Duke of Bedford in the course of the whole Flemish enterprise, as well as during the whole time of his regency in France, had shown considerable foresight in understanding that it would be beyond his power to maintain and control a state of perpetual warfare with Burgundy, with his unfortunate and rash campaign Gloucester had probably lost what fame he had gained in the French campaigns as a good tactician; he had made himself unpopular with the temporary check he put to trade with Flanders, had revealed in full to Council and Parliament the great if ill-directed ambition that governed his acts, and had made a few very powerful enemies, above all the Duke of Burgundy. Besides, he had left free rein to the Council, who had governed in his absence, and to Henry Beaufort, Bishop of Winchester, who had become chancellor. The tension between Gloucester and Beaufort rose to the point that on 30 October 1425 a riot broke out between their respective supporters in London, and the Council had to call the Duke of Bedford to England, acting for some time as protector. Bedford went back to France only in 1427, which meant that during these two years his far less powerful and politically able younger brother was seriously hampered, while his ambition received an almost definitive check. Gloucester's adventure on the continent, when he was for the first time his own master in the art of war, had thus turned out a failure on almost all accounts, and can be considered the beginning of Humphrey's political downfall, and of the second rise of the Bishop of Winchester. It may also be argued that the series of disastrous mistakes he had made drove the Council to anticipate the date of the new King's coronation: when Henry of Windsor was formally invested with royal power over England, on 6 November 1429, he was little more than eight years old.[70]

It is more difficult to assess the impact that the episode had on Humphrey's hitherto excellent relation with the middle classes. On

---

[70] His French coronation was performed slightly later.

the one hand, he might have made himself more popular in London, since he encouraged anti-Flemish feelings, and possibly also drove the merchants to envisage the possibility of greater gains in the event of his conquest. The episode of the London riots between his and Henry Beaufort's faction that has been mentioned above seems to support this hypothesis. Henceforth, Humphrey was associated more than ever with a pro-war party that saw in the Duke of Gloucester the chief defence against the arch-enemy, the Duke of Burgundy. On the other hand, Humphrey's desertion of Jacqueline of Hainault and his rather indiscreet affair with Eleanor Cobham diminished his popularity with some sections of the London population, as seems demonstrated by the protest of a number of London housewives— and up to her trial, it must be noted that the new Duchess of Gloucester never seemed to enjoy much popularity, either among her peers or the commoners, though her trial and condemnation partly turned public opinion in her favour.[71]

We can find an account of the Flemish campaign in Aeneas Silvius Piccolomini's *Commentarii*: the humanist's rather dry comment on Humphrey's final failure is that "homo non tam armis quam plumis et libidinibus aptus magnificis que iactauerat uerbis haudquaquam satisfecit nec tanti famam, quanto uitam duxit".[72] It is probably in this passage, rather than in the heavily biased portrait of contemporary and later English chronicles, that we can have a glimpse of the contemporary observers' judgement upon the Duke of Gloucester's personality. Piccolomini undoubtedly had in mind Vegetius's condemnation of lechery in a good knight, which we find often quoted in medieval texts on good government, such as the numerous versions of the *Secreta Secretorum*. The accusation of lechery carries with it an implicit assumption of lack of political ability, as had done the accusation of sodomy for English kings in the fourteenth century, and would become one of the charges most frequently levelled at the Duke. However, the marriage first and then the desertion of Jacqueline of Hainault, together with the abortive Flanders expedition, received general censure even on the part of English chroniclers

---

[71] Compare what Vickers writes, pp. 203–4.
[72] "A man suited to plumes and pleasures, which he abhorred in magnificent words, rather than to arms; he was never worthy of his fame for the time he lived". *Pii II Commentarii rerum memorabilium que temporis suis contigerunt*, ed. by A. van Heck, Città del Vaticano: Biblioteca Apostolica Vaticana, 1984, p. 535.

that might otherwise be interested, for a number of reasons, in the glorification rather than the vituperation of the man who, particularly after his death, became in common parlance "the good duke Humphrey". Thus writes, for instance, Richard Grafton:

> Homfrey Duke of Gloucester eyther blynded with ambicion or doting for loue, maried the lady Iaquet or Iacomin daughter and sole heire to William of Bauier Duke of Holland, which was lawfull wyfe to Iohn Duke of Brabant then lyuing, which mariage chaunced much to his dishonor. For surely the sweete tast of this plesaunt mariage, brought after a sowre sauce, both to the amorous husbande, and to the wanton wyfe.[73]

Seen in terms of long-term policy or popularity, the episode is equally disastrous. Vickers's comment is entirely appropriate: "Another venture which, though dictated by his main characteristic—ambition, was entirely inconsistent with his desire to be supreme in England".[74] What Gloucester did and what he failed to do in this case are a clear instance of his almost complete lack of far-sightedness in political matters. We have noted above how difficult was the position in which he was placed both by his brother's will and by the Council's subsequent decision as concerns his position in England: it is clear that even the ablest and most tactful politician would have found it difficult to profit from this situation and to find his way back into the Council's favour. On the other hand, Gloucester's decisions in some instances seem particularly and obstinately ill-advised, and this was clearly one of those instances. His first marriage, by putting him in direct competition with Philip of Burgundy, had considerably worsened the precarious position of the Lancastrian rule in France; his second marriage in no way improved this matter, and only made him more enemies in England.

At length, Gloucester's reiterated claims both to Hainault and to the regency were explicitly withdrawn, even before the new King's coronation.[75] By 1428 Humphrey definitely knew that his marriage with Jacqueline of Hainault had brought him very little in terms of

---

[73] *Grafton's Chronicle; or History of England (a facsimile of the 1569 edition)*, London: Johnson, Rivington, et al., 1809, I, p. 551. Compare, for an analogous description of the episode, the slightly later Raphaell Holinshed, *The Third Volume of Chronicles*, London: Johnson et al., 1808.

[74] Vickers, p. 125.

[75] Harriss, p. 168.

power and wealth, and had done nothing to further his ambition or to help his cause with the King's Council—which may be one of the reasons why he decided to marry Eleanor Cobham, possibly being driven in this case by personal rather than political considerations. Once Henry VI was crowned King of England, in 1429, Humphrey was no longer protector, but only chief councillor. His power was thus effectively diminished, and he had no authority to contrast the Council's decisions any longer. The King, of course, was still extremely young, and an abler politician might have held a great influence over him for many years to come, but this does not seem to have been the case with the Duke of Gloucester.

The care and education of the future King

It seems, however, that Humphrey was no such politician. We do not have proof of any great personal attachment between uncle and nephew—on the contrary, Henry VI's attitude towards his uncle in the last years of the latter's life shows that the young King would show no scruple in hastening Gloucester's downfall, and possibly his death. On the other hand, Gloucester's loyalty towards the young King with whose protection he had been entrusted seems never to have wavered. During Henry VI's minority, his uncle tried to wrest power and control from the Council, but apparently never with the idea of deposing the young King. It must be added that in those years, even if the young King had not become of age and had not been crowned so early, the heir presumptive would not have been Humphrey but his eldest surviving brother, John, Duke of Bedford. In later years, after Bedford's death, Humphrey was for a long time (indeed, until his own death), heir presumptive, but such was the Council's control over him at this point that it seems difficult to hypothesise any royal ambition on his part—the accusations levelled at him on the eve of his death seem, then as now, rather preposterous. As to the formative years of Henry's life, it is difficult to estimate the influence his uncle might have had upon him, though presumably his title and the duties with which Henry V had invested him gave the Duke of Gloucester free access to the young King's household and person. His position, his age, his relation to young Henry of Windsor, his self-appointed role as the representative and executor of the dead King's wishes, his attentive cultivation of Henry

V's memory, are all elements that might have helped Humphrey gain more and more ascendancy over Henry VI. To a certain extent, Humphrey might even have expected the young King to recognise him as his mentor or teacher, the living embodiment of the qualities that had made Henry V a hero and a memorable King; as the only brother of Henry V that was constantly living near his son, Humphrey was asked, so to speak, to transmit these same qualities to a child that had not been in time to witness his father's greatness. The hypothesis has its charm, and in some recent studies, an attempt has been made to demonstrate it, to the extent of pointing out the books Humphrey might have chosen, among those he ordered or commissioned, to further his didactic cause and shape the young King's ideology;[76] but many elements of the historical evidence we possess conspire to undermine the possibility of its being a practicable scheme, even if it might have been one of Gloucester's aims.

To begin with, Henry V's will and codicils did not entrust Humphrey with the young King's education, but only with the defence of his person and goods—no personal care being involved. Instead, this task was specifically entrusted to the Duke of Exeter, whose responsibility towards the prince included "persone sue regimen et gubernationem"—a phrase which seems to include also the care of education.[77] The Duke of Exeter was Thomas Beaufort, brother to the Bishop of Winchester; his relations with the Duke of Gloucester seem to have been always devoid of any rivalry or animosity, to the point that in 1426 he was part of the Commission that was set up to help settle the dispute between Gloucester and Henry Beaufort. His role in the King's upbringing has never been put seriously in doubt, and in this sense he is frequently mentioned by contemporary chroniclers: in the *Brut*, for instance, we find this passage in a description of Henry V's last moments, when the King makes his testamentary dispositions:

> And sir Vmfrey, the Duke of Gloucestre, his othir brothir, was tho made the kyngis Lefetenaunte of Engelond in his absence, to kepe and governe the Rewme in alle degreis, in saufynge of the pepull and of the lond, that God maynten and kepe in good pees and reste, with good loue and charite to endure! [. . .] And he [Henry V] comyttid

---

[76] Saygin, pp. 30–47.
[77] Strong, p. 100.

thanne the kepynge of Henry, his yonge sone, to Syr Henry Beauford his vncle, the Bisshop of Wynchestire, and to Sir Thomas Beauford, his othir vncle, Duke of Exetre, and charged hem bothe to his good gouernaunce and kepyng in his tendir age.[78]

The passage shows that, though there was considerable uncertainty among chroniclers as concerns Humphrey's actual role, the possibility of his being entrusted with the prince's personal care is never discussed. The same is written in Tito Livio Frulovisi's *Vita Henrici Quinti*, which was, as we have seen, written under the Duke of Gloucester's personal supervision, and which, addressed as it is to Henry VI, may be read in some passages as an almost explicit declaration of Humphrey's own intentions and understanding of his own role; in the case of the Duke of Exeter's responsibility, there is also a clear reference to the *doctrina* of the young King, which is obviously meant as instruction or education:

> Testamento tamen ante tui tutelam primasque defensiones & curam Humfredo Gloucestriae duci, serenissimo tuo patruo, qui te summa fide tuaque tutatus est ad hos dies quibus te florentem & faustum videmus: mores autem, custodiam corporis, & doctrinam tuam illi Thomae Excestriae duci, ducatus vero Normanniae proventus omnes tuo patruo Johanni Bedfordiae duci ad eam provinciam & regnum tuum Franciae bene regendum & gubernandum legavit.[79]

It is evident from the passage that Humphrey of Gloucester himself was aware of the fact, and did not try to contest this disposition. Even after Exeter's death, on 31 December 1426, the charge of Henry of Windsor's education did not go to Gloucester: Vickers, quoting from the *Rotuli Parliamentorum*, indicates that in 1427 Richard de Beauchamp, Earl of Warwick, was empowered by the Council with the role of tutor to the young prince.[80] Nothing, either in the chronicles or in the surviving official documents, shows that the Duke of Gloucester concerned himself in any way with young Henry's intellectual upbringing.

---

[78] *The Brut or the Chronicles of England*, II, pp. 429–30.

[79] "In his testament he confided you especially to the care of your uncle Humphrey, Duke of Gloucester, who protected you with great loyalty, since we see you happy and well-growing to this day: he also confided your personal protection and education to Thomas, Duke of Exeter, and confided the duchy of Normandy to your uncle John, Duke of Bedford, so that he could well rule that province and your kingdom of France". *Titi Livii Forojuliensis Vita Henrici Quinti Regis Angliae*, p. 95.

[80] Vickers, pp. 210–11.

The hypothesis we have mentioned above concerning an intellectual and ideological project on the part of the Duke of Gloucester has thus no real foundation, nor is it supported by any factual element as concerns the texts Saygin identifies as part of this programme, as we shall see in the following chapters. It is probably nearer to the truth to hypothesise the attempt on the part of Humphrey to strike an original attitude after the failure of his political attempts on the wake of Henry V's enterprises, and to propose a Lancastrian intellectual programme that had little to do with the education of the young prince, and much to do with the imitation, more or less conscious, of models proposed from the rest of Europe, and from Italy in particular. Though, as we have seen before, a moderate passion for books and learning seems to have run in the Lancastrian royal family, in the case of Humphrey it took a very special form, informing of itself his political vicissitudes. During his protectorate, he may have thought of himself as a new Seneca, in charge of the education of the future King. Thus he might attempt to complement his limited political skills by means of the acquisition of an intellectual position that surpassed any analogous effort on the part of his more successful brothers.

Whether this was an explicit political calculation, or whether he was animated by a genuine love for books, Humphrey spent much time and energy in recovering, collecting or commissioning books. Following the ebb of a political career that had never seen real splendour, he also attempted to create a humanist court—his Greenwich palace was the meeting point of Italian humanists such as Tito Livio Frulovisi, Pietro del Monte and Antonio Beccaria, as well as of English writers such as John Lydgate, Thomas Hoccleve, and possibly George Ashby and Thomas Norton. He also got in touch with the best known humanists at a European level, commissioning, for instance, Leonardo Bruni to translate Aristotle's *Politics* into Latin, or Pier Candido Decembrio to translate Plato's *Republic*. Above all, he collected an astonishing number of manuscripts, mainly in Latin and French but also in some cases in English. And whether he actually read them or not—a question that should rarely be asked in the case of patrons—he certainly donated a good many of them to Oxford University Library. Today, the most beautiful part of the Bodleian still bears his name. Historians and literary scholars may have different views of Humphrey's merits, but the validity and the (partial) success of his attempt remain unchallenged. As Carol Meale writes:

In Humphrey's assiduous pursuit of Italian scholars and humanist texts, and his adoption of the essentially public rôle of university benefactor, it is possible to detect a careful fostering of the European renaissance ideal of princely 'magnificence'. The depth of Humphrey's scholarship may be open to doubt—there are indications in contemporary sources that his preferred reading matter was in French rather than Latin—but it is clear that he recognized the status which could accrue in the political sphere from acts of literary patronage.[81]

But the fact remains that Duke Humphrey's political attempt failed, and that it was probably never accompanied by a conscious ideological attempt that concerned the King's person or his upbringing: either during Henry VI's minority or after his coronation, his uncle never reached the height of power, and he never really played Seneca to Henry VI's Nero, except perhaps in his death. This political failure finds its deep-seated reasons not only in the Duke's character, but also in the fact that he never fully reckoned with the strength of ecclesiastical power in England. His great political opponent was the already mentioned Bishop of Winchester, who foiled any attempt on the part of the Duke to overcome either Parliament decisions or the power of the bishops; most of the Duke's personal history is the history of an almost life-long rivalry that involved, if only marginally, also his activity as a patron. Neither ultimately won, but such rivalry could not but be exhausting to both, and possibly detrimental to the nation. Without doubt, it helped hasten the downfall at least of the Duke of Gloucester, besides being a powerful weapon in the Council's hands.

But there is another element that needs taking into consideration. Most political and intellectual historians analysing the figure of Duke Humphrey have tended to underestimate the role of the King, and to consider him a mere pawn in the hands of more experienced or crafty courtiers. Much has also been made of Henry VI's alleged weak-mindedness; it should be remembered, however, that his first spell of mental incapacity (what modern historiography has tentatively identified with depressive stupor) occurred only in August 1453 (lasting that first time for eighteen months), that is, well into the King's majority, and long after Duke Humphrey's own death. Only

---

[81] Carol M. Meale, "Patrons, Buyers and Owners: Book Production and Social Status", in *Book Production and Publishing in Britain 1375–1475*, ed. by J. Griffiths and D. Pearsall, Cambridge: Cambridge University Press, 1989: 201–38, p. 204.

after this long bout, and a temporary return to normality, did the
King's madness become an established and recurring fact. As a young
King, we find no disparaging comment on his intellectual qualities
but only praises of his comeliness, piety, dignity, mildness, though
these of course might have been conventional expressions on the
part of courtiers, visiting potentates and ambassadors, or chroniclers.
It should be noted, therefore, that during his years as Lord Protector
first and First Councillor afterwards, Humphrey would have to contend eventually with the King's youth or with his stubbornness, but
not with any serious mental impairment.

Gloucester's cultural activity thus needs another, more complex
explanation than either the desire to compensate for the lack of political success, or the project to influence the new King and possibly
to re-shape Lancastrian ideology by means of a didactic program.
As I shall show in the following section, his activity as a patron, at
least in its early stages, went together with his political engagements,
and acted for a time as complementary to it.

The 1430s and the beginning of Humphrey's activity as a patron

Though, as we have seen, the Flemish expedition first and then the
political coming of age of the King had effectively checked the Duke
of Gloucester's ascent to power, he did not remain long absent from
the English political scene. Throughout the 1430s he was still one
of the foremost men of the realm, as is shown by a number of
episodes: in 1432, for instance, he renewed his attacks against the
Bishop of Winchester, who had been surprised while attempting to
take away his treasure from England and ship it secretly to Calais,
possibly with the intention of taking it to Rome, or to seek asylum
in the friendly Burgundian court, since his fortunes in England were
then uncertain. Henry Beaufort had no license to export gold, and
Gloucester heard of the attempt and had the ship seized before it
sailed.[82] The episode might have found its conclusion in Beaufort's
definitive ruin, but once again Gloucester's exaggerated reaction, and
his decision to dismiss from office all the Cardinal's supporters,
brought about in the end the possibility for the Bishop to escape

---

[82] For a detailed account of the episode see Harriss, pp. 214–28.

political disgrace, at some cost for his personal fortunes. Once again, "it was a classic instance of the folly of overkill; plainly Gloucester lacked the arts of Machiavelli".[83] The episode, however, is useful to show the real power Gloucester still had—it helped him to re-establish, at least temporarily, his authority over Council.

Another instance that showed him as one of the most relevant English politicians of the realm, in those same years, was the role he played in the matter of the English intervention at the Council of Basel. The Council was meeting in spite of Pope Eugenius IV's bulls of dissolution, and was negotiating with the excommunicated Hussites. Its declared aims were the reform of the Church and the pacification of Christendom, and since it had thus set itself in opposition with the expressed wishes of the Pope, it needed all the political and ecclesiastical support it could get. Thus in 1432 Geraldo Landriani, Bishop of Lodi, visited England as an ambassador of the Council, in order to address the King and Parliament, and to urge the importance of the presence in Basel of an English delegation. The already present delegation was withdrawing, and Landriani needed an ally at the English court to stop this move. He sought, and found, such an ally in the Duke of Gloucester, who helped the Bishop by pleading directly with the King, and persuading him not to send another delegation to Bologna, where another, papal Council was taking place. Landriani and Gloucester thus struck an alliance that was profitable to both, and not only in political terms. Apparently, this interest in the furtherance of activity at the Council of Basel does not accord with Humphrey's religious opinions, which tended to be strictly orthodox: in the same years, as is remembered by some contemporary texts (including John Lydgate's *Fall of Princes*, mentioned above in this chapter), the Duke was energetically contributing to the repression of Lollardy, a movement whose links with the Hussites were, even at the time, extremely clear: A.N.E.D. Schofield, studying Gloucester's role and the presence of the English delegation at the Council of Basel, notes how "the Duke of Gloucester had been a vigorous enemy of Lollardy during the protectorate from 1430 until 1432; the ruthless suppression of Jack Sharpe's rising in 1431 was a spectacular demonstration of his determination to

---

[83] Harriss, p. 218.

maintain order and orthodoxy".[84] It was therefore not a benign interest in the heretical movements that were spreading in Europe at the
time that drove Gloucester to support the Council's petition to the
English King; nor was it, as it has been argued, the interest Gloucester
and Landriani shared in the new classical studies,[85] even if the two
kept up a correspondence that revolved as much on intellectual as
on political issues. Rather, the Duke seems to have shown an awareness of the importance of conciliar trends at the time, and to have
looked with interest at the evolution of the Church at an international level. A further proof of this interest is given by the fact that
later the Duke bought from the testamentary executors of Thomas
Polton, Bishop of Worcester (who had been at the Papal court in
the 1410s, then at the Council of Constance, and had died in Basel
in 1433), a collection of the decrees, or, as they were recorded at
the time, of the *Ordinationes, statuta, constitutiones, decreta et alia acta et
gesta* of the Council of Constance which he kept in his library; the
book was not part of Humphrey's known donations to the University
of Oxford, but is one of the extant manuscripts with a very clear
indication of Humphrey's ownership: "Cest livre est a moy Homfrey
duc de Gloucestre le quel j'achetay des esecuteurs maistre Thomas
Polton feu eveque de Wurcestre" is written on f. 192v.[86]

I have quoted these episodes to show how in the early 1430s the
Duke was still very much one of the potentates of the realm, active
in many fields of English and international politics. It has been argued
that Duke Humphrey's cultural patronage became active only once
his interest in politics began to dwindle,[87] but the most relevant signs
of his interest both in patronage and in the diffusion of Italian humanism in England appear in the same years in which he successfully

---

[84] A.N.E.D. Schofield, "The First English Delegation to the Council of Basel",
The Journal of Ecclesiastical History 12: 1961, 167–96, p. 176.
[85] Schofield also refutes this hypothesis (see p. 175).
[86] Sammut, p. 108.
[87] W.L. Newman, for instance, examines the correspondence between Duke
Humphrey and Decembrio as concerns the translation of Plato's *Republic*, and writes:
"the duke of Gloucester's quest of classical books seems to have become keener as
his political influence declined [. . .] Collecting books had been a passion with the
duke from his youth upwards, and his correspondence with Decembrio shows that
his zeal as a collector was in no way diminished by these disasters and affronts.
Perhaps, indeed, they drove him back from politics to literature". See his "The
Correspondence of Humphrey, Duke of Gloucester, and Pier Candido Decembrio",
The English Historical Review 20: 1905, 484–98, p. 491.

worked for the Council, or scored such a notable if short-lived victory over the Bishop of Winchester. His book-collecting activity had already begun at least in the 1420s, as is shown by the earliest extant books that were in his possession.[88] In chronological terms, his support of Landriani's cause coincided with his invitation to Leonardo Bruni to come to England and become his secretary, and shortly preceded his commission to the same Bruni for the translation of Aristotle's *Politics*, a translation that occupied the humanist from 1434 to 1438.

So, rather than an escape from political duties that were becoming intolerable, we might read Humphrey's activity as a book-collector, his commissions of translations and other works, and his relations with Italian humanists, as a new phase in his political career. The furtherance of the Lancastrian cause, and above all his self-appointed role as the natural inheritor of Henry V's qualities, both as a leader of men and as a military strategist, were never far from Humphrey's thoughts, even in this new field of activity—it must also be noted that Bedford's death, which took place on 14 September 1435, made him heir apparent, as well as depriving Beaufort of a valuable ally, and could thus newly give vent to his ambition.

Duke Humphrey's next great political adventure, the Flanders campaign of 1436, can be analysed not only in its political implications, as the last great enterprise of the Duke, but also as an example of the use the Duke of Gloucester was making of the intellectual and cultural means at his disposal. Shortly after Bedford's death, the Duke of Burgundy had withdrawn his former alliance with the English crown and signed a new treaty at Arras with Charles VII, King of France; for once, Gloucester and Beaufort agreed with each other and with the rest of the Council in considering Burgundy an enemy of England. At the same time, Gloucester was receiving some of the responsibilities and duties that had formerly belonged to his brother Bedford.[89] On 1 November 1435 he had been appointed Lieutenant of Calais and of the adjacent territories—an area of the utmost strategic importance, since it was still a vital centre for the wool trade (though by the 1430s it was perhaps of less importance than the

---

[88] Everest-Phillips dates the beginning of this activity in 1425, "in the period after the fruitless expedition to Hainault" (p. 306).

[89] For a detailed account, see Vickers, pp. 247–54.

pro-war propaganda made it believe), and the safeguard of English trade on the continent. The defence of Calais thus was near to the interests not only of the crown, but of the English merchants and traders. Giving Gloucester this appointment meant recognising his importance and ability—at the same time, the Duke's wife Eleanor Cobham received public recognition as Duchess of Gloucester for the first time, while her father, Sir Reginald Cobham, was given custody of the most important French prisoner in England, Charles d'Orléans.

By June 1436 the Duke of Burgundy was advancing against Calais. Already in the April of the same year, the English had been forced to abandon Paris, and were struggling to retain Normandy. By the end of July Gloucester had received his commission as Lieutenant-General of the army that reached Calais at the beginning of August. In spite of the hurry, the English army raised for the occasion might be estimated at around ten thousand men,[90] against Burgundy's thirty thousand. But Burgundy's army consisted mainly of young and insubordinate Flemish soldiers, and the arrival of the English forces seems to have left them in a state of utter confusion—they broke up their camp and fled, leaving Burgundy no alternative but to flee in his turn. Gloucester pursued him into Flanders, pillaging and burning villages. His raid on Flanders carried no lasting political consequence, but provided his men with booty, while his humiliation of the Duke of Burgundy gave him great popularity with the war party in England. Towards the end of August he crossed the Channel once again, leaving Calais securely in English hands. His reception in London was magnificent, and even if the victory over Burgundy was of short duration, his command and the care he took of his troops were justly praised. Once again he had shown that, if not a great strategist, he was at least a very good tactician, and over a short period of time could also be an excellent leader of men.

What is interesting about this episode is not only its political outcome, or the fact that for once Gloucester had been able to overcome his great enemy Burgundy, and to give a concrete if temporary help to the English fortunes in France. We must also note that the whole enterprise was attentively managed from the point of view of propaganda, to the point that the rather undue importance which

---

[90] Vickers, p. 249.

contemporary chroniclers attribute to the Calais victory and the Flemish raid may be owing in part to some clever engineering on the part of the war party and of the Duke of Gloucester in particular.[91] James A. Doig acutely highlights the distance that separates the actual relevance of the episode from the weight it was given in contemporary accounts:

> One experienced campaigner who had long recognised the value of public support to his enterprises was Humphrey, duke of Gloucester [. . .] his role in the propaganda campaign against Burgundy and the Flemings may have been crucial [. . .] The duke of Gloucester had marshalled the physical and mental resources of the kingdom for a confrontation with Burgundy which, as one commentator astutely observed, he perhaps hoped would make him a worthy successor to Henry V as vanquisher of France. In the end, however, Gloucester's role was negligible. By the time he arrived at Calais at the head of the relief force on 2 August, the siege was abandoned; the heroics of the Count of Montain, the nephew of Gloucester's old adversary, Henry Beaufort, were perhaps decisive in Burgundy's humiliation. Denied the chance of personal glory, Gloucester launched a savage *chevauchée* into Flanders which accomplished little. Yet, on his return to London late in August, he quickly attempted to immortalise his role as the triumphant rescuer of Calais.[92]

The extent of his victory can be quickly assessed. Calais was securely back into English hands, but that, as Doig's article shows, had actually been accomplished even before Humphrey's arrival, and was due more to the cowardice of the Flemish recruits than to the bravery of the English soldiers. During his (relatively unjustified) raid on Flanders he had had a number of towns burnt and pillaged, thus giving vent to his men's frustrated energy, but had not met Burgundy's by now dispersed army, and after some time he decided to interrupt his progress and go back to England. Yet, to judge from contemporary political poems and songs, and later chroniclers, the enterprise acquired an almost undue importance. The events of 1436 caused a spate of ballads and libels, whose general trend was an unstinting praise of Gloucester's military qualities, coupled with derisive comments

---

[91] On this point see also Derek Pearsall, "The Idea of Englishness in the Fifteenth Century", in *Nation, Court and Culture. New Essays on Fifteenth-Century English Poetry*, ed. by H. Cooney, Dublin: Four Courts Press, 2001: 15–27, p. 21.

[92] James A. Doig, "Propaganda, Public Opinion and the Siege of Calais in 1436", in *Crown, Government and People in the Fifteenth Century*, ed. by R.E. Archer, Stroud: Sutton, 1995: 79–106, pp. 91–7.

upon Burgundy's role and behaviour, while the role of the Count of Montain was generally forgotten: this is what we find in one of the earliest chronicles,[93] while in the *Brut* the whole operation is described as the result of careful strategy on the part of Duke Humphrey in his quality of Lieutenant, and of the men he had chosen.[94] Equally revealing are the contemporary poetic texts. In a fifteenth-century ballad we find the conviction that the Duke of Burgundy was a secret ally of James, King of Scots, both conspiring against England:

> Quamvis falsidicus hic dux noster amicus,
> Nobis multa dedit ut ab obsidione recedat,
> Angligenis vinceps [sic] tum Scotus rex habeatur,
> Est falsus princeps, quia principi falsificatur. [. . .]
> Dux Burgundicus et rex Scoticus insidiantur,
> Sed rex Anglicus et grex publicus his dominantur.
> Anglia regna premit, Burgundia dedecus emit,
> Francia fracta tremit, Scotia victa gemit.
> Undique concursus stat et Anglia fortis ut ursus;
> Anglia dum rugit, circula terra fugit.[95]

In other poems, particularly in the ones written in English that may have been supposed to have had a popular origin or at any rate a more universal diffusion, the vituperative tone against Burgundy is more generic, but there is a particular insistence on his own and his men's lack of courage:

> O thou Phelippe, fonder of new falshede,
> Distourber of pees, capiteine of cowardise,
> Sower of discorde, Repref of all knyghthode,
> Whiche of all burgoigne (that is so grete of pryse)
> Thou clepist thiself duc—whan wiltow rise,

---

[93] *An English Chronicle of the Reigns of Richard II., Henry IV, Henry V., and Henry VI.*, ed. by J.S. Daniel, Camden Society, London: Nichols, 1856, pp. 55–6. Written before 1471, it is attributed to Richard Fox. It may be noted, incidentally, that even on Vickers's part there is a slight exaggeration of Gloucester's role, to the detriment of the Count of Montain (p. 254).

[94] *The Brut or the Chronicles of England*, II, pp. 571–84. In this passage the Duke of Burgundy is shown as peculiarly evil and crafty, engineering his own father's death (p. 572) and ordering his soldiers to sink twenty ships laden with stones in the haven of Calais, so as to stop any naval passage to the town (pp. 579–80).

[95] "Even if this duke, falsely calling himself our friend, gave us many occasions to retire from the siege, and even if the King of Scotland is believed such by the English, he is a false prince, since he is made false by another prince [. . .] The Duke of Burgundy and the King of Scotland lay traps for us, but the English King and people will prevail. England holds the sceptre, Burgundy covers itself with shame,

And in pleyn felde doo mustre with thy launce?
Se how all knyghthode thy werre dothe despise,
Wite thyn ovne falsnes al thy myschance![96]

In the same poem, the Duke of Gloucester is celebrated, explicitly contrasted to the cowardly Duke of Burgundy, and the Flanders raid made to appear as the logical conclusion of his campaign:

Beholde duc humfray with knyghtly desire
To meve thy courage the felde forto take;
He soght the in flandres with swerd and with fyre,
Nyne daies brennyng, no pees did he make.[97]

The same tone can be found at the conclusion of another poem, "The Siege of Calais", in which the town, saved by a sort of avenging angel in the person of the Duke of Gloucester, becomes a symbol of the royalty of England, the support of the crown itself. Burgundy is shown, towards the end of the poem, fleeing with his men:

For thay had verray knowyng
Of the Duc of Gloucester commyng,
Calais to Rescewe;
And because they bode not there,
In flandres he sought them fer and nere,
That they may euer Rewe.

O, oonly god, in whom is all,
Save Calais, the tovn Riall,
That euer it mot wel cheve
Vnto the Crovn of England,
As longe as the world shal stonde,
That noon enemys it greve. Amen.[98]

The fact that both English poems are to be found in the same manuscript (Rome, English College, 1306),[99] which is a Lydgate anthology,

---

France in ruins trembles, and Scotland defeated weeps. From everywhere they come, but England is as strong as a bear; when England roars, the whole world runs away". See "Philippe of Burgundy and James of Scotland", in *Political Poems and Songs Relating to English History, Composed during the Period from the Accession of Edw. III. to the Reign of Ric. III.*, pp. 150–1.

[96] "A songe made of the duc of Bourgone", ll. 1–8. The poem is edited in Rossell Hope Robbins, "A Middle English Diatribe against Philip of Burgundy," *Neophilologus* 39: 1955, 131–46, pp. 138–40.

[97] "A songe made of the duc of Bourgone," ll. 97–100.

[98] "The Siege of Calais", ll. 157–68. The poem is printed in Ralph A. Klinefelter, "'The Siege of Calais': A New Text," *Publications of the Modern Language Association* 67: 1952, 888–95.

[99] A list of the contents of the manuscript can be found in Ralph A. Klinefelter,

shows how the two texts might have been born in the same milieu. In these cases, however, there is nothing (apart from their link with Lydgate, who found in Gloucester one of his most powerful patrons) to show conclusively that the pro-Gloucester party could have been behind their composition or diffusion. Lydgate himself is attributed at least one work on the subject, *A Ballade, in Despyte of the Flemynges*;[100] it is well known that Lydgate would compose occasional poems at the slightest provocation, so the presence of this work in the Lydgate canon proves the momentousness of the occasion rather than any allegiance that he may have felt for the Duke of Gloucester. The poem is an invective against the Flemings and against the Duke of Burgundy, without any reference being made to Gloucester. Besides, there is a clear reference to the Calais episode, again without any mention of Gloucester, in Lydgate's *Debate of the Horse, Goose and Sheep*, when the horse tells the sheep:

> Thi wolle was cause & gret occasion
> Whi that the proude Duke of Burgouyn
> Cam befor Caleis with Flemynges nat a fewe,
>   Which yaff the sakkis & sarpleres of the toun
> To Gaunt & Brugis his fredam for to shewe,
>   And of thi wolle hiht hem pocessioun;
>   But his boistous baistill first was bete doun;
> He vnethe escapid with the liff:
> What but thi wolle was cause of al this striff?[101]

Here, what is evident is Lydgate's disillusion with war and its causes.

But we know of at least one poem that was sponsored and directly inspired by the Duke of Gloucester, and that was Tito Livio Frulovisi's *Hunfroidos*, probably composed around 1437.[102] Written in extremely dubious Latin hexameters, the poem centres explicitly upon the siege

---

"A Newly-discovered Fifteenth-century English Manuscript", *Modern Language Quarterly* 14: 1953, 3–7.

[100] *The Minor Poems of John Lydgate. Part II: Secular Poems*, ed. by H.N. MacCracken, Early English Text Society, London: Oxford University Press, 1934: 600–01.

[101] Lines 412–20, in *The Minor Poems of John Lydgate. Part II: Secular Poems*, ed. by H.N. MacCracken, Early English Text Society, London: Oxford University Press, 1934: 539–66.

[102] This is Roberto Weiss's hypothesis; the scholar believes the poem to have been composed at the same time in which Frulovisi was engaged in the composition of the *Vita Henrici Quinti* (see his "Humphrey Duke of Gloucester and Tito Livio Frulovisi", in *Fritz Saxl 1890–1948. A Volume of Memorial Essays from his Friends in England*, ed. by D.J. Gordon, London: Nelson, 1957: 218–27, p. 223). David Rundle slightly antedates the poem (David Rundle, "Of Republics and Tyrants: Aspects of Quattrocento Humanist Writing and Their Reception in England,

of Calais and the Flanders campaign that followed, covering the period from the alliance established at Arras between France and Burgundy in 1435 to the Duke's triumphant homecoming in August 1436, and celebrating Gloucester as the victorious and worthy successor of his brother Henry. The structure of this text, even from a purely stylistic point of view, and its ideological purpose are different from the other work Humphrey commissioned to Frulovisi, the *Vita Henrici Quinti*. There the intent was the celebration of a dead king who had acquired the status of an *exemplum*, a model proposed to that same King's son: as C.W.T. Blackwell writes, "the *Vita* was written not just as a piece of political propaganda for Humphrey, Duke of Gloucester's French policy but to transform Henry V into a model of the virtuous active life".[103] The *Humfroidos*, roughly contemporary to the *Vita*, has quite a different purpose, since it celebrates a living nobleman and his successful deeds at exactly the moment in which this celebration might have contributed to turn his fortunes, and make him once more, and this time permanently, the key-figure of the realm "transforming Humfrey's uneventful Calais expedition of 1436 into something close to an epic encounter".[104] A complete different case is *The Lybelle of Englyshe Polycye*, written between 1436 and 1437, in the wake of the Calais enterprise.[105] This text is far from representing a straightforward propaganda piece, and yet it sheds some very interesting light upon Gloucester's policy and, we may argue, his use of writing for ideological purposes. The *Lybelle* purports to be a verse treatise on the use of sea-power, and as such it gives us enormously interesting information on the English trading links with other countries in Europe: the Low Countries and Spain first, but also Portugal, Italy, France. As well as establishing facts, however, it also envisages an active policy on the part of England that might make use of the country's advantageous position

c. 1400–c. 1460", D.Phil., Oxford, 1997, p. 122), but both agree in its being a celebration written shortly after the Calais campaign.

[103] C.W.T. Blackwell, "Humanism and Politics in English Royal Biography: The Use of Cicero, Plutarch and Sallust in the *Vita Henrici Quinti* (1438) by Titus Livius de Frulovisi and the *Vita Henrici Septimi* (1500–1503) by Bernard André", in *Acta Conventus Neo-Latini Sanctandreani: Proceedings of the Fifth International Congress of Neo-Latin Studies*, ed. by I.D. McFarlane, Binghamton: Medieval & Renaissance Texts & Studies, 1986: 431–40, p. 432.

[104] David Rundle, "Humanism before the Tudors: On Nobility and the Reception of *studia humanitatis* in Fifteenth-Century England", p. 26.

[105] *The Libelle of Englyshe Polycye. A Poem on the Use of Sea-Power*, 1436, ed. by G. Warner, Oxford: Clarendon Press, 1926.

with respect to sea-trade, in order to establish its superiority as a naval and commercial power. The author's updated and detailed information shows that he was in contact not only with the centres of commerce, but also with the centres of power, and it has been argued that the poem was both factually and ideologically informed by the Duke of Gloucester.[106] I reserve a fuller discussion of this point to chapter 5, in which I shall analyse the relation between Humphrey's patronage and a number of literary texts connected to the Calais campaign, including the *Libelle* and the *Hunfroidos*; however, it was useful to insert a mention of both at this point to show how propaganda, especially in a pivotal episode such as the Calais expedition (touching, as we have seen, not only political but commercial interests), could take more complex forms than a mere invective against Philip of Burgundy, or a praise of Gloucester's military tactics.[107]

The 1440s: Duke Humphrey's downfall and death

Once again, however, Humphrey seemed to have misjudged the long-term effect of his enterprise. The immediate echo of his Calais expedition was great, and well supported by propaganda, but did not ultimately help the Duke overcome a situation of instability that became the prelude to his downfall. Calais was his last military undertaking, and from this point on his importance in the realm diminished steadily. This change is due as much to Humphrey's own character—incapable, as usual, to profit over a long period of time from a fortunate moment, he preferred to turn his interest and energies in quite another direction—as to the steady decline of health he was suffering, and to the turning tide in English politics. There

---

[106] The argument is presented by George A. Holmes in his "The 'Libel of English Policy'", *English Historical Review* 76: 1961, 193–216.

[107] It must be noted, however, that in the case of the *Hunfroidos* "no evidence suggests that the work was in fact propagated among the English political community: the only extant copy was written in Italy" (David Rundle, "Humanism before the Tudors: On Nobility and the Reception of *studia humanitatis* in Fifteenth-Century England", p. 26). Weiss's unsupported hypothesis is that the copy of Frulovisi's *De Republica* that Duke Humphrey gave to Oxford included the poem (Roberto Weiss, "Humphrey Duke of Gloucester and Tito Livio Frulovisi", p. 222). The unique manuscript of the poem is now in Seville (Biblioteca Colombina, 7/2/23).

was, initially, no definite episode marking a sudden fall from favour, but only Gloucester's progressive retirement from public affairs. The last years of the 1430s thus mark the beginning of Humphrey's political decline in the sense that the governing centres of the kingdom saw less and less of him. At the same time as his cultural interests began to dominate over his political ones, he also turned his attention to personal comforts, and in particular to the establishment of a small court of his own: already between 1432 and 1437 he had expanded his possessions around his Greenwich mansion of Plesaunce, acquiring seventeen acres of land formerly belonging to the Carthusian monastery of Jesus of Bethlehem at Shene.[108]

I have maintained above that the beginning of the Duke of Gloucester's activity as a book collector and a patron does not coincide with his political failure, not can it be said to be motivated by it; it may rather be argued that his cultural interests, originally pursued as part of his ideological project, gradually took the place of what must have appeared to the Duke a disappointing series of contentions and compromises. In the late thirties and early forties we see Gloucester more and more actively engaged with the pursuit of intellectual patronage, keeping up a correspondence with a number of Italian humanists, encouraging writers to work in his Greenwich Palace, and actively helping the University of Oxford. In the meantime, the English King was attempting a very difficult recomposition of the peace with both France and Burgundy, with Henry Beaufort at the head of the peace party—a commercial truce with Burgundy was signed in September 1439.

Though Gloucester was still identified with those who were in favour of a continuation of the war, we have very little evidence of his direct intervention, except in episodes such as the release of the noble French prisoner, Charles d'Orléans, a release which he tried to prevent with all his might. Orléans had been a prisoner in England since the battle of Agincourt, and had been lately in the care and custody of Gloucester's father-in-law. His release would have had a high symbolic significance—as it turned out later, it was only symbolic, since once back in France the Duke of Orléans took little or no interest in politics and lived a retired life, dedicating himself solely to poetic and intellectual pursuits.

---

[108] Everest-Phillips, p. 86.

Literary scholars have often expressed some disappointment at
Gloucester's animosity against Orléans in this particular instance.[109]
The two, after all, might be supposed to have shared intellectual
interests, and it is tempting to imagine a friendship between a great
writer and a great collector—and perhaps reader—of books. But
Gloucester's opposition to the release of Orléans may more profitably
be read in the light of the political ideology Gloucester had whole-
heartedly supported throughout his life. By remaining a prisoner in
England, the French Duke remained a symbol of the greatest victory obtained by Henry V, a witness of the most glorious moment
England had experienced in this almost secular war against France.
Consciously or unconsciously, Gloucester felt that once Orléans left
England—without even a suitable exchange of prisoners, or some
other form of adequate compensation—England had lost yet another
link with a recent victorious past whose memory he had striven to
keep alive in the young King. This is evident if we read the declaration Humphrey wrote to the King on this occasion, a most interesting document for us since it is also, as far as we know, one of
the very few instances left to us in which we can hear the Duke's
own voice—unlike what happens in his correspondence with Italian
humanists, here the text is in English.[110] In the document there is a
vehement denunciation of the Bishop of Winchester, whose machinations are held to be responsible for the proposed release of Orléans
(Henry Beaufort is also accused of analogous machinations in the
case of the release of James I of Scotland) and for estranging the
King from his uncle; but also constant reference is made to "my
lord of blessed memorie, youre fader"—and it is his will on the matter rather than Humphrey's that is constantly underlined, as a sort
of sacred charge.[111] Gloucester's storming out of the church in which

---

[109] Tino Foffano, for instance, sees much promise in the contact between two
intellectuals such as Orléans and Gloucester, but has to admit in the end that none
of Orléans's poems reveals the influence of Humphrey's intellectual circle ("Charles
d'Orléans e un gruppo di umanisti lombardi in Normandia", *Aevum* 41: 1967,
452–73, p. 452).

[110] Another document in English, also concerning Charles d'Orléans, is the
"Protestatio contra Elargationem Ducis Aurialensis" (Thomas Rymer, *Foedera, conventiones, literae, et cujuscumque generis acta publica, inter reges Angliae, et alios quosvis imperatores, reges, pontifices, principes, vel comunitates, ab ineunte, saeculo duodecimo, viz. ab Anno
1101, ad nostra usque tempora, habita aut tractata*, Hagae comitis: Apud Joannem Neaulme,
1741 (3rd edn), pp. 76–7).

[111] "Protest of Humphrey, duke of Gloucester, against the liberation of the duke

Orléans was swearing never to bear arms against the English King, on 3 November 1440, is not only an instance of his flair for flamboyant gestures, and an open disapproval of the decision of the King and Council; it was also a sort of farewell to a political life in which the Duke could no longer recognise himself. The gesture must have been very impressive, and to have struck the general public, since we find it mentioned even in the Paston Letters. Thus Robert Repps writes to John Paston I:

> The Duk of Orlyawnce hath made his ooth vpon the sacrement, and vsyd it, neuer for to bere armes ayenst Englond, in the presence of the Kyng and all the lordes except my lord of Gloucester; and in pre-vyng my seyde lord of Gloucester agreyd neuer to hys delyueraunce, qwan the masse began he toke hys barge, &c. God yef grace the seide lord of Orlyaunce be trewe, for this same weke shall he toward Fraunce.[112]

From a purely political point of view, Bertram Wolffe sees a clear connection between this extremely outspoken gesture against d'Orléans and the triggering of the royal displeasure that led to Gloucester's ultimate downfall. Put in these terms, the episode might seem trivial, little more than a flamboyant gesture on the part of the Duke. Yet Wolffe sees in King Henry VI a number of unpleasant traits, "weakness and inaction [. . .] vindictiveness and a degree of credulity which jars with the popular, pious and enlightened image of the founder of Eton and King's".[113] On the other hand, the historian highlights also the fact that, by setting his opposition "on record by exemplification under the great seal",[114] Gloucester was openly attacking the Cardinals Beaufort and Kemp, whom he held responsible for the decision, and implicitly considering of little account the King's own will in the matter.

There is little to be added to our sketch of the political career of the Duke of Gloucester. The most serious and spectacular blow to his reputation was given by the Eleanor Cobham scandal and the

---

of Orleans", in *Letters and Papers Illustrative of the Wars of the English in France during the Reign of Henry the Sixth, King of England*, ed. by J. Stevenson, Rolls Series, London: Longman et al., 1864: 440–51. The phrase mentioned above occurs repeatedly throughout the text.

[112] *Paston Letters and Papers of the Fifteenth Century*, ed. by N. Davis, Oxford: Clarendon Press, 1976, II, p. 22.

[113] Bertram Wolffe, *Henry VI*, London: Eyre Methuen, 1981, pp. 125–6.

[114] Wolffe, p. 126.

following trial, in 1441. On 28 June 1441 Eleanor, then Duchess of Gloucester, was accused of conspiring with two clerks, Roger Boling-broke and Thomas Southwell, and a woman, the so-called Witch of Eye, Margery Jourdemayne, to secure the death of Henry VI. According to the accusation that was moved against her, she attempted this by recurring to the black arts. Roger Bolingbroke, an astronomer, perhaps a necromancer, and an Oxford priest and scholar (who had been at one time Principal of St Andrew's Hall), had some con-nection with the house of Gloucester,[115] while Southwell had grad-uated in medicine from Oxford in 1423 and was one of the physician-examiners in the Faculty of Medicine, whose rector was Gilbert Kymer, Gloucester's personal physician and a collaborator in the latter's activity of book-collection and patronage.[116] The Duke himself had been associated with astrological practices in the past: in 1419 one Friar Ralph or Randolf (the Parliament Rolls call him Friar John Randolf) had been implicated in the charges against the Dowager Queen, Joan of Navarre, who had been accused of using sorcery to destroy the king; the same friar was also serving Duke Humphrey, and later, in 1425, he would be again implicated in a dispute between the Bishop of Winchester and the Duke. The same Franciscan friar is attributed, in a manuscript (London, British Library, Sloane 407, ff. 223–6), "the authorship of a set of tables with aspects of the planets, written at the request and with the full support of Humphrey".[117]

The scandal was enormous—in attempting to cause in some way the death of the King, Eleanor was giving the crown to her hus-

---

[115] Wolffe goes so far as to say that Bolingbroke was a "member of Humphrey's household" (p. 127). On Roger Bolingbroke's and Thomas Southwell's activities as astrologers, see J.D. North, *Horoscopes and History*, London: The Warburg Institute, 1986, pp. 143–9.

[116] For a full account of the Cobham affair, see Ralph A. Griffiths, "The Trial of Eleanor Cobham: An Episode in the Fall of Duke Humphrey of Gloucester", *Bulletin of the John Rylands Library Manchester*, 51: 1968–9, 381–99, as well as his *King and Country. England and Wales in the Fifteenth Century*, London: The Hambledon Press, 1991, pp. 233–52. Another account of the affair and of the role of Eleanor Cobham's accomplices is to be found in Hilary M. Carey, *Courting Disaster. Astrology at the English Court and University in the Later Middle Ages*, London: Macmillan, 1992, pp. 138–53. See also Maura B. Nolan, "Necromancy, Treason, Semiosis, Spectacle. The Trial of Eleanor Cobham, Duchess of Gloucester", *Proteus* 13: 1996, 7–11.

[117] Hilary M. Carey, "Astrology at the English Court in the Late Middle Ages", in *Astrology, Science and Society: Historical Essays*, ed. by P. Curry, Woodbridge: The Boydell Press, 1987: 41–56, pp. 51–1.

band, still heir presumptive. A trial that would have been insignificant if it had been confined to the two clerks and the supposed witch thus assumed unexpected proportions. The Duchess of Gloucester reacted promptly, fleeing to sanctuary in Westminster—a move which probably saved her life, since she would then be judged by an ecclesiastic rather than by a secular court. On July 22 she appeared before an ecclesiastical court, and, thanks also to the evidence that Bolingbroke gave against her, she was remanded in custody till October 21. She claimed that she had been practising magic, with the help of Margery Jourdemayne, only to acquire a potion that would ensure her husband's love, and to attempt divination and see whether she would be able to give Gloucester a male heir (which in itself might be read as suspicious, since a son might have given the heir presumptive the male descendant whom the King was still lacking). In the end, she was condemned to a public, humiliating penance, performed in London (13–17 November 1441): she had to walk on pilgrimage to different churches, bareheaded and in an attitude of humiliation. Then she was "committed into the care of Sir Thomas Stanley on a yearly pension of 100 marks for the rest of her life".[118] At the same time, on 6 November, Archbishop Chichele and Cardinal Beaufort pronounced her divorce from the Duke— henceforward we find her described in official documents as "Eleanor, lately called Duchess of Gloucester".[119] Southwell died in prison, Bolingbroke was hanged, drawn and quartered, Jourdemayne was burnt as a relapsed heretic. Eleanor Cobham remained a prisoner until her death in 1452.

It is difficult to understand how much truth the Cobham trial unearthed, how much was the result of superstitious hysteria, and how much was a simple political machination against Humphrey. Modern scholars note that "a series of politically motivated sorcery trials in fourteenth-century France and the papacy and fifteenth-century England reveal the interplay of politics and superstition",[120] nor were charges of treachery and witchcraft against royal ladies a complete novelty in England;[121] G.L. Harriss, among others, explicitly

---

[118] Carey, *Courting Disaster*, p. 139.

[119] Vickers, p. 274.

[120] William R. Jones, "Political Uses of Sorcery in Medieval Europe", *The Historian* 34: 1972, 670–87, p. 670.

[121] As hinted at above, Joan of Navarre, wife to Henry IV, had been similarly accused twenty years before, even if she did not have to submit to a trial.

links the trial with an attack against the Duke, though admitting that
we have no evidence in this sense:

> the records give no hint of what precipitated this or who instigated it
> [. . .] Although there is no contemporary suggestion that the prosecu-
> tion had a political motive, there can be little doubt that the duke was
> the real target [. . .] Eleanor's conviction rendered Humphrey's acces-
> sion to the throne impossible; for whatever the truth of the allegations,
> their inherent credibility and the strong revulsion they aroused made
> the duke a political outcast and permanently suspect.[122]

If this was a political machination, Eleanor was an easy target—
never particularly loved either by her peers or by those middle classes
that had occasionally been enthusiastic supporters of Humphrey, she
had been marked from the beginning as an ambitious upstart, and
an accusation of sorcery and treason moved against her would surely
have disgraced her, and by implication her husband, even if it had
been less founded. What is interesting in this case is not so much
the accusation, which as we have seen had numerous precedents,
but the prompt reaction on the part of both accusers and accused,
and the great publicity this trial had. Equally interesting is Humphrey's
reaction: though the scandal dealt a fatal blow to his position and
reputation, he appeared very little in the affair, and there are recorded
no explicit interventions on his part to save his wife.[123] Wolffe sees
this as a demonstration of "Gloucester's inability to protect his wife
[and] the ruin of his influence over his nephew".[124] But we might
also read Gloucester's passiveness as an attempt to diminish the
importance the affair assumed; if this is so, this policy did not work,
since the detailed accounts we find in contemporary chroniclers tell
us that the echo was enormous, and perhaps disproportionate. In
some way, it even gave Eleanor Cobham some of the popularity she
had never acquired previously, given the great number of ballads
and lamentations were written on her. An anonymous "Lament of
the Duchess" composed in 1441, for instance, seems to accuse her
more of folly than of wickedness, and is careful to disassociate the
Duke from the deeds of his wife:

---

[122] Harriss, p. 322.
[123] Saygin, however, links the episode to one of the donations of books Humphrey
made to the University of Oxford; this point shall be discussed in the next chapter.
[124] Wolffe, p. 127.

All women that ar ware of wark,
My mischeue may ye haf in mynd;
To gef credence to any clerk [. . .]
My best friend now is my foo,
My owne deere lord I dar not see;
Alas, that we shuld twynne in too—
All women may be ware by me.[125]

The chronicler Richard Grafton is more explicit, linking the trial to a revenge against Gloucester (though this position, in its turn, may be motivated by propaganda against the Lancastrian king and even more against Queen Margaret, who was thereafter dubbed as one of Gloucester's arch-enemies):

> Venime will once breake out, and inwarde grudge will sone appere, which was this yere to all men apparaunt: for diuers secret attempts were aduaunced forward this season, agaynst the noble Duke Humfrey of Gloucester, a farre of, which in conclusion came so nere, that they bereft him both of lyfe and lande.[126]

Curiously enough for the wife of a staunch defender of religious orthodoxy, praised in his own time for the repression of Lollardy, Eleanor also appears as a martyr in John Foxe's *Acts and Monuments*, in which she is portrayed as a true Wycliffite hated by the clergy.[127] This instance is a further proof that, in the case of such complex and contradictory personalities as those of the Duke of Gloucester and his wife, historiography could be driven by ideological purposes— something that Duke Humphrey himself seems to have understood very well. As Nolan writes, the Cobham scandal "became a potent metaphor for the authority of the church and the King, the ravages of fortune, the dangers of pride, the wickedness of women, and the slipperiness of Oxford clerks".[128]

The death of the Duke of Gloucester, which took place a few years later than the Cobham trial, was equally open to wide speculation on the part of chroniclers and historians. In spite of the fact

---

[125] "The Lament of the Duchess", ll. 49–51, 69–72. The poem is printed in *Historical Poems of the XIVth and XVth Centuries*, ed. by R.H. Robbins, New York: Columbia University Press, 1959.

[126] *Grafton's Chronicle; or History of England*, I, p. 622.

[127] *Acts and Monuments of John Foxe*, ed. by G. Townsend, New York: AMS Press, 1965, p. 707.

[128] Nolan, p. 7.

that both Humphrey and some of Eleanor's accusers tried to disassociate him from the scandal, the consequence for him was political ruin—after all, it would have been unthinkable for his enemies not to make the most of the affair. We have no public appearance of Duke Humphrey on the political stage after the trial against his wife, until the year of his death—the accusation at Eleanor can be said to be directly linked to the charge of treason that was levelled against Humphrey in 1447. The 1440s see the Duke of Gloucester live a mostly retired life, either in his palace of Plesaunce or in the monastery of St Albans, where he also had his tomb built. His decline paralleled Henry Beaufort's: they died in the same year, though the Bishop of Winchester's death was far from premature and mysterious. The man in the ascendant at this point was William de la Pole, Earl of Suffolk, who had accompanied Margaret of Anjou on her trip to England and to marriage with the English King in 1445. Suffolk was to play a prominent role in the last stages of Humphrey's fall, to the point of being (probably wrongly) remembered by later tradition as Humphrey's murderer.

It is difficult to understand whether the charge of treason that was the ultimate cause of Humphrey's death was simply the result of a conspiracy of his enemies, or was motivated by the fear that the presence of the man who was still the most prominent spokesman for the war party could jeopardise the delicate negotiations with France. By the end of 1445, however, Gloucester was denied access to the court, and removed from the Privy Council. In 1447, he was summoned to a Parliament at Bury St Edmunds—a Parliament that seems, in retrospect, to have been called with the sole purpose of laying accusations of treason against him; as a contemporary chronicler writes,

> and in the moneth of Feuerer next aftir, the x. day thereof, began the parlement at saint Edmundis Bury in Suffolk; the whiche Parlement was maad only for to sle the noble duke of Gloucestre.[129]

Caught unawares, Gloucester opposed no resistance to his arrest, and a few days later, on 23 February, he died. At the same time some of his retainers, as well as his natural son Arthur, were arrested

---

[129] *An English Chronicle of the Reigns of Richard II., Henry IV, Henry V., and Henry VI.*, ed. by J.S. Davies, Camden Society, London: Nichols, 1856, p. 62. Written before 1471, this chronicle is attributed by the editor to Richard Fox.

with the same charge and sent to confinement. The fact that, shortly after his death, Humphrey's body was exposed, seems to demonstrate that he still enjoyed a certain popularity, and that the Council was afraid of the consequences of this sudden death, and of the suspicions it might raise. Even modern historians entertain some doubts as to the manner of this death,[130] and some contemporary chroniclers use the mysterious circumstances surrounding the event to level all sorts of accusations at the Earl of Suffolk, Queen Margaret, or the King. We have, actually, no evidence pointing to murder, and no reason to disbelieve the report of a natural death. Humphrey of Gloucester was not a healthy man—there is more than one instance during his lifetime of his being too sick to attend the Council, and Gilbert Kymer's *Dietarium*, a medical and prescriptive treatise composed for the Duke, seems to confirm this hypothesis. Without doubt, his death came as a relief to many, since by now the Duke, even in this self-effacing role, was a hindrance rather than a support, in a phase of English policy that needed all the support it could get. But the discontent generated by what many saw as an abuse of power on the part of the Earl of Suffolk and an unfounded condemnation of a fundamentally innocent man proved very deleterious to the Lancastrian cause, and was soon used by the Yorkist propaganda to demonstrate the evil of the opposite faction. By the end of the 1440s some of the contemporary texts register a sense of desolation at the death of so many valiant councillors, statesmen and military men:

> The Rote is ded, the Swanne is goone,
> The firy Cresset hath lost his hyght;
> Therefore Inglond may make gret mone
> Were not the helpe of Godde almyght.[131]

---

[130] See, for instance, B. Wilkinson, *The Later Middle Ages in England 1216–1485*, London, 1969, p. 266. On the other hand, the *English Chronicle* quoted above maintains that the Duke "deide for sorow" (p. 63).

[131] "On the Popular Discontent at the Disasters in France", ll. 1–4, in *Political Poems and Songs Relating to English History*, pp. 221–3. The poem was probably composed in 1449. The *Rote* is a reference to Bedford's badge, the *Cressett* to Exeter. Then the poem continues bemoaning the death of Somerset, Beaufort, Norfolk and other peers. The *Swan* was part of the badge of the House of Bohun, to which Humphrey's mother belonged. The Duke of Gloucester had adopted this badge.

An analogous poem, written circa 1462–3, also mourns for the death of Gloucester, but this time uses this death to underline, with a more explicit accusation, Henry VI's "gret foly":

> The good duc of Gloucestre, in the season
> Of the parlement at Bury beyng,
> Was put to dethe; and ay sithe gret mornyng
> Hathe ben in Ingeland, with many a scharp soure,
> Falshode, myschyef, secret synne upholdyng,
> Which hathe caused in Engeland endelez langoure.[132]

The chroniclers who believe in foul play generally accuse Margaret of Anjou,[133] or, in more generic terms, a "fals traytour".[134]

It thus seems that Duke Humphrey of Gloucester was destined to be, at least on the chronicler's pages, greater in death than in life; there is no doubt that the mysterious manner of his death gave a decisive contribution to the myth of "the good Duke Humphrey" that formed part of the Yorkist, anti-Lancastrian propaganda—a myth we also find in Tudor chronicles, as well as in Shakespeare's history plays. Yet, even if he had lived longer, it is reasonable to suppose that Humphrey's political career was doomed, and had been so since the Cobham scandal. Humphrey's political project—his continuation of what he saw as Henry V's policy, and his struggle for a form of absolute power that could be independent of both Parliament and Council—was ill-attuned to the times, and to the very difficult situation that was created in England with Henry V's death. Once Henry VI effectively became King, it was almost inevitable for Humphrey, who had none of the qualities of the King's advisor, to suffer a diminution of importance. On the other hand, his activity as a patron, though to a great extent depending upon and influenced by his political project, could also continue after his political downfall. The following chapter shall show, among other things, how Humphrey attempted to make his patronage part of his policy.

---

[132] "A Political Retrospect", ll. 35–40, in *Political Poems and Songs Relating to English History*, pp. 267–70.
[133] *Grafton's Chronicle; or History of England*, p. 629; Holinshed, p. 211.
[134] "Historical Memoranda," in *Three Fifteenth-Century Chronicles*, ed. by James Gairdner, Camden Society, London: Nichols, 1880, p. 95.

CHAPTER FOUR

"THAIR LIBRAIR VNIUERSAL":
COLLECTING AND DONATING BOOKS

Building a library: the shape of ideology

The contrasting critical evaluations on the size and importance of
Humphrey of Gloucester's library are, at least in part, the result of
a very imperfect knowledge of the state of private libraries in fifteenth-
century England. It is true, though it may be read as an easy generalisation, that "compared with our knowledge of the great collections
of France and Burgundy, information about secular libraries in
England is extremely scanty";[1] it is also true, on the other hand,
that the confusion generated by the variable reports we have on the
extent and quality of these libraries is, if anything, increased by the
changes and developments in the English book-trade, particularly
significant between the fourteenth and the fifteenth century. A struc-
tural study and interpretation of the information provided by what
survives of late medieval English libraries is still missing,[2] but a number of scholars have offered interesting contributions throughout the

---

[1] Richard Firth Green, *Poets and Princepleasers: Literature and the English Court in the
Late Middle Ages*, Toronto: University of Toronto Press, 1980, p. 91. Green adds
that "the earliest surviving inventory of an English royal library, probably made by
a Flemish visitor, dates from 1534/5" (p. 92). It is somewhat surprising, though,
that in a study concerned with noble or royal English libraries in the late Middle
Ages, very little attention is paid to Duke Humphrey's.
[2] The indispensable tool to study late medieval manuscripts is still Neil Ripley
Ker's *Medieval Libraries of Great Britain*, London: Offices of the Royal Historical Society,
1941 (2nd ed. 1964), together with the four volumes of *Medieval Manuscripts in British
Libraries*, written in collaboration with Alan J. Piper, Oxford: Clarendon Press,
1969–82. R.A.B. Mynors wrote a fascinating account of the creation and develop-
ment of a college library between the thirteenth and the fifteenth centuries in the
Introduction to his *Catalogue of the Manuscripts of Balliol College Oxford*, Oxford: Clarendon
Press, 1963, pp. xi–liii. A great deal of information can also be found in *The History
of the University of Oxford, vol. 2: Late Medieval Oxford*, ed. by J.J. Catto and R. Evans,
Oxford: Clarendon Press, 1992, and in *The History of the University of Oxford, vol. 3:
The Collegiate University*, ed. by J. McConica, Oxford: Clarendon Press, 1987. The
most recent survey on the subject is probably *The Cambridge History of the Book in
Britain, vol. 3: 1400–1557*, ed. by L. Hellinga and J.B. Trapp, Cambridge: Cambridge

twentieth century. Various sources of information have been taken into account, from the too few catalogues, to wills (which, however, offer little information on the type of book that was being bequeathed, since they tend to list books generically or inaccurately),[3] to letters or journals, but there is no denying that often "one is thrown back on inference",[4] as regards both libraries and readers. It may be interesting to begin this necessarily brief account of the state of English fifteenth-century libraries with Pearl Kibre's study "The Intellectual Interests Reflected in Libraries of the Fourteenth and Fifteenth Centuries";[5] though over fifty years old now, it is a very useful account of the general intellectual trends that can be identified through a survey of the contents of late-medieval libraries, and I should like to take it as the starting point of my analysis, integrating it with more recent works that will be indicated in the footnotes. Kibre warns us, first of all, against contemporary reports concerning the size of libraries, since these tended to be exaggerated or radically altered; this could be due to technical reasons, such as the practice of binding several texts in a single volume but then listing the several items separately in a catalogue; in other cases, the compiler might have increased the size of the library in his report in order to pay homage to the noble owner. As concerns size, however, Kibre concludes that "a library of about 800 or 900 items might be said to constitute a very fair-sized collection",[6] which helps us to understand how important Duke Humphrey's book-donations to the University of Oxford were, quite independently from the size of the Duke's personal library. The scholar's estimate, which appears to be the result of an average of data drawn from surviving catalogues of European libraries, can be usefully compared with more accurate data we possess about Italian private libraries: a useful instance is constituted by Federico da Montefeltro, who became Duke of Urbino in 1474 and had a much-praised library including 1100 manuscripts

---

University Press, 1999. See also *Medieval Scribes, Manuscripts and Libraries. Essays Presented to N.R. Ker*, ed. by M.B. Parkes and A.G. Watson, London: Scolar Press, 1978.

[3] J.B. Trapp, "Literacy, Books and Readers", in *The Cambridge History of the Book in Britain, vol. 3: 1400–1557*, ed. by L. Hellinga and J.B. Trapp, Cambridge: Cambridge University Press, 1999: 31–43, p. 33.

[4] Trapp, "Literacy, Books and Readers", p. 33.

[5] Pearl Kibre, "The Intellectual Interests Reflected in Libraries of the Fourteenth and Fifteenth Centuries", *Journal of the History of Ideas* 7: 1946, 257–97.

[6] Kibre, p. 258.

(the incunabula which he also possessed are not taken into account here). Even more interesting for our purposes may be the case of Niccolò Niccoli, since his would be a humanist library put together with completely private means, and without the help of the gifts and presentations that might constitute such an important part of a prince's library. Unfortunately there can be no accurate evaluation of the size of Niccoli's library, as there is in the case of Federico, but the humanist Poggio Bracciolini, in the oration he delivered on the occasion of his friend Niccoli's funeral, claimed that the humanist had collected more than 800 volumes; even allowing for some friendly exaggeration, it is an impressive estimate.[7] Partly on the basis of these comparisons, and partly judging from the size of the donations, Roberto Weiss calculates that Duke Humphrey's library could include no less than 500 or 600 volumes;[8] but this hypothesis is to be considered merely an estimate, without any other factual ground.

As for the languages present in the manuscripts, they constitute a more complex question: Greek codices are extremely rare throughout the fifteenth century outside Italy,[9] while the most obvious languages as far as English libraries are concerned are Latin and French. For understandable reasons, a university library or a monastery library would include almost solely manuscripts in Latin; vernacular texts, whether in English or in French, tend to be confined to private libraries. There would be an occasional Italian text, though as a rule vernacular manuscripts appear almost solely in their respective countries.[10] On this point the situation in England seems to follow a unique pattern, since the reading and speaking knowledge of French was still common among the aristocracy during the protectorate and in the early years of Henry VI's reign, while English was becoming the official language of chancery and administration; this situation of *de facto* bilingualism is obviously reflected in the manuscripts. In

---

[7] See Berthold L. Ullman and Philip A. Stadter, *The Public Library of Renaissance Florence. Niccolò Niccoli, Cosimo de' Medici and the Library of San Marco*, Padova: Antenore, 1972, pp. 59–60.

[8] Roberto Weiss, "The Private Collector and the Revival of Greek Learning", in *The English Library before 1700*, ed. by F. Wormald and C.E. Wright, London: The Athlone Press, 1958: 112–35, p. 118.

[9] Kibre, p. 264.

[10] In a European perspective, Kibre states that "the vernaculars other than French and Italian were for the most part localized in the collections of their respective countries" (p. 273).

their survey of the history of the book in England from 1400 to 1557, Lotte Hellinga and J.B. Trapp note that "the evidence, unsurprisingly, suggests a growing reluctance [. . .] on the part of English men and, perhaps rather less in some categories of reader, English women to read and write works not in their own language. This is equalled, indeed surpassed, by the reluctance of readers of other nationalities to read works in English".[11] The chronological perspective in this case takes into account also the first decades of printing, which radically altered reading patterns in England, but it is undeniable that the tendency noted by Hellinga and Trapp is to be observed in its embryonic stages in Humphrey of Gloucester's time. The increased interest in works in English coincides with a decreasing interest in French manuscripts, to the point that it is possible to claim that "at the beginning of the fifteenth century, French was still commonly used, but by the middle of the century it had been superseded by English".[12] In this perspective, we shall note that Humphrey still maintains an interest in French manuscripts, especially as they constituted a more immediate read for their owner than Latin texts.

Even more interesting is the situation we find in English libraries as concerns topics and authors. Once again, we turn to Pearl Kibre, whose first observation on the subject is that "the persistent regard for many of the favourite writings of the earlier medieval period is reflected in the inclusion in many of the libraries of the works of the church fathers, with a particular leaning towards St Augustine".[13] Kibre's conclusion, after a survey of significant authors and titles to which we shall come back later, is:

> In content these libraries of the so-called renaissance of the fourteenth and fifteenth centuries may thus be seen to reveal no sharp line of cleavage between the interests of these centuries from those immediately preceding. The humanistic works (litterae humaniores), products of the enthusiasm for and renewed interest in the classics of Greek and Roman antiquity, supplemented but did not replace the hallowed classics of the more immediate past.[14]

---

[11] Lotte Hellinga, J.B. Trapp, "Introduction", in *The Cambridge History of the Book in Britain, vol. 3: 1400–1557*, Cambridge: Cambridge University Press, 1999, pp. 1–30, p. 15.

[12] David N. Bell, "Monastic Libraries: 1400–1557", in *The Cambridge History of the Book in Britain, vol. 3: 1400–1557*, ed. by L. Hellinga and J.B. Trapp, Cambridge: Cambridge University Press, 1999: 229–54, p. 232.

[13] Kibre, p. 279.

[14] Kibre, p. 297.

Kibre's words are confirmed by a number of subsequent studies on the subject, and warn us against a too clear-cut distinction between a "medieval" and a supposedly "humanist" library. From this perspective scholarly investigations into both secular and monastic libraries have yielded very similar results. Besides, another factor noted by Kibre that has been but rarely taken into account when discussing the contents of a fifteenth-century library is that part of its contents may constitute the heritage of the preceding centuries, and that a catalogue may not be a safe indicator of the intellectual taste of the owner, whether it be a private individual or an institution: "the science of library cataloguing did not really develop until the fourteenth century, and fifteenth-century catalogues obviously include books [. . .] acquired at much earlier dates. In some cases, in fact, the vast majority of the books listed predate the catalogues that list them by more than a century".[15] A number of factors thus contribute to cloud the issue, and above all to make the distinction between "medieval" and "humanist" impossible. It remains to be asked, however, whether such a distinction would have a practical utility. We might note in some libraries, especially secular ones, a component that is absent or little evident in monastic libraries, and that might point towards humanist interests on the part of the owner or collector; additions are to be expected, and to be especially observed, rather than radical innovations. The passage from a medieval to a humanist library should thus be, and generally is, marked by continuity.

Having said this, the main obstacle remains the lack of consistent data and in some cases even of sufficient information, especially as concerns secular libraries. David N. Bell has recently attempted a comprehensive evaluation of monastic libraries between 1400 and 1557,[16] and his reading of some of the extant catalogues offers precious indications as concerns both contents and organisation of the manuscripts preserved in the English monasteries. We shall come back to Bell's observations when analysing the list of Duke Humphrey's donations to the University of Oxford; but even at this early stage it may be interesting to see what subjects and authors found most favour in English monastery libraries. The Bible and biblical glosses obviously had a place of honour, though Bell doubts whether the

---

[15] David N. Bell, p. 231.
[16] David N. Bell, "Monastic Libraries: 1400–1557", quoted above in this chapter.

latter volumes constituted simply a legacy from the previous centuries or were still in use. Commentaries on various books of the
Bible were likewise common, and authors such as Augustine or Peter
Lombard were in particular evidence. Together with this section,
one could find patristic authors, and what Bell generically calls
"medieval authorities":[17] Augustine again, Jerome, Origen (present
in Latin in the catalogue of the Premonstratensian library at Titchfield), Isidore, Thomas Aquinas, Albert the Great, Bernard of Clairvaux (in particular evidence in Cistercian houses), Aristotle and his
commentators. These observations accord with Pearl Kibre's, when
she notes in European late-medieval libraries the constant presence
of St Anselm, St Bernard of Clairvaux, Hugh of St Victor, Peter
Lombard, William of Auvergne, Bonaventura, Albert the Great,
Thomas Aquinas, and, among Greek classics in translation, a predominance of Aristotle over Plato.

A monastic library would follow patristics with hagiography and
sermons, and then with canon law. These texts may have been present, if to a lesser extent, also in secular libraries; civil law, especially as represented by Justinian, would often appear in both. Medicine
could also be fairly represented in both, which should probably make
us beware of excessive enthusiasm over Duke Humphrey's considerable medical collection, which will be discussed below; but sometimes the section devoted to medicine would include little more than
standard and often outdated authorities, as in the case of Titchfield.
Standard medical treatises would include Hippocrates, Galen, Celsus,
Albucasis, Averroes, Avicenna. The same would happen with the
section the Titchfield catalogue labels *grammatica*, though an element
of interest in this case is given by the fact that this section includes
a number of classical poets: Ovid, Horace, Virgil and Maximianus
in Titchfield; Ovid, Lucan and Sallust in the Cistercian house at
Meaux, together with Seneca and Cicero. The library of the Austin
friars at York even possessed copies of Caesar's *De Bello Gallico*.
Scientific treatises would come under the heading of "volumina de
diversis materiis",[18] which may reflect the little attention paid to these
subjects on the part of the monastic libraries. Kibre, however, lists
a fairly large number of authors under the heading "scientific and

---

[17] David N. Bell, p. 237.
[18] David N. Bell, p. 239.

pseudo-scientific works": Ptolemy commentated by Haly, Arabic and Hebrew astrologers in Latin translation, Peter of Abano; among the English astrologers John of Eschenden enjoyed a European reputation. The mathematical treatises include Euclid, Nemorarius, Sacrobosco, Boethius, and some libraries might include music treatises such as those of St Augustine, Boethius, Guido of Arezzo. Then there might be agricultural treatises, such as Hesiod, Varro, Cato, Palladius, Petrus Crescentius, while architecture would be represented by Vitruvius. A small place was also destined to geography, with Ptolemy and Strabo, while more considerable importance had alchemy, with the volumes attributed, more or less accurately, to Hermes Trismegistus, Michael Scot, Richard of Furnival, Albertus Magnus, Aristotle, Raymond Lull. Curiously, Bell does not mention the very popular encyclopaedists, such as Bartholomaeus Anglicus (which found diffusion all over Europe), Alexander Neckam (particularly in English libraries), and the three *Specula* by Vincent de Beauvais. Very popular would also be the *Secreta Secretorum* and the *Picatrix*.

To come back to English monastic libraries, volumes in English might include translations of devotional texts, and sometimes different material: thus the monastery library in Titchfield lists a copy of *The Owl and the Nightingale* and a translation of *The Golden Legend*. Sometimes, even in monastic libraries, there could be manuscripts in French: works on law, for instance, but in some cases what we would unhesitatingly classify as literature of entertainment, particularly romances; they could occasionally belong to a monk, such as the Benedictine from St Augustine's who left to the library of the monastic house his copies of *Guy de Warwick, Ipomedon, Les quatre fils Aymon, Lancelot, L'Estoire del saint Graal, Perceval le Gallois*, and *Histoire de Guillaume le Maréchal*;[19] in other cases similar material could be obtained from a donation, as in the case of the Cistercian abbey of Bordesley which received twenty-seven books in French, mostly romances, from Guy de Beauchamp, Earl of Warwick. This could be an amusing and even endearing trait, especially when we think of the romance-lover monk; but it also reflects the relatively haphazard way with which volumes could be acquired, occasionally mirroring the whim of the donor, occasionally determined by simple coincidence, and stopping us from perceiving a real policy of book-acquisition on the part of

---

[19] David N. Bell, p. 237.

the monastery. All in all, however, we cannot but agree with Bell
when he concludes his examination of monastery library catalogues
with these words:

> What they give is an overwhelming impression of age. The collections
> they record are old collections, and there is little evidence of any inter-
> est in acquiring contemporary books by contemporary authors. In other
> words, they may be fifteenth-century catalogues, but they are not cat-
> alogues of fifteenth-century books.[20]

The same is true when the catalogues post-date the introduction of
printing in England. One startling exception is constituted by what
is known of the library of the Brigittine brethren at Syon; Here, the
fact that the house was a fifteenth-century foundation and the catalogue a sixteenth-century one determines considerable differences:
many printed books are present, and among them Renaissance volumes such as Giovanni Antonio Sulpizio's *Grammatica*, or the works
by Hermolaus Barbarus, Marsilius Ficinus, Erasmus, Coluccio Salutati,
Leonardo Bruni, Poggio Bracciolini, Poliziano, Pico della Mirandola,
Colet and Linacre.[21] It is evident that this library belongs to the second, fuller phase of English humanism, to the age of Erasmus and
Thomas More.

What is still missing, however, is a catalogue that might enlighten
us as to the transition between Middle Ages and humanism, and
this, I would contend, is what we see in the traces that are left of
Duke Humphrey's library. It is in the fist half of the fifteenth century that the distinction between a medieval and a humanist library
becomes blurred, and we can note the insertion of new material into
the standard structure of medieval learning. The already mentioned
Brigittine house at Syon obviously possessed, along with the Renaissance
volumes we have listed, its share of Bibles, glosses and scholastic and
patristic authors; it is not in the absence of medieval interests that
we see a sure sign of change, but in the appearance of new texts
devoted to those same disciplines. The attention humanists had for
education means that the subjects of the *trivium* and *quadrivium* would
still form the topics of reference for the new learning, though they
might be considered from different angles.[22] If the perspective is one

---

[20] David N. Bell, p. 242.
[21] David N. Bell, pp. 245–6.
[22] Kibre also deals with the question of the liberal arts as they were discussed

of continuity rather than radical innovation, then the actual innovations will be more easily detected.

Another factor to be taken into consideration when we examine what survives of Duke Humphrey's library is that what we have in this case can be classified neither as a private nor as an institutional library. Though Humphrey did collect books as a private individual, he also received them, as was naturally due to his institutional role; besides, his donations to the University of Oxford (it must be remembered that the lists of some of these donations are still our most precious source of information on the extent and quality of the Duke's library) were made to an institutional library, and deliberately sought, I believe, to confer a particular imprint to the University and its curriculum. Besides, even as concerns the Duke's own book collection in Greenwich, its owner's role made it, to a certain extent, accessible to a number of readers and scholars. Richard Firth Green makes the same point when discussing royal libraries:

> royal libraries were not necessarily exclusive and jealously guarded institutions whose contents were intended more for show than use; the less expensive volumes, at any rate, may well have circulated amongst the king's intimate companions and the staff of his chamber with a minimum of formal control, and, whether through public reading or private study, have reached a number of courtiers.[23]

The readership was thus more composite than we tend to believe. Besides, royal and even aristocratic libraries rarely coincided with a single location, or were housed in a specific room, as would happen with monastic or university libraries. We shall see later the dispositions given by some members of the Lancaster house on this point; but we may note now that the habit of kings, and of some of the greater nobles, to travel from one place of residence to another, meant that part of the library might travel with its owner, and that the rest might be scattered over various houses, and occasionally left

---

by the humanist authors, though she arrives at slightly different conclusions: "Fifteenth century libraries also reflected the continuity as well as the blending of medieval interests with those of the humanists in other fields. The first two subjects of the *trivium*, that is grammar and rhetoric, which had formed the basic pillars of the medieval interest in the liberal arts, now provided the focal points for humanistic interests and achievements" (p. 280).

[23] Richard Firth Green, *Poets and Princepleasers: Literature and the English Court in the Late Middle Ages*, Toronto: University of Toronto Press, 1980, p. 99.

in the care of a member of the royal or aristocratic *familia*.[24] This situation makes the hypothesis of a complete catalogue very tenuous in these cases. It also makes us reflect upon Humphrey's decision to house his books in one residence, in Greenwich, and to collect a circle of friends and readers here between the late 1430s and the early 1440s, as is attested by the proem of the Middle English translation of Palladius's *De Agricultura*.[25] The decision on Humphrey's part appears to demonstrate not only the Duke's heightened interest in the collection, preservation and use of manuscripts, but also the diminution of his political interests.

Even once all these factors are taken into consideration, it is difficult to determine whether Duke Humphrey, in his assiduous activity of collection and donation of manuscripts, could be considered a singular exception in an aristocratic society that still cared very little for books, either as means of instruction, of entertainment or as an enhancement of their social status, or whether he was *primus inter pares*; this is why the following section of this chapter will include a brief survey of what is known of the cultural activity of other members of the Lancaster house, such as Humphrey's two brothers, Henry V and the Duke of Bedford, and his nephew Henry VI. Humphrey's intellectual activity begins in that phase, shortly before the introduction of printing, when the book-trade sees its first significant changes: though manuscripts remain very expensive, and illuminated manuscripts are generally luxury goods conceived for exhibition rather than actual use, the increasing specialisation in the English booktrade, with the emergence of professional figures such as the scribe, the illuminator, the parchment-maker, or the bookbinder is extremely revealing.[26] These craftsmen would still be found as permanent employees in royal or noble households, occasionally being hired in private households as happened, for instance, in the case of the Pastons,[27]

---

[24] Green, p. 93.
[25] *The Middle-English Translation of Palladius De Re Rustica*, ed. by M. Liddell, Berlin: E. Ebering, 1896. See in particular lines 97–104.
[26] See H.E. Bell, "The Price of Books in Medieval England", *The Library* 4th series, 17: 1937, 312–32, p. 313. On illuminated manuscripts, and their incidence in manuscript production, see also Kathleen L. Scott, "*Caveat Lector*: Ownership and Standardization in the Illustration of Fifteenth Century English Manuscripts", in *English Manuscript Studies 1100–1700*, ed. by P. Beal and J. Griffiths, Oxford: Blackwell, 1989: 19–63.
[27] See H.S. Bennett, *The Pastons and their England. Studies in an Age of Transition*, Cambridge: Cambridge University Press, 1932, pp. 112–3.

but at the same time they would also start to work in shops that could cater to a wide or diversified range of customers, whether in London or in the university towns.[28] This passage indicates the increased diffusion of books, and of a network of book commission and exchange that connects England with the rest of Europe, as will be clear in the case of the Duke of Gloucester.

Book-collecting in the Lancastrian house: The Duke of Bedford and Henry V

In chapter 3 a short account has been given of the passion for books shared by many members of the Lancastrian family, especially as concerned John, Duke of Bedford. Traces of the same passion can be detected also in the case of the other brother, Henry V, though scholarly attention towards this aspect of the King's activity, which could influence both the personal and the public sphere, has been often superficial, and has frequently stopped at generalisations.[29] Thus J.B. Trapp, in an otherwise excellent study on the book in the fifteenth century, has written: "Though Henry V possessed a substantial library, there is no surviving evidence of his use of it. Of the more bookish sort, Henry VI has left no trace in the form of annotation".[30] The sentence highlights a generic but commonly accepted distinction between a warlike Henry V and a bookish Henry VI—a distinction underlined also by images well-known to readers and historians, such as the long line of English kings a visitor to York Minster can admire on the choir screen, all belligerently brandishing

---

[28] An instance is described in Kathleen L. Scott, "A Mid-Fifteenth-Century English Illuminating Shop and its Customers", *Journal of the Warburg and Courtauld Institutes* 31: 1968, 170–96. See also the essays collected in *Book Production and Publishing in Britain 1375–1475*, ed. by J. Griffiths and D. Pearsall, Cambridge: Cambridge University Press, 1989.

[29] As for the third brother, Thomas Duke of Clarence, he "seems to have been indifferent to learning; at least no books are mentioned in his will" (K.B. MacFarlane, *Lancastrian Kings and Lollard Knights*, Oxford: Clarendon Press, 1972, p. 116). However, A.I. Doyle and M.B. Parkes note a manuscript (now Oxford, Christ Church 148), a copy of Gower's *Confessio Amantis*, "where the arms indicate that the volume was completed, and possibly commissioned, not before 1405, for one of the sons of Henry IV, probably Thomas, Duke of Clarence" ("The Production of Copies of the *Canterbury Tales* and the *Confessio Amantis* in the Early Fifteenth Century", in *Medieval Scribes, Manuscripts and Libraries. Essays Presented to N.R. Ker*, ed. by M.B. Parkes and A.G. Watson, London: Scolar Press, 1978: 163–210, p. 208).

[30] Trapp, "Literacy, Books and Readers", p. 41.

a sword, with the sole exception of the last of the line, devoted and
meek Henry VI who is reading from a book. Yet evidence might
point in a different direction.[31]

Though we begin to speak of a Royal Library in England only
with Edward IV, commonly considered its founder,[32] this may be
due to little else but the lack of adequate information on the cultural activity of previous kings. Inventories or catalogues for the fourteenth and early fifteenth centuries are lacking, unlike what happened
in other royal libraries, as for instance in France. What we know of
French libraries has also influenced our view of the Lancastrian cultural patronage: paradoxically, the more complete data we have concerning the Louvre library have turned John of Bedford into a more
important collector of books than either of his brothers. Jenny Stratford
notes that "separate inventories were [. . .] made of the great Louvre
library of Charles V and Charles VI in 1373, 1380, 1411, 1413 and
in 1424, when the books were bought by John, Duke of Bedford,
as Regent of France; after 1429 they were brought via Rouen to
the Duke's wardrobe in London".[33] This means that we know with
a fair degree of certainty what Bedford was appropriating, and this
is a great help if we consider that over one hundred Louvre manuscripts are known to this day (Bedford's acquisition, completed in
1425, included 843 volumes). John of Bedford's incessant political
activity on either side of the Channel and his premature death prevented him from making full use of his acquisition, and prevent us
from understanding clearly the direction his cultural patronage would
take; but his acquisition of the Louvre books must also, to a certain
extent, have reflected upon the reading habits of other members of
his family, who had, together with John, the possibility of reading
and copying a large number of previously unapproachable texts.
Even in this context Humphrey of Gloucester deserves a special men-

---

[31] "Given the dispersal which took place during the majority of Henry VI and
at his own volition, it is perhaps rather Henry IV and Henry V who should be
thought of as bibliophiles and founders of the royal library" (Jenny Stratford, "The
Royal Library in England before the Reign of Edward IV", in *England in the Fifteenth
Century. Proceedings of the 1992 Harlaxton Symposium*, ed. by N. Rogers, Stamford: Paul
Watkins, 1994: 187–97, p. 197).

[32] Jenny Stratford, "The Early Royal Collections and the Royal Library to 1461",
in *The Cambridge History of the Book in Britain, vol. 3: 1400–1557*, ed. by L. Hellinga
and J.B. Trapp, Cambridge: Cambridge University Press, 1999: 255–66, p. 255.

[33] Stratford, "The Early Royal Collections and the Royal Library to 1461",
p. 256.

tion: we know that some of the manuscripts acquired by the Duke of Bedford were sent to him as gifts. Thus in 1427 Humphrey received an illuminated Livy in the French translation of Pierre Bersuire,[34] and a manuscript of *Le Songe du Vergier*, which had been made for Charles V in 1378;[35] these volumes are among the few of his library to have survived. Scholarly attention has generally concentrated on these two volumes, and especially on the Livy, given the importance that has always been paid to the humanist side of Humphrey's book-collecting activity, but among the extant ones we find at least another manuscript that was donated by Bedford to Gloucester, a volume including *La quête du Saint Graal* and *La mort au roi Artus*.[36] Other manuscripts belonging to Humphrey were formerly the property of Charles V and might have arrived to Gloucester through the same channel, though in this case it is more difficult to prove that the Duke of Bedford donated them; among them we may mention *Le livre de linformacion des princes*, a French version of the anonymous Latin treatise *De administratione principum*,[37] and a French

---

[34] The manuscript, previously belonging to Charles V, is now in Paris, Bibliothèque de Sainte Geneviève, franç. 777. On f. 433v a fifteenth-century hand has noted: "Cest livre fut envoyé des parties de France et donné par mons le regent de royaume, duc de Bedford, a mons le duc de Gloucestre, son beau frère, l'an mil quatre cens vingt sept". It is tempting to think that this is the same book that Humphrey sent to the King of Naples, Alfonso V, and to which he refers in a letter to the King, written in July 1445. See Alfonso Sammut, *Unfredo duca di Gloucester e gli umanisti italiani*, Padova: Antenore, 1980, p. 122; the letter to Alfonso is transcribed on pp. 215–6. See also Jenny Stratford, *The Bedford Inventories. The Worldly Goods of John, Duke of Bedford, Regent of France (1389–1435)*, London: Society of Antiquaries, 1993, p. 96.

[35] Now London, British Library, Royal 19.c.iv. The manuscript is described in Sammut, pp. 107–8. See also Julia Boffey, "English Dream Poems of the Fifteenth Century and their French Connections", in *Literary Aspects of Courtly Culture*, ed. by D. Maddox and S. Sturm-Maddox, Cambridge: D.S. Brewer, 1994: 113–21, p. 117. In these articles the text is attributed to Philippe de Mézières, adviser to Charles V and tutor to Charles VI. Elsewhere (see Lièvre below) the book is attributed to Raoul de Presles or, less probably, Évrard de Trémangon. It was originally written in Latin, presumably in 1376, for Charles V, and then translated. On the manuscript and its inclusion in the inventory of Charles's library, see Marion Lièvre, "Notes sur le manuscrit original du 'Songe du Vergier' et sur la librairie de Charles V", *Romania* 77: 1956, 352–60.

[36] Now Bruxelles, Bibliothèque Royale, 9627–8. The manuscript, bearing Humphrey's ex-libris, is described in Sammut, p. 98. It is curious to note that Humphrey's natural son, of whom there is very little trace in the chronicles, was named Arthur.

[37] Now London, British Library, Royal 19.a.xx. The manuscript is described in Sammut, p. 107. The book was also at some time the property of Robert Roos, Humphrey's cousin (see below).

version of Jacopo da Varazze's *Legenda Aurea*.[38] These volumes did
not form part of any of Humphrey's donations to Oxford University
library, but as far as it is known remained in his possession; this,
however, is not surprising, since the Oxford donations did not include
manuscripts in languages other than Latin.

Yet, apart from exhaustive information on the Louvre library and
its acquisition on the part of the Duke of Bedford, very little is known
of the latter's activity as a book-collector. The Bedford inventories
have recently been made the object of very thorough research, but
what has been found concerning non-Louvre manuscripts, of which
eleven survive today, is slightly disappointing.[39] The surviving texts
include the Bedford Psalter and Hours, lavishly illuminated, dated
about 1420, and generally associated with the London workshop of
Herman Scheere; then there are chapel books and a multi-volume
Bible. All these manuscripts are in French. The presence of Scheere's
handiwork shows that Bedford "was patronising scribes and illuminators who had already produced manuscripts for the Lancastrian
monarchy, and who were chosen by other noble and ecclesiastical
patrons during the first decades of the fifteenth centuries";[40] unfortunately the Psalter and Hours constitute the only surviving volume
which is known to have been commissioned in England. A fascinating characteristic of this manuscript, described by Sylvia Wright,
is that "two hundred and ninety of the 300 minor text divisions are
illustrated with portrait heads; a national portrait gallery of Lancastrian
friends and foes is concealed in the initials of carefully selected texts".[41]
As far as is known, the Duke of Bedford did not set out to acquire
manuscripts in Latin or in English; still less did he show any interest in the new, humanist learning—in this respect, Humphrey differed
from both his brothers. Stratford arrives at the same conclusions
when, after her survey of the Bedford manuscripts, she writes:

---

[38] Now Paris, Bibliothèque Mazarine, 1729. The manuscript is described in
Sammut, p. 122.
[39] Stratford, *The Bedford Inventories* (the manuscripts are described on pages 91–6).
See also Jenny Stratford, "The Manuscripts of John, Duke of Bedford: Library and
Chapel", in *England in the Fifteenth Century: Proceedings of the 1986 Harlaxton Symposium*,
ed. by D. Williams, Woodbridge: The Boydell Press, 1987: 329–50.
[40] Stratford, *The Bedford Inventories*, p. 108.
[41] Sylvia Wright, "The Author Portraits in the Bedford Psalter-Hours: Gower,
Chaucer, and Hoccleve", *British Library Journal* 18: 1992, 190–201, p. 190.

Bedford's reputation as a great patron rests today largely on the three opulently decorated liturgical manuscripts begun or adapted for him and for Anne of Burgundy in Paris between 1423 and 1432 [. . .] The luxury manuscripts associated with Bedford and Anne of Burgundy are liturgical books. The secular manuscripts made for Bedford, or with dedications to him, are not of the same very high quality. They are mainly medical astrological or devotional in content. There is nothing to compare with the interest in Humanism of Bedford's brother, Humphrey, duke of Gloucester.[42]

The acquisition of devotional manuscripts which would also show the wealth or the importance of their owner is not unexpected in a fifteenth-century nobleman; had Bedford not acquired the contents of the Louvre library, his rank as a book collector would not be higher than that of any contemporary nobleman with no specific intellectual interests. However, the acquisition of Charles VI's books was a major enterprise, even presumably in financial terms,[43] and we have other clues to Bedford's literary tastes, which unfortunately he was prevented from cultivating more. As highlighted in the brief survey devoted to Bedford's cultural pursuits in chapter 3, fragmentary evidence goes to show that he intended to patronise one or more universities, and that the University of Oxford on more than one occasion appealed to his generosity. Yet anything beyond this is mere conjecture, and however much he may have surpassed his younger brother as a politician, he never reached his status as an intellectual patron.

As written above, we have such detailed information on the Duke of Bedford's activity as a book collector only because the inventories made of the Louvre library prior to and on the occasion of his acquisition were exceptionally informative. On the other hand, there are no reliable estimates of books possessed by or associated with English kings or queens before Edward IV, and speculation on this point has brought scholars to rather gloomy evaluations; thus Stratford, in what is probably the most recent study on the subject, believes that "even the most optimistic calculation, however, scarcely exceeds two dozen".[44] Once again, it may be conjectured that such a meagre estimate depends largely on the paucity of information available.

---

[42] Stratford, *The Bedford Inventories*, pp. 120–2.
[43] It is uncertain how much he paid for the books.
[44] Stratford, "The Early Royal Collections and the Royal Library to 1461", p. 256.

If we know very little about the books the Lancastrian kings owned or used, we know rather more concerning the provisions they made for housing these books. Henry IV, for instance, while having Eltham Palace (which was to be one of his favourite residences) rebuilt, included in the reconstruction a new study among the rooms attached to the King's chamber, as shown in the 1401–2 payments:

> The study was furnished with two desks, listed among the "necessaria": "Et in uno magno deske facto de ij stagez pro libris intus custodicndis cum ij formulis emptis de Rogero Joynour pro studio regis, xxs. Et in uno alio deske minore empto de Johanne Deken pro dicto studio regis, xiijs. iiijd".[45]

It is inconceivable that the King would have made such elaborate preparations for housing little more than two dozen volumes. Besides, he did not neglect intellectual patronage: the *Munimenta Academica* show that he was also a patron of the University of Oxford, even if the surviving documents are not very specific as to the nature of his donations.[46]

As for Henry V's literary tastes, equally little is known, though a few important clues are provided by occasional notes (such as the receipt by a London scrivener in 1421 for £12. 8s. 0d. for making copies of twelve books on hunting),[47] by a list of the books captured at Meaux in 1422,[48] and especially by his testament. In his 1421 will, Henry V was very careful about the destination of his books. Thus among the legacies, in money or in precious objects, to religious houses we read "legamus monasterio sancti Salvatoris secundum sanctam Brigittam vocat' Syon bibliam in tribus voluminibus glosatam",[49] and "legamus ecclesie Christi Cantuar' quoddam volu-

---

[45] Stratford, "The Early Royal Collections and the Royal Library to 1461", p. 261. On this point see also Joyce Coleman, "Lay Readers and Hard Latin: How Gower May Have Intended the *Confessio Amantis* to Be Read", *Studies in the Age of Chaucer* 24: 2002, 209–35, p. 213.

[46] *Munimenta Academica*, ed. by H. Anstey, Rolls Series, London: Longmans, Green, Reader and Dyer, 1868, vol. 1, p. 266.

[47] MacFarlane, p. 117.

[48] The list is printed in MacFarlane, pp. 233–8. The document has been edited by G.L. Harriss. It must be noted that the volumes presented in this list do not seem to have been specifically mentioned in Henry V's will, with the possible exception of the volume described as "Gregorius in pastoralibus" in the list, which may have figured in the donation "ecclesie Christi Cantuar", quoted in this page.

[49] "We bequeath to the monastery called of St Saviour behind St Bridget in Syon a glossed Bible in three volumes".

men continens omnes libros beati Gregorii",[50] while an unspecified
number of presumably religious or devotional works is left again to
Syon, with one important exception:

> Item legamus abbatisse et conventui de Syon omnes libros nostros
> modo existentes in custodia sua, excepta magna biblia nostra que fuit
> bone memorie metuendissimi nobis patris et domini, quam quidem
> bibliam volumus remanere successori nostro.[51]

This seems to show that while in England Henry V, whether or not
still using the desk ordered by his father for Eltham Palace, was also
confiding some of his books in the care of a trusted religious house.[52]
Syon was particularly favoured in that it was left also a considerable sum of money. The abbey is mentioned once again in what
seems a repetition of the previous legacy: "volumus quod abbatissa
de Syon habeat et gaudeat ad usum illius monasterii libros nostros
sibi accomodatos".[53]

The religious houses, though, were not to be left the totality of
Henry's devotional manuscripts. Books to be used for religious purposes are mentioned also in the opening lines of the long section
devoted to the rich legacy to Henry's wife Catherine, for whom the
King shows special consideration:

> Item legamus carissime consorti nostre Katerine omnia illa jocalia
> aurea, argentea deaurata et de argento, ac omnia alia ornamenta altaris
> et capelle nostre, una cum vestimentis et libris que pro xx clericis que
> post transitum nostrum in dicta capella nostra in hospitio dicte consortis
> nostre deo et sibi servituris remanebunt: que omnia in indentura inter

---

[50] "We bequeath to Christ's Church in Canterbury a volume with all the works
of the blessed Gregory". Henry V's last will is published in Patrick and Felicity
Strong, "The Last Will and Codicils of Henry V", *The English Historical Review* 96:
1981, 79–102, p. 93.

[51] "We bequeath to the abbey and abbess of Syon all our books now in its custody, with the only exception of our great Bible which belonged to our very reverend father and Lord, since we wish this Bible to remain in the possession of our
successor". Strong, p. 93. The "magna biblia" has been tentatively identified with
a Bible now in the British Library, Royal 1.e.ix, dated to the reign of Henry IV,
decorated by Herman Scheere and other artists associated with the Lancastrian
house. See Stratford, "The Early Royal Collections and the Royal Library to 1461",
p. 263.

[52] There is good reason to think that he would still be using the Eltham Palace
room, since this residence remained a favourite one for all three Henrys. It was
sometimes used for the Christmas festivities during the reign of Henry VI, as demonstrated by John Lydgate's *Mumming at Eltham*, written in 1424.

[53] "We wish the abbess of Syon to have and use our books destined to her for
the use of her monastery". Strong, p. 94.

reverendum patrem Thomam Dunelmen' episcopum, cancellarium
Anglie, et decanum capelle nostre predicte volumus specifice specificari.[54]

The last sentence may show the care Henry had for the custody of
his books. Neither the Duke of Bedford nor the Duke of Gloucester
were left books, but rather horses or costly items of furniture; on
the other hand, Henry Beaufort, Bishop of Winchester, was left "portiforium nostrum in duobus voluminibus scriptum per Johannem
Frampton",[55] while Thomas Langley, Bishop of Durham, was left
"missale et portiforium que habuimus ex dono carissime avie nostre
comitisse Hereford' et sunt eiusdem scripture"[56]—a detail that shows
how well King Henry knew his books. Identical legacies (even supposing the value of the individual manuscripts to have been lower)
are destined to a number of the King's "clerks", that is, the almoner
and three chaplains: John Snel, Walter Tryngowgh, John Holbrok
and Roger Gates.[57] The last article of Henry's will devoted to books
goes back, in more detail, to "Syon et Cartusien", distinguishing
between the two houses' different tasks, but Oxford also makes an
appearance:

> Item legamus et volumus totum residuum librorum nostrorum, sive
> sint de meditationibus aut utiles ad predicandum evangelium, distribui
> inter monasteria nostre fundationis de Syon et Cartusien', secundum
> discretionem executorum nostrorum; quos ad hoc accipere volumus
> avisamentum clericorum et religiosorum qui ad hanc distributionem
> convenienter faciendam et sciunt et volunt eos cosulere. Libros autem
> ad predicandum ut prefertur utiles assignari volumus monasterio de
> Syon memorato considerato, quod ipsi ex vi religionis tenentur predi-
> care verbum Dei, et Cartusien' secundum regulas sui ordinis prohi-
> betur. Totum vero residuum librorum nostrorum juris aut materie
> scolastice in theologia, legamus comuni librarie universitatis Oxonie ad
> cuius constructionem juvamen prestitimus.[58]

---

[54] "We bequeath to our very dear wife Katherine all our gold, gold-plated and
silver ornaments, and all the ornaments of our altar and chapel, together with the
vestiments and books which will remain after our death in the chapel for our twenty
clerics who will serve her and God: and let all of them be specified in an indenture between the reverend father Bishop Thomas of Durham, Chancellor of England,
and the dean of our chapel". Strong, p. 93.

[55] "Our breviary in two volumes written by John Frampton".

[56] "The missal and breviary which we received from our very dear grandmother
the Countess of Hereford, which are of her writing".

[57] Strong, pp. 94–5.

[58] "We bequeath all our remaining books, both of meditations and useful to
preach the Gospels, to be distributed among the monasteries of Syon and Cartusian,

This detailed list did not exhaust Henry's library resources, since the section of the will devoted to the King's unnamed successor leaves him, among other things, "omnes libros nostros superius non legatos".[59] In the codicil following the 1421 will, the Queen is left yet another missal, while Henry's successor, here named, is left "libros [...] capelle nostre his exceptis que aliis in testamento nostro aut supra vel infra reliquimus per legatum".[60] This is followed, a few lines later, by another mention of books: "volumus quod omnes libri nostri, cuiuscumque fuerint facultatis aut materie, in nostro testamento aut codicillis non legati, filio nostro remaneant pro libraria sua".[61] The reference to his son's own library may allude to a Lancastrian use, established by Henry IV, to keep books for personal use in a room furnished on purpose. Besides, it is interesting to note that in one of the codicils the gift to the religious houses is somewhat qualified, presumably to favour the King's successor: "volumus quod neque abbatissa, confessor et conventus de Syon neque prior et conventus de Bethleem juxta Shene ex legato nostro habeant libros aliquos eiusdem continentie duplicatos, nec predicti prior et conventus de Bethlem habeant aliquos libros sermonum".[62] The specification that the religious houses were not to have any duplicates might further reflect on the number of the books possessed by the King.[63]

Such a list goes, even at the most prudential evaluation, well beyond the two dozen books mentioned by Stratford. The scholar herself, however, analyses the King's testament, saying that "there can be little doubt that by 1421, and before he obtained the books

---

to the discretion of our testamentary executors; and the clerics and ecclesiastics who know about such matters must be consulted for an optimal distribution of these books. But we would rather give the books for preaching to Syon, since they by the force of their religion must preach the word of God, while the Cartusians cannot do this. We wish to leave to the common library of the University of Oxford, towards whose building we contributed, all our remaining books of law and scholastic theology". Strong, p. 94.

[59] "All the books which we have not previously bequeathed". Strong, p. 96.

[60] "The books in our chapel apart from those which we have left to others elsewhere in our testament". Strong, p. 99.

[61] "We wish that all our books, of any faculty or subject, not other wise bequeathed in our testament or codicils, be left to our son for his own library".

[62] "It is our desire that neither the abbess, the confessor or the monastery in Syon, nor the prior and convent in Bethleem near Shene have two copies of the same books, nor that the prior and convent of Bethleem have books of sermons". Strong, p. 100.

[63] Stratford, "The Early Royal Collections and the Royal Library to 1461", p. 262.

from the Market of Meaux in 1422, Henry possessed a considerable learned library".[64] Not only did Henry V evidently possess a vast store of manuscripts, which he valued and knew well; he also seems to have envisaged for them various destinations that corresponded not only to his obligations as a King, but also to the different practical purposes of the volumes themselves. In this he showed far more attention and care than his son, Henry VI, whose books were in great part dispersed during his own lifetime, and rather resembled his younger brother Humphrey who would show considerable care in his donations to the Oxford University library, as shall be seen below.

Before turning our attention to Henry VI, however, it is interesting to see what happened to the Oxford legacy. In leaving his legal and scholastic volumes "comuni librarie universitatis Oxonie", Henry had set an example that Humphrey was later to follow; but the University library of Oxford, evidently unlucky with legacies, was not to receive the King's generous bequest. Some considerable time later, on 2 April 1437, the library was still trying to obtain the manuscripts that were its due. At this stage the library had already received an unspecified gift of books and money from Duke Humphrey, as shown in a letter dated 11 May 1435, and had already relied on the Duke, whether directly or through the mediation of Gilbert Kymer, to help it in a number of controversies;[65] so it was only natural that it should turn once again to the Duke to obtain help in recovering Henry V's manuscripts. The letter, included in *Epistolae Academicae Oxonienses*,[66] is extremely obsequious, as is the case of all letters the University directed to Gloucester, and feels sure the noble patron will express his approbation of the course of lectures undertaken: "novimus enim lecturam ordinariam et exercicium in septem scienciis liberalibus et tribus philosophiis fore vestre serenitati placita".[67]

---

[64] Stratford, "The Early Royal Collections and the Royal Library to 1461", p. 262. After the capture of Meaux, in 1422, Henry V had taken 110 books. According to G.L. Harriss, the books "formed the collection of one or more of the religious houses of the town" (see Harriss's edition of the book list in MacFarlane, p. 233).

[65] *Epistolae Academicae Oxonienses*, ed. by H. Anstey, Oxford: Clarendon Press, 1898, pp. 114–51.

[66] Pp. 151–3.

[67] "We know that the ordinary course and practice of the seven liberal arts and the three philosophies will be approved by your Highness".

But there are many expenses—most of all, the University needs a larger supply of books: "desunt enim nobis et librorum copia et habendi facultas".[68] The letter thus asks the Duke, in general terms, to give his help so that more books may be acquired; and it is tempting to see in this passage a reminder to the effect that Humphrey might continue with his policy of book-donation, already begun in 1435. But within this general request there is a more pointed reference to the acquisition of those books "quos invictissimus et illustrissimus princeps frater vester Henricus quintus oratrici vestre Universitati Oxoniensi et nobis legavit".[69] It is not clear whether Oxford managed to recover the books of Henry's legacy, but it seems improbable—in later letters to Humphrey, we read once again desolate exclamations on the depleted state of the library. However, the connection between the role of the two brothers as concerned the increase of the University library was thus clearly established.

In the case of Henry VI, we have evidence of intellectual interests (especially in his founding King's College in Cambridge, as well as the school at Eton), but he seems not to have been a careful book-keeper: "perhaps the dispersal of a considerable proportion of Henry VI's books to Oxford and Cambridge should be seen as yet another example of his dangerous tendency towards excessive open-handedness after the end of his minority, as well as evidence of his patronage of learning".[70] In accordance with the dispositions included in his father's will, the Council kept a number of books in the Treasury during Henry VI's minority—Stratford estimates that there were over 140 Latin books, most of which were given, in 1440, to university colleges, as it happened to the books left by Humphrey after his death, books which were meant for the University library at Oxford. The King kept a few of his father's and of Humphrey's books, particularly French illuminated manuscripts, and had a few made for him during his lifetime, such as the presentation copy of John Lydgate's *Life of St Edmund and St Fremund*,[71] but could not equal his father in the collection of an impressive library to distribute

---

[68] "We lack both the abundance of books and the means to obtain them".

[69] "Which your victorious, reverend and princely brother Henry V bequeathed to the University of Oxford and to us".

[70] Stratford, "The Early Royal Collections and the Royal Library to 1461", p. 265.

[71] Now British Library, Harley 2278.

among his friends and followers at his death. On the other hand, he did not show himself particularly responsive to Italian humanists' solicitations for patronage.[72] In this light, the two previous kings may be considered bibliophiles with more justice than Henry VI, since they shared, at least to some extent, Humphrey's passion for the collection and donation of manuscripts.

The library of Duke Humphrey

A little over forty manuscripts survive today of a library whose real size it is impossible to estimate with any degree of accuracy.[73] Duke Humphrey's library has had a curious fate in that it is better known for those volumes their owner alienated, donating them to Oxford, than for those he kept. No inventory or catalogue, if ever one was made, survives of the library as it stood in the Duke of Gloucester's time; almost all we know of it has been patiently collected and described by Alfonso Sammut, and the resulting volume is our best instrument to discuss a collection that was celebrated in its day as one of the most important in England.[74] Sammut's book presents in

---

[72] On this point see David Rundle, "Of Republics and Tyrants: Aspects of Quattrocento Humanist Writing and Their Reception in England, c. 1400–c. 1460", D.Phil., Oxford, 1997, pp. 232–3, and his "Humanism before the Tudors: On Nobility and the Reception of *studia humanitatis* in Fifteenth-Century England", in *Reassessing Tudor Humanism*, ed. by J. Woolfson, Basingstoke: Palgrave Macmillan, 2002: 22–42, pp. 24–5.

[73] A.C. De La Mare and Richard Hunt are even less sanguine in their estimate of the number of surviving and recognisable manuscripts belonging to the Duke: "About thirty manuscripts belonging to Duke Humfrey can be identified, either from his *ex-libris*, or from the opening words of the second leaf of the text, or because they bear his arms" (*Duke Humfrey and English Humanism in the Fifteenth Century. Catalogue of an Exhibition Held in the Bodleian Library Oxford*, Oxford: Bodleian Library, 1970, p. 2). It must be added, however, that between the publication of their catalogue and the present time new manuscript discoveries have been made.

[74] Sammut's book (Alfonso Sammut, *Unfredo duca di Gloucester e gli umanisti italiani*, Padova: Antenore, 1980) has been only very slightly updated, as far as the information on Humphrey's library is concerned, by A.C. De la Mare, "Duke Humfrey's English Palladius (MS. Duke Humfrey d.2)", *The Bodleian Library Record* 12: 1985, 39–51, and by David Rundle, "Two Unnoticed Manuscripts from the Collection of Humfrey, Duke of Gloucester", *The Bodleian Library Record* 16: 1998, 211–24, 299–313. A manuscript unnoticed by Sammut (British Library, Ashmole 66, discussed below) is mentioned and briefly discussed in Hilary M. Carey, "Astrology at the English Court in the Late Middle Ages", in *Astrology, Science and Society: Historical Essays*, ed. by P. Curry, Woodbridge: The Boydell Press, 1987: 41–56, p. 47.

an orderly form all the sources that might help us in this discussion: it lists the extant manuscripts (including the one whose ownership is dubious, and listing apographs in a separate section), tracing as far as possible their history, besides presenting the list of the manuscript donations to Oxford as it appears in *Epistolae Academicae Oxonienses*, and thus providing future scholars with the two most important elements for a reconstruction of the library. It also edits and presents the 1452 catalogue of King's College, Cambridge, since after Humphrey's death Henry VI, contravening his uncle's express wishes, gave a great part of the remaining volumes to Cambridge rather than to the University library of Oxford. It is thus reasonable to infer that the catalogue would list manuscripts formerly belonging to the Duke of Gloucester—an inference proved by the fact that three of the extant volumes appear also in the King's College catalogue.[75] For the sake of completeness, Sammut includes in his book also John Leland's list of the volumes seen "Oxoniae in bibliotheca publica" at some stage in the early sixteenth century.[76]

It should be added that this reconstruction forms only a part, if a substantial one, of Sammut's book, which is mostly devoted to the relation between Humphrey and Italian humanists, with an edition of the letters exchanged between the Duke of Gloucester and Italian scholars such as Leonardo Bruni, Pietro del Monte, Antonio Beccaria, Pier Candido Decembrio, and of the dedications inserted in the volumes the humanists would present to Humphrey. It is on this point that most of Sammut's discussion concentrates. This is also the aspect on which recent scholarship has most worked, as has been shown in chapter 1 of the present volume. But Sammut's *tour de force* enables us to turn our attention also to the library in itself, and to see that the great attention given to the humanist side of Humphrey's activity has perhaps blinded us to equally interesting issues. This may be

---

[75] Sammut, p. 58. De La Mare and Hunt go as far as to say that in the Cambridge fifteenth-century library "the number and range of classical and humanistic works in the collection is due to Duke Humfrey" (*Duke Humfrey and English Humanism in the Fifteenth Century*, p. 10). In a review to Sammut's book, however, Mariangela Regoliosi is not of the same opinion, believing that only a fraction of Humphrey's books went to Cambridge, and that King's College mostly had manuscripts copied from Humphrey's, as the different *secundo folio incipit* demonstrate (the review is published in *Aevum*, 56 (1982): 352 4).

[76] From *Ioannis Leland Antiquarii de Rebus Britannicis Collectanea*, ed. T. Hearnius, III, Oxoniae 1715, pp. 58 9. See Sammut, pp. 95 7.

said to be the case even with Sammut's own work, as early reviewers
were quick to notice. In a review of *Unfredo duca di Gloucester* published in 1982, for instance, B. Barker-Benfield made some interesting observations:

> It would be unfair to criticize Dr Sammut for failing to produce the
> definitive study of the Duke's library when he only intended this sec-
> tion as an appendix to the central topic of Italian contacts. But [. . .]
> the library contained more solid medieval texts than classico-human-
> istic ones; the non-Italian aspect of Duke Humphrey's intellectual life
> is not entirely alien to Dr Sammut's theme, for somehow it had made
> him susceptible to humanistic ideas.[77]

It is true that today the real value of Sammut's book lies in its central section, with its careful reconstruction of Duke Humphrey's
library, rather than in the investigation of the relationship between
the Duke and the Italian humanists, an investigation that has been
amply superseded by later studies.[78] Even Barker-Benfield, though
correctly noting the sheer size of the "solid medieval" part of
Humphrey's library, prefers to read it as part of the Duke's education and preparation to the humanist principles he was to espouse,
a sort of introductory section to the classico-humanist library. Yet,
once the relevant evidence has been analysed, it can be seen that
the medieval library constitutes by far the most relevant part of Duke
Humphrey's intellectual legacy. Of the forty-six extant manuscripts
that can be associated with him (including those whose ownership
is rather dubious), only twenty can be considered humanist or are
associated with the Italian humanists working for the Duke;[79] in the
donations to Oxford the humanist texts are only one element of a
much larger collection.

---

[77] B. Barker-Benfield, "Alfonso Sammut, *Unfredo duca di Gloucester e gli umanisti italiani*", *The Library* 6th series 4: 1982, 191–4, p. 193.

[78] In particular, see David Rundle, "Of Republics and Tyrants" and "Humanism
before the Tudors", quoted above; see also his "On the Difference between Virtue
and Weiss: Humanists Texts in England during the Fifteenth Century", in *Courts,
Counties and the Capital in the Later Middle Ages*, ed. by D.E.S. Dunn, New York: St
Martin's Press, 1996: 181–203. See also Susanne Saygin, *Humphrey, Duke of Gloucester
(1390–1447) and the Italian Humanists*, Leiden: Brill, 2002.

[79] Interestingly enough, the four manuscripts whose relation with Humphrey is
most dubious are all humanist; it is legitimate to think that the scholars' desire to
add one more proof of the Duke's attention towards the new learning may have
slightly forced facts.

Of all the other circumstances that might throw light on Humphrey's library, very little is known, so that any attempt on our part to reconstruct the library not only as it stood but as it worked, and to compare it with contemporary European libraries, is doomed to be little more than a tentative hypothesis.[80] We know that very often the Duke would mark his manuscripts with a note of ownership: this often tends to be an ex-libris in the form of a short sentence, "ce livre est a Humfrey duc de Gloucestre", or "cest livre est a moy Homfrey duc de Gloucestre," sometimes completed by a note on the provenance of the manuscript; sometimes we read Humphrey's own motto "mon bien mondain", occasionally coupled with his name. In the case of humanist books, or books of Italian provenance, sometimes there is an analogous ex-libris in Latin; thus in the collection *Duodecim Panegyrici Latini* we read, on f. IVv, "Est illustrissimi domini ducis Cloucestrensis", followed by a list of contents, apparently in the scribe's own hand.[81] The ex-libris or note of ownership has been in many cases erased, so that it can sometimes be read only with the help of an ultra-violet lamp;[82] as far as it has been possible to ascertain, however, it appears on at least twenty-nine of the extant volumes, though rarely on the opening folio, more often appearing immediately after the end of the text.[83] The use of the title might help us with the dating of these acquisitions: Humphrey became Duke of Gloucester in 1414, which means that all the relevant volumes must have been inscribed, if not actually acquired, after that date.

Less frequently we can see the Duke's coat of arms on the books: in at least one volume, it has been added once the manuscript became the property of the University of Oxford.[84] In this volume,

---

[80] Thus we may read as unsubstantiated Weiss's statement that "his collection of manuscripts was representative of classical, humanistic, and medieval learning, so that if quality is to prevail over quantity, there is hardly any doubt that his collection was the most important in England at his time" (Roberto Weiss, *Humanism in England During the Fifteenth Century*, Oxford: Blackwell, 1941, p. 61).

[81] Paris, Bibliothèque Nationale, lat. 7805. Described in Sammut, pp. 118–9, and in *Duke Humfrey and English Humanism in the Fifteenth Century*, p. 6.

[82] For instance in the manuscript containing a collection of bestiaries, (olim) London, Sion College, Arc. L.40.2/L.28. The manuscript was privately bought in 1977. See Sammut, p. 110.

[83] This last observation, however, is difficult to verify, since re-binding or restoration of the manucripts in the following centuries might make the opening folio particularly prone to destruction.

[84] London, British Library, Harley 33. See Sammut, p. 103.

a copy of William of Ockham's *Dialogus inter magistrum et discipulum de heresi et hereticis*, the label of the old University library of Oxford includes Gloucester's coat of arms and the inscription "Deologus Oc(ham 2°) fo. Jesu tamquam. Ex dono illustrissimi principis et domini Humfridi, filii, fratris regum et patrui, ducis Gloucestrie, comitis Pembrochie et Magni Camerarii Anglie". As De La Mare and Hunt correctly observe, "the label, now stuck down on a flyleaf, must originally have been fixed to the binding of this MS., probably under a horn cover".[85] It seems evident that in this case the library was closely following Humphrey's own practice in styling himself, and might even have been acting according to the Duke's own instructions. Besides, as Doyle and Parkes correctly note in the case of vernacular manuscripts, coats of arms were not usual: "the incorporation or addition of such insignia in the illumination of vernacular manuscripts in England seems to have been less common than might be expected when one considers that a significant portion of potential customers must have been armigerous".[86] The same scholars, describing a manuscript belonging to Humphrey and containing a number of John Gower's works in Latin, English and French, note

> at the top of f. 1 "Mon b[ien mondain] Gloucestre" and on f. 201v below the colophon "Cest livre est A moy Homfrey Duc De gloucestre", both legible under ultra-violet light. The unusual medieval binding of polished light-coloured skin over bevelled boards is blind-stamped with some tools not found (so far as we know) elsewhere, of which one, a Lombardic capital **M**, might refer to Humfrey's motto and another is a small fleur-de-lis: not the tools on bindings connected with Gilbert Kymer, his physician.[87]

In this case the presence, not elsewhere noted, of what we might call a personalised binding could indicate that this volume was meant for private perusal and not for a donation. That the volume was composed to meet a particular buyer's requirements may also be seen by other characteristics noted by the two scholars: "whereas the quality of script, pictures and illuminated borders in the manuscript is very high, the secondary initials are simply flourished, and such a discrepancy suggests the intervention of a personal choice in the

---

[85] *Duke Humfrey and English Humanism in the Fifteenth Century*, p. 2.
[86] Doyle and Parkes, p. 208.
[87] Doyle and Parkes, p. 208. The manuscript (now Oxford, Bodleian Library, Bodley 294) is also, if less accurately, described in Sammut, pp. 112–3.

finishing of the copy, if not at the commencement of its production".[88] As we shall see in the case of the presentation copy of the
Middle English translation of Palladius's *De Re Rustica*, written for
Humphrey, in some cases the patronage of the Duke of Gloucester
could also determine a precise choice in the decoration and illumination of the text.

In a few cases we have a dedication, whether from the author,
the translator (particularly in the case of Latin translations of Greek
texts prepared by Italian humanists), or the donor. Thus in a manuscript including Tito Livio Frulovisi's *Vita Henrici Quinti* we have,
on f. 132r, the name "Humfry", and, on f. 1v, in red ink, an inscription in the form of an elegiac couplet probably to be attributed to
the Italian humanist's own hand:

> Hoc tuus exiguo te munere donat amator
> Nemo carens magnis tradere magna potest.[89]

In this case the dedication follows the standard humanist practice of
concluding with a *sententia*, though I have not been able to identify
a particular classical or medieval source for it. Elsewhere the inscription strikes a more personal note: in the Latin version of an Arabic
Antidotarium we read, on f. 230v, "Loyale et belle a Gloucestre loyale-
ment Vostre la Duchesse".[90] The frequent appearance of the ex-
libris in what seems to be the Duke's own hand, or of what may be
read as a note of ownership, may suggest that Humphrey was especially careful of the volumes in his possession. Roberto Weiss goes
further than this, assuming that there was a note of ownership in
all Gloucester's books, and that he would also mark the volumes in
other ways: "once in his library his volumes seem to have had a
small vellum label on the outer cover of the binding, where was
indicated not only the title of the volume, or of the first item in it,
but also, again, how it had been acquired, the label being protected
by a transparent sheet of horn." According to Weiss, this is proof

---

[88] Doyle and Parkes, pp. 208–9.

[89] "He who loves you presents you with this small gift. Nobody can give great
things, if he lacks what is great". The manuscript is now Cambridge, Corpus Christi
College, 285. See Sammut, pp. 98–9.

[90] Now London, British Library, Sloane 248. See Sammut, p. 102. Commenting
on this inscription, Vickers correctly notes that "Loyale et belle" had been adopted
by the Duke as his motto (Kenneth H. Vickers, *Humphrey Duke of Gloucester. A
Biography*, London: Constable, 1907, pp. 433–4).

that Humphrey personally supervised his library.[91] It might be closer
to the truth to assert that he was very concerned with the ownership of his volumes, and treated them with the same respect and
care with which he would treat the rest of his "bien mondain". The
same attitude, after all, was shown by his brother Henry: if the books
listed in the latter's will are as carefully indicated as his most precious items of furniture, it means that he valued them as highly, at
least from the purely financial point of view.

In the absence of a catalogue or inventory, of even of satisfying
information on other traits of a prosperous private library such as
the employment, occasional or otherwise, of illuminators or book-
binders, the presence of Gloucester's ex-libris remains one of the
most important elements to trace back manuscripts to their owner.
The dispersal of the Duke's library after his death makes it difficult
to identify as his property a volume which does not bear a very
clear identification, in the form of an inscription, a motto or a dedication. However, even a cursory survey of the manuscripts bearing
such an ex-libris or an annotation concerning ownership tells us that
Italian humanists or "middlemen" were far from being the only
providers.[92] As a member of the royal family and one of the most
prominent political figures in early fifteenth-century England, Humphrey
of Gloucester would inevitably receive unsolicited presentation volumes, or dedications of new works (this seems to have been the case,
for instance, with John Capgrave's Biblical commentaries *In Genesim*
and *In Exodum*, which will be discussed in the following chapter); yet
this does not mean that he did not actively search books, or acquire
them by other means. If we only consider a list of donors, we may
note how diverse was their origin and probably their intention in
giving manuscripts to the Duke: the list includes Italian humanists
or intellectuals whose gifts were generally far from disinterested,
English writers or scholars looking for patrons, relatives or lesser
noblemen, Humphrey's own wife.[93] Italian humanists or middlemen

---

[91] Roberto Weiss, "Portrait of a Bibliophile XI: Humphrey, Duke of Gloucester,
d. 1447", *The Book Collector* 13: 1964, 161–70, p. 163.
[92] "Middlemen" is the term employed by Susanne Saygin in her book to describe
those Italian agents (generally prelates who held important functions in Anglo-Papal
politics) who helped Duke Humphrey to establish a connection with the leading
Italian humanists of his time.
[93] In his "Portrait of a Bibliophile XI: Humphrey, Duke of Gloucester, d. 1447",

are the most obvious source for humanist books;[94] but even in this field a glance at the English donors or givers may reserve a few surprises.

As we have seen in the previous paragraph, the Duke of Bedford gave his brother a number of French manuscripts that could be read for pleasure as well as for learning. We have some traces of the reading tastes shared by the two brothers: for instance, both seem to have been interested in geomancy, as well as medicine, and "Bedford also commissioned a long and elaborate *Summa* of physiognomy from Roland Scriptoris, the author of [Humphrey's] geomancy".[95] In giving him books in French, Bedford may have known he was indulging his brother's taste: if we believe what Humphrey writes in a letter to Alfonso V, the Duke preferred to read Livy in the French version his brother had given him rather than in the Latin original, though the 1443 donation to Oxford shows that he did possess the Latin text and even an epitome (also in Latin) of the same work.[96] This fondness for literature in French is also revealed in a letter by Antonio Beccaria to the Duke: the humanist, announcing the completion of his Latin translation of Boccaccio's work *Il Corbaccio*, praises (perhaps excessively) his patron's ability to read Latin and his curiosity for books in other languages, and with a few extravagant images gives a short sketch of Humphrey's reading habits:

> Verum etiam si quid est quod alieno sermone aliqua cum dignitate confectum sit, id etiam studere ac cognoscere non desistis. Omitto nunc gal[l]icas historias aut potius romanas eo sermone conscriptas, quas ita memoriter tenes, ut caeteros te audientes in tui admirationem atque stuporem saepius converteris, cum nulla res sit ex suis ac caeterarum

---

Roberto Weiss draws a somewhat inaccurate list of Humphrey's book-donors, though in some cases the manuscripts seem to have been given or sent to order. Among the donors Weiss lists John Capgrave, Jacqueline of Hainault, John, Duke of Bedford, Richard Beauchamp, Earl of Warwick, Lord Carew, Sir John Roos, Sir John Stanley, Zenone da Castiglione, Bishop of Bayeux, John Whethamstede, Andrew Holes, Pier Candido Decembrio, Pietro del Monte (p. 163). The list repeats the one presented in Weiss's *Humanism in England during the Fifteenth Century*, p. 61.

[94] Their role is amply discussed in Saygin, pp. 139–200. Since their contribution to Humphrey's library has occupied most recent scholarship on the Duke's patronage, I prefer to dedicate this section of the present volume to other, less known areas of patronage or book-collection.

[95] Carey, "Astrology at the English Court in the Late Middle Ages", p. 47. Humphrey's geomancy is now London, British Library, Ashmole 66.

[96] The letter is published in Sammut, pp. 215–6.

nationum rebus festis, quam non tibi notiorem esse constet quam vig-
ilantibus lyncis oculis orientem solem.[97]

The letter is couched in the usual flattering terms, yet Beccaria seems
to wish to avoid patent untruths: thus, when it comes to the Duke
reading Greek texts, the humanist adds "quae [. . .] tibi in latinam
linguam convertantur". The term *historiae* may equally well refer to
the Livy as to other manuscripts given to Humphrey by the Duke
of Bedford, such as *La quête du Saint Graal* and *La mort au roi Artus*,[98]
but may also apply to other volumes in Humphrey's library. *Le Songe
du Verger*, for instance, is a treatise of civil law presented under the
courtly form of a dream narrative. It may be added that Humphrey's
fondness for reading narratives in French (possibly in preference to
Latin, as the Pierre Bersuire translation of Livy demonstrates) is
shown also by other manuscripts in his library such as the *Chronique
de France ou de saint Denis*,[99] Laurent de Premierfait's version of
Boccaccio's *Decameron*,[100] *Le roman de Renart*,[101] Du Vignay's version of
Jacopo da Varazze's *Legenda Aurea*[102] or Frère Laurent's *La somme du
roi Philippe ou Somme des vices et des vertus*.[103] The little group of French
manuscripts might therefore give us an idea of Humphrey's reading
tastes. In all, twelve manuscripts in French have survived, plus a collection of the works of John Gower which is partly in French. Barker-
Benfield adds as a further proof of Humphrey's taste the fact that
the French manuscripts formed no part, as far as it is known, of
Humphrey's donation to the University of Oxford.[104] I would argue
that the choice of exclusively Latin manuscripts for the donation was

---

[97] "Yet if something worth perusing is in a foreign tongue, this does not stop
you from wishing to study and know it. I will not speak of those French histories,
or rather Latin histories translated into French, which you know by heart, so that
often you move listeners to wonder and admiration, since there is no notable event
of their own or other nations which is not known to you, more than the sunrise
to the attentive eyes of the lynx". The letter is published in Sammut, pp. 162–5
(this passage p. 163).

[98] Now Bruxelles, Bibliothèque Royale 9627–8.

[99] Now London, British Library, Royal 16 G.IV. The manuscript is described
in Sammut, pp. 106–7.

[100] Now Paris, Bibliothèque Nationale, franç. 12421. Described in Sammut,
p. 121.

[101] Now Paris, Bibliothèque Nationale, franç. 12583. Described in Sammut,
p. 121.

[102] Now Paris, Bibliothèque Mazarine, 1729. Described in Sammut, pp. 122–3.

[103] Now Reims, Bibliothèque Municipale, 570. Described in Sammut, pp. 123–4.

[104] Barker-Benfield, p. 193.

deliberate on the part of the Duke: Latin was the current language
of the university, and Latin were the texts the students and scholars were supposed to read, even if it must be admitted that donations to college or monastery libraries were often made with little
attention to this important detail.[105] In this case, Humphrey's linguistic choice would simply demonstrate his greater care in the choice
of the manuscripts to give to a university library, in comparison with
an average donor. On the other hand, Bedford's choice to give his
brother the manuscripts mentioned above would seem to show that
he knew Gloucester's tastes, from the point of view of both language
and literary genre, and that at least in some cases his gifts expressed
the intention to further his younger brother's desire for entertainment
by giving him narratives of a historical or allegorical character, as
well as straightforward romances. The French section of Humphrey's
library, however acquired, seems to have been also the most private
section, and the one he most willingly perused, and it was mostly
constituted by narratives, with a certain predilection for romances
and dream literature. Such predilection was shared not only by some
of the Benedictine monks of St Augustine's, as has been seen above,
but by other English arictocrats, and by kings: Richard II, for instance,
owned no less than three Arthurian romances, including Chrétien's
Conte del Graal.[106] Commenting on what survives of Humphrey's library,
Roberto Weiss discovers with apparent surprise that "neither poetry
nor plays were plentiful among his books, and possibly never exercised a strong appeal for him".[107] The observation is anachronistic—
dramatic writing, though representing possibly the most important
form of literary production in the fifteenth century, would have no
right of place in libraries for a long time yet, and the presence of
a play would be more surprising than the absence. We should rather

---

[105] As shown by David N. Bell in his exhaustive survey "Monastic Libraries:
1400–1557", quoted above. Evidence for donations to university libraries before
Duke Humphrey's is much scantier: see Elisabeth Leedham-Green, "University
Libraries and Book-sellers", in *The Cambridge History of the Book in Britain, vol. 3:
1400–1557*, ed. by L. Hellinga and J.B. Trapp, Cambridge: Cambridge University
Press, 1999: 316–53.

[106] On the popularity of French romances in fourteenth- and fifteenth-century
England, see Rosalind Field, "Romance in England, 1066–1400", in *The Cambridge
History of Medieval English Literature*, ed. by D. Wallace, Cambridge: Cambridge
University Press, 1999: 152–76.

[107] Weiss, *Humanism in England during the Fifteenth Century*, p. 68.

turn, for an indirect but very apt comment, to Italo Calvino, who wrote in the catalogue for an exhibition of books of chivalry:

> Il millennio che sta per chiudersi è stato il millennio del romanzo. Nei secoli XI, XII e XIII i romanzi di cavalleria furono i primi libri profani la cui diffusione marcò profondamente la vita delle persone comuni, e non soltanto dei dotti.[108]

Calvino, using also Dante's description of Paolo and Francesca reading the story of Lancelot in *Inferno* V, underlines the identification of chivalric romances and semi-historical narratives with a literature of entertainment that, far as it was from religious or devotional literature, constituted yet a genre that the upper and middle classes could both enjoy without any specific literary preoccupation; we might suppose Duke Humphrey to belong to this wide group of readers.

Within Humphrey's immediate family circle, another donor besides the Duke of Bedford was Humphrey's wife. As we have seen above, she gave him a manuscript that might have been written for the occasion, a copy of Albucasis sive Albukasem Khalaf Ebn Abbas Al-Zaharaiar's *Antidotarium per Lodaycum Tetrafarmacum e lingua arabica translatum*, a medical treatise translated into Latin in 1198.[109] What seems to have escaped scholarly attention is that another manuscript may have come from the Duchess. It is an autograph collection of the works of Nicholas of Clemanges; the ex-libris on f. 119v reads "Cest livre est a moy Homfrey duc de Gloucester du don maistre guill(aum)e Errard docteur en theologie chanoyne nostre dame de Rouen", but on f. 120r we read "Loyale et belle a Gloucester", a partial repetition of what we could read in the dedication of the *Antidotarium*.[110]

---

[108] "The millennium now drawing to a close has been the age of romance. In the eleventh, twelfth and thirteenth centuries the books of chivalry constituted the first lay literature which was widespread to the point of leaving a lasting impression on the life of those who were not especially concerned with the humanities". Italo Calvino, "Books of Chivalry—Libros de caballerias", in *Tesoros de España. Ten Centuries of Spanish Books. Catalogue of an Exhibition in the New York Public Library, October 12–December 30, 1985*, New York: The New York Public Library, 1985: 231–2, reprinted in *Perché leggere i classici*, Milano: Mondadori, 1995: 62–7.

[109] Listed in Lynn Thorndike and Pearl Kibre, *A Catalogue of Incipits of Medieval Scientific Writing in Latin*, Cambridge, Mass.: The Mediaeval Academy of America, 1963, p. 1284.

[110] The manuscript is now in Oxford, Bodleian Library, Hatton 36 (S.C. 4082), and is described in Sammut, pp. 113–4. David Rundle reads "Loyale et belle a Goucester" as simply Humphrey's motto ("Respect for the Dead: The Habits of

It seems probable that the manuscript was given from Clemanges to Errard, but though Humphrey's ex-libris demonstrates the provenance of the manuscript, it does not necessarily demonstrate that Errard was the actual donor, though the word *don* in this as in the other ex-libris obviously refers to a gift, and could not be confused with *dom* meant as Errard's title.[111] There remains a doubt on the identity of the *Duchesse* of the *Antidotarium* dedication. In listing Gloucester's book-donors, Roberto Weiss appears to assume that she is to be identified with the Duke's first wife, Jacqueline of Hainault,[112] but I would argue an identification with Eleanor Cobham as more probable, given the contents of the manuscript as well as the interest Eleanor seemed to have in her husband's intellectual pursuits: we know that Roger Bolingbroke, the Oxford scholar who was to be implicated in the Cobham scandal, was the author "of at least one treatise dedicated to the Duchess of Gloucester which gives a brief introduction to judicial astrology, including questions concerning how a man might die".[113] Humphrey's interest in medical books, as well as the most active stage of his policy as a book-collector and patron, belongs to a later phase of his life, and coincides with the ripening of his friendship with Gilbert Kymer, who was in the Duke's employment as medical advisor in the 1420s and became chancellor of the University for the first time in 1431; significantly, Humphrey began to show an active interest in the University by 1430, when he suggested some changes to the curriculum; his subsequent relations with the University often saw Kymer acting as an intermediary. The establishing of a time frame for Humphrey's medical interests, however, can only be very vague. Eleanor Cobham, whom Humphrey married in 1428 but had probably known much earlier, shared to a certain extent her husband's intellectual interests; the group that

Manuscript-collecting and the Dispersal of the Library of Humfrey, Duke of Gloucester", forthcoming in *Lost Libraries*).

[111] The formula used by Humphrey is nevertheless slightly ambiguous. One would expect a preposition such as *de* or *du* after the word *don*; there are also confusing instances such as the inscription "cest livre est a moy Homfrey duc de Gloucestre du don treschier en Dieu l'abbe de seint Alban" (Oxford, Corpus Christi College, 243, f. 197v), in which the expression "treschier en Dieu" would make more sense with reference to the giver, rather than to the gift.

[112] Weiss, "Portrait of a Bibliophile XI: Humphrey, Duke of Gloucester, d. 1447", p. 163.

[113] Carey, "Astrology at the English Court in the Late Middle Ages", p. 52. The manuscript is now Gloucester Cathedral 21.

was involved in the scandal that determined her downfall in 1441 included Roger Bolingbroke and Thomas Southwell, connected both with Gloucester and with the University of Oxford, where Southwell had graduated in medicine in 1423 and to whose faculty of medicine he still belonged. It may be said that the scientific coterie that gravitated around Duke Humphrey could very well include Eleanor Cobham; in this context a gift such as the *Antidotarium* makes more sense if coming from her hands. If, besides, we accept the inscription in the Nicholas de Clemanges manuscript as proof that this book came from the same donor (or possibly, in this case, an intermediary) as the *Antidotarium*, then in this case the donation can be no earlier than 1432, the year in which Errard became a canon in the church of Notre Dame in Rouen. By this time Jacqueline of Hainault was completely estranged from the Duke, and Eleanor was recognised as the new Duchess of Gloucester.

Other members of the Lancaster family (with a more or less close relationship) figure among Humphrey's donors, as is shown from the surviving manuscripts, even if we must remember that the word *cousin* that is to be found in some of Humphrey's ex-libris could refer simply, in English as in French, to another member of the nobility. One of them, and in some ways an interesting one, is Robert Roos, who gave Humphrey a volume including the French translation of Vegetius's *De Re Militari* by Jean de Vignay, together with a fragment of the French version of Aegidius Romanus's *De regimine principum* by Henry de Gauchi. In this case the inscription, at the end of the Vegetius section, reads "Cest livre est a moy Homfrey duc de Gloucestre du don mess. Robert Roos Chevalier mon cousin".[114] Another proof of the closeness between the Duke and Robert Roos may be given by a manuscript containing a French version of the anonymous Latin treatise *De administratione principum*;[115] while on f. 2r we read a variation upon Humphrey's usual ex-libris, "Mon bien mondain Gloucestre

---

[114] Originally, however, it was a larger manuscript, so it might have included the entire translation of *De regimine principum*. The manuscript is now Cambridge University Library, Ee. 2. 17. See its description in Sammut, pp. 100–1. See also Charles F. Briggs, *Giles of Rome's De Regimine Principum. Reading and Writing Politics at Court and University, c. 1275–c. 1525*, Cambridge: Cambridge University Press, 1999, pp. 65–6; Briggs also describes the manuscript, pp. 153–4.

[115] Now London, British Library, Royal 19.a.XX (described in Sammut, p. 107). According to Sammut, the treatise was translated into French by the Carmelite friar Jehan Golein or Goulain for Charles V.

au duc", on f. 152v we read "Ce livre de linformacion des princes est a moy Robert Roos chivaler". It is not clear whether one of the two noblemen donated it to the other, but the double inscription is at least proof that the manuscript passed from the one to the other. Robert Roos, as well as being related to the Duke, may have formed part of his intellectual coterie, and may have used the books in Humphrey's library.[116] The family connection was somewhat distant—Eleanor Cobham was related to Robert's wife—but the use of the term *cousin* suggests a certain closeness, even if not necessarily a blood relation. A copy of the *Livre des seyntez medicines* was donated to Humphrey by Thomas Carew, a statesman and soldier who had always been a strong supporter of the Lancaster (the author of the treatise, Henry of Lancaster, was also Humphrey's great-grandfather, since he was Blanche Chaucer's father, and was also inserted in John Capgrave's *De Illustribus Henricis*);[117] in this case, we know that the manuscript must have been donated before 1430, the year of Thomas Carew's death.[118] The first page of the manuscript has an illuminated border decorated with seven escutcheons, one of which can be identified with the arms of Beauchamp, Earl of Warwick.[119] In this case the value of the volume probably resided in the fact that the author had been the first Duke of Lancaster. The editor of the modern edition even hypothesises that the copy given to Humphrey, composed in the fourteenth century, was a "family copy", that is,

---

[116] Ethel Seaton supposes that Robert's son Richard formed also part of Humphrey's intellectual circle, and composed poetry now attributed to John Lydgate, to Geoffrey Chaucer, and even sonnets and other short pieces now attributed to Thomas Wyatt. Apart from these sometimes far-fetched suppositions, her study is an interesting exploration of intellectual life in the Lancastrian court. See Ethel Seaton, *Sir Richard Roos (c. 1410–1482), Lancastrian Poet*, London: Rupert Hart-Davis, 1961. I have discussed Ethel Seaton's contribution in chapter 1 of the present volume. However, according to Douglas Gray's contribution to the *Dictionary of National Biography*, Richard was the son not of Robert but of William Roos, who died in 1414.

[117] *Johannis Capgrave Liber de Illustribus Henricis*, ed. by F.C. Hingeston, Rolls Series, London: Longman, Brown, Green, Longmans, and Roberts, 1858, p. 161.

[118] The manuscript is now in Stonyhurst College, Lancashire. A description can be found in Sammut, p. 101. There is some uncertainty as concerns the year of Carew's death; the *Dictionary of National Biography* opts for 1430 or '31. The *Livre* is now published as *Le Livre des Seyntz Medicines. The Unpublished Devotional Treatise of Henry of Lancaster*, ed. by E.J.F. Arnould, Anglo-Norman Text Society, Oxford: Blackwell, 1940. For a biography of the author and a presentation of the work, see Arnould, "Henry of Lancaster and his *Livre des seintez medicines*", *Bulletin of the John Rylands Library* 21: 1937, 352–86.

[119] Arnould, ed., *Le Livre des Seyntz Medicines*, p. ix.

written under Henry of Lancaster's supervision, or in any case a direct copy of the original.[120] The Earl of Warwick in his turn, once again mentioned in Humphrey's ex-libris as "mon treschier cousin" gave him a French version of Boccaccio's *Decameron*, a volume which forms part of that small but significant group of narratives in French that Humphrey apparently kept in his library even after the munificent Oxford donations. We should probably follow Roberto Weiss[121] in identifying the Earl of Warwick mentioned in the ex-libris with Richard de Beauchamp (1382–1439), who was a follower of Henry IV and then of Henry V, Lord High Steward at the latter's coronation, and then named deputy of Calais (in this capacity he undertook a number of diplomatic missions for the King). Beauchamp took part in the French wars, receiving the surrender of Caen Castle in 1417, and being a protagonist during the siege of Rouen in 1418 and of Melun in 1420. He was also one of the guardians appointed during the minority of Henry VI. A proximity with the Duke of Gloucester is therefore easy to deduce, though there is no indication of the Earl of Warwick having been a great or discriminating patron of arts.

It can be seen that donors who were somewhat related to Humphrey did not choose to give him texts that might be put in relation with the new, humanist learning, though of course it might be argued that the wide range of interests shown by the books we have listed so far already constitutes a humanist trait,[122] if Pier Candido Decembrio, in his prologue to the seventh book of his version of Plato's *Politics*, could work it into a flattering remark for the Duke:

> Nam et musice disciplinam et gymnastice, ut intelligo, sic una imiscuisti et in anima vicissim moderate contulisti, ut verus et perfectus musicus pre cunctis habere. Neque notus, ut Plato inquit, sed iustus et legitimus princeps sis omnino, quippe qui in laborum cura ac stu-

---

[120] Arnould, ed., *Le Livre des Seyntz Medicines*, p. xi. In a study devoted to the book, Arnould writes of this manuscript that it "a toute l'apparence d'un exemplar de famille. Son exécution artistique et la qualité de son texte font présumer qu'il est proche de l'original et peut être daté d'environ 1360" ("has all the outward appearance of a family manuscript. Its artistic execution and the quality of the text make me think that it is close to the original, and possibly dated around 1360". E.J.F. Arnould, *Étude sur le Livre des saintes médecines du duc Henry de Lancastre*, Paris: Didier, 1948, p. lxx).

[121] "Portrait of a Bibliophile XI: Humphrey, Duke of Gloucester, d. 1447", p. 163.

[122] See Barker-Benfield, p. 193.

diorum non claudus mancusve sed rectus atque integer cum gymna-
siorum venationumque sis cupidus, ac militiam abunde tueris, non
minus tamen legendi et audiendi veritatemque inquirendi curam habes,
nec ad veritatem dignoscendam tuam aiemus animam errare, que spon-
taneum mendacium odio susceperit graviter que se mentiri ferat, tum
aliis quoque mentientibus permaxime succenseat.[123]

On the other hand, these particular donors' choices may also go to
show that Humphrey was a real innovator, since, though continuing the Lancastrian tradition of book-collection and intellectual patronage, he decided to turn his attention, at least in part, to the new
works produced by Italian humanists: one important difference between
Humphrey's library and that of his brothers is that neither Henry
V's nor the Duke of Bedford's collections included humanist texts.
The same can be noted if we consider Humphrey's donations to
Oxford: "though humanist texts are not numerically the largest components in his gift, they do not figure at all in the libraries of his
brothers, Henry V and John, Duke of Bedford. Some of Humfrey's
manuscripts later served as exemplars for copyists in England".[124]

But it must also be noted that not all humanist texts in Humphrey's
possession were given him by Italian scholars or middlemen. A copy
of Coluccio Salutati's *De laboribus Herculis*, for instance, bears on f.
179v the inscription "Cest livre est a moy Homfrey duc de Gloucester
du don [maistre An]-drew Holes".[125] Probably Holes bought the manuscript in Florence, where he lived from 1439 to 1444. A Fellow of
New College in 1414–20 and then a king's proctor at the Papal
Curia, Holes studied canon law in Padua and thus came in touch
with a number of Italian humanists. More difficult to establish is his
link with Duke Humphrey: Holes may have been a protégé of Thomas
Bekynton, who in his turn had been in Duke Humphrey's service

---

[123] "You bring together and alternate in moderation the disciplines of music and
gymnastics, so as to be a perfect and prominent musician. You thus are not simply a well-known prince, as Plato says, but a just and honest one, since in your
work and study you are not lame or defective but correct and virtuous, as you love
exercise and hunting, and devote yourself to the art of war, you are no less devoted
to reading and listening to the truth, and we won't say you fail in recognising the
truth, and you have a natural hate of lying and detect it immediately, feeling rage
at those who lie". The prologue is transcribed in Sammut, pp. 209–11 (this quotation pp. 210–1).

[124] Trapp, "Literacy, Books and Readers", p. 295.

[125] Biblioteca Apostolica Vaticana, Urbinate lat. 694. The manuscript is described
in Sammut, pp. 123–4.

as Chancellor in 1420. Bekynton was later to recognise Humphrey
as a lifelong benefactor—it is thus possible that he put the possible
patron and the young scholar in touch. In another case, there is a
manuscript containing Francesco Petrarca's *De remediis utriusque fortunae* and including also Pietro Paolo Vergerio's *Vita Petrarce*, which
Humphrey was given by Nicholas Bildeston, as attested by an inscription on f. 5r, "Cest livre est a moy Homfrey duc de Gloucestre [du
don mai]stre Nichol Bildeston doian de Salisbury".[126] While Andrew
Holes may have been needing Humphrey's patronage, Bildeston
seems to have already acquired a powerful patron in the Bishop of
Winchester, Henry Beaufort, whose Chancellor he was. Bildeston
was also a friend of Poggio Bracciolini, and in the 1420s, while in
Rome, had bought, following Niccolò Niccoli's advice, a number of
classical and Petrarchan texts.[127] So in this case the manuscript donation to Humphrey may have had different motivations, but it is interesting to observe how both givers decided that the donation of a
humanist's text or collection of texts may have pleased the prospective patron. If scholars like Andrew Holes, rather than noblemen
like Duke Humphrey, were the true link between Italian and English
humanism, as David Rundle maintains,[128] then we must conclude
that they also saw in the Duke of Gloucester a natural receptacle
for learned dedications or donations. J.L. Trapp reconstructs the
interesting history of this manuscript, noting the conventional portrait of the Italian writer and what he considers a gothic hand,
though the manuscript was written in Italy.[129] Trapp supposes that
Bildeston had this volume transcribed in Italy. As for its being a gift
to Humphrey, Trapp presumes it to have been extorted, as might
have happened in royal circles.[130]

To the manuscript of Petrarca's *De remediis* just described we must
add another manuscript which passed from Bildeston to the Duke
of Gloucester, a text whose history has been recently reconstructed

---

[126] Paris, Bibliothèque Nationale, lat. 10209. The manuscript is described in
Sammut, pp. 119–20. Bildeston was dean of Salisbury from 1435 until his death
in 1441.
[127] See Rundle, "Humanism before the Tudors", p. 25.
[128] See Rundle's "Humanism before the Tudors".
[129] Sammut instead believes the hand to be "umanistica libraria italiana" (p. 119).
[130] J.B. Trapp, "Il libro umanistico tra Italia e Inghilterra dal '400 al primo '500",
Scrittura e civiltà 22: 1998, 319–37, pp. 323–4.

by David Rundle.[131] The manuscript, now Cambridge, Gonville and Caius 183/216, is an Italian copy of Seneca's *Epistulae*, probably dating to the early fifteenth century. The ex-libris on f. 151r reads: "Cest livre est A moy humfrey duc de gloucestre le quel Je achatay des executres maistre Nichol bildeston jadis doyen de salisbury". We shall see presently another case in which Humphrey bought manuscripts from testamentary executors. Bildeston died in 1441, which gives us an approximate date for Humphrey's acquisition.

Another English donor, and a man who seems to have enjoyed a close friendship with the Duke was John Whethamstede, the abbot of St Albans who in his turn befriended Italian humanists such as Pietro del Monte, and who knew Leonardo Bruni's work. Whethamstede is also inserted in that list of friends of Humphrey, or members of his *familia*, who work in his Greenwich library together with the anonymous translator in the latter's version of Palladius's *De Re Rustica*: "Whethamstede, and also Pers de Mounte, Titus, and Anthony."[132] Among the surviving manuscripts in Sammut's list we may notice a copy of the *Historia Anglorum* by Matthaeus Parisiensis, together with the last part of the *Chronica Majora 1254–9*, which was probably given to him by Whethamstede.[133] There is also another manuscript that has survived, a miscellaneous collection of philosophical, medical and astrological texts including Albertus Magnus's *De divinatione*, Raymond de Marseille's *Liber cursum planetarum* and Aristotelian or pseudo-Aristotelian texts, together with medieval translations of Plato's *Phaedo* and *Meno*, as well as a commentary on Timaeus.[134] In this case the provenance can be established with more certainty, since the ex-libris on f. 197v reads "Cest livre est a moy Homfrey duc de Gloucestre du don treschier en Dieu l'abbe de seint Albon". Whethamstede also gave Humphrey a copy of his own *Granarium de viris illustribus*, which then formed part of the last Oxford

---

[131] Rundle, "Two Unnoticed Manuscripts from the Collection of Humfrey, Duke of Gloucester". Rundle describes the manuscript on pp. 299–301.

[132] *The Middle-English Translation of Palladius De Re Rustica*, ed. by M. Liddel, Berlin: E. Ebering, 1896, ll. 102–3. The list, besides Whethamstede, includes Pietro del Monte, Tito Livio Frulovisi and Antonio Beccaria.

[133] The manuscript is now London, British Library, Royal 14 C. VII. Described in Sammut, p. 106.

[134] Now Oxford, Corpus Christi College, 243. Described in Sammut, pp. 115–6. See also Hilary M. Carey, *Courting Disaster. Astrology at the English Court and University in the Later Middle Ages*, London: Macmillan, 1992, p. 55.

donation: in the list the three volumes of the work are registered as
"granarium Johannis de Loco Frumenti".[135] On the other hand, it
is unclear what John Leland saw "Oxoniae in bibliotheca publica"
in the sixteenth century, since in his list we read "Granarium, ingens
volumen, Joannis de Loco Frumenti: Whethamsted, abbatis S. Albani,
ad Humfredum, ducem Gloucestriae, de viris illustribus".[136] The
description might refer to the above-mentioned *Granarium*, rebound
to form one volume, or it might refer to another manuscript now
in the Bodleian (Auct. F. inf. 1.1), a copy of Valerius Maximus's *De
dictis et factis memorabilibus* which did belong to Whethamstede (and
was possibly composed in his abbey) but which Sammut does not
put among the manuscript that can be considered with some certainty to have belonged to Humphrey.[137]

Barker-Benfield thus underlines the many analogies between Humphrey and Whethamstede:

> Whethamstede, a sophisticated product of the monastic and university
> tradition, cheerfully maintained his ornate Latin style and "medieval"
> cast of mind in spite of correspondence with Pietro del Monte and
> visits to Italy; the same catholicity enabled Duke Humphrey to act as
> patron to Bruni and Decembrio in Italy and to Lydgate and Capgrave
> at home.[138]

The nature of Whethamstede's gift to Humphrey seems to confirm
this interpretation. The Duke showed equal appreciation for a medieval
and a humanist translation of Plato, only in the latter case the value
of the text was enhanced by the fact that the translation was made
(almost) to order. A gift, obviously, may reveal much about the donor
and very little about the receiver; yet the friendship between the two
in this case seems to have been lasting and of an intellectual nature,
and, as in the case of the Duke of Bedford, the abbot may have
had a fairly accurate idea of what Humphrey would appreciate. We
shall see in the following chapter how Whethamstede's friendship
was heartily reciprocated by gifts in kind on the part of the Duke,
and this may throw further light on the (often discussed) intellectual

---

[135] Items 63, 64 and 65 of the list published in *Epistolae Academicae Oxonienses* and
reprinted in Sammut, pp. 72–84.

[136] Leland's list, first appearing in *Ioannis Leland Antiquarii de Rebus Britannicis
Collectanea*, ed. by T. Hearnius, III, Oxoniae 1715, pp. 58–9, is also reprinted in
Sammut, pp. 95–7. For all references to Leland, I use Sammut's version of the list.

[137] See Sammut, p. 132.

[138] Barker-Benfield, p. 194.

circle forming around the Duke of Gloucester and possibly centring upon his library. I should like to note at this point Weiss's comment on Whethamstede's intellectual activity: he was "one of the last of the English mediaeval polymaths rather than one of the early English humanists".[139] It may be added that in those historical and cultural circumstances the difference is extremely tenuous.

Sometimes books were not given but otherwise acquired: as in the case of the copy of Seneca's *Epistulae* described above, in some of the surviving manuscripts the addition to the usual formula of the ex-libris seems to indicate that Humphrey bought the volume; an instance is the *Chronique de France ou de saint Denis*, in which the ex-libris on f. 445r reads "Cest livre est a moy Homfrey duc de Gloucestre du don les executeurs le seigneur de Faunhope".[140] John Chandos, Earl of Fawnhope, died in 1428. Sammut infers from the ex-libris that Chandos was the donor, but it is at least equally probable that Humphrey bought the volume from the testamentary executors. In this case the choice of a French chronicle would confirm our previous reflection on Humphrey's literary tastes. A similar instance, only more clearly defined as an acquisition, can be seen in the case of a miscellaneous volume, where the ex-libris, on f. 192v, reads "Cest livre est a moy Homfrey duc de Gloucestre le quel j'achetay des executeurs maistre Thomas Polton feu eveque de Wurcestre".[141] The Bishop of Worcester died in 1433. Three manuscripts are perhaps too little to assume that Humphrey made a practice of buying books from testamentary executors; David Rundle, taking into considerations only the two manuscripts coming from the surviving property of Bildeston and Polton, notes that both former owners were in somewhat friendly terms with the Duke, and decides to downplay the possibility of an interest in the actual manuscripts on the part of the buyer:

> Might it be that Humfrey's purchases from executors were a way of paying back service done to him by their former owners? In other words, could it be that these purchases were a method of showing respect to the dead? It might be objected that the decision to buy a manuscript should be governed by the desirability of its text; even if that were the case, Humfrey's indulging of his penchant for a detailed

[139] Weiss, *Humanism in England during the Fifteenth Century*, p. 38.
[140] London, British Library, Royal 16 G. VI. Described in Sammut, pp. 106–7.
[141] London, British Library, Cotton Nero E. V. Described in Sammut, p. 108.

ex-libris in each of these instances suggests he was willing to remember his acquisitions by association with its previous owner.[142]

It seems to me that in this case the scholar's desire to reduce the impact of Humphrey's patronage on early English humanism has made him prefer an improbable possible to the quite plausible possibility that the Duke was interested in the texts he was buying. The French chronicle and the classical Latin texts correspond to analogous choices Humphrey made in other cases. It is worth noting that he should be particularly interested in the miscellany formerly belonging to Thomas Polton, since this collection includes the Acts of the Council of Constance. In the previous chapters the importance of this Council has been already underlined, both as concerns its political and religious implications and as an occasion for a number of humanists and their perspective patrons to get in touch with each other, as was the case with Poggio Bracciolini and the Bishop of Winchester. We still lack a comprehensive study of the cultural implications of the Council; but it is fair to say that it provided the occasion and a great incentive for the transmission of humanist thought to northern Europe. In the case of this particular manuscript, however, we may assume that the interest for the Duke of Gloucester was more political than intellectual; as A.C. De La Mare writes,

> Thomas Polton, elected Bishop of Worcester in 1426, died at Basel, where he was attending the Council, on 23 August 1433. Duke Humfrey was one of his executors. Polton had earlier been at the Roman Curia from *c*. 1394, when he became a papal chaplain, and he attended the Council of Constance, where he was the main English representative on the Secretariat of the Council. In 1417 he was the principal protagonist in the struggle by the English to maintain their privileges and position at the Council as a separate "nation".[143]

In thus acquiring what De La Mare considers "one of the most complete collections of the general *acta* of the Council, which lasted from 1414 to 1418",[144] Humphrey probably meant to pursue the question of the independence of English home policy from the interference of the Papal curia, a question that had provoked serious dissension

---

[142] Rundle, "Two Unnoticed Manuscripts from the Collection of Humfrey, Duke of Gloucester", p. 305.

[143] A.C. De la Mare, "Manuscripts Given to the University of Oxford by Humfrey, Duke of Gloucester", *The Bodleian Library Record* 13: 1988, 30–51, 112–21, p. 114.

[144] De La Mare, p. 114.

during Henry V's reign, particularly with the Bishop of Winchester, as we have seen in chapter 3.

Little information can be drawn from the remaining extant manuscripts, always excluding those given by or commissioned to Italian humanists. A copy of Pierre Le Manguer's *La Bible Historiée ou Les histoires écolâtres* is notable for a particularly verbose ex-libris on f. 511r: "Le dixiesme jour de septembre l'an mil quatre cens vingt et sept fut cest livre donné a tres hault et tres puissant prince Humfrey, duc de Gloucestre, conte de Haynnau, Hollande, etc., protecteur et difenseur d'Engleterre, par sire Jehan Stanley, chevalier, ledit prince estant en l'abbaye Nostre Dame a Chestre".[145] More interesting is a twelfth-century Hebrew psalter with Latin *marginalia* in an English gothic hand, registered in a catalogue of the abbey of St Augustine, in Canterbury, with the indication "in manibus ducis Glocestrie perditur".[146] The manuscript is splendidly illuminated, which might explain why Humphrey took it from the abbey library (and since *perditur* maintains in the late Middle Ages the connotation of disapproval it has in classical Latin, the choice of the verb evokes an image of Humphrey stealing books from a library like many a modern reader). On the other hand, it must be noted that among the extant manuscripts belonging to the Duke there is another psalter, this time in Latin, with an ex-libris giving Humphrey's full titles but no indication of how he acquired the book,[147] and a volume with extracts from the Latin psalter, presumably commissioned by Humphrey himself who chose the extracts, if we interpret the ex-libris correctly: "Cest livre est a moy Homfrey duc de Gloucestre des seaulmes les quelx *jay esleus* du sautier".[148] The presence, on f. 8, of a devotional image representing the Duke "presented by St Alban to Christ as Man of Sorrows in a Trinitarian context"[149] reinforces the impression of a volume he commissioned and whose setting and illumination he, to a certain extent, supervised. Analysing this image, Nigel Morgan writes:

---

[145] Paris, Bibliothèque Nationale, franç. 2. Described in Sammut, pp. 120–1.

[146] "It fell in the hands of the Duke of Gloucester". Leiden, Bibliotheek der Rijksuniversiteit, Or. 4726. The manuscript is described in Sammut, pp. 101–2, with references to the St Augustine catalogue.

[147] London, British Library, Yates Thompson, 14. Described in Sammut, p. 109.

[148] London, British Library, Royal 2 B. I. Described in Sammut, pp. 104–5. Italics mine.

[149] Nigel Morgan, "Patrons and Devotional Images in English Art of the International

Duke Humphrey's scroll is affirming his belief that he is the recipient of the love of Christ as the suffering Man of Sorrows. The image is combined with that of the Trinity which probably signifies the freely given love of God imparted through the grace of the Holy Spirit. The Duke's scroll has the words "Your pity (*pietas*) O Lord has been worked in me" implying the effects of Christ's suffering in his passion and the effects of the grace which that sacrifice has given to humanity. There is also a eucharistic element in the blood flowing from the Man of Sorrows into a chalice with a Host above.[150]

It may be added the both the choice of psalms and some details of the image on f. 8 (such as Christ's blood flowing into a chalice containing the host), as well as of other images, are unique to this manuscript, which is a clear indication of the patron deciding the structure and the details of the text. As Kathleen Scott observes:

> A patron capable of selecting his own anthology of psalms would also have been able to initiate instructions for the concepts that he wished to see expressed in an introductory picture, and it is quite likely that Duke Humfrey did so here [. . .] Although the presence of an active, knowledgeable patron caused displacement on this book, it also increased rather than depleted the pictorial rewards.[151]

It may be noted that the burial chamber of Duke Humphrey in St Albans Abbey, built around 1442, had on its eastern wall a painting of the crucifixion, in which four chalices collected water and blood from Christ's wounds—in this case, too, the Duke, being buried in the chamber, would find himself at Christ's feet.[152] Three versions of the psalter in a collection in which no other book of the Bible survives are a lot; besides, the 1439 donation to Oxford includes a psalter which, though it has not survived, does not seem to coincide with any of those mentioned above,[153] while the 1443 donation

Gothic c. 1350–1450", in *Reading Texts and Images. Essays on Medieval and Renaissance Art and Patronage*, ed. B.J. Muir, Exeter: University of Exeter Press, 2002: 93–121, p. 100.

[150] Morgan, p. 100. Everest-Phillips suggests that the emblem on the Duke's robe refers to the foliage of his heraldic badge (p. 346).

[151] Scott, "*Caveat Lector*: Ownership and Standardization in the Illustration of Fifteenth-Century English Manuscripts", p. 29.

[152] The painting is now almost completely faded, but the details have been reconstructed from eighteenth-century antiquarian pictures. See Jane Kelsall, *Humphrey Duke of Gloucester, 1391–1447*, St Albans: The Friends of Saint Albans Abbey, 2000, p. 14.

[153] As shown by the "secundo folio" evidence.

Fig. 2. Duke Humphrey kneeling before Christ as Man of Sorrows.

Fig. 3. Tomb of Duke Humphrey.

includes Nicholas Trevet's commentary on the psalter (in this case the donation, however, includes other commentaries on other biblical texts). Psalms were often inserted in books of private devotions, and psalters would be among the most frequented books of the Bible for private perusal, but in this case there seems to be a decided preference on the part of the Duke, particularly in the case of the Hebrew psalter, since it is inconceivable that Humphrey could read the language; perhaps the beauty of the manuscript in this case motivated the Duke's desire. The Duke's much discussed bibliophilia (if we use the term in its etymological sense) is more in evidence here than with many humanist volumes.

The question of the Hebrew psalter leads us to consider another issue connected with Humphrey's library—namely, the languages in which the books in his possession were written. The book donations to Oxford, as we have already seen, included only manuscripts in Latin, with the partial exception of a volume described in the University document as "verba greca et interpretaciones lingue latine", and explained by Weiss as "probably one of those medieval etymological compilations which were almost as far removed from Greek scholarship as Humphrey himself was".[154] Latin is evidently considered by Humphrey not only the language spoken at the University, but also a language particularly apt for the transmission of culture and of relatively new works coming from the rest of Europe: this explains the inclusion, for instance, of Giovanni da Serravalle's Latin translation of and commentary on Dante's *Divina Commedia* in the 1443 donation to Oxford. The list referring to this donation includes two volumes, oddly placed at some distance from each other (while the various volumes of works by Petrarch, for instance, or by Boccaccio are generally placed together): one is called *commentaria Dantis*, the other *librum Dantis*. Their presence deserves further discussion.

Giovanni Bertoldi da Serravalle, Bishop of Firmano, was a Franciscan who attended the Council of Constance. The Council dragged on for four years, and it is conceivable that between sessions the participants had more than one occasion to meet and discuss not only the issues of the Council, but also a number of other topics. Serravalle befriended two Englishmen, Nicholas Bubwith, Bishop of Bath and Wells, and Robert Hallum, Bishop of Salisbury, and, possibly at their

---

[154] Weiss, *Humanism in England during the Fifteenth Century*, p. 63.

prompting, possibly inspired by his own admiration for the Italian poet, he decided to translate the *Commedia* into Latin for their benefit, and completed the work, together with a Latin commentary, in 1416. In the incipit to the commentary, Serravalle declared that the work was undertaken "ad preceptum et instantiam" of the two Englishmen.[155] It must be added that the commentary was not very successful in Italy, and is still underestimated by Dante scholars, but it marks the fifteenth-century diffusion of Dante in England, and indeed in northern Europe. Both English Bishops were connected with Oxford (Hallum, who died before the conclusion of the Council, was Chancellor of the University, while Bubwith may have studied at Oxford, and in his will left money both for the poor priests studying at Oxford and for the building of a new cathedral library at Wells).[156] Their connection with Oxford may have been the means through which Duke Humphrey heard of the existence of a Dante translation and commentary and decided to acquire a copy, which he subsequently donated to the University library. Another possible link might have been Thomas Bekynton, who had been Duke Humphrey's Chancellor before becoming Bishop of Bath and Wells, and who was to recognise the Duke as a lifelong benefactor. Serravalle's commentary (whether Humphrey's actual manuscript or another copy) was still in Oxford in the sixteenth century, since John Leland includes in his catalogue "commentarii Joannis de Seravala, episcopi Firmani, ordinis Minorum, Latine scripti, super opera Dantis Aligerii, ad Nicolaum Bubwice, Bathon. et Wellensem episcopum, et D. Robertum Halam, episcopum, Sarisbur. Commentarii editi sunt tempore Constantiensis concilii". Leland's use of the word *commentarii*, like the *commentaria* appearing in the 1443 list, suggests more than one volume; we may perhaps accept Paget Toynbee's hypothesis that the word *commentaria* included both Serravalle's commentary and his translation— and indeed, one would not have made sense without the other.[157]

---

[155] For a full account of the undertaking of the translation and commentary see David Wallace, "Dante in Somerset: Ghosts, Historiography, Periodization", in *New Medieval Literatures 3*, ed. by D. Lawton, W. Scase and R. Copeland, Oxford: Oxford University Press, 1999: 9–38, p. 13. Another dedicatee of the work was Cardinal Amedeo of Saluzzo. It may be noted that a copy of Serravalle's commentary written in what appears to be a fifteenth-century English hand is to be found in London, British Library, Egerton 2629.

[156] Wallace, "Dante in Somerset", pp. 14–5.

[157] Paget Toynbee, "The Dante MSS. presented to Oxford by Duke Humphrey",

Serravalle's work was meant as a popularisation of what he evidently considered a major work of poetry; Dante's choice of the vernacular would otherwise have condemned the book to a limited diffusion. In translating Dante to make it more accessible, as David Wallace correctly observes, "Bertoldi thus effects a neat reversal of roles habitually accorded to vernacularity and *latinitas*: Latin here assumes the role of a vernacular (a language of everyday speech) in shaping to serve an illustrious mother tongue".[158] Once in England, moreover, the Latin version would acquire yet another layer of meaning, since the enforcement of Arundel's Constitutions would make the Latin language of the book its only passport: "the Latinity which Bertoldi employed to popularize (among a clerical élite) could also serve as a veil to obscure the view of a wider English populace".[159]

What is Humphrey's role in this complex transaction? The lists of the Oxford donations reveal a particular curiosity on the part of the Duke regarding late-medieval Italian writers: Petrarch and Boccaccio are extensively represented, together with a number of minor authors—but in most cases, the works listed were originally written in Latin, as is the case with the numerous works by Petrarch. However, in the case of the Italian Boccaccio, Humphrey's curiosity seems to have been awakened more than with the less known Italian Petrarch: not only did he possess Laurent de Premierfait's French version of the *Decameron*, as we have seen above, and a number of Boccaccio's Latin works (the 1443 donation includes what is now considered the later, humanist part of his work, as opposed to the medieval *Decameron*: erudite works such as *Genealogia deorum gentilium*, *De casibus virorum illustrium*, *De mulieribus claris* and *De montibus, silvis, fontibus, lacubus, fluminibus, stagnis et paludibus, et de nominibus maris*) but he also commissioned a translation of the *Corbaccio* to Antonio Beccaria. As Antonio Beccaria writes in the prologue to his translation, written in the form of a letter to the Duke:

> Sensisti enim Bocacium, virum ingenio et doctrina praeditum, librum quendam adversum mulieres in suo sermone edidisse, eundem etiam ut intelligeres affectasti, iussistique, ut tibi in lucem latinae linguae

---

The Times Literary Supplement, 18 March 1920, 187. See also Toynbee's *Dante in English Literature from Chaucer to Cary (c. 1380–1844)*, London: Methuen, 1909.

[158] Wallace, "Dante in Somerset", p. 16.

[159] Wallace, "Dante in Somerset", p. 21.

traducerem, non ut adversum mulieres aliquo concitareris odio, sed ut
viri illius ingenium in hoc quoque dicendi genere prospicere posses, et
perspectum laudares quo nihil potest esse praestantius. Quod quidem
ut tuae parerem voluntati, eo libentius feci, quo videbam rem tibi
gratissimam ac iocundissimam [me] facturum ob eam maxime, quam
in literarum studia caritatem geris. Feci igitur ut iussisti, serenissime
princeps, hacque opera mea Bocacium ipsum et tibi et mihi obliga-
tum reddidisti: tibi in primis, quod sic iussisti, mihi vero quod tibi
paruerim, atque eius librum latinae linguae splendorem illustrarim fecer-
imque immortalem.[160]

Beccaria's concluding sentence in this passage somewhat echoes
Serravalle's intention in translating the *Commedia*: the Latin version
makes the Italian original more accessible, and even (though this
sentiment seems to belong to Beccaria but not to the humbler Serravalle) more splendid. It is worth noting that the manuscript preserving the Latin *Corbaccio* (though undoubtedly an apograph, and
not Humphrey's original volume) includes also Leonardo Bruni's
Latin translation of the first *novella* of the fourth *giornata* of the
Decameron, narrating the love of Tancredi's daughter for the humble
Guiscardo, and her father's terrible punishment of the lovers. It is
difficult to say whether this later manuscript is a faithful copy of
the earlier one, belonging to Humphrey, or whether the fifteenth-
century English scribe copied from Humphrey's manuscript only the
Latin version of the *Corbaccio*. If the former hypothesis were true,
the collection of amorous tales accompanying Boccaccio's texts (including Petrarch's story of Griselda, and Piccolomini's *De duobus aman-
tibus*)[161] would give us an interesting indication on the Duke's literary
tastes, and would help us understand some of the allusions in Thomas

---

[160] "You heard that Boccaccio, a man of great wit and knowledge, had written
a book against women in his own tongue, and wishing to understand it, you ordered
it to be translated into Latin, not to generate hate against women, but so that you
could understand the wit of this man in any manner of writing, and having understood it you could praise what was worth praising. To obey your will, I did it willingly, because I saw it was delightful to you, since you take pleasure in literary
studies. So I did as you had ordered, noble prince, and translated Boccaccio for
you and myself: for you first, since you had ordered it, but for myself too, since I
saw clearly that I had obeyed you and shown the wonder of this book in Latin,
and made it immortal". Oxford, Bodleian Library, Lat. Misc. d. 34, ff. 5v–6r. The
prologue is also edited in Sammut, pp. 162–5.
[161] On this point see also Julia Boffey and A.S.G. Edwards, "Literary Texts", in
The Cambridge History of the Book in Britain, vol. 3: 1400–1557, ed. by L. Hellinga and
J.B. Trapp, Cambridge: Cambridge University Press, 1999, 555–75, p. 571.

Hoccleve's *Dialogue*, in which the poet discusses with a friend the subject he should choose in order to write something for the Duke; after taking into consideration and discarding a number of possibilities, the friend says:

Thow wost wel/on wommen greet wyt[e] & lak
Ofte haast thow put/Be waar/lest thow be qwit.
Thy wordes fille wolde a quarter sak
Which thow in whyt/depeynted haast with blak.
In hir repreef/mochil thyng haast thow write
That they nat foryeue haue/ne foryite.

'Sumwhat now wryte in honour & preysynge
Of hem/so maist thow do correccioun
Sumdel of thyn offense and misberynge.[162]

The idea that the Duke might appreciate this choice of subject probably derives from precise knowledge of the patron's taste on the part of the poet. This also tallies with Piccolomini's description of the Duke, quoted in the previous chapter, as "homo non tam armis quam plumis et libidinibus aptus".[163] Apparently this aptness extended also to his favourite reading. It is likewise significant that, though the *Corbaccio* belongs, along with Boccaccio's Latin works quoted above, to the second, "humanist" phase of the Italian writer, and though it bears a strict relationship with Dante's *Commedia*, to the point of being considered a parody of the earlier work, the Duke did not include it in his third, more humanist donation of manuscripts to the University of Oxford, while he did give to the library his copies of Boccaccio's Latin productions.

A small detail leads us to think that Humphrey's curiosity for Italian authors, and for Dante in particular, may have gone even deeper than this. The *commentaria Dantis* in the 1443 Oxford donation has already been discussed, but the same donation includes another manuscript, described thus: "librum Dantis secundo folio *a te*".[164] This book, in the absence of a clearer description, is more difficult to identify, and Toynbee initially had attempted an identification

---

[162] *Dialogue*, ll. 667–75. See *Thomas Hoccleve's Complaint and Dialogue*, ed. by J.A. Burrow, Early English Text Society, Oxford: Oxford University Press, 1999, pp. 66–7.

[163] *Pii II Commentarii rerum memorabilium que temporis suis contigerunt*, ed. by A. van Heck, Città del Vaticano: Biblioteca Apostolica Vaticana, 1984, vol. 2, p. 535.

[164] Number 120 in the list. See Sammut, p. 83.

with *De Monarchia*, which, however, does not present the phrase *a te* in any point that might reasonably correspond to a beginning of the second folio.[165] There is no proof that the text might be a copy of *De Monarchia* apart from Humphrey's interest in this kind of literature, and Toynbee himself later rejected this hypothesis for a more enticing one: the volume could be the *Commedia* in the original Italian version, in which case "a te" would correspond to *Inferno* I.91, "A te convien tenere altro viaggio".[166] In Serravalle's Latin version there is no passage that could fit the *secundo folio* description, and though in his commentary the relevant Italian line is quoted, this quotation occurs too late to make it possible its insertion in the second page of a manuscript.[167] Beccaria's praise would then be revealed as fundamental truth—though unable to read languages other than English, French or (probably) Latin, the Duke showed much curiosity for texts in other languages: "si quid est quod alieno sermone aliqua cum dignitate confectum sit, id etiam studere ac cognoscere non desistis".[168] We could even go one step further and argue that "cum dignitate confectum" could refer to the text itself in the case of Dante, Boccaccio, or the Greek writers, but could also be interpreted as referring to the beauty of the decoration and writing in texts such as the Hebrew psalter.

Having discussed Humphrey's interest in texts in French and Italian, and reserving a fuller discussion of his Latin manuscripts for the section devoted to the Oxford donations, there now remains to discuss the presence in his library of manuscripts in English. What we find may seem rather disappointing: the list of extant manuscripts includes only two volumes in English belonging with any certainty to the Duke. Indeed, one of them is only partly in English: it is a

---

[165] Toynbee, "The Dante MSS. presented to Oxford by Duke Humphrey", p. 187.

[166] Paget Toynbee, "Duke Humphrey's Dante, Petrarch, and Boccaccio MSS.", *The Times Literary Supplement* 22 April 1920, 256. See also H.H.E. Craster, "Duke Humphrey's Dante, Petrarch, and Boccaccio MSS.", *Times Literary Supplement* 13 May 1920, 303. This article is an answer to Toynbee, confirming the former's hypothesis.

[167] Serravalle's translation and commentary are published in *Fratris Iohannis de Serravalle ord.min. Episcopi et Principis Firmani Translatio et Comentum totius libri Dantis Aldigherii cum textu italico Fratris Bartholomaei a Colle eiusdem ordinis*, ed. by M. da Civezza and T. Domenichelli, Prati: Ex Officina Libraria Giachetti, 1891. The line "A te convien tenere altro viaggio" is translated by Serravalle with "aliud iter te oportet tenere".

[168] Oxford, Bodleian Library, Lat. Misc. d. 34, f. 5r. See Sammut, p. 163.

collection of the works of John Gower, which includes the *Confessio amantis* in Latin and English and other, minor works, mainly in Latin, though one, the *Traitié pour essampler les amantz marietz*, is in French. The manuscript has been already discussed above in this chapter, and we have noted how some of the characteristics of the binding and of the illumination suggest the probability of its having been either commissioned by the Duke, or at least acquired by him, who also suggested some last-minute interventions. Here it may be added that the presence of Gower's works in a manuscript that does not seem to be a gift or a presentation copy indicates an interest in the previous generation of English poets that is particularly fitting in one of the most renowned patrons of the English writers who lived in his own times. Once again, we should not perhaps pay particular attention to differences, or supposed differences, between a medieval and a humanist element in Humphrey's library, and consider him a reader who was trying to understand the element of continuity between the literature of the past—both of the medieval and the classical past—and the literature of the present, particularly of present-day England.

The other English manuscript present in the Duke's library is the Middle English translation of Palladius's *De Re Rustica*.[169] In this case the translation was commissioned by the Duke, and the manuscript is explicitly dedicated to him—in the proem there is also, as already written above, a passage that is fundamental for our understanding of Gloucester's intellectual circle. The passage will be discussed more in depth in this and the following chapter; there remains to be noted here that the extreme care with which the illumination and the setting of at least the first part of the translation is executed suggests that Humphrey followed the execution not only of the translation

---

[169] Oxford, Bodleian Library, Duke Humfrey d.2. Described in Sammut, pp. 125–6, and more in depth in A.C. De la Mare, "Duke Humfrey's English Palladius (MS. Duke Humfrey d.2)", *The Bodleian Library Record* 12: 1985, 39–51. See also Alessandra Petrina, "The Middle English Translation of Palladius's De Agricultura", in *The Medieval Translator. Traduire au Moyen Age 8*, ed. by R. Voaden, R. Tixier, T. Sanchez Roura and J.R. Rytting, Tournhout: Brepols, 2003: 317–28. The text, as presented in Duke Humphrey's manuscript, is published as *The Middle-English Translation of Palladius De Re Rustica*, ed. by M. Liddell, Berlin: E. Ebering, 1896. Another edition (*Palladius on Husbondrie*, ed. by B. Lodge, Early English Text Society, London: Trübner, 1873) publishes an incomplete text, which has survived in another manuscript (see note below).

but of the manuscript. Of the three manuscripts that have preserved this translation for us,[170] only this presents the proem in its entirety, and its outward appearance is such as to underline its noble destination. Ruled in purple ink, with brilliant gold initials,[171] the manuscript is at its most splendid in the proem, that is, the part that does not appear in the Latin original and that is explicitly dedicated to Humphrey. Here the words are written in four different colours, probably underlining, as has been supposed, the intricate rhyme-scheme, varying for each stanza and including internal rhymes;[172] the rest of the manuscript, instead, is written in one colour, with coloured initials (generally with red ink filling in the already drawn black letters) and rubrics. The stanzas added as an epilogue to the various books, corresponding to the months of the year, are likewise coloured, whether they refer to the patron or not. They thus seem to answer a double purpose: on the one hand, they celebrate the patron to whom this splendid homage is made; on the other, they indicate to the reader which parts of the text are unrelated to the Latin original. This latter might seem a far-fetched hypothesis, but is supported by the fact that this compiler is extremely attentive to the reader's needs: for this purpose he inserts a *tabula* at the beginning of the book that is not to be found in the original. George R. Keiser thus writes on this point:

> textual divisions were determined by the book-structure of the source, each devoted to a month of the year. While this ordering has an obvious value, the translator, perhaps at the patron's recommendation, provided a supplementary finding system. In the dedication copy, Bodleian MS Duke Humfrey d. 2, arabic folio numbers and stanza letters in the text correspond to those found with entries alphabetically arranged in a *tabula*. Not surprisingly, late copies preserve this apparatus, which facilitated access to specific information.[173]

---

[170] The other two are London, British Library, Additional A. 369 (the first manuscript to be identified in modern times, and the basis for the Early English Text Society edition of the text, without the proem or the epilogues to the various months) and Glasgow University, Hunter 104 (probably the same version as the Bodleian Library manuscript, but badly mutilated).

[171] De la Mare, "Duke Humfrey's English Palladius (MS. Duke Humfrey d.2)", p. 39.

[172] An interesting analysis of the manuscript is to be found in D.R. Howlett, "Studies in the Works of John Whethamstede", D.Phil., Oxford, 1975, pp. 207–20.

[173] George R. Keiser, "Serving the Needs of Readers: Textual Division in Some Late-Medieval English Texts", in *New Science out of Old Books. Studies in Manuscripts*

Such detailed attention to the pictorial details of the manuscript diminishes as we proceed in the perusal of the text; the splendid project seems to have lost its impetus, so that the mentions of the patron decrease as we proceed, and the last books do not even include the usual epilogue. The manuscript has other peculiar characteristics in its make-up: the leaves which contain the epilogues for January and February, most explicit in their praise of the patron, were added at the end of complete quires, as if the presentation copy itself was evidence of work in progress. The presentation copy of the Middle English translation of Palladius's *De Re Rustica* thus becomes doubly precious: not only does it preserve for us a proem that gives such interesting information (albeit couched in too flattering terms to be completely reliable) on the Duke's intellectual activity; it is also constructed in such a way as to allow us a glimpse into Humphrey's relation with his *scriptorium*. Unfortunately, we have too little information on the presence of copyists and illuminators in the Duke's employment; but in a case like this it is inconceivable that the Duke would ignore the elaborate preparation that the production of this manuscript would entail. What may rather be deduced is a patron requiring of the translator and the scribe (assuming them not to have been the same person) a close collaboration, so that the decorative element should also help the reader towards a better, more immediate and complete understanding of the text, particularly when the text, as in this case, had a practical value and could be used for reference. If anything, the manuscript strikes us as somewhat over-elaborate for an agriculture manual, though it may be assumed that, since Humphrey had commissioned the translation, he also wanted the dedication copy to have a symbolic value.

It is also worth noting that the manuscript lacks one image we would have expected, that is, the image of the writer presenting his work to the patron. Everest-Phillips sees this absence as corroborating "the suggestion, based on extant volumes belonging to the Duke, that Duke Humphrey was not altogether particularly keen on illuminated manuscripts for the sake of illuminations, and valued the content more than the illumination".[174] This suggestion is probably

---

and Early Printed Books in Honour of A.I. Doyle, ed. by R. Beadle and A.J. Piper, Aldershot: Scolar Press, 1995: 207–26, pp. 209–10.

[174] L.C.Y. Everest-Phillips, "The Patronage of Humphrey, Duke of Gloucester. A Re-evaluation", Ph.D., York, 1983, p. 116.

confirmed by another observation: when there is an image of the writer presenting the work to the patron, either it refers to a book Humphrey had not commissioned (as in the case of the two Biblical commentaries by John Capgrave) or to the manuscript that was completed after Humphrey's death (as in the case of the copy of Lydgate's *Fall of Princes* with this particular illumination). Illumination for Humphrey appeared interesting only in so far as it enhanced the clarity of the work, or included organised motifs, such as the coat of arms, that could sustain a symbolic rather than a pictorial celebration of the duke. I quote once again Everest-Phillips, who sees at this point a correspondence between this mode of celebration and what Thomas Hoccleve does when he discusses the symbolic meaning of the Duke's name.[175]

Only hypotheses can be formulated on the existence of other manuscripts in English in Humphrey's possession. Since John Lydgate's *Fall of Princes* is also a work he commissioned, and which is explicitly and repeatedly dedicated to him, he must have had a presentation copy of the manuscript, but if so, it has not survived. The same could be said with regards to one of Thomas Hoccleve's works, alluded to in Hoccleve's *Dialogue*, though in this case the reference is more uncertain (and will be discussed in depth in the following chapter). Since the Duke possessed (and might have ordered) a manuscript with Gower's works, it is surprising not to find works by Geoffrey Chaucer in his collection, given this poet's popularity in the fifteenth century, the relatively high number of manuscripts of his works that has survived, and especially the constant references made to Chaucer as "my maistir" by John Lydgate, one of the English poets who worked most for the Duke of Gloucester[176]—but again, there can be no founded hypotheses as to what he actually possessed but has not survived, apart from the Latin manuscripts donated to Oxford and appearing in the University lists. Sammut mentions a miscellaneous volume as probably Humphrey's: the manuscript (now Cambridge University Library, Gg. 4. 27) contains a

---

[175] Everest-Phillips, p. 352. For Hoccleve's play on the name "Homfrey" see lines 596–97 of his *Dialogue* (*Thomas Hoccleve's Complaint and Dialogue*, ed. by J.A. Burrow, Early English Text Society, Oxford: Oxford University Press, 1999).

[176] It must be noted that there are a number of references to Geoffrey Chaucer in Lydgate's *Fall of Princes*, a work commissioned by Duke Humphrey.

number of major Chaucerian works, such as *Troilus and Cryseide*, *The Canterbury Tales*, *The Legend of Good Women*, *The Parlement of Foules*, together with John Lydgate's *Temple of Glas*. Sammut, however, does not explain on what foundation he bases this hypothesis, other than the obvious inference that Humphrey *must* have possessed a manuscript with Chaucerian works. Another manuscript in English has been tentatively inserted in the Duke of Gloucester's list, since in this case there is a note, on f. 1r, "a vous me ly Gloucestre";[177] but, as Sammut correctly observes, the name could refer to Thomas, Duke of Gloucester. The issue in this case is further complicated by the content of the manuscript: it is a Wycliffite version of the *New Testament*. Humphrey's owning of this particular text would be rather surprising, since he was known and celebrated as a strenuous defender of orthodoxy, and a cruel persecutor of a number of Lollards. For analogous reasons, it is not conceivable, as Barker-Benfield observes, that the Duke possessed no work by Reginald Pecock, "in spite of the fact that the latter had written at least 6 books between the 1430's and the 1450's, and that the two had been reasonably close".[178]

As we have seen above, we have few elements that allow us to discuss Humphrey's role as concerns the illumination of the manuscripts he commissioned or ordered; scholars who have devoted specific studies to Duke Humphrey, such as Weiss, Sammut, Rundle or Saygin have generally devoted very little attention to this point. Generally speaking, they have tended to assume that Humphrey either did not employ illuminators or used their services very sparingly, as seems to have been the standard practice in fifteenth-century England: "There was no patronage of scribes or illuminators in England to come anywhere near equalling that of the Dukes of Burgundy and the Kings of France and the members of their court circles, or of the Renaissance princes in Italy."[179] However, we have seen while discussing the presentation copy of the Middle English

---

[177] New York, Public Library, 67. Sammut mentions the manuscript on p. 131, reporting information received by A.I. Doyle.

[178] Barker-Benfield, p. 194. For a tentative chronology of Pecock's works, see Nicholas Watson, "Censorship and Cultural Change in Late Medieval England: Vernacular Theology, the Oxford Translation Debate, and Arundel's Constitutions of 1409", *Speculum* 70: 1995, 822–64, p. 863.

[179] J.J.G. Alexander, "Foreign Illuminators and Illuminated Manuscripts", in *The Cambridge History of the Book in Britain, vol. 3: 1400–1557*, ed. by L. Hellinga and J.B. Trapp, Cambridge: Cambridge University Press, 1999: 47–64, p. 61.

translation of Palladius's *De Re Rustica* that the scribe could use colours and setting, if not actual illumination, as a means to make the text more immediately understandable to the reader, and thus that Humphrey, or in any case his *scriptorium*, gave due importance to the visual quality of a manuscript. Besides, A.C. De La Mare and Richard Hunt observe some interesting visual analogies in a number of manuscripts belonging to Humphrey; describing the presentation copy of Tito Livio Frulovisi's *Vita Henrici Quinti* (now Cambridge, Corpus Christi College, 285; the manuscript is probably Frulovisi's autograph), they write:

> The illuminated initial on fol. 4 contains the royal arms of England. Initials in the same style, with monsters and caricature heads and rather muddy coloured acanthus leaves, in pink, blue, green and orange on scalloped grounds of gold and colours are also found in the two other manuscripts of Frulovisi's works written in England [another copy of the *Vita Henrici Quinti*, equally presented to the duke, now London, College of Arms, Arundel 12, and Frulovisi's Latin comedies, now Cambridge, St John's College, C. 10], in the two manuscripts written by Antonio Beccaria for Duke Humfrey [St Athanasius's theological treatises, now London, British Library, Royal 5 F. II, and St Athanasius's *Orationes contra Arianos*, now Cambridge, King's College 27], and in Duke Humfrey's choice of Psalms [London, British Library, Royal 2 B. I].[180]

This would show that Humphrey's Latin secretaries could at least pay equal attention to the setting and decoration of their manuscript as the anonymous Palladius translator did. The presence of both Italian and English scribes in Humphrey's *scriptorium* can be deduced by the nature of the manuscripts; see, for instance, De La Mare and Hunt's description of Humphrey's manuscript containing his choice of psalms, and particularly of the miniature with border at the beginning:

> Duke Humfrey kneels before Christ as Man of Sorrows. Behind him stands saint Alban. The border is in the same style as those [in Frulovisi's and Beccaria's manuscripts, described above]. The Italian element in the style is all the more remarkable in an English gothic book. Note the groups of dots on the background, which are not found in purely English manuscripts.[181]

---

[180] *Duke Humfrey and English Humanism*, p. 3.
[181] *Duke Humfrey and English Humanism*, p. 5.

Thus even in the case of the illuminations just described we may infer that they were realised in the same *scriptorium*, and that Humphrey's intellectual activity extended also to his supervising the production of manuscripts he had commissioned. There is even less information concerning the binding, though it may be noted that Humphrey's copy of Coluccio Salutati's works, a manuscript including *De saeculo et religione, De fato et fortuna*, and *Declamationes*, is in a fifteenth-century English blind-stamped binding, where the stamps "include some which are found on books which were bound at Salisbury c. 1459–63 for Gilbert Kymer, who was then dean of Salisbury".[182] Kymer was Humphrey's physician, and Chancellor at the University of Oxford in 1431–34, and then again in 1446–53. It is also know that he played an important role in the establishment and maintenance of cordial relations between the University and the noble patron, relations that culminated with the donations of books.

It is therefore evident that, in spite of his almost proverbial stinginess, the Duke of Gloucester spent much time, care and money on his library. The Duke has often been accused, by contemporary poets and humanists as well as by modern scholars, of being too miserly to recompense adequately work done for him. Thus the request for money becomes a recurring *motif* in Lydgate's *Fall of Princes*, elaborated through a number of metaphors and more or less veiled allusions, to the point that David Wallace has seen in this a precise ideological move on the part of the patron: Humphrey, according to Wallace, "managed to keep Lydgate in a subservient role by being stingy with his *largesse*. In pursuing his patron through the whole length of the *Fall of Princes*, Lydgate becomes ever more exhausted and alienated from his own intellectual labour".[183] The less dependent Italian humanists could express their need more openly: in the Introduction to the present volume we have already quoted Antonio Beccaria's epigram *Ad principem Humfredum*, in which the complaint is quite explicit: the Duke is very good at making promises, less prompt in maintaining them, always procrastinating his payments: "nihil est quod mihi mane datur".[184] Pier Candido Decembrio, once

---

[182] *Duke Humfrey and English Humanism*, p. 10.
[183] David Wallace, *Chaucerian Polity: Absolutist Lineages and Associational Forms in England and Italy*, Stanford: Stanford University Press, 1997, p. 333.
[184] "You give me nothing in the morning". Durham, North Carolina, Duke University Library lat. 37, f. 10v. The epigram is printed in Sammut, p. 165.

his translation of Plato's *Republic* was completed, felt himself in a position to refuse the Duke's offer—a hundred ducats to be paid annually—and asked instead to be given the money to buy Petrarch's house: "pretium ville olim Francisci Petrarce piis precibus ab eadem postulavi".[185] Humphrey's silence prompted him to a series of half-anguished, half-irritated questions: "Quis enim provocatus a principe tanta humanitate, tanta munificentia non respondeat? Quod si minus prudenter responsum est a me, vincat[ur] tamen offerentis benignitas acceptantis lenitate. Quorsum hec?"[186] But we may infer from the following letters that Decembrio never received what he wanted, though in this case it is difficult to understand whether the Duke was once more showing his stinginess, or whether Decembrio was being more than usually extravagant in his demands.[187] Appeals to the patron's munificence were a matter of course in humanist transactions, since humanists rightly thought that theirs was an intellectual profession and should be compensated accordingly, while too often the patron seemed to believe that the honour of having their names on the work's opening page should be compensation enough for the writers. In the case of Humphrey, there has been perhaps overmuch stress on his thrifty attitude; after all, in the *Fall of Princes* Lydgate alternates complaints with expressions of jubilation at having received the money, which leads us to conclude that he was paid at least sometimes; and the books commissioned in Italy were almost certainly paid for, otherwise the middlemen would not have continued their activity.

We could better understand Duke Humphrey's attitude towards money, and thus estimate more accurately the weight of what we

---

[185] "With pious prayers I asked for the price of the house once belonging to Petrarch". Milan, Ambr. I 235 inf., f. 17r. The letter is reprinted in Sammut, pp. 200–03.

[186] "Who, being moved by a prince with such humanity and generosity, should not answer? Even if I have answered to you less than wisely, yet the generosity of the giver should be won by the indulgence of acceptance. Why then?" Milan, Ambr. I 235 inf., f. 17v (see Sammut, p. 201).

[187] "Duke Humphrey's offer of a hundred ducats appears extremely generous from an English point of view but should be regarded from Decembrio's point of view. Poggio Bracciolini received six hundred pieces from Alfonso of Naples [. . .] for Xenophon's *Cyropedia* [. . .] Vespasiano says that Alfonso spent as much as twenty thousand ducats a year as salaries for scholars" (Everest-Phillips, p. 275). The scholar lists a number of other examples, concluding that "this indeed makes Duke Humphrey's hundred ducats seem paltry" (p. 276).

might call his cultural expenses, if we had a more exact idea of his financial situation, and of the other expenses he incurred. Kenneth Vickers observes that "the Lancastrians had always been poor, and [. . .] the constant sinking of money into the bottomless morass of the French wars had reduced the dynasty and kingdom to a very low financial state".[188] On the other hand, Humphrey's role as Protector of England during Henry's minority and later as First Councillor granted him considerable emoluments: Vickers notes that in 1431 he was receiving two thousand marks per annum as First Councillor, and four thousand when the King was absent; in the same year, after his activity against heretics and especially against Jack Sharpe, the salary was increased to five thousand marks a year.[189] Even for a nobleman in his position, it was a very handsome allowance, and it might have allowed more generosity in the pursuit of his intellectual activities. There is reason to believe, however, that apart from the expenses he obviously incurred during enterprises such as his raid in Flanders, he also spent much of his money on houses and land. In this activity, too, he may have followed the ideal of princely magnificence according to the model proposed by Italian noblemen in the fifteenth century.[190] One tends to remember the manor of Plesaunce in Greenwich as the centre of Humphrey's intellectual circle; it may be added that in the last years of his life, when he had almost retired from active politics, he invested much in lands, buying "the Hundred of Wootton and the Manors of Woodstock, Handborough, Stonesfield, and Wootton, all in the neighbourhood of Oxford".[191] Besides, in the past he had held court in Pembroke Castle, and in his manor of Penshurst in Kent, while there is less certain evidence of his having resided near St Albans, at Leicester and at Pontefract. He obviously possessed a house in London. Some of his letters to Italian humanists are dated "ex Placentia diversorio nostro",[192] which Sammut reads as a reference to the manor of Pleshy (which belonged to the dukedom of Gloucester), though it might

---

[188] Vickers, p. 228.
[189] Vickers, pp. 226–8.
[190] See Peter J. Lucas, "The Growth and Development of English Literary Patronage in the Later Middle Ages and Early Renaissance", *The Library* 6th series, 4: 1982, 219–48, p. 226.
[191] Vickers, p. 258.
[192] Sammut, p. 199.

equally well refer to Plesaunce, Humphrey's palace in Greenwich.[193] The Greenwich manor itself had been a royal residence for Henry IV and Henry V; the latter had given it to Thomas Beaufort, and it had become Humphrey's within two years of Beaufort's death. In the late 1430s the Duke increased his possessions in the immediate neighbourhood of the manor, developing also the park and surrounding the manor with a wall.[194] In the last years of his life, we see him supervising the building of his tomb in St Albans Abbey. Such pursuits were bound to be extremely expensive, and it is probable that Humphrey reserved most of his income to his investments, leaving only a lesser part to the commission or acquisition of manuscripts. After all, however we read the donation to the University of Oxford—whether we consider it the act of an enlightened patron or the manoeuvre of a defeated politician—there is no doubt that it was an enormously generous gift on the part of a man who could reasonably expect many more years of life, and was thus expected to invest in his gift. This point, however, will be further discussed in the next section.

Another question to be asked when considering Humphrey of Gloucester's intellectual project is whether he was following a model. It has been generally assumed that the Duke was attempting to import Italian humanism in England, or, more brutally, that circumstances, and the insistence of humanists in offering their services, induced him to commission even books in which he was not particularly interested. This is David Rundle's position—examining manuscripts in Humphrey's possession, the scholar sees him as the still (and basically empty) centre of a circle of activity. The volumes Rundle takes into consideration

> are linked by a negative feature: beyond his characteristic *ex libris*, there is little sign of Humfrey's in these manuscripts. They may attract attention because their ownership by a famous aristocrat has previously been unnoticed, but the information to be garnered from them tells us much more about those around the duke than about the man himself. His library is, as it were, a poor *speculum principis* in which to see

---

[193] Other letters, however, are dated "ex Granuico diversorio meo", and in this case there is no doubt the reference is to Greenwich. See, for instance, Sammut, p. 216.

[194] See Vickers, pp. 444–5.

his reflection; it is, however, a well-placed window from which to view the interests and activities of the duke's less exalted contemporaries.[195]

But what has been observed in this chapter on the acquisitions and commissions of books in various languages, on how Humphrey would occasionally seek or acquire a book by other means than donations and presentations, on the care he spent in supervising the work of his scriptorium, would rather lead us to think that behind the Duke's intellectual activity there was a policy, the pursuit of an ideological conviction. It has already been observed in the previous chapter that Humphrey's model throughout his life seems to have been his elder brother; in the years of his protectorate the Duke tried to continue Henry V's policy, to the cost of setting himself against most of the King's Council, and even when Henry VI was crowned and Humphrey's role became more and more marginal he attempted to set himself as the continuator of the dead and glorious King's policy, as unfortunate episodes such as Humphrey's strenuous opposition to the liberation of Charles d'Orléans demonstrate. The commission of the *Vita Henrici Quinti* to Tito Livio Frulovisi is likewise significant, since he wanted to inscribe the memory of his brother in the classical frame of humanist historicism. As regards his policy of book-acquisition, however, Humphrey's attitude appears to diverge from that of his brother, and indeed from Lancastrian policy as a whole. Acquisition of books for both Henry V and Bedford meant essentially a financial investment, and an acquisition of prestige; both acquired a large number of books by buying or appropriating entire libraries—the Louvre library in the case of Bedford, the books obtained with the capture of Meaux for Henry V. Neither set out to acquire individual volumes, with the possible exception of Bibles or prayer books—in some cases, as with the Bedford Psalter and Hours, books whose splendid illumination made them precious objects rather than materials for reading. Neither acquired or commissioned individual books in Latin or translations; neither showed any interest in the new humanist learning. It may be, as Rundle claims, that Humphrey fell easy prey to humanist insistence; but humanists must have known

---

[195] Rundle, "Two Unnoticed Manuscripts from the Collection of Humfrey, Duke of Gloucester", p. 311. Rundle is referring to Cambridge, University Library, Gg.i.34(i), and Cambridge, Gonville and Caius, 183/216, mentioned above, whose ownership on the part of the Duke he has recently rediscovered.

that their requests or offers would have found a more willing ear
with the Duke of Gloucester than with other English noblemen.
Humanist praise may sometimes be an obvious way for the writer
to ingratiate himself with the patron; but when we read passages
such as the following, we may think of a different interpretation:

> Legi cupide, que scripsisti miratusque sum Romanam facundiam in
> Brittaniam usque profectam esse. Sed fuerunt et alii apud Anglos
> Tulliane cultores eloquentie, inter quos venerabilem Bedam nemo non
> posuit. Petrus Blesensis longe inferior fuit, cujus epistolis hanc tuam
> perbrevem antepono. Congratulor tibi et Anglie, quia jam verum dicendi
> ornatum suscepisti. Sed magne ob hanc causam referende sunt grates
> clarissimo illi et doctissimo principi, Clocestrie duci, qui studia human-
> itatis summo studio in regnum vestrum recepit, qui, sicut mihi rela-
> tum est, et poetas mirifice colit et oratores magnopere veneratur.[196]

The passage comes from a letter written by Aeneas Silvius Piccolomini
to Adam de Moleyns. With this letter Piccolomini championed humanistic studies in England, and he probably saw in Moleyns a possible
promoter of these studies, but it is difficult to see what advantage
he would draw from his praise of the Duke of Gloucester. The letter is dated 1444, when Humphrey's star was no longer in the ascendant; Moleyns was at the time English Protonotary of the Holy See,
and would become Bishop of Chichester and keeper of the Privy
Seal in two years' time; he certainly was no friend of the Duke, and
would later seal the warrant for his arrest. Rather than thinking of
an elaborate and misplaced compliment on the part of Piccolomini,
it is thus more economical to infer that he was simply impressed by
the reports he had concerning the Duke as a patron of humanistic
studies, and used his name in the letter as one of the most evident
examples of the advancement of the new learning in England.

Thus, if Humphrey actively pursued his policy of acquisition and
commission of texts with a specific ideal in mind, it would be inter-

---

[196] "I avidly read what you wrote and I wonder that the Latin eloquence has so
far entered Britain. But there were also others in England who admired the eloquence of Cicero, among whom is the venerable Bede. Peter of Blois was far inferior, and I put his letters before your own very short one. And I congratulate you
and England, since you care for the art of rhetoric. But we should also be very
thankful for this to that famous and learned prince, the Duke of Gloucester, who
has welcomed humanist studies in your kingdom with great attention, as I hear, and
admires and cares for poets and orators". From a letter written by Aeneas Silvius
Piccolomini to Adam de Moleyns, 29 May 1444. See *Der Briefwechsel des Eneas Silvius
Piccolomini*, ed. by R. Wolkan, Wien: Alfred Holder, 1909, p. 325 (letter n. 143).

esting to see why and how he developed and changed the original Lancastrian attitude, paying attention to a form of learning which had been hitherto extraneous to English culture. Patronage of the new vernacular tradition had been already undertaken by Henry V, as is evident in the case of Hoccleve's *The Regement of Princes* and Lydgate's *Troy Book*; Humphrey combined this form of patronage with a new appreciation of the classics, attempting a meeting of the Latin humanist and classical texts with the contemporary production in the vernacular. John Lydgate's *Fall of Princes*, conflating Boccaccio's *De casibus virorum illustrium* (with the help of Laurence de Premierfait's French version) with Chaucer's contribution to the *de casibus* literature in his *Monk's Tale*, is probably the most outstanding result of this enterprise; but the Middle English translation of Palladius's *De Re Rustica* belongs to the same policy, and illustrates the attempt on Humphrey's part to give literary dignity to the vernacular by introducing it to the classical tradition of Latin texts. He may have followed not only the example of his brother, but also the model of an Italian *signore*, particularly in his dealings with humanists;[197] it is interesting to note, for instance, that in recurring to professional advice to build his library he was imitating contemporary Italian princes. Speaking of the latter's intellectual activity, Weiss observes that "Cosimo de Medici is known to have relied on Tommaso Parentucelli, later Pope Nicholas V, while reorganising the library of San Marco, Florence, while Federico da Montefeltro, Duke of Urbino, followed the suggestion of his Florentine bookseller, Vespasiano da Bisticci, when assembling his famous library."[198] The Duke of Gloucester seems to have relied in particular on Pier Candido Decembrio in the choice of manuscripts to acquire, as is shown by the epistolary exchange between them. It may be inferred that Decembrio, *mutatis mutandis*, played with Humphrey the same role he was playing, closer to home, with the Duke of Milan; as Alfonso Sammut observes, "come il Decembrio orientò Filippo Maria Visconti nella scelta dei libri così influenzò Unfredo nell'acquisto di determinati testi".[199]

---

[197] J.B. Trapp observes that "Humfrey seems to have conceived the idea of modelling his household on a contemporary Italian princely court. Why, and on whose advice, is not clear" ("The Humanist Book", p. 293).

[198] Weiss, *Humanism in England during the Fifteenth Century*, p. 58.

[199] "As Decembrio helped Filippo Maria Visconti in his choice of books, so he

Humphrey's closeness with Pier Candido Decembrio may have been
related to his admiration for the Duke of Milan, as seems to be
shown by his attention in underlying Decembrio's employment with
the Duke in his ex-libris to his copy of Decembrio's translation of
Plato's *Republic*. A more important clue to Humphrey's attitude towards
Filippo Maria Visconti is probably a letter in which he asked the
Duke of Milan to provide him with a complete catalogue of his
library, which included a number of Petrarch's manuscripts. Gloucester
then wrote to Decembrio, relating his request:

> Scripsimus etiam ad principem tuum Mediolanensem litteras nostras,
> una cum tuis quibus rogabamus, ut biblyothece sue tibi daretur copia,
> tum etiam ut nostro nomine te haberet commendatum, proponens sibi
> virtutis tue optima exempla. Quas quidem si accepisti necne, prorsus
> ignoramus. Ideo has quoque ad te mittere cum eodem indice nostro
> instituimus, quo certior sit voluntas nostra.[200]

The passage seems to show that, apart from any consideration of
political or personal admiration, Humphrey of Gloucester saw in the
Duke of Milan, and especially in his library, a possible model to free
his intellectual pursuits from an inevitable imputation of insularity,
and to give a European dimension to his collection of manuscripts.[201]

There remains one question, probably the most important, and it
concerns Humphrey as a reader: "how much, to what an extent,
did Duke Humfrey read and study his books?" Roberto Weiss, having asked this question, answers rather dismissively: "It is of course
quite certain that he had neither Greek nor Italian, and that if there

---

influenced Humphrey in the acquisition of determinate texts". Alfonso Sammut,
"Tra Pavia, Milano e Oxford: trasmissione di codici", in *Vestigia. Studi in Onore
di Giuseppe Billanovich*, ed. by R. Avesani, M. Ferrari, T. Foffano, G. Frasso and
A. Sottili, Roma: Edizioni di Storia e Letteratura, 1984, 2: 613–22, p. 619.

[200] "We also sent a letter to your prince in Milan, asking for a copy of the catalogue of his library, and praising you in our name, and proposing the good example of your virtue. We do not know whether you received it or not. We have
however ordered to have it sent to you together with a catalogue of our own library,
so that you know our wishes". Firenze, Biblioteca Riccardiana, 827, f. 66v. The
letter is printed in Sammut, p. 193.

[201] L.C.Y. Everest-Phillips suggests Alphonso V of Sicily as a possible model: "To
what extent Duke Humphrey was consciously modelling his patronage on his knowledge of the courts of Italian patrons is impossible to assess, but that he was highly
aware of his contemporaries among the patrons in Italy is obvious [. . .] it seems
pertinent to suggest the way in which Alphonso's reputation as a patron may have
influenced Duke Humphrey". Her assumption is based on the fact that Tito Livio
Frulovisi had been in Naples in 1443–4 (p. 44).

was a French version of a Latin classic available, he clearly preferred it to the original".[202] The observation is obviously supported
by what we know of Gloucester's intellectual activity, but here it is
meant as a censure of what Weiss evidently considers a non-humanist
frame of mind on the Duke's part. The same scholar makes the
point more at length elsewhere:

> If we have enough material to establish Humphrey's attitude towards
> humanism, what we have concerning his actual learning is on the other
> hand rather disheartening. That he knew Greek is out of the question,
> and in spite of his having given a Greek name to one of his illegiti-
> mate children [his daughter Antigone, who married Henry Grey, Earl
> of Tankerville], his acquaintance with Greek literature did not go far
> beyond the Latin translations of Plato, Aristotle, Plutarch, and St.
> Athanasius. As for his Latin scholarship, its standards seem doubtful.
> His Latin correspondence was certainly the work of secretaries, and
> he doubtless had a marked predilection for Latin classics in French
> translations. Thus, he is known to have parted with the Latin origi-
> nal of a work, and to have retained a French version of it. Besides
> this, perhaps an index to the shallowness of his Latin learning is pro-
> vided by his notes of ownership on his books, which are invariably in
> French.[203]

Yet even within these linguistic limitations, Humphrey's strategy of
manuscript acquisition, in a few instances, strikes us as evidence of
a reader's mind, rather than simply a book collector's. The much
quoted instance of his preferring French translations to Latin origi-
nals shows an attitude that, from a modern point of view, would be
perhaps objectionable in a Latin scholar but is quite praiseworthy
in an average reader. Finding Livy in the original too difficult, as
would many of us, Humphrey preferred to read it in a vernacular
translation; which argues for an authentic interest in what he was
reading, rather than a complacent assumption of a standardised
(though not necessarily much practised, even in Italy) humanist attitude. In contemporary English patrons, such as the Duke of Bedford,
the acquisition of a manuscript (as in the case of the Bedford Psalter
and Hours) seems to answer a desire to enhance one's status; often
the beautiful, illuminated manuscript is a precious object which exists

---

[202] Weiss, "Portrait of a Bibliophile XI: Humphrey, Duke of Gloucester, d. 1447",
p. 169.
[203] Weiss, *Humanism in England during the Fifteenth Century*, p. 68.

mainly as a statement on its owner's wealth, taste, or authority. Humphrey appears to avoid, generally speaking, this commonly shared pose; the books he acquires are rarely notable for their beauty, or for the gold of their illuminations; more often, they strike the modern scholar for the text they contain. In at least one case the illumination, supervised by the patron, is meant not simply as an embellishment of the volume but as a practical guide for the reader.[204] It is, on the other hand, more difficult to evaluate the Duke's relationship with the writers or scholars he patronised; David Rundle has recently written on this point:

> this image of Humfrey directing 'his' scholars and paying close attention to their works is, I would suggest, more trope than truth. There is, in fact, a lack of evidence to demonstrate his reading of humanist works; his annotations to his manuscripts, confined in the main to adding a French ex-libris or a motto at the beginning or end of a volume, suggest greater concern to demonstrate ownership than readership.[205]

Rundle continues attempting a reversal of the point; in the case of surviving manuscripts acquired by Humphrey through the mediation of his secretary Antonio Beccaria, the latter appears with some marginalia, while the Duke left only his ex-libris: "It is as if the duke's book-buying habits were directed by the literary tastes of his secretary".[206] I shall discuss this issue more in depth in the following chapter; but, if the idea of the patron "directing" his writers may be exaggerated and even slightly preposterous, what is left of the correspondence between the Duke and the Italian humanists, and the tone generally used by English poets when speaking of him or even to him in their works, strikes a more personal note than the usual exchange of courtesies between poet and patron; the writers flatter or, more rarely, challenge, the patron on their own ground. It may be that Humphrey was no great critic; but I would argue he was a very good reader.

---

[204] I am referring to the presentation copy of the Middle English translation of Palladius's *De Re Rustica*, discussed above.

[205] Rundle, "Humanism before the Tudors", p. 26. It should be noted, however, that marginal annotation is not an unmistakable proof of an intellectual reader: in the humanist manuscripts collected by William Gray, now in Balliol College, there is little or no trace of marginal comments.

[206] Rundle, "Humanism before the Tudors", p. 28.

We can derive little information concerning his literary taste from what has remained of his library, and even in this case there is some critical confusion; when Weiss, for example, writes that the Duke's tastes were "quite catholic, but with a definitive bias towards history and political philosophy",[207] he is, I believe, judging on the basis of the lists that have preserved for us the contents of some of Humphrey's donations to the University of Oxford. These lists reveal a quite explicit educational ideology, but it should be remembered that these, were, after all, books Humphrey decided *not* to keep. What little we know of the books he did not donate may be more revealing; thus earlier in this section we have been able to observe his preference for narratives of a chivalric or romance nature, together with his favouring reading matter in French; his interest in a specific book of the Bible, and also, if less markedly, his interest in recent history and contemporary politics, and his interest in medical treatises.[208]

In its very diversity, the portion of Duke Humphrey's library that we can still observe may perhaps be seen as an attempt to create a *bibliotheca universalis*—whether for himself, for the young king whose education he was supervising, or for the future generations of Oxford students. He was, I believe, neither following simply his personal tastes, as a reader or a bibliophile (though they contributed to influence some of his choices), nor supinely accepting such books as would come in his way in the form of gifts or presentations. This is shown by the patient perseverance with which his Italian middlemen were asked to look for books; by the advisory lists requested to the Italian humanists with whom he corresponded; and, no less, by his commissioning, or accepting the dedication, of Latin translations of Greek works.

Another significant element is the presence of "modern" works—works by Petrarch, or Boccaccio, and their successors. This allows us to focus our attention on another side of Humphrey's cultural activity, apart from the collection of manuscripts. I would argue that

---

[207] Weiss, "Portrait of a Bibliophile XI: Humphrey, Duke of Gloucester, d. 1447", p. 169.

[208] J.D. North associates with Humphrey also British Library, Arundel 66, a medical treatise which at one time was mistakenly attributed to Caerleon. See his "The Alfonsine Tables in England", in *Prismata: Festschrift fur Willy Hartner*, ed. by Y. Maeyama and W.G. Saltzer, Wiesbaden, 1977: 269, 301, p. 266, and Carey, *Courting Disaster*, p. 145.

he did attempt to create a humanist court—his Greenwich palace
was the meeting point of Italian humanists such as the already mentioned Tito Livio Frulovisi, Pietro del Monte, Antonio Beccaria as
well as of English writers (in some cases, future English writers) such
as John Lydgate, Thomas Hoccleve, and possibly George Ashby,
Thomas Norton, John Russell. Here again, the discussion is open,
as to what "humanist court" really means in this case, and on what
resources this particular group of people could count. One of the
most interesting testimonies we have on this point is the already
mentioned prologue to the Middle English translation of Palladius's
De Re Rustica. The words of the anonymous Palladius translator, once
he has completed the most conventional part of his prologue, evoke
the image of a circle of scholars and writers, both English and Italian,
gathered under the munificent protection of a patron who is depicted
as adorned of every virtue and proficient in every branch of knowledge, to the point of correcting the writer's own metre:

> For clergie, or knyghthod, or husbondrie,
> That oratour, poete, or philosophre
> hath tretid, told, or taught, in memorie
> Vche lef and lyne hath he, as shette in cofre;
> Oon nouelte vnnethe is hym to profre.
> Yit Whethamstede, and also Pers de Mounte,
> Titus, and Anthony, and y laste ofre
> And leest. Our newe is old in hym tacounte
>
> But that his vertu list vs exercise,
> And moo as fele as kan in vertu do.
> He, sapient, is diligent to wise
> Alle ignoraunt, and y am oon of tho.
> He taught me metur make, and y soso
> Hym counturfete, and hope, aftir my sorow,
> In God and hym to glade; and aftir woo,
> To ioy, and aftir nyght, to sey good morow.[209]

The idea that Duke Humphrey would not only read the translation
as it was being completed, but also correct the metre of the translator, has been the subject of a certain amount of ridicule, as has
been the attribution to Humphrey of some annotations found in the

---

[209] Liddell, p. 22. A full discussion of this point is to be found in Petrina, "The
Middle English Translation of Palladius's De Agricultura".

margin of the Palladius manuscript. I find it interesting, however, that the Palladius translator should have inserted this unusual element in his praise of his patron, and also that in the rest of the prologue Humphrey should be praised not so much as a prince and a politician but as a scholar: the writer underlines Humphrey's intellectual qualities, noting that

<blockquote>
his wit
And grace in sondri place is so fecounde
That sapience in his prudence is knyt.
[25–27]
</blockquote>

Humphrey is remarkable also for "goldon sapience [. . .] intellect, and consel fortitude" (65–66); he appears proficient in natural philosophy, physics, metaphysics, the arts of the quadrivium, morals, ethics, politics, grammar, logic, rhetoric (73–80). More surprisingly, details of his intellectual activity are given: at Oxford the books donated by this lord "hath euery clerk at werk" (90), and students, scattered among the twelve desks, now can avail themselves of a universal library. It could have been, of course, simply sycophantic flattery: but even in this case, the writer would write what the patron wanted to hear, would pander to the patron's wishes. Besides, we find similar tones in Lydgate's *Fall of Princes*, a free rendition of Boccaccio's *De Casibus* (via Laurent de Premierfait's French version) undertaken at Humphrey's request, as the writer explicitly states. In the Prologue he turns to his patron and writes:

<blockquote>
Off hih lettrure, I dar eek off hym telle
And treuli deeme that he doth excelle
In vndirstondyng alle othir off his age,
And hath gret ioie with clerkis to comune:
And no man is mor expert off language,
Stable in study alwey he doth contune,
Settyng a-side alle chaungis of Fortune.[210]
</blockquote>

John Russell, in his *Boke of Nurture*, though written after Humphrey's death, felt it his duty to refer to him:

<blockquote>
an vsshere y Am/ye may beholde/to a prynce of highe degre
þat enioyethe to enforme & teche/alle þo thatt wille thrive and thee.[211]
</blockquote>

---

[210] *Lydgate's Fall of Princes*, ed. by H. Bergen, Early English Text Society, Extra Series, Oxford: Oxford University Press, 1923–27 11.384–90.

[211] "John Russell's Boke of Nurture", in *The Babees Book, Aristotle's ABC, Urbanitatis,*

And an even more comic and domestic reference can help us confirm our hypothesis: Thomas Hoccleve's *Dialog with a Friend*, in which the friend reminds a very dejected Hoccleve

> Thow seidist/of a book thow were in dette
> Vnto my lord/þat now is lieutenant,
> My lord of Gloucestre/is is nat so?[212]

Even these allusions, to which I shall come back for discussion in chapter 5, appear to agree on one point: Humphrey may be considered not a humanist in the accepted sense (being neither a teacher, nor a professional writer), but rather a privileged reader of humanist books. With the Duke of Gloucester we thus have a splendid instance of the humanist audience, as well as "the first Englisman to aim at forming a fairly complete classical library and have recourse to expert advice in the formation of it".[213]

The book donations to the University of Oxford

One of the greatest obstacles towards a full understanding of Gloucester's activity as a book-collector is of course the fact that almost all we know of his library is what he donated. The lists of his book donations to Oxford have constituted the most complete and detailed document of Humphrey's intellectual activity at least until the attempt at reconstructing his library starting from the surviving manuscripts was undertaken by Alfonso Sammut; therefore, inevitably, such lists have become the object of much interest, and have been subjected to a number of varying, often discordant interpretations. To quote only two of the most significant, Roberto Weiss based his reading of the Duke's intellectual personality almost solely on these lists,[214] while more recently Richard Firth Green has con-

---

Stans Puer ad Mensam, The Lytille Childrenes Lytil Boke, The Bokes of Nurture of Hugh Rhodes and John Russell, Wynkyn de Worde's Boke of Keruynge, The Booke of Demeanor, The Boke of Curtasye, Seager's Schoole of Vertue, &c. &c. with some French & Latin Poems on Like Subjects, and some Forewords on Education in Early England, ed. by F.J. Furnivall, Early English Text Society, London: Trübner, 1868: 115–239, ll. 3–4.
[212] *Thomas Hoccleve's Complaint and Dialogue,* ed. by J.A. Burrow, Early English Text Society, Oxford: Oxford University Press, 1999, ll. 532–4.
[213] Weiss, *Humanism in England during the Fifteenth Century,* p. 69.
[214] Weiss, *Humanism in England during the Fifteenth Century,* pp. 62–3.

tended that the manuscripts included in the lists of the Oxford donations "are unlikely to represent a typical cross-section" of the original library.[215] Both attitudes might be disputed. What we should try
and understand is the spirit in which a nobleman in the extremely
singular political position in which Humphrey found himself, and
with what appears to have been a great trust in the power of books,
would make these successive donations: why these books, why these
numbers, why these dates. For a better understanding of these issues,
however, it is useful first of all to look at the state of University
libraries at the time of Humphrey's donations.

The universities in the fifteenth century played a pivotal role as
concerns the acquisition and preservation of learning: for the first
time in England they contrasted the absolute power of monastery
libraries, and proposed themselves as possible alternatives. Besides,
the links between monastery and university libraries were becoming
stronger, if only because monks were regularly required to attend
university in the fifteenth century.[216] At this stage of their development English universities found themselves dealing both with the religious and the secular authority, though the former tended to be
limited to the national representatives: "Like the English clergy in
general, the university in the fifteenth century was well aware that
the pope was too remote to be an effective shield against the secular power: papal censures now carried little weight in England".[217]
In their new role, and working side by side with the English centres of power, it was natural that university colleges would concern
themselves with a systematic policy of manuscript acquisition, and
that former students or public figures would think it right or expedient to donate books to universities. At the same time, the problem of an adequate housing for these books was being raised.

In the early decades of English university life manuscripts were
generally locked in chests, though Merton College already possessed
a *libraria* by 1338.[218] The first English college to have a room specifically

---

[215] Richard Firth Green, *Poets and Princepleasers: Literature and the English Court in the
Late Middle Ages*, Toronto: University of Toronto Press, 1980, p. 8.
[216] David N. Bell, p. 232.
[217] R.L. Storey, "University and Government 1430–1500", in *The History of the
University of Oxford, vol. 2: Late Medieval Oxford*, ed. by J.J. Catto and R. Evans, Oxford,
Clarendon Press, 1992: 709–45, p. 714.
[218] M. Parkes, "The Provision of Books", in *The History of the University of Oxford*,

built in order to house a library was New College, founded in 1379 by William of Wykeham, Bishop of Winchester.[219] As well as founding the college and providing it with a library room (which was opened in 1386, a few years after the college itself), the Bishop of Winchester gave the new foundation 246 manuscripts. He evidently realised the importance of an adequately provided library in a centre of learning, and conversely, the need for books to be adequately housed if they were to be profitably used. By the second half of the fifteenth century many colleges had begun to have an accessible library: this was the case, for example, of Exeter College, or of Queen's College.[220] Generous book donations had already started by that time, and in some cases they were characterised by a systematic approach to the issue of university learning, rather than being the haphazard legacy of the manuscripts possessed by an individual. As Parkes writes:

> The number of books involved, the range of interests covered by the contents of these books, and above all the fact that in several instances there were two copies of the same work, suggest that the books given to the colleges represent not merely the personal collection of one man, nor (since they were to be chained) the wish to provide portable capital, but the intention to provide books for the use of members of these institutions.[221]

We shall see how this attitude, as well as Wykeham's concern about providing a college at the same time with a library and a resonable number of manuscripts, were imitated by Humphrey of Gloucester, who could thus step in the wake of a fairly established tradition by using book donations either as a means of propaganda or as a simple gesture of generosity. Neil Ripley Ker, on the other hand, examining the book donations to the English colleges in the late Middle Ages, observes that the foundation collections in particular tended to be impersonal, though they could occasionally be far more generous in size than even Wykeham's liberal offer: "the emphasis was on numbers, enough books to make a library room look reasonably

---

vol. 2: Late Medieval Oxford, ed. by J.J. Catto and R. Evans, Oxford: Clarendon Press, 1992: 407–83, p. 459.

[219] Parkes, p. 460.

[220] Parkes, pp. 459–60. For a reconstruction of the medieval library of Balliol College see Mynors, pp. xi–xxiv.

[221] Parkes, pp. 461–2.

full".[222] On the other hand, gifts were the most usual means by which manuscripts were acquired by a college or university library; these institutions did not yet have a systematic policy of book acquisition, and probably would not have the necessary funds to implement such a policy. Booklists and inscriptions generally provide modern scholars with sufficient details as to the means of acquisition of a particular manuscript, and while in most cases, as shown above, the acquisitions were the result of a donation, sometimes they came to the college as unredeemed securities, since the college could and occasionally did act as a money lender.[223] The fact that actual buying was recorded is of special interest to us because it indicates not only that the book in question was particularly wanted, but also that the purchase in itself was a relatively rare event. The libraries then tended to reflect the successive layers of the donors' bequests, and not to highlight the intellectual, didactic or ideological attitude of a particular college. In this sense, then, it may be said that Duke Humphrey's donations marked a novelty in the relationship between the donors and the centres of learning, as shall be seen more in detail below.

By the end of the fourteenth century, however, the need for a permanent fund of books was a well-established necessity in university colleges, as was the practice of book donations, which in some cases became almost an obligation: in the case of Merton College, for example, the fellows were required to behave as the monks did with monastery libraries: if a fellow of the college died, or entered a monastic order, he was expected to leave all the books he possessed to the college. This means that by 1375 Merton had benefited from 60 donors, as opposed to equally famous colleges like Balliol (19 donors) or Oriel (18). But this also means that these donors were usually registered for a small number of books (more substantial gifts appeared to have been a feature of the years after 1375), and that the contents of the donations could in no way be determined by the

---

[222] Neil Ripley Ker, "Oxford College Libraries before 1500", in *The Universities in the Late Middle Ages*, ed. by J. Ijsewijn and J. Parquet, Louvain: Louvain University Press, 1978: 293–311, reprinted in *Books, Collectors and Libraries. Studies in the Medieval Heritage*, London: The Hambledon Press, 1985: 301–20, p. 313.

[223] "Money was lent and not repaid and the security for it, usually a book, remained with the lender. This is a kind of buying" (Ker, "Oxford College Libraries before 1500", p. 309).

college authorities.[224] To give an idea of the extent of college libraries by 1375, Ker tells us that there were more that 100 books at Oriel and at least 150 at Balliol.[225] Given the nature of the book acquisitions, inevitably the library catalogue tended to be of a conservative nature, and to abound particularly in theology. An enquiry into the books possessed by Merton College in 1360, for instance, reveals what follows:

> The theological catalogue shows that there was a useful working collection within narrow limits, consisting mainly of glossed books of the Bible [. . .] of postils on the Bible [. . .] of commentaries on the Sentences of Peter Lombard [. . .] and the works of St Augustine [. . .] St Gregory [. . .] and St Thomas [. . .] and many copies of the two great twelfth-century text-books, the *Historia Scholastica* and the Sentences. On the other hand there are only forty-three volumes of everything else, including history and encyclopaedias, which have their place with theology in this catalogue.[226]

Such a list of contents is of almost the same tenor as what we can find in a monastery library. For instance, the catalogue of the Premonstatensiam library of Tichfield, dated 1400, and which can be considered fairly representative of monastery libraries of the time, reveals what follows:

> the catalogue proper [. . .] begins with a list of Bibles and glosses. This is a traditional arrangement which may be seen in all but one of the catalogues we shall be examining [. . .]. To what extent the glosses were used in the fifteenth century is unclear, but we may recall that the location of such volumes at Durham provides us with clear evidence for changing tastes. Mixed in with this biblical material we find the *Historia scholastica* of Peter Comestor and the commentaries on the Psalter by Augustine and Peter Lombard.[227]

The comparison, brief though it is, shows that at this stage the secular college libraries still had to build their intellectual profile, and

---

[224] Ker, "Oxford College Libraries before 1500", p. 311.

[225] As can be seen, this short survey takes into account only secular colleges; however, in the late fourteenth and early fifteenth century secular colleges were only a small part of the University. For instance, before 1400 only seven secular colleges existed in Oxford. There would be other book-owning institutions of a religious nature (not counting, of corse, the University library itself): three Benedictine colleges, the Augustinian abbey and priory, the Cistercian abbey, the friaries.

[226] Ker "Oxford College Libraries before 1500", p. 305.

[227] David N. Bell, p. 237. See the rest of Bell's article for a detailed discussion of the contents of late medieval English monastery libraries.

to find a cultural identification that would distinguish them from ecclesiastical centres of learning. Besides, and no less important, it is evident that donations could hardly obviate a problem specific to university book collections, and that was the necessity for a constant updating in book resources, together with a need to keep in touch (at least to a certain extent) with bibliographical novelties. The acquisition of texts in the various vernaculars was not yet a concern, since Latin remained the official language of learning and communication in fifteenth-century English universities; but even so, a well-organised college or university library would have to direct a part of its efforts towards the acquisition of newly-produced texts, or persuade a prospective donor to acquire the texts that were most urgently needed. University *curricula* could have a great influence both on what was being bought and on what was being donated, if we may assume that the donation or its contents might be occasionally solicited by the university authorities.

The reader will have noted that so far the discussion has concerned university colleges and their libraries. A well-established but still unverified tradition tells us that Duke Humphrey was educated at Balliol College, Oxford.[228] A donation to the college where he had received his education would thus have been not only welcomed but expected. However, one of the important things to be underlined when discussing Humphrey's book-donations is that the recipient was not Balliol or any other college, but the University library, a decision which raises a number of different questions, connected with the central question of why the Duke of Gloucester should decide on such large donations to begin with. A number of hypotheses can be (and have been) formulated in this case: for instance, the Duke might very simply have had problems of space in his manor of Plesaunce, where he seemed to have kept most of his library, and have decided to get rid of a number of manuscripts in Latin, a language he knew but not so well as to make it matter of everyday reading. This interpretation might be supported by the fact that among the books he donated was the Latin Palladius's *De Re Rustica*, a text he had had translated into English. The problem of housing books should not be considered a minor one: Oxford University

---

[228] Vickers, p. 346. Vickers's sources are John Bale and unspecified Italian humanists.

library had to face a similar problem in the early sixteenth century, and the result was the irreparable loss of a great number of medieval manuscripts. Another possible explanation behind Gloucester's donation might be that he wanted to get rid of volumes that had been presented to him on various occasions, but in which he was not particularly interested. Roberto Weiss's hypothesis is slightly more bizarre: "he parted with them because he had other copies of these works in his library".[229] The inevitable conclusion is that, if he had so many duplicates, the number of manuscripts he actually possessed must have been enormous indeed. Weiss himself, however, seems to believe in his own hypothesis only in part, since a few lines later he hastens to modify his conclusions:

> All the same, as every book he gave away cannot have been a duplicate, there must have been a very strong reason for such generosity. The explanation is to be sought above all in Duke Humfrey's outlook. His exchanges with Renaissance Italy had made him a firm believer in the practical value of a faultless and polished Latin in politics and particularly in diplomacy. Such exchanges had also made him painfully aware that such standards had certainly not been achieved so far in England, except perhaps in his own chancery. It seemed therefore imperative to him that something had to be done in order to raise the standards of learning in general and of Latin in particular in England, and because of this he did not hesitate to make these lavish benefactions to Oxford.[230]

This modified explanation certainly makes more sense, but it remains extremely limiting—to endow a library so lavishly solely in order to raise the linguistic standard of the clerical community in England seems a project with very little practical value. There are two other major objections to this interpretation: on the one hand, the manuscripts donated by Humphrey did not by any means represent a fair sample of the polished Latin Weiss is thinking about (I am assuming the scholar is here thinking of humanist Latin); the texts come from different periods—there are the new, humanist translations of Greek texts, and the Latin works of the great contemporary Italian writers, but also medieval medical treatises, Bibles and bibli-

---

[229] Weiss, "Portrait of a Bibliophile XI: Humphrey, Duke of Gloucester, d. 1447", p. 168.
[230] Weiss, "Portrait of a Bibliophile XI: Humphrey, Duke of Gloucester, d. 1447", p. 168.

cal commentaries, medieval encyclopedias—the collection, although including only manuscripts in Latin, is too linguistically diversified to constitute an acceptable model. On the other hand, these are the years in which the English chanceries were developing their own language and style, showing a decided preference for the use of English rather than Latin. As has been shown in chapter 2, the project was strongly supported by Henry V, and it is unlikely that his younger and devoted brother would go in the opposite direction. The preoccupation with a polished Latin in official documents seems to have been fairly extraneous to national politics, though it might well have been a personal concern for Humphrey, who had Italian humanists (though minor ones) working for him as Latin secretaries in the most important years of his career as a public figure.

Berthold L. Ullman's interpretation goes in the opposite direction when he observes:

> It is altogether likely that Humphrey reserved for himself many humanistic manuscripts and gave Oxford those books which interested him least and those which were most needed for the university's traditional curriculum. That, in fact, is clearly indicated by an examination of the donations which Humphrey made. In 1439 he presented 129 volumes, very few of which can be called humanistic.[231]

It is true that the first recorded donation contained few books that could be considered humanistic, but this could have been a matter of convenience rather than choice. Besides, the same could not be said of the third donation, which contained an important percentage of the "new" texts Humphrey had acquired from Italian writers or middlemen in the 1430s. To suppose that the humanist books he donated to Oxford were a small part of those he possessed means to suppose a vast humanist library, probably vaster that his distance from the humanist centres of production allows us to suppose. But the strongest objection to this theory is that there is no true distinction, either in Humphrey's or in the other great libraries of his time, between a medieval and a humanist book. In building his library Humphrey was collecting what he considered important, what came his way and what he liked to read, which is probably the way

---

[231] Berthold L. Ullman, "Manuscripts of Duke Humphrey of Gloucester", *Studies in the Italian Renaissance*, Roma: Edizioni di Storia e Letteratura: 1955: 345–55, p. 349.

most important private libraries were (and are) put together. The donations to the University of Oxford have a different motivation, but again, I believe, do not take into consideration a possible different purpose between medieval and humanist learning. Humphrey did not simply wish to alienate books he did not want or was not interested in; his donations were part of an active policy that required him to give these tests not to a college, however prestigious, but to an autonomous body to which any Oxford student or scholar might make reference.[232] Susanne Saygin's hypothesis that "from 1437 onwards, Gloucester systematically acquired Italian publications with the aim of donating them to the University of Oxford"[233] might thus be enclosed in this wider project, in which he included not only the humanist texts he was acquiring in Italy, but also manuscripts he was buying or receiving in England.

Humphrey's desire not only to endow the University library with a large number of manuscripts, but also to give it an adequate library room, together with his interest in the University curriculum, shows a desire to connect his name to the very core of the University, and to propose (if not to impose) an ideological model that was strongly rooted in Lancastrian propaganda to the generations of future intellectuals, but especially of future clerks, officials, civil servants. In the years of his donations Gloucester established close links between himself and the University, and may have eventually thought of the University as his cultural representative, and of himself as the University's most authoritative interlocutor. Since his relationships with the King's Council were so strained, and even the popular feeling towards him so changeable, he might have looked at Oxford as a possibly unusual but important ally, especially if he was thinking of a long-term project; after all, it must be remembered that until his death he remained the heir apparent to the throne, and that

---

[232] Elisabeth Leedham-Green has shown that the potential readership for the University library was rather large: "when the Oxford library opened in 1412 it was to be open to graduates, to monks and friars of eight years' standing, and to the sons of the nobility, for two hours in the morning and three in the afternoon. From the late 1440s dispensations are recorded allowing access to members of religious houses who were not graduates in arts, sometimes with the proviso that MAs were to have priority, or that contributions should be made to the cost of repairing, or even of purchasing, books" (Leedham-Green, p. 327). This point, however, shall be discussed more in detail below.

[233] Saygin, p. 111.

Henry V's untimely death was no good omen for the life and health of his son. A proof that his policy was taking the desired shape may be found in the special tone his correspondence with the University took; apart from the customary fulsome thanks for the books received, the University authorities constantly appealed to him when their independence and safety were under threat, kept him constantly informed of University life and its politics; in one occasion, in a letter complaining about people who disturb the peace of the University, there is even a quotation from Plato—a rare occurrence in the *Epistolae Academicae*.[234] Apparently this close relation between the University and the Duke contributed to alienate Henry VI's favour to the point that, after the Duke of Gloucester's disgrace and death, the King decided to donate what remained of his uncle's library not to Oxford (which had staked a not unreasonable claim to it, since the Duke's explicit wish was that Oxford should have all his books) but to King's College, Cambridge, the college he had himself founded, as if to underline once more the links between Oxford University and Duke Humphrey.

If this hypothesis is correct, in choosing the University library as the recipient of his donations Humphrey had been unusually far-sighted, since in the 1430s this institution was far from rivalling either the collections or the prestige of some of the more important colleges. A very brief look at the early history of the University library will show some interesting points. The University library should have been officially founded already in 1320, when Thomas Cobham, Bishop of Worcester, while destining his manuscripts after his death for the use of the poor scholars at the University, donated money for the building of a congregation house that could be the property of the University, rather than of a college; a room above the congregation house was meant for the library, and Cobham specified that the books he bequeathed should be chained in this room.[235] Unfortunately, at the moment of Cobham's death, in 1327, his intentions could not be carried into execution. His books had to be pledged in order to pay for his funeral expenses, and Adam of Brome, then provost of Oriel College (a college he had founded the previous year)

---

[234] *Epistolae Academicae Oxonienses*, pp. 128–30. The letter is dated 7 December 1435.

[235] For a full and informative discussion on this point, see Parkes, p. 470.

redeemed them and had them installed in his college. In 1337, however, the proctor intervened and had the books removed from the
college and temporarily replaced in the University, while only in
1367 did the University decree that the books should be installed as
Cobham had originally intended. The dispute, however, was not
finally settled until 1410, when Archbishop Arundel stepped in, giving Oriel College a reimbursement of 50 marks from his personal
funds and thus effectively terminating any contention.[236] Information
as to the contents of the library before Cobham's donation is very
scanty, as shown by Elisabeth Leedham-Green's reconstruction:

> The earliest evidence for books owned by the University of Oxford
> consists of a copy made in 1432 of an inventory of the university's
> property. The lost original is datable to before 1350 and records two
> manuscripts: one a Bible divided into four parts so that, on deposit of
> a surety, scholars might borrow parts to correct their own copies, and
> the other an old copy of Exodus. Their original donor, Roger de
> Holdernesse, or de Skeffling, Dean of York, had been a master in
> Oxford in the 1250's. It appears also, from a copy of a letter from
> the university surviving by chance in the letter formulary of Richard
> de Bury, Bishop of Durham, that Henry de Harkeley, Chancellor of
> the University, bequeathed books to it on his death in 1317. We do
> not know whether the university ever secured the bequest.[237]

The library was thus officially opened to scholars and readers only
in 1412; the room Cobham had indicated in his bequest remained
the seat of the library until 1488, when it was replaced by what is
now known as Duke Humfrey's Library. Unfortunately, however, no
record has survived of the books donated by the Bishop of Worcester,
nor do we know the exact extent and number of subsequent bequests
or book donations that would have enlarged the store of the University
library. Yet Parkes notes that since 1412 "the university seems to
have begun to exert itself to attract donations",[238] even if none of
the early fifteenth-century donations could compare in magnitude or
scope with Duke Humphrey's.

Much of the correspondence between the University of Oxford
and Duke Humphrey has been preserved in Henry Anstey's *Epistolae
Academicae Oxonienses*, and constitutes a precious document to under-

---

[236] Parkes, p. 471. On this point, see also Leedham-Green, p. 317.
[237] Leedham-Green, pp. 316–7.
[238] Parkes, p. 472.

stand the complex nature of the book donations we are discussing. The first donation for which a list survives is dated 5 November 1439, but there is ample evidence that the Duke of Gloucester had proposed himself as a patron to the University long before that date. It must also be noted that the relationship between the nobleman and the institution cannot be fully understood if we do not take into consideration another participant in this story, the physician Gilbert Kymer. Earlier in this chapter it has been noted that Kymer was Humphrey's medical advisor in the 1420s, and became chancellor of the University in 1431; it should be added that we find his name in University documents already in 1412, and that he is concerned with the library in the same year in which it was officially opened to readers. As *Procuratoribus Magister*, he signed a document dated 20 November 1412 in which he declared that, since at last the University was endowed with an adequate library, "universitas *statuit et decrevit*, quod Capellanus idoneus, in sacerdotio constituitus, in custodiam librariae communis in congregatione Regentium solemni eligatur".[239] Kymer's role evidently required him to concern himself with the organization and administration of the library; the same document specifies who may use the library, and under what conditions. On this point the statute is very specific:

> Nullus in Universitatis libraria de caetero studeat, nisi graduati tantum et religiosi possessionati post octo annos in philosophia, juramento prius per eos praestito, coram cancellario in praesentia custodis librariae, illos se octo annos in hac Universitate habere, una cum juramento quod caeteri Universitatis graduati praestabunt, cujus tenor infra statuto proximo continetur; filii vero dominorum, qui in Parliamento regio sedem habent, cum quibus ex gratia speciali ingrediendi facultatem Universitas ordinavit, ad idem, sub forma simili praestandum, sacramentum noverint se astrictos.[240]

---

[239] "The University orders and decrees, that an apt chaplain, in holy orders, may be chosen in a solemn congregation of the governors for the custody of the common library". *Munimenta Academica*, p. 261.

[240] "Nobody can study in the University library, apart from graduate students, ecclesiastics who have studied philosophy for at least eight years, having taken an oath, in front of the chancellor and of the librarian, that they have been eight years in this University, together with the oath taken by all University graduates, that will be contained in the next statute; and also the sons of those who sit in the King's Parliament; the University orders that they may be given licence to enter the faculty, once they take the same oath". *Munimenta Academica*, p. 264.

The granting of the right of access to the library to the sons of the members of Parliament is particularly interesting. Finding itself among the most important centres of secular learning in England, Oxford did not want to remain a privileged but isolated institution, and tried to establish links with political power which would, on the one hand, ensure the financial survival of the University, and on the other, make it part of the political debate. The discussion on Humphrey's donations will also show whether they had any relation with this attitude on the part of the University.

In the same year, and in the same document, we see the Duke's name associated with Oxford, probably for the first time. Humphrey is included in a list of benefactors to the library, who shall be remembered especially at the Masses. It is, however, unlikely that this mention originated by an act of generosity on the part of the Duke, who was 22 at the time and had not yet become a public figure. It is more probable that he was named simply as a member of the royal family. Later, in 1427, the University addressed him in person to resolve a problem connected with a minor friar who had disgraced himself. The late 1420s would then appear to indicate the beginning of a direct interest on the part of the Duke in the affairs of the University. It should be noted that this interest is not limited to the state of the library, but embraces also questions of internal policy, of administration, of funding. More important still, the Duke appears to have concerned himself with the University curriculum. A letter from the University, dated 6 July 1431, regrets that at the moment it is impossible for the University to carry out the reforms proposed by the Duke, though it promises to try again in future. Unfortunately Humphrey's proposal has not survived, but the tenor of the University's letter may provide us with some clues on the matter, as can be seen in the following extensive quotation:

> Nos enim a nostra mente labitur, sed totum in viscera merito se diffundit, quod vestris graciosissimis litteris ad reformacionem trium, que significantis eisdem, nimietate amoris in presenti termino, vestra dignacio voluit nos hortari. Et licet jussionibus dominacionis vestre simus, et semper erimus, obtemperare parati, partim tamen ob quorundam nostrorum absenciam, partim eciam ob brevitate signati temporis et gravitatem operis recommissi, non juxta vota modo valuimus mandata vestra sufficienter, ut cupimus, adimplere; sed confisi desuper regnantis influxu, ad laudem sibi complendam vestram, et ad nostros speciales honorem et commodum, quos, velut metimur ex opere, corditer affectatis, ante festum natalis Domini, coädunatis professori-

bus omnium facultatum, celerius quo sufficimus hec tria curabimus salutare.[241]

The curriculum for the Faculty of Arts was established by a document dated 10 December 1431, in which Kymer was named as *Cancellarius*.[242] Lack of complete information makes Humphrey's role and weight in the establishing of a new art course unclear, but his interest seems beyond doubt. At the same time the tenor of the letter, together with the fact that the Duke is addressed with the formula "Illustrissimo principi, atlete fidei et studii protectori, duci Gloucestrie, locum tenenti Anglie, &c., nostro refugio singulari"[243] suggests that Humphrey was already singled out as a special benefactor. The formula will be repeated, with some variation, in the future correspondence between the University and the Duke; on the other hand, no other benefactor or public figure is addressed in a similar way in the extant documents.

It is difficult to see whether there is a connection between this interest in the arts curriculum and the book donations that followed. The special emphasis on rhetoric and classical literature seems to indicate a support of the humanist cause that would be also furthered through the subsequent donations, though humanist texts were included mainly in the last donation.[244] Susanne Saygin sees Humphrey's interest as part of a standard practice, commenting on his reform proposals with these words: "if it is assumed that they concerned the arts course at Oxford, they would have had their

---

[241] "We let slip from our mind, but kept in our heart, the exhortations of your Highness towards the reformation of the three arts, which you made so clearly and with so much love. We are and always will be ready to obey your wishes and commands, though in this case, partly because of our absence, partly because the time is so little and the work so important, we have not evaluated your wishes as completely as we wanted; but confiding in the influence of the king, to obtain praise for you, and for our honour and convenience, we shall gather the professors of all the faculties before the feast of Christmas, and take care of the three arts more quickly than we did". *Epistolae Academicae Oxonienses*, p. 65.

[242] *Munimenta Academica*, pp. 285–7. The document includes also a detailed description of the curriculum.

[243] "To the illustrious prince, defensor of the faith and protector of studies, the Duke of Gloucester, *locum tenens* of England, &c., our special refuge".

[244] "Certainly his books could have furthered the humanist cause in Oxford since not all of them were in fact to be confined to the library. Books relevant to the new arts course were to be kept in a special chest for loan to lecturers and, if not so required, to the principals of halls for the use of their pupils" (Leedham-Green, p. 317).

equal in Bedford's patronage of lectures in the *artes liberales* and the
three philosophies during the early 1430's".[245] However, patronage
is not the same thing as specific proposals of reform, which presume
that the Duke had occasion or time to consider the issues at hand.
In these years both Gloucester and the Duke of Bedford are often
appealed to, so that they might lend their assistance (generally of a
financial nature) to Oxford; but there seem to be letters of thanks
only in the case of Humphrey. At the same time, Gilbert Kymer is
occasionally asked in other letters to use his influence with the Duke
to obtain the latter's assistance when the peace at Oxford was dis-
turbed. The pattern seems clear: Humphrey was selecting Oxford
University as the main recipient of his patronage; the University was
appealing to him in matters concerning not only the library, but the
everyday running of the institution; Kymer (to whom the University
once refers, in a letter to Humphrey, as "celsitudinis vestre clericum")[246]
was often acting as an intermediary. The relationship becomes more
definite from 1435, a year in which the Duke's political fortunes
seemed to be clearly in the ascendant: in the same year the Duke
of Bedford had died, which made Humphrey heir apparent; in the
following year, the Flanders campaign would confer on him, though
briefly and perhaps spuriously, military glory. It is possible that, as
with most of Humphrey's political and military decisions, this form
of intellectual patronage modelled itself on the policy of Henry V;
as Saygin correctly notes, the Duke may have considered it "an
opportunity to project his self-image as protector of his dead brother's
will beyond the confines of the court, and publicise it to a wider
audience".[247]

There certainly were book donations on the part of the Duke of
Gloucester before 1439, that is, before the earliest list in our possession. It is unfortunate, and somewhat tantalising, that we should
have no indication either of the size or of the type of the other
donations, apart from the three recorded; but this does not mean
that they were exiguous, or of no importance.[248] A letter from the
University dated 11 May 1435 speaks of "magnificis donis librorum

---

[245] Saygin, p. 84.
[246] "Clerk to your serene Highness". *Epistolae Academicae Oxonienses*, p. 256.
[247] Saygin, pp. 85–6.
[248] As Saygin seems to assume (p. 84).

et auri",[249] and of the light these gifts will shed upon the liberal sciences. In the following year there is an even more generic letter of thanks, but with a clear reference to the arts curriculum: "O precelsa serenitas, o celica inspiracio, cujus ope et mandato septem liberalium arcium triumque philosophiarum studium et doctrina, olim fere in oblivionem lapsa, renovata fuerant et in actum redacta".[250] It is difficult to see how else Humphrey could have contributed to this renovation, if not with gifts, either in money or in books. Again, other gifts are alluded to between the donations we know of: on 28 February 1440 there is a letter of thanks for seven manuscripts donated to the library.[251] A letter dated 14 July 1445[252] thanks the Duke for an unspecified but presumably high number of manuscripts—this could be a reference to the third recorded donation, but if so it would come rather late (the donation was made on 25 February 1444); besides, there is already a letter of thanks for this donation.[253] What is interesting about the 1445 letter is that it refers not only to Latin but to Greek volumes: "hic enim prisca Greci Latinique sermonis majestas, quam incuria hominum infinitis pene seculis obscuravit, patrocinio vestro in lucem traducta reflorescit".[254] It may be argued that the reference is simply to Greek texts in Latin translation, as was the case with many of the humanist books Humphrey acquired; but the use of the word *sermonis* might make us think of volumes in the Greek tongue. It should be added, however, that there is no other proof of this. Anstey's collection records another letter of thanks in 1446, with a reference to Humphrey's munificence.

Such observations make it even more awkward to consider the three lists we have a reliable source on Duke Humphrey's library, if only because they appear more than ever incomplete. If we assume

---

[249] "A magnificent gift of books and gold".

[250] "O celestial serenity, o divine inspiration, by whose work and order the study and doctrine of the seven liberal arts and of the three philosophies, once almost fallen into oblivion, have been renovated and brought into being". *Epistolae Academicae Oxonienses*, p. 139.

[251] *Epistolae Academicae Oxonienses*, pp. 197-9

[252] *Epistolae Academicae Oxonienses*, pp. 244-6.

[253] *Epistolae Academicae Oxonienses*, pp. 240-2.

[254] "The original majesty of the Greek and Latin tongue, almost obscured by human oblivion for so many centuries, is now blossoming once again, brought back to light by your patronage". *Epistolae Academicae Oxonienses*, p. 245.

that they were part of an ideological project on the part of the Duke, we must also remember that the magnitude of this project escapes us, not only because there is evidence of unspecified donations, but because Humphrey's death, and the *damnatio memoriae* that immediately followed it (including Henry VI's arbitrary disposing of the remaining manuscripts), abruptly interrupted any project of this kind. By late medieval (and Lancastrian) standards, Humphrey's death may not have been premature, but it was certainly sudden; the fact that the correspondence with Oxford continues until the year of the Duke's death shows that his relationship with the University was by no means concluded. The modern scholar is left with very incomplete clues.

With this proviso, the records of the three donations may be profitably discussed since, taken individually, they show consistencies and differences which may be very informative. They constitute a document of difficult interpretation, since they include books of all types, books that might belong to a medieval library and books that might be more easily classified as humanistic. There is very little indication of the Duke's tastes, or of his favourite subjects. The Church Fathers, from Augustine to Jerome to Ambrose to a number of others, are well represented, together with Peter Abelard and with more recent Italian authors—there are a number of Latin works by Petrarch and Boccaccio, as well as Giovanni da Serravalle's Latin version of Dante's *Divina Commedia*; there are works by medieval English writers, such as Bede or John of Salisbury, Latin classics such as Seneca, Ovid, Sallust, Pliny and Livy, together with the *Cato moralizatus*, Plato and Aristotle in Leonardo Bruni's or Antonio Beccaria's translations, along with a surprising number of books on medicine (the standard medieval library on the subject), Avicenna and Albertus Magnus, texts of astronomy and astrology, John Capgrave's biblical commentaries, Whethamstede's *Granarium*, and so on. No systematic analysis of the subjects included in these donations has yet been undertaken, though Weiss observes that

> a perusal of the lists of manuscripts given to Oxford bears out the catholicity of his tastes but suggests a certain predilection for medicine and astrology. These last two subjects, and works of medieval learning, theological and otherwise, formed perhaps the majority of his books. Still classical works and the neoclassical writings of his contemporaries were so far from being negligible that, apart from other

evidence, they would suffice in themselves to show the strong bent of his mind towards classicism.[255]

A more detailed description is offered by J.B. Trapp, who notes how the first donation sees a predominance of medical texts, together with astronomical or astrological books, theological treatises, Bibles and medieval encyclopedias, as well as rhetorical treatises. The humanist component is certainly more noticeable in the third donation, which however includes also scholastic texts (about one fifth of the whole gift), books of civil or canon law (one eighth), patristic texts (one tenth). Yet there is no doubt that the point of interest of the third donation, for modern scholars but also for fifteenth-century Oxford readers, is constituted by the new books: Boccaccio and Petrarch, what Trapp calls the "native humanist component", represented for instance by the works of John Whethamstede, and the new Latin translations of Greek texts. In all donations, besides, there is a section devoted to Latin classics.[256]

Once the analysis is focused on the single lists, interesting details emerge. The first detailed donation, dated 5 November 1439, saw Gilbert Kymer, together with Ralph Drewe, as an intermediary. Kymer was then Chancellor of the University, and brought the 129 manuscripts to Oxford himself.[257] Susanne Saygin attempts to link this donation to a specific moment in Humphrey's political life: in September of the same year the Duke of Gloucester had summoned Parliament to gather at Oxford at the beginning of November, attempting to stop the Council's decision to release Charles, Duke of Orléans, who was then prisoner in England.[258] It has been shown in the previous chapter that Gloucester's opposition to the projected release took an almost violent tone, as is shown in the Duke's written document of protest,[259] and there is no doubt this episode marked

---

[255] Weiss, *Humanism in England During the Fifteenth Century*, p. 62.

[256] Trapp, "Il libro umanistico tra Italia e Inghilterra dal '400 al primo '500", pp. 323–4. Trapp's analysis is presented again, with some amplifications, in his "The Humanist Book", in *The Cambridge History of the Book in Britain, vol. 3: 1400–1557*, ed. by L. Hellinga and J.B. Trapp, Cambridge: Cambridge University Press, 1999: 285–315.

[257] Parkes, p. 473. See also *Epistolae Academicae Oxonienses*, p. 179.

[258] Saygin, pp. 86–7.

[259] "Protest of Humphrey, Duke of Gloucester, against the liberation of the Duke

one of the moments of most heated conflict between Gloucester and
Henry Beaufort. We also know that Gloucester's protest against the
release of Orléans, when there was no opposing the decision, would
assume an ostentatiously public form: he stormed out of the church
in which the former prisoner was swearing never to bear arms against
the English King, on 3 November 1440. Thus it is conceivable that
the considerably large 1439 donation had been timed in order to
acquire the favour of Oxford during the negotiations with the
Parliament. The collection of *Epistolae Academicae* includes for the year
1439 a letter to the Parliament about the Duke's gift; the letter is
in English, and seems to have been dictated (at least in spirit) by
Humphrey himself:

> Wherfore we besege your sage discrecions to consider the gloriose yiftes
> of the graciose prince to oure sayde Universite, for the comyn profyte
> and worschyp of the reme, to thanke hym in tyme commyng, when
> goode dedys ben rewarded.[260]

Many of the Oxford students would be the sons of the representatives gathered in Parliament; besides, the library, as has been noted
above, was open to the sons of the parliamentarians whether or not
they belonged to the University. The Duke of Gloucester often set
himself against the King's Council, but equally often found support
in non-aristocratic sections of the population: "Humphrey, because
of his ambitions and his pride, stood largely alone; but he had the
intermittent support of the *plebs*, notably the Londoners and the
Commons in Parliament".[261]

Thus, Saygin's hypothesis is plausible, but the timing of the donation seems rather tight. The donation, as we have noted, was made
on 5 November; the indenture between the Duke and the University,
in which the latter acknowledged the receipt of the volumes and
listed them, is dated 25 November. If the summons to the Parliament
had been made in September, and the actual meeting took place at
the beginning of November, it is unlikely that Humphrey's generosity

of Orleans", in *Letters and Papers Illustrative of the Wars of the English in France during
the Reign of Henry the Sixth, King of England*, ed. by J. Stevenson, Rolls Series, London:
Longman, 1864: II.440–51.
  [260] *Epistolae Academicae Oxonienses*, p. 184.
  [261] B. Wilkinson, *The Later Middle Ages in England 1216–1485*, London: Longmans,
1969, p. 260.

had time to make itself publicised, however prompt the University's letter to the Parliament may have been. Besides, it is conceivable that it would be some time before the manuscripts listed in the indenture could actually be made accessible to the readers. Therefore, though probably the Duke of Gloucester was trying to find a powerful ally in the University through his gifts, and though he probably was "inspired by his wish to publicise his self-image as faithful executor of Henry V's will",[262] it is less likely that in this case there was such a strict concatenation of cause and effect.

As to the contents of the donation,[263] the list follows, though far from faithfully, the usual order proposed in contemporary library catalogues, discussed above in this chapter. The very first items to be catalogued are Nicholas de Lyra and a "diccionarium" in four parts which Sammut believes to be Pierre Bersuire' *Dictionarium seu Repertorium morale*;[264] then there is a Bible and a Bible concordance, followed by a number of ecclesiastical histories, biblical glosses, theological works. This section follows traditional patterns, and the authors listed do not excite particular surprise; we might note that Bede is represented by a respectable number of works: his *Historia Ecclesiastica Gentis Anglorum*, a commentary on the Acts of the Apostles and the treatise *De Temporibus*. Equally interesting is the fact that in this first, "ecclesiastical" section, including approximately thirty-nine volumes,[265] Petrarch's *De vita solitaria* is included. Other works by Petrarch follow at some distance: his *Rerum memorandarum libri* and *De remediis utriusque fortunae*. Already this first donation shows a particular interest in Petrarch, whose Latin works were beginning to be known in England.[266] On the other hand, the collection of Latin and Greek classics is rather reduced but of some interest: there are medieval versions such as Filippo di Bergamo's *Cato Moralizatus sive speculum regiminis*, the so-called "Aristotelis de anima cum commento"

---

[262] Saygin, p. 87.

[263] The complete lists have been published, with some annotations, in Sammut, pp. 60–84.

[264] Sammut, p. 61.

[265] The estimate is offered with some hesitation: some of the books listed are of difficult identification.

[266] On this point see Nicholas Mann, "La prima fortuna del Petrarca in Inghilterra", in *Il Petrarca ad Arquà. Atti del convegno di studi nel VI centenario (1370–1374)*, ed. by G. Billanovich and G. Grasso, Padova: Antenore, 1975: 279–89, and "Petrarch Manuscripts in the British Isles", *Italia Medioevale e Umanistica* 18: 1975, 139–509.

which may correspond to the anonymous *Quaestiones in tres libros de anima*, Isidore of Seville's *Ethymologiae* and John of Salisbury's *Polycraticus*, but also Plato's *Phedro* in Leonardo Bruni's translation, and the translations by the same humanist of Aristotle's *Ethics* and *Politics*. The Latin translation of Aristotle's *Politics* had been promised by Leonardo Bruni to Duke Humphrey in 1434; in a letter dated 1 November 1438 the humanist declares his satisfaction in hearing that the Duke has received the translation; the donation to Oxford followed after only a year, which may mean that Humphrey had the University library in mind from the beginning of his commission, or that he realised very quickly how important it would be for the library to have these new versions. It is true that the first donation has only a small percentage of humanist books, as compared to the third; it must also be noted that Humphrey's relations with Italian humanists (as opposed to his employing Italian secretaries) were still in their relatively early stages.

But the largest section of the donation is constituted by medical books. The difficulty in cataloguing a medieval manuscript as scientific or medical has been already highlighted by Linda Ehrsam Voigts when she asks: "how can we identify a 'scientific book' if what is called *science* is not what medievals understood as *sciencia*?". To this we may add another problem, constituted by the fact that often theological or logical treatises might debate questions of physical science. Yet the same scholar gives a useful definition for medical manuscripts, defining medicine in the Middle Ages as a "technology for maintaining or restoring health",[267] and this is what we have in the texts included in Gloucester's donations. Examining the lists, Vern L. Bullough in 1961 attempted a reconstruction of the Duke's medical library. The first donation includes thirty-two texts (there will be three more in the third donation, none in the second), but this considerable number, according to Bullough, does not seem to include any real novelties:

> Surprisingly, these are mostly from the twelfth or thirteenth centuries and are not the current works which were finding their way into the

---

[267] Linda Ehrsam Voigts, "Scientific and Medical Books", in *Book Production and Publishing in Britain 1375–1475*, ed. by J. Griffiths and D. Pearsall, Cambridge: Cambridge University Press, 1989: 345–402, p. 345.

university curriculum [. . .] They indicate that the Duke himself was
not as prepared to break new ground in this field as he was in others.[268]

The same opinion is expressed by F.M. Getz:

> There were no dangerous novelties here: many of these sources had
> been known to Bacon and Bartholomew nearly two hundred years
> before. The collection was hardly representative of what would be
> called medical humanism.[269]

This seems particularly surprising if we think that Gilbert Kymer,
former chancellor of the University and apparently an intermediary
in this donation, was a physician, and might be thought to have had
a particular interest in the search for new books belonging to this
field, while Humphrey's correspondence with Italian humanists shows
that he was interested in completely different subjects. There is no
evidence in his correspondence that he meant to acquire medical
books from Italy, or that he was particularly interested in novelties.
On the other hand, Kymer's only surviving medical work, the *Dietarium*
written for Duke Humphrey, showed the same intellectual attitude:

> Gilbert Kymer's sole medical work, a regimen of health written for
> Humfrey, duke of Gloucester in 1424, about a year after Kymer had
> obtained his DM, encapsulated what learned medicine was supposed
> to be, and by its citations of Roger Bacon and the *Secreta Secretorum*
> marked a return to the thirteenth-century medical attitudes from the
> Galenism represented by fourteenth-century Mertonian scholars.[270]

The medical books included in the first donation include well-known
medieval texts such as Averroes, Avicenna, Bartholomaeus Anglicus,
Galenus, Gerardus Carmonensis, Gilbertus Anglicus, Hippocrates,
Haly Abbas, Petrus Hispanus, Willelmus de Saliceto—standard medical works of an old fashioned curriculum, in which the only fourteenth-century book is Bernardus de Gordonio's *Lilium*. In such a
collection perhaps the only thing to be noticed is the attention given
to English-born authors—a characteristic that recurs also in other

---

[268] Vern L. Bullough, "Duke Humphrey and His Medical Collections," *Renaissance News* 14: 1961, 87–91. Bullough indicates also the most obvious deficiencies in the donation.
[269] F.M. Getz, "The Faculty of Medicine before 1500", in *The History of the University of Oxford, vol. 2: Late Medieval Oxford*, ed. by J.J. Catto and R. Evans, Oxford: Clarendon Press, 1992, 2: 373–405, p. 403.
[270] Getz, "The Faculty of Medicine before 1500", p. 398.

sections of this and the other donations. It is true, as Bullough maintains, that in this way Humphrey contributed but little to the progress
of this branch of learning; it is also true, however, that the University
library, depleted as it was, would probably welcome traditional volumes that could help establish the medical core reading of the students. The size of this part of the donation, together with the fact
that there are no medical books in the second donation and only
three (of which one is another copy of a text already appearing in
the first donation) in the third, may perhaps show that the Duke of
Gloucester was answering a precise request on the part of Kymer
or of the University authorities, while he had no specific interest in
what he was giving. None of the medical books included in the
donations seems to have survived. The only books of medical interest in the Duke's collection that have survived are the *Antidotarium*
given to the Duke by his wife, described in the previous section and
probably a copy of the already mentioned *Dietarium de sanitatis custodia* written by Gilbert Kymer. The manuscript now preserved in the
British Library has no indication of ownership, but since it was explicitly devoted to the Duke's health it was unthinkable that the latter
would not possess a copy, if not the only copy, of it.[271] As for the
question of the relation between what was clearly a medieval medical collection and Humphrey's humanist interest, Paul Oskar Kristeller
reminds us that

> The humanist criticism of medieval science is often sweeping, but it
> does not touch its specific problems and subject matters. Their main
> charges are against the bad Latin style of the medieval authors, against
> their ignorance of ancient history and literature, and against their con-
> cern for supposedly useless questions. On the other hand, even those
> professional scientists who were most profoundly influenced by human-
> ism did not sacrifice the medieval tradition of their field [. . .] If we
> care to look beyond the field of the humanities into the other fields
> of learning as they were cultivated during the Italian Renaissance, that
> is, into jurisprudence, medicine, theology, mathematics, and natural
> philosophy, what we find is evidently a continuation of medieval learn-
> ing and may hence very well be called scholasticism.[272]

---

[271] The manuscript is now British Library, Sloane 4, ff. 63r–98v. The text is
partly published in *Liber Niger Scaccarii*, ed. by T. Hearne, Oxonii: E Theatro Sheldoniano, 1728.
[272] Paul Oskar Kristeller, "Humanism and Scholasticism in the Italian Renaissance",
Byzantion 17: 1944–45, 346–75, reprinted in *Renaissance Thought and its Sources*, New
York: Columbia University Press, 1979, pp. 92, 99.

The medical section of Humphrey's donation is followed by a number of philosophical treatises, with volumes such as Plinius's *Naturalis Historia*, books attributed to Aristotle such as *Liber philosophorum moralium antiquorum* and *De mundo*, Avicenna and Albertus Magnus; but what is more interesting at this point is the conspicuous presence of astrological books. There are at least thirteen astrological volumes in this donation, once again covering traditional fields: there is Roger Bacon's *De caelo et mundo*, Haly Abenragel in two volumes, Albumasar, Egidius's *De cometis*, Zael's *De iudiciis astrorum* and *De vita hominis*, Ptolemy's Almagest and another work called *Tripertitum*, an unspecified work by Thebit ben Chorat, John Ashenden's *Summa astronomiae*, and a number of books of astronomical tables. As in the case of the medical books, the astrological texts are almost solely concentrated in the first donation; the third donation will only include only Ptolemy's *Cosmographia*.[273] Hillary M. Carey links this part of the donation, once again, to Gilber Kymer:

> It is quite likely that the selection of works on astrology in Duke Humphrey's bequest reflects the interest of his "special messenger" Gilbert Kymer, rather than his personal taste. Surprisingly, among the forty-four extant manuscripts which bear Duke Humphrey's autograph, only one touches on the sciences of astrology and astronomy, namely Oxford Corpus Christi College MS 243. This book was given to the Duke in 1440 by John Whethamstede, abbot of St Alban's, and it contains the *De divinatione* by Albertus Magnus, a tract *De signis aquarum*, and the *Liber cursum planetarum* by Raymond of Marseille. However, undoubtedly the chief attraction of the book to the humanist reader was not these tracts but the Latin translations of Plato's *Phaedo* and *Meno* in the same volume. What a prince might consider essential for a university library was not necessarily what he would regard as essential reading for himself.[274]

We can therefore see the same pattern emerging in the case of the medical books: as far as this donation is concerned, there is a distinction between what Humphrey was receiving and requesting and what he was donating. Since in other cases the opposite happens, we may infer that in this first donation Gilbert Kymer played a major role

---

[273] Hillary M. Carey includes in the list also "the ubiquitous *Secreta Secretorum*", which is indeed included in the first donation, though it is difficult to consider it merely an astrological book. See her *Courting Disaster*, p. 55.

[274] Carey, *Courting Disaster*, p. 55.

in requesting specific volumes or volumes relating to specific subjects, which however did not involve the Duke's personal interest. The difference with the third donation in this sense is striking. On this point, Sammut presents a very interesting hypothesis: this donation might have been modelled upon a bequest made by Simon Bredon in 1372. Bredon, a physician and a Fellow of Merton College, left his rich collection of medical and astrological manuscripts to Balliol, Merton, Queen's and Oriel. The University library, moving its first tentative steps in the 1430s, might have proposed this model to the prospective donor, possibly through Kymer's mediation.[275]

The rest of the donation includes a number of Latin authors, particularly rhetoricians: there are six volumes of works by Cicero (his orations and letters, but also the pseudo-Ciceronian *Rhetorica ad Herennium*), Quintilian's *Institutio oratoria*, Priscianus's *Institutionum grammaticarum libri*, Valerius Maximus and Aulius Gellius. There are also a few works we can consider proto-humanist, such as Giovanni Boccaccio's *Genealogia deorum gentilium* or Coluccio Salutati's letters. Yet there is little doubt that the most important part of this donation for the receivers would be constituted by the medical and astrological collections, and thus that in this first list we see only little connection with Humphrey's interest in the arts curriculum. Equally interesting is the fact that the following donations, which include little or nothing of medical or astrological interest, are not connected with the name of Gilbert Kymer. It may be added that the University took immediate care of the books: in a document dated on the same day as the donation, there are dispositions concerning the safekeeping of the volumes.[276] They are to be kept under lock and key in a special chest which is then called "cista trium philosophiarum et septem scientiarum liberalium", the chest of the three philosophies and seven liberal sciences. The document also decrees that while no book can be sold, alienated, exchanged or even removed from the library if not to be bound, an exception can be made if the Duke asks to borrow one of the volumes.

The second donation of which there survives a complete record is dated 10 November 1441, and includes only ten manuscripts. Six of them are works by Augustine, and there is another patristic author,

---

[275] Sammut, p. 71.
[276] *Munimenta Academica*, pp. 326–30. The same document appears in *Epistolae Academicae Oxonienses*, pp. 187–91.

Rabanus Maurus. The remaining three manuscripts include Livy, Seneca and a text described as "novum opus super Aristotelis ethicam". If medicine and astrology characterised the 1939 donation, this donation clearly seems to be meant for the faculty of divinity.[277] If so, it might mean that the Duke's donations answered specific requirements on the part of the various faculties which would make use of the University library. Again, Susanne Saygin links this donation to a particolar moment in Humphrey of Gloucester's political life: this was the year of the Eleanor Cobham scandal, and Humphrey might have chosen books destined to the faculty of divinity in order to influence his wife's impending trial:

> Since several members of that faculty were sitting on the committee that was to adjucate in Eleanor's case, it seems likely that the donation of November 1441, may not, as has hitherto been presumed, have been just another indication of the duke's enlightened and disinterested promotion of learning, but a desperate attempt to impress Eleanor's judges in her favour.[278]

Once again, however, it must be noted if this was the Duke's intention, he did not move with much promptness. Eleanor and her associates were arrested towards the end of June 1441; she admitted she was guilty of a part of the charges on 25 July; her formal divorce from Gloucester was pronounced on 6 November; three days later she was sentenced to her public penance; yet the gift to the University was inventoried only on 10 November 1441, and on the same day the University thanked the Duke with a letter.[279] As for Saygin's hypothesis for the third recorded donation, it is less connected to a specific event:

> It is here proposed that in the aftermath of the Cobham affair, the duke perceived his second major donation to Oxford as a way to prevent the appropriation of his posthumous reputation by Suffolk's regime and as an opportunity to provide for his own spiritual welfare after his death. In 1444, Gloucester was in his early fifties; by aristocratic standards this was not very old, yet his brother Bedford had died in his mid-forties and Gloucester himself may have had a history of poor health.[280]

---

[277] As noted by Saygin, pp. 101–2.
[278] Saygin, p. 102.
[279] *Epistolae Academicae Oxonienses*, pp. 202–4.
[280] Saygin, pp. 112–3.

This might be a reasonable explanation not only for this specific gift but for a number of other decisions on Humphrey's part: for instance, in 1443 he had allocated £433 6s. 8d. to the establishment of his chantry tomb at the Abbey of St Albans, where he would be buried in 1447. As for his supposedly poor health, this hypothesis might be supported by the contents of Kymer's *Dietarium*. Yet once again it is difficult to believe in a close connection: if Humphrey was thinking of his posthumous reputation, it is conceivable, for instance, that in the 1443 donation he would include not only Tito Livio Frulovisi's *De Republica* but also his *Vita Henrici Quinti*, which was probably Humphrey's most important commission finalised to Lancastrian propaganda (especially if we consider the popularity this book enjoyed in England), and perhaps the eulogistic *Humfroidos*.[281]

Whatever the political reasons behind this donation, there is no doubt that it is the most interesting from the point of view of the students of English humanism. It includes 135 volumes, and the humanist element is particularly prominent. Many of the books listed had been formerly objects of discussion between the Duke and his Italian correspondents, or had been presented to him on various occasions. Even more interesting, there is at least one Latin volume of which Humphrey had ordered a translation into the vernacular, that is, Palladius's *De Re Rustica*, and other volumes of which he possessed and retained an English or a French translation.

A good part of the donation, however, is still medieval. The theological section, listed at the beginning, includes Anselm of Canterbury, Augustine, Johannes Chrysostomus, Ambrose, Albertanus Causidicus Brixiensis and William of Ockham, but also Nicholas Trevet's commentary on the Psalter (and his Boethian commentary) and what seems the whole group of manuscripts John Capgrave had presented to the Duke. Between 1437 and 1439 Capgrave had sent or personally delivered (presumably) unsolicited copies of his Bible commentaries, *In Regnum I* and *III* (that is, I Samuel and I Kings), *In Genesim* and *In Exodum* to Humphrey. The fact that the whole series was made over to the University library may argue for a lack of interest on the part of the Duke—as will be shown in the next chapter, it is difficult to consider Capgrave a representative of the native

---

[281] Sammut, however, believes the *Humfroidos* to have been included in the manuscript of the *De Republica* given to the University library.

humanism Humphrey actively patronised. Two of Capgrave's manuscripts have survived,[282] together with Athanasius's theological trac-
tates, also donated in 1443,[283] and already discussed in the previous
section. A group of manuscripts are of French origin; among them
there is a volume described as *sompnum viridarium* which might be the
Latin original of *Le songe du Vergier*, attributed to Philippe de Mézières,
which John, Duke of Bedford had donated to Humphrey.[284] The
hypothesis is supported by the fact that the *sompnum viridarium* is
inserted in a group of texts on canon and civil law, constituting
about an eighth of the whole donation.[285] As R.H. Helmholz notes,

> The canon law provided the principal source of the jurisprudence in
> the English ecclesiastical courts. These courts, held by every bishop
> and archdeacon, as well as by many lesser clerics, played a wide and
> important role in the legal life of medieval England. Indeed, they held
> significant jurisdiction over the law of marriage, wills and probate, and
> part of the law of defamation, well into the nineteenth century.[286]

Given its importance, canon law was formally taught in English universities until the canon law faculties were abolished in the 1530s.[287]
Thus books on canon law would be considered an essential part of
a University library. I would argue that, as in the case of medical,
astrological, and perhaps also theological books, Duke Humphrey's
gifts did not express his personal taste but his acknowledgement of
the University's needs. Here, too, the collection includes strictly traditional texts, such as the principal commentators on the texts of the
Corpus iuris canonici (Johannes Andreae, Panormitanus) together with
some volumes of the *Corpus iuris canonici* itself. There is also the volume containing the Acts of the Council of Constance, which Humphrey
had bought in 1433 from the testamentary executors of the Bishop

---

[282] Now Oxford, Oriel College 32 and Oxford, Bodleian Library Duke Humfrey b.1.

[283] Now London, British Library, Royal 5 F.II.

[284] Now London, British Library, Royal 19 C.IV. Described in Sammut, pp. 107–8.

[285] According to J.B. Trapp's calculations. See Trapp, "The Humanist Book", p. 295.

[286] R.H. Helmholz, "The Canon Law", in *The Cambridge History of the Book in Britain, vol. 3: 1400–1557*, ed. by L. Hellinga and J.B. Trapp, Cambridge: Cambridge University Press, 1999: 387–98, p. 387.

[287] Helmholz suggests that the subject was still studied informally afterwards (pp. 387–8).

of Worcester.[288] Civil law, also studied in fifteenth-century English universities, is represented by equally traditional authors such as Johannes Faber or Baldus.[289]

This section is followed by a considerable collection of Vincent de Beauvais's works: the *Speculum historiale, Speculum naturale* and *Speculum doctrinale* are all present, followed by books of history, both ancient (Eusebius, Trogus Pompeius, Daretes Frigius, Livy, Flavius Josephus, Suetonius, the younger Pliny), and modern, or at any rate nearer in space; there is a copy of Matthew of Westminster's *Eulogium historiale Anglie* and Ralph Higden's *Polychronicon*, together with John Whethamstede's *Granarium* (once again, presumably the copy Whethamstede himself had given the Duke). These books mark the transition between the "medieval" and the "humanist" section of the donation, with a special emphasis on Italian writers. The list includes four works by Giovanni Boccaccio (*Genealogia deorum gentilium, De casibus virorum illustrium, De mulieribus claris* and *De montibus*, already discussed above), together with no less than seven works by Petrarch (*Epistolae, De remediis utriusque fortunae, Secretum, De viris illustribus*, possibly *De vita solitaria* and two other works of more difficult identification). Both Boccaccio and Petrarch were already present in the first donation, which argues for Humphrey's extreme interest in late-medieval Italian authors. The list also includes Andrea Domenico Fiocchi's *De romanis magistratibus* and the two volumes associated with Dante, possibly his *Divine Comedy* and Bertoldi's commentary, already discussed in the previous section. The humanist influence is also recognisable in the choice of classical authors: many Greek texts are in the new, humanist translations; there is a very high number of Plutarch's *Vitae* translated by the younger Lapo Castiglionchio, Francesco Barbaro, Antonio Pacini, Antonio Beccaria, Leonardo Bruni and others,[290] together with Eschines in Bruni's translation. There is also a volume

---

[288] Now London, British Library, Cotton Nero E V. Described in Sammut, p. 108.

[289] On books of civil law in fifteenth-century English libraries, see Alain Wijffels, "The Civil Law", in *The Cambridge History of the Book in Britain, vol. 3: 1400–1557*, ed. by L. Hellinga and J.B. Trapp, Cambridge: Cambridge University Press, 1999: 399–410.

[290] Among the Plutarchian material there is also a *Demetrius* whose translator I have been unable to identify, since the only humanist version known to us is by Donato Acciaiuoli, not earlier than 1454.

described as "novam traduccionem tocius policie platonice", which is Pier Candido Decembrio's translation of Plato's *Republic*; the manuscript still survives.[291] More interesting still is a volume described as "verba greca et interpretaciones lingue latine", which, as has been seen above, might have been simply a medieval etymological compilation, but might equally well have been a more modern attempt at a dictionary.

Even in this section, however, full as it is of novelties, there is no real distinction between medieval and humanist books: together with what we have listed above, there are more reassuringly traditional items such as Boethius, Pierre Bersuire's *Ovidius moralizatus*, or a lapidary. The list is completed by Peter Abelard's *Epistulae*, Nicholas of Clemanges, Vitruvius, Caesar's *Commentarii*, another copy of Willelmus de Saliceto's *Summa conservationis et curationis*, Terence, Sallust and others. There are also a number of contemporary, humanist works, which Humphrey had probably acquired from their authors: Pietro del Monte's *De virtutum et vitiorum inter se differentia*, Pier Candido Decembrio's *Declamationes*, the already mentioned *De republica* by Tito Livio Frulovisi and a book generically described as "libri Leonardi" which might correspond to Leonardo Bruni's *De interpretatione recta*, since in the second paragraph we find the word *interpretem*, which might have been imperfectly transcribed by the compilers of the Oxford list when they wrote "secondo folio *-terpres*".[292] This work was written by Bruni around 1420, after his translation of Aristotle's *Nicomachean Ethics*, dedicated to Pope Martin V, and since in 1434 Humphrey expressed interest in Bruni's original works, this authoritative *summa* of the Italian humanist's theories on translation would have been an obvious choice for Zeno da Castiglione who had received from the Duke the commission to purchase for him books by Guarino and Bruni.[293] So it would seem that, after devoting different sections of this and the previous donations to the various

---

[291] Now Vatican Library, Vatic. Lat. 10669. Described in Sammut, pp. 124–5. On the margins there are annotations by Decembrio addressed to Humphrey, such as "Attende, princeps" on f. 152v.

[292] See Leonardo Bruni, *De interpretatione recta*, in *Opere letterarie e politiche di Leonardo Bruni*, ed. by P. Viti, Torino: Unione tipografico-editrice torinese, 1996: 145–93; the word occurs on p. 152.

[293] Vickers, p. 351. The other possibility is Bruni's *Vita Ciceronis*, where we can read "ut interpretes" in the third paragraph, but this seems less likely.

faculties of the universities, Humphrey concluded his gift with the
books he had lately acquired, and which constitute the real novelty
of his donation.

It is tempting to see a connection between the humanist books
contained in this donation and the list of recommended books
Decembrio had sent the Duke in 1440; unfortunately it has not survived, but Sammut presumes it to have been a copy of a list of volumes "ex latinis scriptoribus magis necessaria" preserved in the
Biblioteca Ambrosiana.[294] According to Sammut, there are at least
twenty-three cases in which there is a similarity; yet this confirms a
connection between Decembrio's activity and Humphrey's donation,
rather than the intention on the part of the Duke to give the University
library the same books the Italian humanist considered indispensable. Once again, this type of hypothesis is destined to flounder
against the paucity of data at our disposal.

I would then argue that the humanist component of Humphrey's
donation was, actually, only a component, and that the subsequent
history of the library of Oxford, together with the subsequent history of culture, has helped in giving it more importance perhaps
than the Duke himself meant. Of these donations Barker-Benfield
has written that

> in his demand for dedications from Bruni and Decembrio, the Duke
> seems concerned more for personal glory than *utilitas publica*. But by
> giving the books to Oxford—and not to one College, like Whethamstede
> or Grey, but to the whole University—he consigned his private enthu-
> siasms to the public domain [. . .] These books provided the exem-
> plars for many English copies of humanistic texts. Before the Oxford
> manuscripts were dispersed, English humanism had already flowered
> in men like Linacre or More. The great empty room which Sir Thomas
> Bodley reopened in 1602 for the use of *Oxonienses et respublica literato-
> rum* had already served those clients well.[295]

Yet very little of this could have been Humphrey's intention. He
was probably aware that the new translations and treatises by men
such as Bruni or Decembrio introduced important novelties in the
history of culture—or, if he was not, his Italian correspondents would

---

[294] Milano, Biblioteca Ambrosiana, R 88 sup., ff. 172v–173r. Published in Sammut,
pp. 37–8.
[295] Barker-Benfield, p. 194.

have made this point very clear to him—but they remained additions, not elements of revolutionary change. It is otherwise inconceivable that he should have inserted them in a list that includes so many medieval, traditional books.

As has been seen above, Humphrey's relations with the University did not cease with this donation. Gilbert Kymer was elected chancellor again in 1447, and this seems an evident manoeuvre on the part of the University to secure the Duke's goodwill on a permanent basis—unfortunately, Humphrey died only sixteen days later. There may have been other gifts; there certainly was the intention of leaving all remaining books to Oxford. The squabble between the Oxford University library and King's College, Cambridge over the possession of these books goes to show that the volumes Humphrey had already donated were far from constituting the totality of his library. Besides, Humphrey intended to offer financial help towards the building of an adequate library room, though the promised sum was never received by the Oxford authorities. But there are other signs of a continued relationship between the Duke and Oxford; one of the most interesting is a note dated 13 January 1445, in which the University registers the fact that a copy of Plato's *Phaedo* has been lent to Humphrey.[296] It had been established in the previous indentures that, though the donated books would belong to all intents and purposes to the University library, the Duke reserved the right to consult and even borrow them, so this note might simply show that the Duke was exercising his privilege. Yet Plato's *Phaedo* does not appear in either of the three list; on the other hand, it is included in the manuscript of miscellaneous philosophical and astrological texts John Whethamstede gave Humphrey.[297] This might support the hypothesis that there were other donations besides the three analysed here; or (but this is a far-fetched hypothesis) it might mean that the Duke wanted to compare different versions of the same text.

Humphrey's patronage of Oxford University met with an effective stumbling block in his nephew Henry VI's intellectual patronage. In 1440 Henry VI had had his foundation of Eton College rationalised in letters patent, dated 11 October. Shortly before this, on 14 September of the same year, the royal commissioners had acquired

---

[296] *Epistolae Academicae Oxonienses*, p. 246.
[297] Now Oxford, Corpus Christi College, 243. Described in Sammut, pp. 115–6.

for Henry land at Cambridge, previous to the creation of what would have become King's College, and that officially came into existence in 1441, when on 2 April the King himself laid the foundation of the building.[298] We do not know whether the King acted in imitation of his uncle's patronage, or following his father's model. But he certainly used his newly founded Cambridge college as a means to contrast his uncle's last wishes. The fact that Humphrey intended to give "all his Latyn bokes" to the University of Oxford is demonstrated by a document redacted shortly before the Duke's death.[299] However, Humphrey's wishes were not carried into execution, and the successive story of his remaining manuscripts is instructive in itself.[300] He died on 23 February 1447; on the same day, with a special grant,[301] Henry VI made over to his own recently founded King's College, Cambridge, all the property Duke Humphrey had held in the parish of St Andrew in the ward of Baynard's Castle. The property stood in the City of London, and was mentioned in the college accounts as "Gardrobe Duke Humphrey" until the nineteenth century. It was an extremely munificent gift, and obviously very much needed by the new-born college. The college provost, rightly enough, interpreted this as a political act: Henry was re-affirming his supremacy, and his hostility to Oxford, by means of his generosity to the Cambridge college he had founded—and this generosity would involve no expense on his part. Thus on 21 March of the same year the provost, together with the provost of Eton, addressed a petition to Henry VI. After lamenting the needs of the new foundation, especially as concerned books, both for divine offices and study, and "ornements" (that is, vestments required for divine services and other occasions), the provost asked the King to grant the college first choice "of alle such goodes afore eny other man and in especiall of alle maner Bokes ornementes and other necessaries as nowe late were perteyning to the Duke of Gloucestre".[302] The proposal might be

---

[298] For more information on Henry VI as founder of colleges, see Bertram Wolffe, *Henry VI*, London: Eyre Methuen, 1981, pp. 135–45.

[299] *Epistolae Academicae Oxonienses*, p. 294.

[300] For this reconstruction of the ultimate destiny of Humphrey's manuscripts, see A.N.L. Munby, "Notes on King's College Library in the Fifteenth Century", *Transactions of the Cambridge Bibliographical Society* 1: 1951, pp. 280–6.

[301] *Rotuli Parliamentorum*, V, 132.

[302] Petition preserved in the Public Records Office. Here it is quoted from Munby, p. 282.

considered rather bold, though the provost probably knew he was
playing on fairly safe ground. At any rate, it gives us an idea of the
consideration in which Duke Humphrey's library was kept, even after
the large donations to Oxford.

We do not know whether King's College knew of Humphrey's
previous promise to Oxford—if so, their petition was an act of considerable hostility. The University of Oxford, however, had also acted
with great promptitude, sending its own petition to the King,[303] so
that the latter had to set up a commission to administer and dis-
pose of the deceased Duke's property. The haste with which this
commission was put together (on 23 March 1447, that is, two days
after the Cambridge petition), tells us something of the great pressure that was exercised on this matter from all sides. There is little
certainty as to the outcome of the dispute: the commission was rather
biased in favour of King's College, while Oxford was sending other
letters proving its claim. However, there is no registration of large
acquisition of books for Oxford University library in those years,
while the 1452 library catalogue for King's College contains "a number of classical and neo-classical books which feature in no other
fifteenth-century Cambridge catalogue and which could hardly have
been derived from any other source".[304] King's College appears to
have made good use of the volumes thus acquired:

> At King's College in Cambridge, where Henry VI had envisaged a
> huge library room, 110 by 34 feet, not to be realized, a major scoop
> was achieved with the acquisition in the late 1440s of many of the
> books, rightly due to Oxford, of Duke Humfrey of Gloucester. Among
> these were what were almost certainly the only classical and neo-clas-
> sical books to be found in Cambridge institutional libraries at that
> time. Use was made there of some of Duke Humfrey's texts: a man-
> uscript of Jacobus de Cessolis's *De ludo scacchorum*, signed and dated by
> Simon Aylward in 1456, was probably based on the copy in the library
> at King's.[305]

Still, some manuscripts may have gone elsewhere: after all, King's
College would be supposedly interested only in manuscripts in Latin,
while Humphrey's collection included texts in French and in English.
In part, the administrators of the Duke's estate after his death (some

---

[303] *Epistulae Academicae Oxonienses*, pp. 251–2.
[304] Munby, p. 283.
[305] Leedham-Green, p. 322.

of whom were later accused of embezzling goods) may have taken advantage of their position: for instance, the copy of Seneca's *Epistulae* Humphrey had acquired from the testamentary executors of Nicholas Bildeston passed into the hands of John Somerset, one of these administrators.[306] Some books may have remained in Henry VI's possession: "Henry seems to have kept a few of Duke Humfrey's books, choosing the French illuminated manuscripts for himself".[307]

After Humphrey's death, the vicissitudes of the Oxford University library during the reign of Edward VI seem to have been in part the Duke of Gloucester's unwitting fault: "Because it was largely the collection given to Oxford by Duke Humfrey its destruction is a supreme example of enmity to fifteenth-century Oxford by persons highly placed in the University".[308] On the other hand, there is little doubt that Duke Humphrey's donations sparkled a new interest in humanistic books, and that his collection inspired English humanists such as Robert Fleming or William Gray, while giving the colleges the possibility of copying some of these texts.[309] Another effect of Humphrey's patronage may be that after his death, the establishment of a patron became usage: "the university had come to regard the unofficial position of protector as established in practice, and necessary".[310] On March 14, 1447, that is, three weeks after Duke Humphrey's death, the same University of Oxford sent a letter to William de la Pole, marquess of Suffolk, in which the chancellor and congregation asked him to become their protector. Ironically enough, de la Pole had been the prime instigator of Humphrey's arrest. The University, however, did not forget its former benefactor, and in 1452 decreed that proper, though belated, obsequies should be tributed to the Duke.[311]

---

[306] Rundle, "Two Unnoticed Manuscripts from the Collection of Humfrey, Duke of Gloucester", pp. 306–9.

[307] Stratford, "The Early Royal Collections and the Royal Library to 1461", p. 266.

[308] Neil Ripley Ker, "The Provision of Books", in *The History of the University of Oxford, vol. 3: The Collegiate University*, ed. by J. McConica, Oxford: Clarendon Press, 1987: 441–77, p. 466.

[309] Ker, "Oxford College Libraries before 1500", p. 313. Leedham-Green adds: "William Gray, who entered Balliol College, Oxford, in 1431 had copies made, in 1442, of books from the library of Duke Humfrey—Valerius Maximus and a volume of Latin panegyrics which contained also works by Bruni and Giannozzo Manetti—the first humanist texts, perhaps, to be copied in Oxford" (p. 321).

[310] Storey, "University and Government 1430–1500", p. 719.

[311] *Munimenta Academica*, p. 735.

CHAPTER FIVE

CURIOSITY AND ERUDITE HUMANISM:
DUKE HUMPHREY AS A PATRON OF LETTERS

This chapter is devoted to an aspect of Duke Humphrey's patronage that has been generally underestimated. While his relations with
Italian humanists have been minutely scanned, and there is ample
documentation on the subject, much less has been said of his relations with native intellectuals, writers and scholars.[1] This neglect may
be due to a number of reasons: on the one hand, the underestimation involves the whole of fifteenth-century English literature, generally considered, as has been noted in the previous chapters, poor
and derivative in comparison with the splendours of the fourteenth
century (always excluding drama); on the other hand, the links
between Italy and England in the passage from the Middle Ages to
the Renaissance have been perhaps overestimated, especially by twentieth-century scholars.[2] Duke Humphrey entertained close epistolary

---

[1] Recent studies show a new awareness of the subject. See, for instance, allusions to Humphrey's patronage in Lee Patterson, "'What is me?': Self and Society
in the Poetry of Thomas Hoccleve", *Studies in the Age of Chaucer* 23: 2001, 437–70;
Larry Scanlon, *Narrative, Authority, and Power: The Medieval Exemplum and the Chaucerian
Tradition*, Cambridge: Cambridge University Press, 1994; James Simpson, "Bulldozing
the Middle Ages: The Case of 'John Lydgate'", *New Medieval Literatures 4*, ed. by
W. Scase, R. Copeland and D. Lawton, Oxford, Oxford University Press: 2001,
213–42; Paul Strohm, "Hoccleve, Lydgate, and the Lancastrian Court", *The Cambridge
History of Medieval English Literature*, ed. by D. Wallace, Cambridge, Cambridge
University Press: 1999, 640–61. In earlier years, L.C.Y. Everest-Phillips attempted
to reconcile attention to the influence of Italian humanism and English poetical
production in her "The Patronage of Humphrey, Duke of Gloucester. A re-evaluation", Ph.D., York, 1983. There remains, however, a lamentable gap between
scholars working on fifteenth-century English literature and scholars working on
Italian humanism and its repercussions in England.

[2] It is also true, however, that this overestimation has far-reaching roots, if in an
"Imaginary Conversation" Walter Savage Landor (1775–1864) makes Chaucer say
to Boccaccio and Petrarch: "I will attempt to show Englishmen what Italians are:
how much deeper in thought, intenser in feeling, and richer in imagination, than
ever formerly; and I will try whether we cannot raise poetry under our fogs, and
merriment among our marshes". This is quoted, without irony, in Laurie Magnus,
English Literature in its Foreign Relations, 1300 to 1800, London: Kegan Paul, Trench,
Trübner, 1927, p. 10. Magnus's comment is: "This conversation, though 'imaginary,'
is true."

relations with Italian humanists and let himself be guided by them in the choice of the manuscripts he acquired, but he had equally close relations with a number of English writers, commissioned works to them, and used their talents for ideological purposes. In this chapter I will therefore concentrate on his commissions of books in England: leaving aside his contacts with Italian humanists resident in Italy (an aspect of his activity that has been amply discussed), the focus of my analysis will be either original works or translation he directly commissioned or works that were written for him or dedicated to him by English writers, whether in English or in Latin, or by non-English writers who were members of Humphrey's household.

Of course, even in the patronage of native talent Humphrey may have modelled his activity on that of the Italian princes, as he may have done in the case of his collection of manuscripts. Lotte Hellinga and J.B. Trapp remind us that "England of the time could boast no commissioner of manuscripts on the scale of Duke Federico of Urbino, the Medici, Cardinal Giovanni d'Aragona in Italy; Louis XII or Cardinal Georges d'Amboise in France; or Raphael de Marcatellis, abbot of St Bavo, or Louis de Gruythuse in the Low Countries".[3] In this perspective, Humphrey may be considered the last great patron before the age of printing, the last to influence the production of manuscript texts in England. The advent of the age of printing determined a great change in the relation between writer and audience, since it formed a collective readership rather than building upon a single reader: availability became easier, and at this point "the primary factors influencing book ownership were need and means. Thus, the chief owners of books were university-educated and university-educators, that is to say, the secular and regular clergy, including theologians, and other professionals such as lawyers and doctors".[4] In the case of Humphrey we can still speak of a single individual determining a cultural choice through his patronage, and some of the presentation copies dedicated to him that have survived address the patron as if he was considered the only reader of the book.

---

[3] Lotte Hellinga, J.B. Trapp, "Introduction", in *The Cambridge History of the Book in Britain, vol. 3: 1400–1557*, ed. by L. Hellinga and J.B. Trapp, Cambridge: Cambridge University Press, 1999: 1–30, p. 16.

[4] Margaret Lane Ford, "Private Ownership of Printed Books", in *The Cambridge History of the Book in Britain, vol. 3: 1400–1557*, ed. by L. Hellinga and J.B. Trapp, Cambridge: Cambridge University Press, 1999: 205–28, p. 205.

Even more than his ideology, Humphrey's patronage reflects his culture: "Literary patronage has its roots in literacy, because only the literate patronize literature".[5] Peter Lucas's statement may be refined further: the nature of the books commissioned or for which the writer receives some sort of support reflects the intellectual attitude of the patron. It would be a mistake to see the Duke of Gloucester as undiscriminating or too easily guided in his choice of books to be acquired, commissioned, donated. The donations to the University of Oxford, analysed in the previous chapter, reflect a precise policy on the part of the donor. The same may be said as concerns his commissions.

Yet a first look at the works commissioned by or dedicated to Humphrey may be disappointing: there are no great works of literature, no memorable poems. The most important translation of a Latin classical text he commissioned concerns an agricultural manual, which does not strike a modern reader as the most fascinating of texts. But against this disappointment we must set other factors, such as a concept of *Fachliteratur*, meant as utilitarian or scientific writing, which may have no place in modern literary canons but certainly had one in the late Middle Ages. Humphrey was not motivated simply by a generic love of reading, even less by a conception of literature as entertainment. His intellectual activity was primarily functional to the construction of an ideological myth: the great Lancastrian house, guiding England in the achievement of a consciousness of itself as a nation, according to the lines set down by Henry V. Both Henry's and Humphrey's attention to the affirmation of the vernacular goes in this direction: if Henry sought to make English the official language of chancery and foreign politics, Humphrey attempted to give it the dignity of a literary language. Most of his commissions concern translations of Latin texts, particularly texts which had long been recognised as authoritative in a number of different fields; if the collection of manuscripts pointed towards an attempt to create a *bibliotheca universalis*, the works undertaken within his intellectual circle reflect the attempt to create a library in the vernacular, to give English the dignity of a language for literature.

---

[5] Peter J. Lucas, "The Growth and Development of English Literary Patronage in the Later Middle Ages and Early Renaissance", *The Library* 6th series, 4: 1982, 219–48, p. 220.

As in the cases of manuscript acquisition and donation, examined in the previous chapter, here too the extant evidence tends to be fragmentary at best. It could be assumed that the existence of a richly illuminated manual, set as a presentation copy to the Duke, would be an indication either of his commission, or at least of his grateful reception of the volume, since the expense involved could scarcely be met by an author who did not have a reasonable hope of receiving some sort of financial return;[6] on the other hand, the case of John Capgrave, which will be discussed presently, goes to demonstrate that sometimes such investments on the part of the writer would have very little return, while Humphrey's only inter-mittent generosity is often the cause of lament or even of direct expostulation, particularly if the writer had received a commission and felt thus entitled to expect a reasonable reward.

Before dealing with Humphrey's activity, it may be interesting to consider briefly a poem that was dedicated to him and his brothers when they were still being tutored. The poem is Henry Scogan's *Moral Balade*, written in 1407.[7] Very little is known of its author, but he was a member of the royal household, and a friend of Geoffrey Chaucer; the other mention of his name occurs in the latter's *Envoy to Scogan*. The dedicatees of the *Balade* enjoy a double status, since the poet addresses them as "my noble sones, and eek my lordes dere" (l. 1). The double address gives an immediate indication of the ambiguity inherent in the poem: was it meant as actual moral advice to the young noblemen, as the phrase "this litel tretys" (l. 3) seems to indicate, or is it simply a piece of conventional flattery?

---

[6] On this point see Richard Firth Green, *Poets and Princepleasers: Literature and the English Court in the Late Middle Ages*, Toronto: University of Toronto Press, 1980, p. 98.

[7] The *Balade* is published in *Chaucerian and Other Pieces*, ed. by W.W. Skeat, Oxford: Clarendon Press, 1897: 237–44. The dedication mentioning Henry IV's sons has been added by John Shirley; it may be noted that, while Henry is called "the Prince", Thomas, John and Humphrey are given the ducal titles they would acquire only much later. The colophon says "Thus endeth the traytye wiche John Skogan sent to the lordes and estates of the kynges hous". Very little critical attention has been dedicated to this work, which is nevertheless discussed in May Newman Hallmundsson, "Chaucer's Circle: Henry Scogan and his Friends", *Medievalia et Humanistica* 10: 1981, 129–39, Lee Patterson, *Chaucer and the Subject of History*, London: Routledge, 1991, and Andrew James Johnston, *Clerks and Courtiers: Chaucer, Late Middle English Literature and the State Formation Process*, Heidelberg: Universitätsverlag C. Winter, 2001, pp. 227–50.

The tone is of moral advice: old and infirm (though he could not have been more than forty-six years old), the poet asks his pupils to take warning from him, and avoid youthful folly, lust and vice; in particular, they are instructed not to forget that virtue does not come through ancestry, but through "leeful besinesse Of honest lyfe" (ll. 75–6). The tone of the poem is at times almost indignant, which makes me think that it sprang from a particular instance of reprehensible behaviour on the part of the pupils. Particularly interesting is a reference to "my mayster Chaucer [. . .] that in his langage was so curious" (ll. 65–6); Scogan seems to underline a "genealogical" affinity between himself and Chaucer,[8] and to propose the latter as a model for his readers, quoting his *Balade of Gentilesse* in full. There follow allusions to Boethius, Cicero, Julius Caesar, Nero, Balthasar, Antiochus; in short, a brief evocation of a classical setting of positive and negative *exempla*. The poem in itself, of course, cannot in any way be connected with Humphrey's patronage; I propose it here simply as an example of the kind of moral and advisory writing which the Duke was later to encourage, particulary with his commission of Lydgate's *Fall of Princes*, and to which he was evidently exposed from an early age.

The translations and the new role of the vernacular

A significant part of Humphrey's intellectual efforts seem to have been directed towards the translation of Latin works into the vernacular. The modern scholar may be reminded of King Alfred's attempt to bring a corpus of European literature into English, though Humphrey's work strikes us as much more fragmentary, possibly because interrupted by political cares, by the Duke's own changeable nature, and in the end by his sudden death. Yet it is possible to identify a pattern, according to which Humphrey donated to the University of Oxford a number of Latin texts whose translations (in English or, more occasionally, in French) he either possessed or commissioned. It is hardly surprising, as has been underlined in the previous chapter, that the donations to Oxford should be almost exclusively of Latin manuscripts, since this was the official language of learning;

---

[8] The observation is made by Patterson, *Chaucer and the Subject of History*, p. 16.

it is more interesting that the Duke should provide himself with vernacular translations, possibly for his own use, as is demonstrated by
the less-than-favourable reports of his proficiency in Latin. Yet, if
this were the only explanation, the language to which Humphrey
would naturally turn could have been French almost as probably as
English. In a moment in English history in which the transition
between French and English as the language of politics and officialdom
was being undertaken, there is little doubt that the Lancastrian households would be conversant with both languages, but the question of
what was Humphrey's mother tongue is a fascinating one. The surviving specimens of his ex-libris are in French, though this may be
no more than the imitation of a use observed in some of the manuscripts he had acquired; the official documents and correspondence
coming from him are in Latin, with one significant exception, that
is, his intervention to protest against the liberation of the Duke of
Orléans, which is in English.[9] Humphrey is described as reading a
French translation of Livy,[10] and some of his French manuscripts
contain texts that would be normally read for entertainment, such
as romances. Of many of the Latin manuscripts which he donated
to Oxford he had French versions, but in the case of commissions
he decidedly turned to English. This linguistic orientation may be
less the result of a personal preference and more part of a policy of

---

[9] *Letters and Papers Illustrative of the Wars of the English in France during the Reign of Henry the Sixth, King of England*, ed. by J. Stevenson, Rolls Series, London: Longman, 1864, pp. 440–51. In slightly modified terms, but also in English, is the "Protestatio contra Elargationem Ducis Aurialensis" (Thomas Rymer, *Foedera, conventiones, literae, et cujuscumque generis acta publica, inter reges Angliae, et alios quosvis imperatores, reges, pontifices, principes, vel comunitates, ab ineunte, saeculo duodecimo, viz. ab Anno 1101, ad nostra usque tempora, habita aut tractata*, Hagae comitis: Apud Joannem Neaulme, 1741 (3rd edn), pp. 76–7). This change in Humphrey's "public" language, especially if we think of a former document, in Latin, addressed to the lords of the first Parliament in Henry VI's reign in 1422, is consistent with what was happening to official language in England; for instance, John Fisher notes that "The Rolls of Parliament were regu-larly in Latin and French, but occasional entries indicate that the discussion was in English. In an entry of 1426, the exposition is in Latin, but the lines spoken by the witnesses are in English. In another of 1432, the clerks of the Royal Chapel present a petition in Latin, but the introduction is in English" (John H. Fisher, "A Language Policy for Lancastrian England", *Publications of the Modern Language Association* 107: 1992, 1168–80, p. 1169). In the case of the declarations against Orléans, Humphrey may have rejected Latin to ensure a prompter understanding in his audience, and French for ideological motives.

[10] As shown in a letter from Humphrey to Alfonso V of Naples, quoted in Alfonso Sammut, *Unfredo duca di Gloucester e gli umanisti italiani*, Padova: Antenore, 1980, pp. 215–6.

encouragement of the use of English as the language of culture; to have a work such as Palladius's *De Re Rustica* translated meant to create and propose to future readers an English vocabulary of agriculture, a lexicon sanctioned by the existence of a standard text on the subject.

In this project Humphrey was far from alone: the early fifteenth century is characterised by a collective effort in this direction, with a number of translations or prose versions of standard works of various nature being commissioned and performed. Eleanor Prescott Hammond offers us a brief survey of this activity:

> At the opening of the century John Trevisa, the protégé of Lord Berkeley, made for his patron prose translations of Bartholomaeus' De Proprietatibus Rerum, of Higden's Polychronicon, and of delle Colonne's De Regimine Principum. The Polychronicon was printed by Caxton in 1482, emended by the editor-printer because of its "rude and old Englysshe, that is to wete certayn wordes which in these dayes be neither vsyd ne understanden." The De Regimine was one of Hoccleve's sources for his verse Regement of Princes, dedicated to Henry V while Prince of Wales; and another of his sources, the Secreta Secretorum, so widely popular in the Middle Ages, was turned into English prose by James Young for the Earl of Ormonde about 1420, and into verse by Lydgate and a pupil a generation later. It was about 1410 that John Walton made his stanzaic translation of Boethius' De Consolatione at the commend of Lord Berkeley's daughter. Another didactic work, de Guilleville's three-part Pilgrimage, was turned into English several times before 1500, one verse-rendering of its second part being by Lydgate to the Earl of Salisbury's order. Much of Lydgate's activity, indeed, was as a translator. He went over into the romantic-epic field at the bidding of Henry V, with his Troy Book; he may have pleased himself with his Siege of Thebes, his Churl and Bird, his Dance Macabre; but his principal business was that of a large-scale didactic translator, from the saints' lives done for Henry V and for Henry VI, for the Countess of March, for the Abbot of St. Albans, to his heaviest undertaking, the 36,000 lines of the Fall of Princes, executed for Humphrey of Gloucester. Didactics mingled with narrative we find in the saints' legends of Bokenam, Bradshaw, Capgrave, in the Assembly of Gods, the Court of Sapience, the Book of La Tour Landry printed by Caxton, and so on; and didactics were abundant unmixed, as in Cato, in Peter Idle's Instructions to his son, in Ashby's Activa Pollecia Principis, in Barclay's Mirror of Good Manners, in the whole group of Regements and Secrees on the one hand, of books of nurture on the other.[11]

---

[11] Eleanor Prescott Hammond, *English Verse Between Chaucer and Surrey*, London: Duke University Press, 1927, pp. 15–6.

To this widespread activity the Duke of Gloucester seems to have contributed not only with his own commissions, but with a change of attitude towards the original text and its rendition in English, as is demonstrated by the translation he commissioned of Palladius. Humphrey might have applied to his idea of translation what he was learning thanks to his contacts with Italian humanists, or he might have been awakened to the importance of an accurate and elegant translation through the humanists' activity; as Bruni, Decembrio and many others were translating Greek texts into Latin, as Humphrey himself was employing Italian scholars to translate Greek and Italian texts into Latin, so he would employ English scholars to translate Latin texts with a closeness to the original that might constitute the real novelty of his contribution. In the previous chapter it has been proposed that the Duke possessed a copy of Leonardo Bruni's *De Interpretatione Recta*; one of Bruni's letters to Humphrey confirms that the humanist would expose his theories on translation and urgently defend them even in his correspondence.[12]

Of only two translations we can say with absolute certainty that they were commissioned by Humphrey, and they are the anonymous translation of Palladius's *De Re Rustica* and John Lydgate's *Fall of Princes*, the latter a version of Giovanni Boccaccio's *De casibus virorum illustrium*, though Lydgate's direct source might have been not Boccaccio but a French prose version by Laurent de Premierfait. Lydgate's work shall be discussed below, in a separate section dedicated to this poet.

The translation of Palladius has been often mentioned in the previous chapters, since its proem gives us interesting clues concerning the existence of an intellectual circle around Duke Humphrey, of scholars and writers possibly working in his own library.[13] We should now discuss what prompted the Duke to commission this type of translation. It was the first complete translation into English of Palladius's work, but the Latin writer was by no means unknown in

---

[12] The letter is published in Sammut (pp. 146–8), who dates it March 1434, and in Francesco Paolo Luiso, *Studi su l'epistolario di Leonardo Bruni*, Roma: Istituto storico italiano per il Medio Evo, 1980, pp. 122–3; Luiso is more uncertain on the date, and adds to the letter a tentative "1428–1434".

[13] Some of the arguments presented in this section have already appeared in Alessandra Petrina, "The Middle English Translation of Palladius's De Agricultura", in *The Medieval Translator. Traduire au Moyen Age 8*, ed. by R. Voaden, R. Tixier, T. Sanchez Roura and J.R. Rytting, Tournhout: Brepols, 2003: 317–28.

England: parts of his work appear in a *Godfridus super palladium* which is "a vernacular translation of a Latin work compiled from various sources, including the *De re rustica* of Palladius, by an otherwise unknown Geoffrey of Bologna, perhaps originally a German from Franconia, in the mid fourteenth century".[14] All over Europe Palladius's work enjoyed "a splendid popularity" from the ninth century, and the Latin text had been available in England since the Norman conquest.[15] On the other hand, Humphrey seems to have been interested also in other classical agricultural treatises: in a letter to Pier Candido Decembrio, dated 1444, he says he has received some manuscripts, but laments that others have not arrived; among these are Cato's and Varro's works on agriculture.[16] He certainly possessed the Latin Palladius, which appears in the list of his third recorded donation to the University of Oxford. Though, as we have seen, this work had a number of precedents in England as far as the translation of Latin texts was concerned, Humphrey's commission can be considered the first direct translation of a Latin classical text into Middle English, closely followed (an accurate chronology is impossible, and the two translations are roughly contemporary) by the translation of Claudian's *De Consulatu Stilichonis*, commissioned by Richard, Duke of York.[17] The particular quality of the translation and the exceptional layout of the presentation copy show the interest Humphrey had, at least initially, for this enterprise.

A modern reader may find it somewhat disconcerting that a fifteenth-century English prince should choose to make available in the vernacular a fourth-century Latin treatise on agriculture; yet Palladius was established as one of the canonical texts on the subject,

---

[14] George R. Keiser, "Practical Books for the Gentleman", in *The Cambridge History of the Book in Britain, vol. 3: 1400–1557*, ed. by L. Hellinga and J.B. Trapp, Cambridge: Cambridge University Press, 1999: 470–94, p. 481.

[15] R.H. Rodgers, *An Introduction to Palladius*, London: University of London Institute of Classical Studies, 1975, p. 15; Mauro Ambrosoli, *The Wild and the Sown. Botany and Agriculture in Western Europe: 1350–1850* (original title *Scienziati, contadini e proprietari*, Torino: Einaudi, 1992), transl. by M. NcCann Salvatorelli, Cambridge: Cambridge University Press, 1997, pp. 12–17.

[16] The letter is published in Sammut, pp. 197–8.

[17] See A.S.G. Edwards, "The Middle English Translation of Claudian's *De Consulatu Stilichonis*", in *Middle English Poetry: Texts and Traditions: Essays in Honour of Derek Pearsall*, ed. by A.J. Minnis, York: The Boydell Press, 2001: 267–78. The translation is also analysed in Sheila Delany, *Impolitic Bodies. Poetry, Saints, and Society in Fifteenth-Century England. The Work of Osbern Bokenham*, New York, Oxford: Oxford University Press, 1998, pp. 133–43.

and though it had a number of powerful rivals, such as Columella, or the already mentioned Cato and Varro, it had the advantage of a clear, sober style, which gave it immediate practical value.[18] One of the most striking qualities of the Middle English translation is that it strives to maintain the same concise elegance, the same readability as the original. This attitude has been earlier explained with Humphrey's interest in the new humanist effort towards "rectitude" and elegance in the humanist translations of Greek texts: the easy flow and readability of the Palladius translator may mirror what Bruni and Decembrio were aiming at in their translations of Plato, Plutarch and Aristotle. On the other hand, there is no doubt that Humphrey did not consider the translation a mere humanist exercise in style, but saw the treatise as a useful manual, to be ranged together with the various translations of Vegetius's *De Re Militari*, or even of Boethius's *De Consolatione Philosophiae*. The acquisition of Latin manuals of internationally recognised value in the national language contributed to the establishment, so to speak, of a national library, and the Middle English *De Re Rustica* may be seen as Humphrey's contribution, or perhaps as one of his contributions to this project. This is shown not only by the nature of the translation, but by the way the text is graphically manipulated. The layout of the English text, as it appears in the presentation copy,[19] highlights not only the translator's devotion to the patron but also this practical aspect: to the basic text was added, together with the proem, an apparatus of arabic folio numbers and stanza letters corresponding to an alphabetically arranged *tabula* that made it possible to consult the text quickly and easily.[20] The sections including a praise of the patron are highlighted by the use of different inks, and coloured inks in the prologue as well as in the epilogues to each book evidentiate a complex structure of internal rhymes.[21] The desire for greater clarity goes

---

[18] Ambrosoli writes that Columella's *Res rustica* "would have presented too many difficulties [. . .] its size discouraged translation as it had discouraged its circulation in previous centuries" (p. 25). He adds that "in England Palladius' *Opus Agriculturae* was the recognized text of noble agriculture. It reflected the interest and curiosity that the upper classes felt for exotic plants and crops, exotic and Mediterranean being one and the same to them" (p. 26).

[19] Now Oxford, Bodleian Library, Duke Humfrey d. 2.

[20] On this point, see also Keiser, p. 484.

[21] "It is this feature of the MS which clinches the suggestion that this was the copy presented to Duke Humphrey, for when he took it in his hands, all the stanzas addressed to him are readily discernible" (Everest-Phillips, p. 108).

hand in hand with the praise of the patron in the translator's mind, as well as in the illuminator's (both seem to have worked under Humphrey's supervision, and the decoration is highly functional to the understanding of the text). This is also the double purpose of the sections that have been added to the Latin original, such as the prologue, or the epilogues added to the initial books.

The identity of the translator has been the object of much discussion, and a number of hypotheses have been made, though none has any verifiable basis.[22] The tone and contents of the prologue make it clear that he was in the Duke's household and probably in his employment, where he had arrived after much sorrow; it is tempting to think of him as a chaplain, since his sometimes unctuous praise of the patron is often mixed with the praise of God. The same tone demonstrates that the project was Humphrey's, and that his presence dominates the translator's work throughout; this is not the case, as in John Capgrave's Biblical commentaries, of works written first and then presented to the perspective patron. The translator interlaces his praise with references to the subject he is going to discuss: the recurring image of Humphrey as "princis flour" is elegantly inserted in the context:

> Wel myght a kynge of such a flour enioye,
> To seen it sprynge in fyn odour & huys,
> Strength & sauour, hym oueral to ioy,
> In whos fauour science and al vertu is.[23]

The appellative is more meaningful than it might appear: one of the heraldic badges of Duke Humphrey was a spray of flowers, and his tomb in St Albans Abbey has a frequently repeated ornamental

---

[22] D.R. Howlett ("Studies in the Works of John Whethamstede", D.Phil., Oxford, 1975, pp. 216–50) identifies the translator with Thomas Norton, clerk, chancellor and chaplain of Duke Humphrey. He also offers an interesting if occasionally controversial analysis of the translation. Stephen Medcalf ("On Reading Books from a Half Alien Culture", in *The Later Middle Ages*, New York: Holmes & Meier, 1981: 1–55), attributes the translation to one Robert Parke, probably misreading Henry Noble MacCracken's attribution to Robert Parker (see his "Vegetius in English", in *Anniversary Papers by Colleagues and Pupils of George Lyman Kittredge*, Boston and London: Ginn, 1913: 389–403); it may be added that Medcalf's inaccuracy concerns also a number of other points, including even the year of Humphrey's death.

[23] *The Middle-English Translation of Palladius De Re Rustica*, ed. by M. Liddell, Berlin: E. Ebering, 1896, Prohemium, ll. 61–4. The image is alluded to also in ll. 5 and 126 (further references to the text are to this edition).

detail, a device of "daisies in a standing cup" or of "wheat-ears in vases on pedestals".[24] Thus by using what might appear at first only a conventional image, the writer could, as it were, personalise it for the Duke, and at the same time link it with another image that will recur later in the text and will be discussed below, that of Christ as Jesse's flower.

The same topicality recurs throughout the prologue; Humphrey is not simply described in generically eulogistic terms, as a prince and a hopefully munificent patron, as Lydgate could fulsomely do, but specific stress is given to virtues that might not form the aristocratic patron's common stock: his scholarly accomplishments are underlined, with a pedantic emphasis on the disciplines in which he excels. The list of these disciplines, which includes the three parts of philosophy and the arts of the trivium and quadrivium (Prohemium, ll. 73–80), is almost an echo of the Oxford arts curriculum which had recently been the object of the Duke's attention; it may be simply lack of imagination on the part of the translator, but it leads us to think that the activity of patronage directed towards the University and the commission of translations were closely linked, and that the scholars who were part of the Duke's *familia* would be acquainted with both sides of his intellectual interests. Besides, there is an explicit reference to the book donations in the following stanzas of the prologue, which link the Oxford clerks now happily at work thanks to Humphrey's gift of a "librair vniuersal" to the Italian and English scholars working in the Duke's own library, which possesses "uche lef and lyne" of anything that has been treated, told or taught by "oratour, poete, or philosophre" (98–100). Alliteration here helps the flow of a eulogy that is almost cloying in tone; but what is striking is not the tone, but the detail of the praise. Humphrey was one of the foremost men of the realm, heir apparent to the throne, and a prince with a military renown; yet the translator chose to underline his intellectual qualities, and his outstanding library. It may be sycophantic flattery; it may even have been written at Humphrey's direct prompting; it either demonstrates that the Duke did have a library of exceptional proportions, or that he wanted future readers to believe so. The dating of this work is helped by some indications in the

---

[24] As described by T.D. Kendrick in his "Humphrey, Duke of Gloucester, and the Gardens of Adonis", *The Antiquaries Journal* 26: 1946, 118–22.

prologue: after evoking past episodes of the Duke's political and military career, such as his repression of the Lollards,[25] or his triumph in Calais, the writer makes a reference to the donations of manuscripts to the University of Oxford (Prohemium, l. 89); this allusion, accompanied by a marginal notation on the presentation copy in the same hand as the text which reads "plures s. CXXX", points to a period between 1439 and 1443, and the fact that the Latin Palladius was donated in 1443 probably gives us a *terminus ante quem*, since it is difficult to believe that the Duke, however keen a collector, would possess two copies of the same Latin text; on the other hand, the translator would probably need to refer to the original until his work was completed.[26] In the last years of his life, if the hypothesis on the dating of the translation is correct, after a number of serious checks on his political career, Humphrey probably thought it best, or more expedient, or even politically far-seeing, to turn his attention more than ever upon an intellectual career that had earned him so far nothing but praise, even if praise of an interested kind, and in which he had no rivals of the calibre of his political enemies Henry Beaufort or William de la Pole. The Palladius translator, in more detail and showing far more closeness to the Duke than other writers Humphrey had patronised, strove to perpetuate an image that would identify Gloucester no longer with the Calais conqueror (since agriculture is a far from martial occupation) but with a man of letters, a keen reader, an expert versifier, and above all a nobleman concerning himself directly with the intellectual future of his country.

Among the translator's more extravagant claims is the fact that the Duke "taught me metur make" (Prohemium, l. 109). This statement has provoked a certain amount of ridicule among modern

---

[25] "A chronicle kept by monks at St. Albans during the first abbacy of John Whethamstede records the death of the notorious outlaw William Wawe in 1427. It also reports Duke Humfrey's presence at the burning of a heretical priest at Smithfield in 1431 and in the same year his prosecution of John Scharpe, who had attacked the endowed orders". D.R. Howlett, "The Date and Authorship of the Middle English Verse Translation of Palladius' *De Re Rustica*", *Medium Aevum* 46: 1977, 245–52, p. 247.

[26] The prologue alludes also to the Duke of Orléans; in this case it would have been good policy on the part of the translator to insert this reference before the release of Orléans, in November 1440, which effectively marked the end of Gloucester's political career.

scholars; but it was so important to the translator that he reiterated
it at the end of Book II, presenting the reader with an image of the
Duke reading the partially completed work and intervening on its
versification to the point of actually creating the poetry of the text
from the translator's bleak prose:

> And now my lord biholdith on his book.
> ffor sothe al nought, he gynnyth crossis make
> With a plummet and y noot whow his look,
> His cheer is straunge, eschaunge. Almeest y quake,
> ffor ferd y shrynke away, no leue y take.
> ffarwel, my Lord! Do forth for y am heer,
> And metur muse out of this prosis blake.
> [II.480–6]

It is tantalising that in the presentation copy we should find just
such a cross, in the margin against line 52 of the prologue, where
the scribe wrote *unto* for *undo*.[27] Besides, the same presentation copy
contains also an annotation on the margin of f. 53r, corresponding
to III.1183, when the description of various ways of grafting is concluded by the comment: "what harm is forte assay?". Here a hand
tentatively identified with the same hand of the ex-libris on other
manuscripts belonging to Humphrey has written: "unde Ouydius:
sed quid temptare nocebit?".[28] The reference is to Ovid's *Metamorphoses*,
I.397, and the previous chapter has shown that this text, in the
"moralised" version by Pierre Bersuire, was part of Humphrey's third
recorded donation to Oxford. There is yet another reference, though
in more generic terms, to the Duke correcting the translation at the
end of the book devoted to February (III.1212):

> And lo my lord in hande hath ffeueryeer;
> Wul he correcte? Ey what haue y to done?

---

[27] Everest-Phillips believes "unto" to be a deliberate mistake inserted by the translator, "an example of the humour with which the poet embraces his role in the
patronage relationship" (p. 107).

[28] The identification is made by D.R. Howlett in his "The Date and Authorship
of the Middle English Verse Translation of Palladius' *De Re Rustica*", p. 246. Howlett
identifies the hand of the annotation with the ex-libris appearing on f. 197v of a
collection of philosophical and astronomical texts which was given Humphrey by
John Whethamstede (now Oxford, Corpus Christi College, 243, described in Sammut,
pp. 115–6). See also D.R. Howlett, "Studies in the Works of John Whethamstede",
Ph.D., Oxford, 1975, p. 214. David Rundle, however, expresses doubts about this
identification (personal communication).

He wul doon as a lord. Thenne aftir heer,
Asfaste y thynke on sette, At Marchis mone.
[III.1211–14]

Here it is interesting to note that, though the lines belong to the book devoted to February, the writer describes Humphrey who "in hande hath ffeueryeer", which confirms the hypothesis that the envoys were added after the completion of the translation of the various books. This characteristic reappears in the envoy to Book IV, devoted to March:

Now Marche is doon, and to correctioun
His book is goon, as other dede afore,
Of hym that seid "y thy protectioun
ffrom al thy foon aduersaunt, lesse & more,"
And his bihest stedfest is euermore.
[IV.981–5]

Especially in these early books, the Duke's revision seems to be a routine practice.[29]

Thus the lines quoted above, together with what evidence the presentation copy provides, challenge the modern reader's scepticism about the Duke's intellectual accomplishments; it might obviously be an exaggeration to say that the Duke actually taught versification to the translator, and the stanza might also be meant as "a gently mocking parody" of both the translator and the patron,[30] but it could not be an outright invention, or it would sound a very odd sort of praise. Besides, it seems certain that the translator would submit each book, as it was completed, to the patron's approval, at least as far as the early books go; after the first four books the numerous references to the patron gradually disappear, substituted by more conventional praises of Christ, while the image of the "princis flour", earlier applied to Humphrey, is then used for the Saviour, together with the more traditional epithet "Iesse flour". At the same time the marginal decorations in the presentation manuscript diminish in size and significance. Apparently, while the translator was bent on completing his work, the Duke gradually lost interest in the project. Yet up to the final book the references to the "princis flour" are ambiguous enough to

---

[29] A hypothesis confirmed by Howlett, "The Date and Authorship of the Middle English Verse Translation of Palladius' *De Re Rustica*", p. 246.

[30] Everest-Phillips, p. 107.

make it possible to interpret them as allusions to the patron, especially since the opening stanza of the prologue establishes a clear
connection between God and Humphrey, with a rather daring image
that sees the former making provisions for the maintenance of agriculture both in nature and in art, and assigning the latter his role
in each respect. Thus at the end of Book IX we find a rather ambiguous statement:

> Thy princis flour on cleer,
> On cloudy, derk or light he must vpbrynge.
> And y to werk am sette At Septembeer.
> [IX.216–8]

The closing lines of Book XII are resolutely addressed to God, the
King of kings, but do not forget the patron:

> O kyngis Kyng, O Lord, O Thyng hiest,
> Louyng record and rynge her stryngis chaste
> To thyn honour; of fyr sauour that haste
> A flour to taste, odour to caste. Al yeer
> Thy duc attende, of fuke vnblende, or laste
> Vnshende, and ende vs sende of Decembeer.
> [XII.605–10]

By the end of the whole work, the ambiguity is still present, though
the addressee of the envoy is God:

> My wit, my word, my werk The magnifieth,
> O kyngis Kynge, O Lord of lordis hie,
> Whos grace a princis flour honorifieth,
> That in nature hym like is noon to trie.
> [XIII.79–82]

Yet the enthusiasm of the early envoys is lost. As it seems clear that
the various books were translated, prepared in the presentation copy
and decorated one at the time, to be submitted to Humphrey for
correction and approval,[31] we might deduce that the patron lost interest or perhaps was distracted by more pressing matters, so that the
initial magnificence of the work trailed away, till in the last books
there is little more than the bare translation. The discussion of other
texts associated to or commissioned by Duke Humphrey will reveal

---

[31] As D.R. Howlett notes in his "The Date and Authorship of the Middle English
Verse Translation of Palladius' *De Re Rustica*", p. 246.

similar tones in the writer's attitude towards the patron: thus Lydgate, in his *Fall of Princes*, presents a long if not equally detailed list of the Duke's intellectual accomplishments, but finds himself obliged, halfway through his work, to remind Humphrey of his need for at least partial payment.

L.C.Y. Everest-Phillips acutely defines the actual translation "a creative reworking in verse rather than a literal rendering".[32] The translation is striking in that it very rarely deviates from the meaning of the original, preferring to concentrate on the actual advice given on farming than on literary or linguistic questions of faithfulness. The translator completely enters the Latin narrator's persona, and re-enacts his dialogue with the reader, offering a text which finds its cornerstone in its affinity with rather than its literal likeness to the original. There are few exceptions, and they are generally of an extremely practical nature, as in book I, when the Palladius translator describes the approved method of fattening geese:

> Yf thou desirest that thi gees be tendir,
> When they in age ar passid xxx daies,
> Of figis grounde and watir temprid, sclendir
> Gobbettis yef thy gees. But these arayis
> To speke of heere, for nought but myrth & play is;
> Yet as myn auctor spak so wold I speke,
> Sith I translate, and looth am from hym breke.
>   [I.729–35]

"As myn auctor spak" is a key phrase here: the translator is bound to follow his *auctoritas*, and has an almost philological task in front of him, since he has been asked to present this classical text in the English tongue; at the same time the work has a practical purpose, and in the name of this purpose he reacts against a suggestion he considers ridiculous, though it comes from Palladius himself. The Middle English text often wavers uncertainly between georgic poetry and didacticism, but never forgets its primary audience. It addresses the implicit reader, the husbandman for whom the work is written, and who is invited, with the frequent use of the imperative, to take part in his work directly. Technical terms are translated carefully and clearly, with no concessions to Latinisms; Liddell observes that the work presents "a great number of words not elsewhere recorded

---

[32] Everest-Phillips, p. 69.

in Middle-English literature".[33] Occasionally the margins provide the Latin equivalent, particularly in the case of technical terms, and this detail confirms the translator's effort to propose as complete as possible an agricultural lexicon in the vernacular. The clear prose of the Latin original is rendered in the Chaucerian rhyme royal beloved by fifteenth-century English writers.[34] Eleanor Hammond is particularly enthusiastic in her literary evaluation of the text:

> So excellent is the text of Wentworth Wodehouse that its editor, Mark H. Liddell, rarely has to supply a missing word from Bodley Add. A. 396 (formerly at Colchester Castle); and in the first 1,800 lines I note but three cases in which the scribe shows carelessness about inflexional -e [. . .] The iambic flow is completely orthodox; I have not observed any nine-syllabled lines; and in the metrical workmanship one is obliged to recognize not only a very conscious and competent manipulation of rhythm, but strict scribal supervision by men who heard the -e and insisted that it be duly written. The matter of the book is exceedingly unpoetic; but the man behind it was both accurate and able; he twists his verse with a firm hand, varies his pauses and his line-length agreeably, and whenever he has a chance to speak for himself presents the reader with brief *tours de force* in world-play and rhyme-pattern which are as much superior tecnically to Lydgate's envoys on three rhymes or his use of refrain as the Palladius' line management is superior to Lydgate's monotony.[35]

For this effort the unknown translator should certainly be praised; whether the metre is his own or the result of Humphrey's prompting, it is decidedly better than what, for example, Lydgate was producing approximately at the same time, and the lines have a smooth

---

[33] Liddell, p. vii.

[34] Hammond, however, notes a variation on this metrical pattern: "the prologue and the connective-stanzas between books are of eight lines. The author thus uses a slightly different form when speaking in his own person; compare the use of refrain, occasionally of eight-line stanzas, in the envoys added by Lydgate, at Gloucester's command, to the Fall of Princes translation" (*English Verse Between Chaucer and Surrey*, p. 203).

[35] Eleanor P. Hammond, "The Nine-syllabled Pentameter Line in some Post-Chaucerian Manuscripts", *Modern Philology* 23: 1925, 129–52, pp. 148–9. Vickers is of a different opinion: "his name has not survived, and perhaps, considering the quality of his verse, he was wise not to betray his identity" (Vickers, p. 394). Ambrosoli speaks of "clumsy verse" (p. 26). Douglas Gray, instead, sees in the Palladius translator "a remote precursor of the later tradition of 'georgic' poetry" (see his "Humanism and Humanisms in the Literature of Late Medieval England", in *Italy and the English Renaissance*, ed. by S. Rossi and D. Savoia, Milano: Unicopli, 1989: 25–44, p. 41).

flowing that captivates the reader. If the modern reception of medieval texts were not so decidedly biassed against *Fachliteratur*, this translation would certainly deserve a more favourable estimation than much contemporary poetry. As it is, however, its interest remains mainly documentary, as a precious source of information on the Duke's intellectual activity, though it would be equally interesting to study its language, since the lexicon and syntax offer an important contribution to the development of Middle English.[36] The possibility that the book would have also an immediate practical function is not to be discarded, and it has been noted that when the translator writes that

> This kyngis dere vncul, & sone, and brother,
> Hath God prouect, His werkis to conclude,
> His werkis here—or where is suche another?[37]

the reference to *werkis* might be not only to literary works, but to agricultural or architectural enterprises at Greenwich. Once again, however, lack of evidence does not allow either to prove or to disprove this hypothesis.

Whether or not this commission was intended as part of a series, perhaps the first of a reading list of Latin classics that still lacked an English translation, is of course impossible to say, but the care and attention Humphrey appears to have devoted to the project, taking into account his notorious lack of constancy as shown in his political and military enterprises, indicates that he greatly believed in the importance of this translation. In later years, the association of this translation with its patron seems to have hindered the book's reputation, since, as has been seen in the previous chapter, a later manuscript preserved almost intact the body of the translation, while eliminating all references to Humphrey.[38]

---

[36] A perceptive comment on the literary qualities of this translation can also be found in Hammond, *English Verse Between Chaucer and Surrey*, pp. 202–3. As for its linguistic richness, it was pointed out by Mark Liddell in his edition of the text; just such a linguistic study was what Liddell intended to present in the companion volume to his edition, but the volume unfortunately never appeared.

[37] Prohemium, ll. 70–2. The observation is made by Everest-Phillips, p. 87. It might be noted in passing that, by styling the patron's title as he does in line 70, the translator uses the same formula employed by the Oxford University authorities in their correspondence with Humphrey.

[38] London, British Library, Additional A. 369.

Other texts have been associated with the work of the Palladius translator, though in this case there is no demonstrable link with the patronage of Duke Humphrey. One such text is the already mentioned translation of Claudian's *De Consulatu Stilichonis*; the original text was written around 400 AD to celebrate a Roman general and his military and political achievements, and its translation was apparently commissioned by or at any rate written for Richard, Duke of York.[39] The Middle English version, appearing in London, British Library, Additional 11814, is a direct translation, which is one important point in common with the Palladius translation, though the layout is different in that the manuscript presents both translation and Latin original. It was probably completed in 1445, shortly after the Palladius translation. A.S.G. Edwards briefly compares the two works:

> One may be struck by the Janus-like implications of the two translations. If they can be held to signal anything, it is contrasting modes of conduct: the active political life in the Claudian as opposed to rural retreat in the Palladius, which seems to lack any overt or covert reference to contemporary affairs. These antitheses seem so clearly defined as to tempt one to seek a relationship in significance growing out of their relationship in time, form and subject. If the Claudian seems actively to assert Richard's political identity, could the Palladius in contrast be an acknowledgement of Humfrey's own political commitment at this stage in his life? And can we perhaps see in the Claudian among other things an acknowledgement by Richard of Humfrey's humanist achievements that can be linked to a wish to extend a natural literary affinity into the political realm?[40]

These observations are very interesting. It is true that there is no reference to contemporary affairs in the whole of the Middle English Palladius, though the prologue in particular, as we have seen, expatiates at length on the Duke's intellectual pursuits. The prologue thus deliberately isolates the Duke in a world of his own, whose links with political or public life are only mentioned in reference to a glorious past. On the other hand, Richard's decision, a few years after the Palladius translation, to commission an almost specular translation of his own, may testify to the interest Humphrey's intellectual activity was raising, even among his contemporaries. It may be added that in Humphrey's third donation to Oxford there appears "Claudianum

[39] On this point see Edwards, p. 273.
[40] Edwards, p. 277.

minorem secundo folio *anxie*", which Sammut identifies with Claudian's *Panegyricus dictus Probino et Olybrio Consulibus* (circa 395 AD); besides, John Leland's list of the manuscripts in Duke Humfrey, published in 1715, includes a "Claudianus, poeta".[41] Claudian was widely read in the late Middle Ages, perhaps more as a model of poetical technique among late-Latin, neo-classical writers than as a historian. Evidently, the Duke of Gloucester and Richard of York shared an admiration for this poet, and perhaps Richard was following Humphrey more closely than modern scholars suspect.

Another text associated with the Palladius translation is the Middle English version of Vegetius's *De Re Militari*, known as *Knyghthode and Bataile*. Vegetius was widely read in the Middle Ages as a manual of military practice, and Humphrey possessed both the Latin original, which he donated to the University of Oxford in 1443 (John Leland saw the book in 1715),[42] and a French version by Jean de Vignai.[43] The first English translation of Vegetius, according to its colophon, was completed in 1408 for Thomas of Berkeley by a translator generally identified with John Walton.[44] So the popularity of this text was already well established in England by the middle of the fifteenth century, thanks also to French translations such as Christine de Pizan's, which would later be the source for Caxton's version. The second Middle English translation seems to have been prepared in 1458 for John, Viscount Beaumont, as is shown by the reference to "my lord Beaumont".[45] In this case, too, the translation is preceded by a proem, that provides the work with its occasion, since it celebrates the royal entry of Henry VI and his Queen into London.[46] The translator describes himself as a parson of Calais, and has been tentatively identified with Robert Parker. The aim of the

---

[41] Sammut, pp. 83 and 95.

[42] Sammut, pp. 80 and 95.

[43] Cambridge University Library Ee.2.17. Described in Sammut, pp. 100–1.

[44] *The Earliest English Translation of Vegetius' De Re Militari, ed. from Oxford MS Bodl. Douce 291*, ed. by G. Lester, Middle English Texts, Heidelberg: Carl Winter—Universitätsverlag, 1988.

[45] Proemium, l. 47. See *Knyghthode and Bataile. A XVth Century Verse Paraphrase of Flavius Vegetius Renatus' Treatise "De Re Militari"*, ed. by R. Dyboski and Z.M. Arend, Early English Text Society, London: Oxford University Press, 1935.

[46] Much of this information is based upon *The Idea of the Vernacular: An Anthology of Middle English Literary Theory, 1280–1520*, ed. by J. Wogan-Browne, N. Watson, A. Taylor and R. Evans, Exeter: University of Exeter Press, 1999, pp. 182–6.

poem is not only to introduce Vegetius's text, but also to exhort the
King and the English subjects to a more strenuous defense of Calais,
which was becoming a Yorkist stronghold at the time. It is interesting to note that in two later manuscripts the allusion to Henry
VI is replaced by a mention of Edward IV; clearly the poem could
be adapted to political changes, while its central message remained
identical. Even in the older manuscript, however,[47] the opening poem,
corresponding to ff. 1r–2v, is in a separate foliation from the rest of
the book, which makes it possible to suppose that the poem was a
later addition, or perhaps a substitution for something that was no
longer suitable to political circumstances. The year 1458 can therefore be referred with any certainty only to the poem, while the translation might have been completed earlier.

In an article dated 1913, Henry Noble MacCracken proposed the
identification of the Vegetius translator (identifying him with Robert
Parker) with the Palladius translator who had worked for Duke
Humphrey.[48] Both chose to translate the original Latin prose into
verse, and both, showing a keen awareness of the standards of metre,
and of the use of inflexional -e, used an eight-line stanza rhyming
ababbcbc for the proem and rhyme royal for the actual translation.
In both cases the attempt is to render the meaning rather than the
letter of the original, and the result is surprisingly elegant for such
un-poetic subjects. Internal evidence seems therefore sufficient to support MacCracken's hypothesis, a hypothesis confirmed by Everest-
Phillips's analysis.[49] To these two critics' observations I would only
add another similarity, that is, the references to the patron or dedicatee and to Christ which tend to become the same in the two prologues, as if Humphrey's and Henry's religious devotion provided
the writer with an excuse to consider, respectively, agriculture and
warfare as forms of devotional exercise (admittedly, a harder task in
the latter case). From these observations there emerges the image of
a devoted clerk, with an excellent knowledge of classical Latin and
a very good gift for turning his matter into verse (whether or not

---

[47] Cambridge, Pembroke College 243.
[48] See the already mentioned "Vegetius in English", pp. 398–9. MacCracken also
lists a number of verbal analogues, and of similar spelling choices. He also notes
that both manuscripts are provided with detailed indexes.
[49] Everest-Phillips, p. 68.

with the help and guidance of the patron). The ideology he supports in the later work is consistent with Humphrey's political attitude, and if this parson of Calais had spent a few years in the Duke's
household he might have been one of his, unfortunately less influent,
political supporters.

John Lydgate

In his analysis of the Palladius translation and of the manuscript that
constitutes its presentation copy, D.R. Howlett dedicates particular
attention to the brief list of names of scholars appearing in the prologue: John Whethamstede, Pietro dal Monte, Tito Livio Frulovisi,
Antonio Beccaria, and, last and humblest, the translator himself,
working in the Duke's palace and availing themselves of his library
and of his intellectual guidance. The list is somewhat heterogeneous,
and it seems to me to have been conceived and ordered to suit
metre rather than accuracy, and perhaps to impress with its particular stress on the presence of Italian humanists. Howlett however
notes a surprising absentee: "the exclusion of Lydgate's name from
Norton's proem to his translation of Palladius may imply that Lydgate's
work was too slight, too belletristic, to be reckoned among the weight-
ier works of 'serious' scholars".[50] The interpretation is interesting, if
perhaps far-fetched, and posits for this humble and occasionally servile
if very gifted translator a new and unexpected role as a keen literary critic. Yet it is true, setting all value judgments aside, that John
Lydgate, though frequently employed by Duke Humphrey and, among
other things, engaged by him to write his most ponderous work,
could be associated to the Duke's intellectual circle only with some
straining. His contribution to Humphrey's intellectual project is great
but atypical, and requires a reconsideration of the notion of humanism in the Duke's circle. Born around 1370, Lydgate became one
of Humphrey's translators when he had already written much, and
for equally if not more illustrious patrons. He had written for Henry
V, then prince of Wales, for Queen Catherine, and he would of
course write for Henry VI, as well as for a number of lesser noblemen and women, abbots, London notables, and sometimes even with

---

[50] Howlett, "Studies in the Works of John Whethamstede", p. 224.

no commission at all. In the course of a long and extremely busy
life, Lydgate wrote all manner of verses for all manner of people,
explored innumerable literary genres, seemed possessed by inex-
haustible curiosity not only concerning libraries but also the everyday chronicle of his time. This voluble, sententious, but often curiously
endearing gossip apparently set out to reckon, in all humility, with
a number of fathers, sometimes pressing them to death under the
weight of his unstoppable verbosity, but always presenting us with a
remarkable witness of the literary trends of the time. Lydgate is the
all-knowing librarian of fifteenth-century England, recording not only
the heritage of foreign or ancient texts and the necessities of devotional literature but the passage of a fashion, a royal marriage, a
pageant, a mumming, a funeral. He will accord the same delighted
interest to Aesopic fables, Guido delle Colonne's *Historia Destructionis
Troiae*, the life of a saint or the portrait of an ale-seller. It is not true
that he was untouched by the new learning proposed by early humanists visiting England, or by patrons acquiring innovative texts; but
at the same time he heavily felt his debt with medieval literature,
his master Chaucer above all, so that the new authors and scholars
he was reading thanks also to the Duke of Gloucester's mediation
could be for him only an addition to a store of medieval attitudes
to science and literature on which he had long exercised his pen.
He undoubtedly read them and they are quoted in his works, most
notably in the *Fall of Princes*; and he partly shared his patron's literary tastes, such as his admiration for Petrarch.

Critical evaluations on Lydgate have often been content with calling him the last of a line of evolution of medieval literature that
finds its culmination with Chaucer and sees in Lydgate the extreme
representative of decay; at the same time, already in 1951 Walter
Schirmer identified new trends in this poet's writing: "Lydgate, without being fully aware of it, in imitating his admired master discovered
new realms".[51] I contend Lydgate represents among English writers
what Humphrey represents among English book collectors and patrons:
an uneasy transition between Middle Ages and Renaissance, the

---

[51] Walter F. Schirmer, "The Importance of the Fifteenth Century for the Study
of the English Renaissance with Special Reference to Lydgate", *English Studies Today*
1: 1951, 104–10, p. 105. Derek Pearsall, on the other hand, sees almost no trace
of humanism in Lydgate's work. See his *John Lydgate*, London: Routledge & Kegan
Paul, 1970, p. 15.

acceptance of some of the new intellectual attitudes and a curiosity for newly discovered or translated texts that is, sometimes awkwardly, grafted onto a solid and self-sufficient medieval structure.

This attitude is well symbolised, in both poet and patron, by their admiration of Petrarch. Duke Humphrey donated a number of Petrarch's texts to the Oxford University library, and possibly possessed more manuscripts of works by the same poet, as well as Pietro Paolo Vergerio's *Vita Petrarce*. In the prologue to Book IV of the *Fall of Princes* Lydgate painstakingly lists a number of works by Petrarch: clear reference is made to *De remediis utriusque fortune, Bucolicum Carmen, Secretum, Psalmi Penitentiales, Africa, De ignorantia, De vita solitaria*, while the story of Griselda is highlighted among his *Epistolae*.[52] There is also an allusion to a "Cosmographie" which Nicholas Mann identifies with the *Itinerarium breve de Ianua usque ad Ierusalem et Terram Sanctam*.[53] The list, which is followed by a description of themes and motifs in Petrarch's literary production, is extraordinarily detailed even for Lydgate, particularly if we compare it to the more cursory references to classical authors in the same passage. Commenting on this passage, Douglas Gray writes:

> The context of this list is a discussion of literary fame and a defence of writing [. . .] He knows of Petrarch as a 'laureat' writer, but his own work shows no sign of having been influenced by the new learning; it is clearly in the tradition of older medieval humanism. The usual English view of Petrarch seems to have been of him less as a 'humanist' than as the moral author of the *De remediis*.[54]

The observation is correct but maintains a division between a medieval and a humanist Petrarch that perhaps should be substituted by a more comprehensive view. The fifteenth-century reception of Petrarch in England, as it transpires from Gray's comment, seems to have been as limited as our own; instead, though it tended to ignore his poetic production in Italian that now, as in the English sixteenth century, is most appreciated, it showed great curiosity for his Latin works, and did not limit itself to *De remediis utriusque fortunae*, as a

---

[52] Book IV, ll. 106–26. See *Lydgate's Fall of Princes*, ed. by H. Bergen, Early English Text Society, Oxford: Oxford University Press, 1923–27.
[53] Nicholas Mann, "Petrarch's Role in Humanism", *Apollo* 94: 1971, 176–83, p. 181.
[54] Douglas Gray, "Humanism and Humanisms in the Literature of Late Medieval England", p. 36.

long-standing tradition would have it; it certainly did not see a difference between the so-called medieval and the humanist works.[55] Humphrey's own library demonstrates the contrary. Whether medieval or humanist, Petrarch represented the same novel curiosity towards classical learning and writing that characterises humanism and that Lydgate, to a certain extent, shared. The two poets, each in his way, can be made to represent the *trait d'union* between medieval and humanist, that *trait d'union* Humphrey perhaps unwittingly explored and unconsciously symbolised in his library. Petrarch's presence makes itself felt in *The Fall of Princes* in other passages besides the one just mentioned; Nicholas Mann sees a direct link between this extensive knowledge of the Italian poet and Humphrey's library, though the scholar insists on the idea that Lydgate's knowledge was limited to the "medieval" Petrarch—an inference partly disproved by the nature of some of the works mentioned.[56]

As is almost inevitable in the case of so prolific a poet, Humphrey's patronage of Lydgate is demonstrated not only by *The Fall of Princes*, but also by a number of minor, often occasional poems, which occasionally surprise the reader as instances of greater creativity and readability than Lydgate's more famous longer poems.[57] They need not

---

[55] The fundamental refence in this case is Nicholas Mann's study, "Petrarch Manuscripts in the British Isles", *Italia Medioevale e Umanistica* 18: 1975, 139–509. Also interesting are a number of articles the English scholar wrote in the same years: "La prima fortuna del Petrarca in Inghilterra", in *Il Petrarca ad Arquà. Atti del convegno di studi nel VI centenario (1370–1374)*, ed. by G. Billanovich and G. Frasso, Padova: Antenore, 1975: 279–89; "Dal moralista al poeta: appunti per la fortuna del Petrarca in Inghilterra", in *Atti dei Convegni dei Lincei: Convegno Internazionale Francesco Petrarca*, Roma: Accademia Nazionale dei Lincei, 1976: 59–69; "Il Petrarca e gli inizi del Rinascimento inglese", *La Cultura* 15: 1977, 3–18.

[56] Mann, "Dal moralista al poeta: appunti per la fortuna del Petrarca in Inghilterra", p. 61.

[57] John Norton-Smith correctly underlines how Lydgate is at his best "in the translating of everyday event into a compact form", and continues noting that "for the modern reader it is likely that the creative Lydgate will emerge in the short occasional poems where he was able to give events a modest, imaginative form". See *John Lydgate. Poems*, ed. by J. Norton-Smith, Oxford: Clarendon Press, 1966, pp. xi–xii. Helen Cooper notes that "Lydgate is now being revealed as just such a commentator on the tangled politics of power and dissent in the early decades of the century, with their dread of heresy, their brief triumph of jingoistic nationalism succeeded by the anxieties attendant on the power struggles around an infant sovereign" (Helen Cooper, "Introduction", in *The Long Fifteenth Century. Essays for Douglas Gray*, ed. by H. Cooper and S. Mapstone, Oxford: Clarendon Press, 1997: 1–14, p. 6).

have been always the result of specific commissions; in the poet, the sense of contemporary history, in its major as well as in its trivial manifestations, is always strong, and an incessant flow of occasional verse accompanies all political or social occasions of fifteenth-century English life. Literary criticism has always been at pains to find derogatory epithets for Lydgate's verse, starting with Ritson's notorious "drivelling monk", but a more profitable evaluation of the poet may stem from considerations such as this, formulated by Eleanor Hammond: "historically, he sums up his age as definitely as did Pope or Dr. Johnson."[58] Thus a number of events in Humphrey's own life were marked by the tribute of Lydgate's poem. In particular, he wrote a "comendable balade", now known as *On Gloucester's Approaching Marriage*, which Hammond calls *Epithalamium for Gloucester*.[59] The occasion was Humphrey's marriage to Jacqueline of Hainault, and can thus be dated around 1422 (the marriage took place between the end of 1422 and the beginning of 1423, but Lydgate in the poem speaks of Henry V as living, and the King died in August 1422). Eleanor Hammond speaks of this poem as conventional, and showing "complacent ignorance of the actual political situation".[60] The tone is indeed generically laudatory, and most references to Cupid and to a number of other classical gods and famous women may sound simply the repetition of a cliché. However, there are some points of interest; one is the complete absence of references to the religious quality of marriage, together with the wholly classical setting, which may show that even the monk of Bury could look with interest at classical lore, and not feel bound by his vocation in his occasional verse. Besides, there are a number of allusions to contemporary history Hammond seems to have overlooked. The sanctity of the marriage oath is guaranteed by Jupiter (l. 14), and here the allusion may sound political rather than matrimonial: a reader conversant with classical mythology would rather expect a reference

---

[58] Hammond, *English Verse between Chaucer and Surrey*, p. 87.

[59] The poem is published in the second volume of *John Lydgate. Minor Poems*, ed. by H.N. MacCracken, Early English Text Society, Oxford: Oxford University Press, 1934, pp. 601–8. Hammond edits the poem in her *English Verse between Chaucer and Surrey*, pp. 142–8. I am using MacCracken's edition for all quotations from Lydgate's minor poetry, unless otherwise indicated.

[60] Hammond, *English Verse between Chaucer and Surrey*, p. 144.

to Jupiter's wife Juno, who presided over marriage. Since the allusion is followed by two stanzas establishing a relationship between marriage and the alliances of provinces, both opposing the possibility of strife, it may be that Lydgate, perhaps over-optimistically, was aware of the political possibilities inherent in this marriage, and chose this occasion to insert a mention of a favourite theme of his, the praise of peace. It may also be that, in his claiming that

> noman may þordeynaunce eschuwe,
> Thinges disposed by cours celestyal,
> Ner destenye to voyde nor remuwe,
> But oonly God þat lordshipeþe al.
> [22–5]

Lydgate was attempting to exorcise the threat of war that this marriage would inevitably pose, since it was clear that Gloucester was aiming, through Jacqueline, at the territories of Hainault, Holland and Zeeland to which his newly-wedded wife had a claim. If this is true, it would also explain why the ballad antedates the actual marriage: as in much of his minor poetry, but also in some passages of the *Fall of Princes*, Lydgate is inserting his personal plea for peace, and perhaps warning Gloucester of the possible consequences of this marriage, of which he however absolutely approves as an act of love. The fact that this plea is supported by "ensaumple in bookes" (l. 29) and in "cronycles autentyk and olde" (l. 36) may be simply an instance of the poet's constant use of *amplificatio*, but it may also refer to a use of history Humphrey would surely understand. Topical are also the allusions to the beneficial effects of Henry V's marriage with Catherine of France, which Lydgate links to his auspices that the duchy of Holland will be obtained through the same peaceful means. The description of Jacqueline, "sooþefast myrrour of beaute and fayrnesse" (l. 67), is the occasion for the introduction of a list of truthful and wise women, a list mainly taken from classical history; the fact that in his list Lydgate prefers to celebrate truth and wisdom rather than beauty or charm may demonstrate his concern about the political consequences of the marriage—fair Helen of Troy is also mentioned, but as a bad example to be avoided. The presentation of Duke Humphrey is conventional in its opening lines: he is a knight and soldier, renowned for his prowess and martial qualities. In his case, too, a list of notable men of antiquity is invoked; first the nine worthies, among whom Paris, Troilus, Hector and Tydeus are mentioned; then the poet praises the Duke's wit "to reede in bookis" (l. 142), and writes of his knowledge of poetry and philosophy. One passage is particularly surprising:

Slouth eschuwing, he dooþe his witt applye
To reede in bookis, wheeche þat beon moral,
In Hooly Writt with þe allegorye,
He him delyteþe to looke in specyal.
[141–4]

Here the tone becomes decidedly less conventional, and the praise more personal, though it is obviously not as detailed as it was in the prologue of the Palladius translation. The allegorical interpretation was generally applied to Biblical books, and, as Hammond notes, Gloucester's donations to Oxford included allegorical readings of various parts of the Bible.[61] The reference could therefore be to a favourite reading practice of the Duke. The list of famous men of antiquity is resumed, this time to include Solomon, Julius Caesar, and surprisingly Cicero: the Duke is

Of rethoryk and eeke of eloquence
Equypollent with Marcus Tulius.
[150–1]

Even if the closing image of Humphrey and Jacqueline will refer to a son of Mars and a fair Duchess, it is interesting that the poet should have felt it necessary to insert unconventional traits in his description of the Duke. David Rundle has seen in these lines a possible allusion to the fact that Humphrey, even in his early thirties, was considered unusually learned by his contemporaries, but then the scholar, with his usual scepticism, adds:

I would suggest that the skill of this passage is that it makes the conventional seem individual. In doing this, it has a close precedent in Lydgate's description of Henry V in the prologue of *The Troy Book*. Of Henry, as later of Humphrey, it is said that he reads in order to avoid "the cursyd vice of slouthe", his specialism being "bokys of antiquite" [Troy Book vol. 1, ll. 79–83]. This choice accords with the work that follows, just as the preferred reading matter in the ballad suits a man preparing to enter holy matrimony. It may be, then, that the reference to a specific genre has more to do with the type of poem in which it is mentioned than with any established penchant of the patron.[62]

[61] Hammond, *English Verse between Chaucer and Surrey*, p. 436.
[62] David Rundle, "Of Republics and Tyrants: Aspects of Quattrocento Humanist

Yet the passage in the *Troy Book* to which the scholar refers is widely different. Henry V, says Lydgate, has great joy in reading "bokys of antiquite", and finds there examples of virtue.[63] There is one reference to a classical author, and that is to Vegetius. The allusion suits, as Rundle notes, the context, but there is nothing that might refer personally to Henry V, distinguishing him from other martial warriors, if not the reference to the love of books, which seems to have been a typical Lancastrian trait. On the other hand, the portrait of Duke Humphrey in the short text we have just examined strikes a different note. Though, as has been already noted, there is much that is conventional in this ballad, I find it difficult to see in the lines just quoted a reference to suitable reading matter for a man who was about to be married. Allegorical reading of the Bible has little to do with the perusal of devotional treatises or religious guides to holy matrimony; and certainly the reference to Cicero, in this context, sounds even less suitable. I would contend that here we have an instance of a personalised eulogy, either accurate in its description of the patron or accurate in its response to that patron's wishes. It is also, as Walter Schirmer contends, "a brilliant solution of a difficult task".[64] This interpretation, which implicitly considers the poem the result of a specific commission, is opposed by Everest-Phillips, who believes the poem to have been unsolicited, and calls it "Lydgate's 'tradesman's sample'".[65] Yet it is difficult to see how, if there was no commission behind, Lydgate could have such a precise knowledge of the Duke's intellectual interest at such an early stage.

Completely different in tone is the *Complaint for my Lady of Gloucester and Holland*.[66] It was written on the occasion of Humphrey's separation and attempted divorce from Jacqueline of Hainault, which of course means that it could not have been commissioned by the Duke,

---

Writing and Their Reception in England, c. 1400–c. 1460", D.Phil., Oxford, 1997, p. 107.

[63] Prologue, l. 80. See *Lydgate's Troy Book*, ed. by H. Bergen, Early English Text Society, London: Kegan Paul, Trench, Trübner, 1906.

[64] Walter F. Schirmer, *John Lydgate, a Study in the Culture of the Fifteenth Century*, London: Methuen, 1961, p. 114.

[65] Everest-Phillips, p. 124.

[66] Published in the second volume of *John Lydgate. Minor Poems*, pp. 608–13. On this poem see also Tony Davenport, "Fifteenth-century Complaints and Duke Humphrey's Wives", in *Nation, Court and Culture: New Essays on Fifteenth-Century English Poetry*, ed. by H. Cooney, Dublin: Four Courts Press, 2001: 129–52.

and might even have been unacknowledged by its author, who hides behind the narrative *persona* of "a Solytarye"; it may be added that MacCracken's inclusion of this poem in the Lydgate canon has been contested by more recent scholars.[67] Though sympathising with Jacqueline's plight, the poem does not accuse Humphrey, trying rather to excuse him for his lack of "stableness"—a quality Humphrey did not seem to possess in any great degree, and for which he was nevertheless praised by both Lydgate and Hoccleve—by attributing the cause of his desertion to witchcraft.[68] The mention of witchcraft is interesting in the light of Humphrey's intellectual interests, which extended to astronomy and medicine, and of the Cobham scandal in 1441. But the image of the "myrmayde" and "fals Circes" who, with the help of her witches, retains and troubles the Duke "ageyns al right" and "agayins al lawe", might even be a direct allusion to Eleanor Cobham, while the chorus of women praying for Jacqueline's return refers to an actual episode that followed the separation between the Duchess and Humphrey.

Other works by Lydgate have been associated with Humphrey, but generally without great foundation. One such is the verse translation of the *Secreta Secretorum*, whose translation was completed by Benedict Burgh.[69] This text was originally attributed to Aristotle, and said to have been written in answer to the request of his pupil Alexander. It is a treatise on the *de regimine principum* tradition, in which, however, there is also the intimation that secret teaching lies there under a veil. No Greek correspondent has been found, while its earliest surviving versions are Arabic.[70] The text, translated into Latin by Philip of Paris in the thirteenth century, was then used by fourteenth-and fifteenth-century English writers, such as Gower, in

---

[67] See, for instance, Pearsall, *John Lydgate*, p. 166. The attribution to Lydgate is due to John Shirley's annotation, in the margin of Bodleian Library, Ashmole 59, f. 57r. The manuscript was compiled by Shirley after Gloucester's death (see Margaret Connolly, *John Shirley. Book Production and the Noble Household in Fifteenth-Century England*, Aldershot: Ashgate, 1998, p. 82).

[68] On this point see Hammond, *English Verse*, p. 144.

[69] *Lydgate and Burgh's Secrets of Old Philosoffres*, ed. by R. Steele, Early English Text Society, London: Kegan Paul, Trench, Trübner, 1894.

[70] DeWitt T. Starnes observes that the Arabic versions might derive from various sources written in Syriac in the fourth century. See the Introduction to his edition of Lydgate's text (*The Gouernaunce of Kynges and Prynces. The Pynson Edition of 1511. A Translation in Verse by John Lydgate and an Anonymous Poet from the Latin of the Secretum Secretorum*, Gainesville: Scholars' Facsimiles and Reprints, 1957).

Book VII of his *Confessio Amantis*, and Hoccleve, through the mediation of Guido delle Colonne. There are a number of fifteenth-century prose versions, one dated 1420, one 1460, one, partial, by John
Shirley, dedicated to Henry VI.[71] It is tempting, given its subject
matter, to see Humphrey's influence in Lydgate's translation, but
such an assumption is completely unproven, and does not fit the
probable date of the work.

Another text whose connection with Duke Humphrey has long
been the object of debate is *The Serpent of Division*.[72] It seems now
established beyond doubt that this prose account of the war between
Caesar and Pompey was written by John Lydgate, though there is
less general agreement on the date of its composition,[73] based on
the reference, in one of the two best manuscripts, to the making of
"this litill translacion, the moneth of decembre the first yere of oure
souvereigne lorde that now ys, King Henry the vjte".[74] It has then
been assumed the work was completed after Henry V's death, in
the later part of 1422 or perhaps in 1423. There is less agreement
as to the occasion of the poem, and whether it was the result of a
specific commission. Given the subject matter (the description of the
Roman civil war gives the poet the occasion to insert his usual plea
for peace) and the classical allusions, it is tempting to believe that
the work was written at Duke Humphrey's command. Though written with little talent for the organisation of the arguments, this work
has historical merit, since it is the first treatment of the Roman civil
wars in English, as well as being among the first political pamphlets written in England; unlike almost contemporary propaganda
works, such as *The Libelle of Englyshe Polycye*, it is not narrowly circum-
scribed to contemporary, local politics, preferring to look back at the
classical past, searching for a historical *exemplum*, that could then be

---

[71] *Three Prose Versions of the Secreta Secretorum*, ed. by R. Steele, Early English Text
Society, London: Kegan Paul, Trench, Trübner, 1898.
[72] *The Serpent of Division by John Lydgate the Monk of Bury*, ed. by H.N. MacCracken,
London: Oxford University Press, 1911.
[73] MacCracken is definite both in his attribution to Lydgate and in his dating it
1422, connecting the image of the serpent with Lydgate's *Siege of Thebes*, generally
dated 1421, and deducing that the two works must have followed each other closely
(*The Serpent of Division*, pp. 4–5). See also Walter F. Schirmer, *John Lydgate*, p. 82.
David Rundle considers the date "doubtful" ("Of Republics and Tyrants", p. 114);
Susanne Saygin prefers the date 1425 for the work (*Humphrey, Duke of Gloucester
(1390–1447) and the Italian Humanists*, Leiden: Brill, 2002, p. 16), but her choice
shall be discussed more in detail presently.
[74] British Library Additional 48031.

compared to the present situation but also have universal value. The final exhortation to lords and princes to remember what the writer has just narrated, and to use "discrecion" in their own wars, is generic enough not to allow the modern reader a comparison with a definite moment in English fifteenth-century history.

The identification of the patron commissioning this work with Duke Humphrey is more the result of critical wishful thinking than based on specific proof, though it has been supported by authoritative scholars. Henry N. MacCracken has been among the first to establish this identification, though without realising that it was at odds with what he himself considered the purpose of the work, that is, "to preserve public tranquillity".[75] This does not seem to have been the Duke of Gloucester's major concern, at any point in his life. If the work was completed in 1422, it was a time in which Humphrey was doing precious little to preserve peace; shortly after Henry V's death he started a controversy with the King's Council on the interpretation of his brother's testament and his own role towards young Henry of Windsor, and this controversy was the beginning of ever-worsening relations, particularly between Humphrey and the Bishop of Winchester. As Walter Schirmer writes, "Humphrey was not, like Bedford, a conscientious father of his country, who skilfully sought to forestall the dangers that threatened it under its infant sovereign".[76] If, on the other hand, the work was completed, or at least commissioned, before Henry V's death, both the King and his younger brother were keener to keep the French campaign going than to concern themselves with tranquillity in England, and Humphrey would not be particularly interested in an exhortation against fraternal strife, since he seemed perfectly content to follow his brother's politics. Yet the hypothesis of a commission on the part of the Duke, which, as David Rundle correctly notes, is at best unproven,[77] is also supported by one of the most important Lydgatian scholars, Derek Pearsall, who writes:

> Gloucester [. . .] was aware of the more immediate perils of domestic faction, and it was probably he who commissioned *The Serpent of Division*, a prose history of the war of Caesar and Pompey designed to warn

---

[75] *The Serpent of Division*, p. 1.
[76] Schirmer, *John Lydgate*, p. 82.
[77] Rundle, "Of Republics and Tyrants", p. 114.

of the dangers of civil strife, the "irrecuperable harmes of division" (p. 66, lines 2–3). The text ends with the author's statement that the work was done "bi commaundemente of my moste worschipfull maistere & souereyne" (p. 66, lines 4–5) [. . .] The reference to the author's "maistere & souvereiyne" is to the king by courtesy of Gloucester who, though not king, spoke in England with the sovereign's voice, as can be seen from the terms of reference of his appointment as protector in England, 15 December 1422, during Bedford's absence in France.[78]

It seems to me that here Pearsall is exaggerating Gloucester's powers; the phrase "maistere & souvereyne" could well refer to two different persons, but Lydgate would never attribute the second title to the King "by courtesy of Gloucester", since it would sound almost as an attribution of this title to the Duke himself.[79] Nor could Gloucester have it so openly claimed that he spoke with the King's voice, given the trouble he was having to have his prerogatives acknowledged by the King's Council. It may be that the sovereign in question is Henry V, and that the work took too long, and was completed only when the King had already died. Or it may be that the annotation quoted above, alluding to the first year of Henry VI's reign, refers to the year of his actual coronation; in this case the work would have been completed in the early 1430s. Even in this case, though, there is little reason to attribute the commission to the Duke of Gloucester—especially since, judging from *The Fall of Princes* and the Palladius translation, he preferred more elaborate references to his presence in the works he commissioned. Besides, though its subject matter is classical history, it is difficult to consider this work an instance of humanist writing—Julius Caesar was of course well known in the Middle Ages, and had often appeared in the *de casibus* literature, including Chaucer's Monk's Tale.

---

[78] Derek Pearsall, *John Lydgate (1371–1449): A Bio-bibliography*, English Literary Studies Monograph Series, University of Victoria: English Literary Studies, 1997, p. 23.

[79] It should also be noted that some manuscripts omit "& souvereyne". Nigel Mortimer believes that the term could have been used for the Duke, given his ambiguous political status in 1422 and Lydgate's desire to flatter his patron (Nigel Mortimer, "A Study of John Lydgate's *Fall of Princes* in its Literary and Political Contexts", D.Phil., Oxford, 1995, p. 86). It should be remembered, however, that Duke Humphrey was not Lydgate's only patron, and that the poet would not have risked displeasing a higher authority for the sake of an epithet that could sound even galling to the Duke.

Susanne Saygin has made this work and the supposed occasion of its commission the cornerstone of her interpretation of the relationship between Gloucester, his brother the Duke of Bedford and their young nephew Henry of Windsor, with Lydgate cast in the role of "one of the leading Lancastrian propagandists".[80] By moving the date of composition to 1425 (which can be done only considering the "first yere" of the British library manuscript a scribal error for "fourth yere"), and reading the initials "J. De V." or "J. De B." at the end of two manuscript copies as indications of a dedication to John of Bedford, Saygin sets Humphrey's supposed commission of the work during the stipulation of an alliance between Gloucester and Bedford, basing her hypothesis mainly on her expectations of a symmetry between the Roman triumvirate described by Lydgate and an analogous situation in England. Thus Humphrey may be identified with Caesar (which would be, however, hardly flattering for his brother), and Pompey with Henry Beaufort, while the commission could be read as an instance of Gloucester's "pragmatic approach to history".[81] This is Saygin's conclusion:

> The leitmotif of the *Serpent*, that as long as unity prevailed, the kingdom would be strong, but ruin would threaten as soon as selfish ambition allowed discord to creep in, acted as a powerful affirmation of the idea of cooperation that was central to Gloucester's treaty of alliance. If it is assumed that the duke attributed equal importance to the literary work and the legal contract, and that both texts were intended to supplement and reinforce each other, this would testify to the practical value Gloucester attributed to literature for the interpretation and formulation of politics, and it would demonstrate how intensely the duke's literary patronage was informed by political motives. In the ensuing decades, the dynamic interrelation between his action in the spheres of political and culture became a hallmark of Gloucester's policy.[82]

Unfortunately, there is simply no proof that this construction is historically based: the scholar's whole hypothesis is based on her own assumptions. It is difficult to reach any conclusion regarding this text and its commission, and it is impossible to use it for a more complete understanding of the Duke of Gloucester's intellectual activity.

---

[80] Saygin, p. 41. For her discussion on *The Serpent of Division*, see pp. 41–5.
[81] Saygin, p. 45.
[82] Saygin, p. 45.

It is probably more profitable to study it as an expression of Lydgate's own ideology, and of his often expressed anxiety about the nefarious consequences of war, and especially of civil war.[83]

One last minor poem dealing with the life of Duke Humphrey that has been sometime, but probably wrongly, attributed to Lydgate is the *Epithalamium eiusdem Ducis Gloucestrie*.[84] The text is in the form of a complaint, with a refrain at the end of each stanza. The commemoration of the Duke is interspersed with invocations to God, Christ and the Virgin, and is set in generic terms, with some personal allusions in lines 73-6:

> He was verray fader and protectour to the land,
> Ingland, I meane, that is thyn owne dowarye;
> Never man had more zele, as I understond,
> Ne redyer to redresse alle transgressis by and by.

There is also a reference to Humphrey's activity as a pillar of the church, but no allusions to his cultural activity, while Lydgate would not spare himself on this point.

But the most important work Lydgate wrote for the Duke of Gloucester is of course *The Fall of Princes*. This huge poem, notorious for being probably the longest in the English language, was begun probably in 1431 and was not completed until 1438 or 1439.[85] It was a translation of Boccaccio's *De casibus virorum illustrium* undertaken with the mediation of Laurent de Premierfait's prose version of Boccaccio, variously called *Des Cas des Nobles Hommes et Femmes*,

---

[83] For an excellent literary evaluation of this work, see Schirmer, *John Lydgate*, pp. 83-9.

[84] It survives in two manuscripts, British Library Harley 2251 (ff. 7r-8v) and British Library Additional 34360. Excluded from MacCracken's edition of Lydgate's minor poems, it has been edited by Rossell Hope Robbins in "An Epitaph for Duke Humphrey (1441)", *Neuphilologische Mitteilungen* 56: 1955, 241-49. Given that the poem quite clearly laments the death of the Duke, Robbins's hypothesis on the year of its composition is surprising.

[85] Pearsall, *John Lydgate*, p. 223. The critic writes: "These were the years when Gloucester was at the height of his power and influence, and the commission to Lydgate was designed to advance the Duke's reputation as a European patron of letters and as the English representative of the new Italian humanist learning. His plans came unstuck, partly because of Lydgate's inert response to the materials, and one suspects that Gloucester gradually lost interest". See Pearsall, *John Lydgate (1371-1449): A Bio-bibliography*, p. 33. An excellent analysis of the relation between poet and patron in *The Fall of Princes* can be found in Nigel Mortimer, "A Study of John Lydgate's *Fall of Princes* in its Literary and Political Contexts".

De la Ruyne des Nobles Hommes et Femmes, or *Des Nobles Malhereux*; once
we consider the English title, it is easy to see that Lydgate's change
from illustrious or noble people to princes (though the latter are by
no means the only protagonists of his book) may have been meant
as a homage to the patron.[86] The relation between the three texts
has been the object of much critical debate, but it is almost certain
that the French version (which occasionally Lydgate decidedly and
surprisingly abbreviates) was not Lydgate's only source; he certainly
glanced at Boccaccio more than once, besides availing himself of a
number of other sources, such as Ovid's *Metamorphoses*, Petrarch, a
version of the story of Lucretia by Coluccio Salutati, and of course
a number of Chaucerian works. Occasionally the references to the
Frenchness of Lydgate's antecedent may sound more like a political
than a literary allusion: in a work begun during Henry VI's royal
progress in France, it was important that the continuity between
French and English culture should be underlined.[87] Both the links
with the humanist texts arriving in Humphrey's library and the references to contemporary history are thus set in the foreground, and
the poem, with its complex system of lengthy prologues, becomes
at the same time a continuation of the medieval *de casibus* tradition
and the celebration of a library that unites classical and new authors
in harmonious continuity.[88] The *Fürstenspiegel* tradition carried with
it an implicit, but never openly expressed, didactic aim: princes were
supposed to profit by it, learning what examples they should avoid,
and drawing from the sad cases of evil or misguided princes an ideal
image of what they should be. This is how they are presented to
the ideal reader, which in this case does not seem to coincide with

---

[86] "Lydgate calls our attention to the importance of rulers and thus emphasizes
at the start the central purpose of his own work" (Alain Renoir, *The Poetry of John
Lydgate*, London: Routledge & Kegan Paul, 1967, p. 106).

[87] As has been noted by Larry Scanlon in his *Narrative, Authority, and Power*,
p. 329.

[88] Everest-Phillips reads the choice of Laurent de Premierfait as a desire on the
part of Humphrey to emulate John, Duke of Berry, at whose command Laurent
had written his version (Everest-Phillips, p. 130). John Watts supports the connection between literature and ideology, reading it however in a different direction
from the critics quoted so far: "Advice-literature did indeed appeal to the literary
tastes of the nobility, [...] its assumptions regarding the enthusiasm of readers for
advice were justified and [...] it may indeed, therefore, have been the chief literary influence on the formation of political views" (*Henry VI and the Politics of Kingship*,
Cambridge: Cambridge University Press, 1996, p. 56).

Fig. 4. The presentation scene of John Lydgate's *Fall of Princes*.

the actual dedicatee. Yet, as Derek Pearsall rightly underlines, they are not to be considered books of instruction, and though princes read them and occasionally, as in this case, commissioned them, the patrons would not expect to be taught their duties, or to be revealed unwelcome truths; they read them "because it was important that they should represent themselves as receptive to sage counsel".[89] Pearsall applies this observation to Thomas Hoccleve's *Regement of Princes*, but it is easy to see that it is equally apt in the case of Lydgate's *Fall of Princes*; only here the poet is perhaps more anxious to reassure the patron on this point.

It is clear that this was a completely different enterprise from the Palladius translation, elegant and carefully laid out as that work is. It is also clear that, whatever his stylistic and technical shortcomings, Lydgate was a different poet from the Palladius translator, with a completely different task in front of him, and would not be content with passively obeying the Duke's dispositions. Throughout his progress among the illustrious men and women who have fallen prey to Fate, Lydgate is also pursuing his own lines of enquiry, into the nature of true regality, and the relation between nobility and virtuous conduct.[90] This, together with the reappearance of the *leitmotiv* of the melancholic reflection on the fate of the mighty, and on the evil consequences of strife, led Lydgate to deviate from Boccaccio's tone. The Italian poet had brought an innovation to the genre, by adopting a tone of derision to the great, falling through their own desert rather than misfortune—a tone that is particularly felt when the victims are members of the clergy.[91] This, together with the striking use of Latin, had probably contributed to the great influence Boccaccio's *De casibus* had in the two centuries following its author's death. Lydgate's lamenting and didactic tone owes more to his other acknowledged master, Geoffrey Chaucer, and to the Monk of his *Canterbury Tales*.[92] Yet, unlike Chaucer's Monk, the fifteenth-century

---

[89] Derek Pearsall, "Hoccleve's *Regement of Princes*: The Poetics of Royal Self-Representation", *Speculum* 69: 1994, 386–410, p. 386.

[90] On this point see Renoir, pp. 106–7. Renoir links this attitude to John of Salisbury's political theory.

[91] See Schirmer, "The Importance of the Fifteenth Century for the Study of the English Renaissance with Special Reference to Lydgate", pp. 105–6.

[92] Mortimer maintains Lydgate also had access to Thomas Hoccleve's *Regiment of Princes* in the Duke of Gloucester's library (p. 62), but there is no evidence Humphrey possessed a copy of this work.

poet carefully avoids any reference to contemporary instances; these will appear in a much smaller work, *Of the Sodein Fal of Princes in Oure Dayes*, whose subjects include Edward II, Richard II, Charles VI of France, Thomas, Duke of Gloucester, and John, Duke of Burgundy; perhaps this poem did not have so powerful a patron behind it. *The Fall of Princes* stops short of mentioning the faults of contemporary princes; indeed, by concluding with king John of France, and his capture at the hands of Edward, the Black Prince, he manages to end on a note of triumph for the English crown.[93] On the other hand, though the work is clearly intended as a *speculum principis*, and though the individual stories are generally concluded by an envoy which briefly summarises what has been going on before and exhorts princes to take heed and profit from what they have read (in addition to Boccaccio's conclusion), Lydgate avoids reading the cases he narrates under a Christian light, and in this attitude he might be nearer to Boccaccio.[94] The relation between Lydgate and his most important *auctoritates* is not without its bearing on the present discussion. It is difficult to relate some of Lydgate's philosophical stances in the poem to the fact of Humphrey's commission, but they can certainly be connected to an intellectual climate that was widely different from both Chaucer's and Boccaccio's. The more careful tone as far as the clergy is concerned, for instance, may derive from Lydgate's own status, but it is certainly connected also to a Lancastrian preoccupation with the Church, whose support was sorely needed by this less than stable monarchy.[95] The same may be said of the issue of bad government, which is not as significant for Lydgate as it was for his predecessors.[96] The Duke of Gloucester was taking charge of his share of the Lancastrian policy of patronage by having some Lancastrian favourite themes transposed into the vernacular, and combining them with a new, humanist appreciation of the classics and of classical history. Lydgate's operation makes the different instances in Boccaccio and Chaucer meet and partly fuse, both poets bringing their authoritative weight to the new work.

---

[93] As David Wallace notes in his *Chaucerian Polity: Absolutist Lineages and Associational Forms in England and Italy*, Stanford: Stanford University Press, 1997, p. 325.

[94] An interesting comparison between Lydgate and Chaucer is drawn by Larry Scanlon in his *Narrative, Authority and Power*, p. 324.

[95] See Scanlon, *Narrative, Authority and Power*, p. 298.

[96] A point made by Mortimer, p. 34.

But one of the most interesting characteristics of *The Fall of Princes*, among the most popular works of Lydgate, is its sustained eulogy of its patron.[97] Unlike what happens in the Palladius translation, here Humphrey's interest does not seem to flag very soon, or perhaps Lydgate was a more patient and persistent *protégé*, while the work was composed in earlier and happier years for the Duke. The first book is introduced by a prologue similar in contents and structure to the prologue in the Palladius translation, though decidedly more diffuse, and occasionally tending to wander off the point. After establishing his more direct sources and the year in which his composition began, and acknowledging both Boccaccio's and Laurent's valiant effort, Lydgate, lamenting the absence of a muse and wondering where he should turn for inspiration, begins to consider a number of other *auctoritates* that are here introduced more for the sake of the *ubi sunt* motif than because of any influence they might have had on the poet; thus Chaucer is mentioned first, followed by Seneca, Cicero and Petrarch. Lydgate also inserts a whole list of Chaucer's works before introducing the new theme of this prologue: these old poets used to be the favourite of kings, who would listen to their advice and teaching; in this country a mighty prince is showing the same commendable attitude. The connection between writers and patrons, literary fame and political interest, is already established here, and is a theme Lydgate shall revisit; as David Wallace writes, "the crucial linkage between the 'renoun' of writers and the status or 'worshipe' of a nation was one that the Lancastrians had long been willing to exploit (and Lydgate and Hoccleve to exemplify)".[98] There is, however, a difference between Humphrey and the kings and princes of old; though loving, like them, to read books, he far excels everybody else in understanding and knowledge.[99] The prince and politician is presented first: this son and uncle of kings (an appellation Humphrey seems to have been particularly fond of) has governed England guaranteeing peace, showing both prudence and knightly qualities: and here Lydgate's own predilection for prudence seems slightly at odds with the necessity of praising Humphrey as a

---

[97] V.J. Scattergood notes how "this work appears to have been extremely popular, for more than thirty manuscripts, some of them highly decorated, have survived" (*Politics and Poetry in the Fifteenth Century*, London: Blandford Press, 1971, p. 151).

[98] Wallace, *Chaucerian Polity*, p. 332.

[99] A point noted also by Everest-Phillips, p. 135.

knight—a dilemma that will be faced also by Tito Livio Frulovisi in his *Hunfroidos*. Then the poet's attention turns to the man of letters, but here the praise strikes the reader as being at the same time more exaggerated and less incisive than what could be read in the Palladius translation; the Duke "hath gret ioie with clerkis to comune" (l. 387), reads various languages and is "stable in study" (l. 389), yet there are no references to specific branches of learning or intellectual activities, nor is there a mention of the scholars working with him. Shortly the poet turns his attention to the patron as an enemy of Lollardy, and it is clear that he finds this side of his patron's personality more striking and worthy of mention than his intellectual attainments. It is perhaps true that Lydgate was less close to his patron than the Palladius translator; besides, by the time he started working on *The Fall of Princes* he had already achieved notoriety and received important commissions, so that he could not adapt himself to his patron's wishes in quite the same way, but had to observe a decorous respect of tradition in his prologue, noticeable especially in his use of formulaic phrases: he will work "with support off his magnificence" (l. 435) and remain "vndir the wyngis off his correccioun" (l. 436), but we miss the amused abandon of some almost jocular passages of the Palladius translation, such as the vignette of Humphrey correcting the translator's work at the end of the first book.

The first mention of Ovid occurs in Book I, l. 2136. The insertion is slightly pedantic, used not to correct but to support Boccaccio's telling of the story of Cadmus and his wife:

> Nor off ther deth I fynde noon other date,
> Sauff that Ouide maketh mencioun,
> And Iohn Bochas the poete excellent
> Seith that . . .
>
> [2135–8]

The mention of Ovid is simply name-dropping at this point: since Lydgate is taking the story from Boccaccio, he would have no real need of Ovid's authority, nor is he juxtaposing two versions of one myth; he is just showing off his erudition. The same happens in a number of other passages: the story of Medea evokes the double authority of Ovid and "moral Seneca" (Book I, ll. 2383–4, 2411), the story of Minos is narrated "takyng witnesse Metamorphoseos" (Book I, l. 2443), and so on.[100] Generally only Ovid is mentioned,

---

[100] This observation is supported by a similar observation in Schirmer, *John Lydgate*,

and the book used is his *Metamorphoses*, though in IV.94–105 there
is also a list of Ovid's work, analogous to what Lydgate had done
with Chaucer and Petrarch. This constant reference strongly reminds
the reader of the marginal annotation on f. 53r of the presentation
copy of the Palladius translation, discussed above: there, too, the
annotator had mentioned Ovid, essentially to support and repeat a
statement already made in the text. In the case of the Palladius,
however, the allusion to Ovid's authority was far less pertinent than
in this case, and seems simply the self-conscious observation of an
erudite reader. In both cases it does not add much. I am tempted
to see also in Lydgate's use of Ovid the evidence of Humphrey's
hand, his loading the translator and his work with extra reading
matter that in many cases could only conform to what was to be
found in Boccaccio. There are other points of similarity between *The
Fall of Princes* and the Palladius translation, such as the addition of
prologues, and of an envoy at the end of each story: the envoys in
particular, though in part they are meant to reiterate the motif of
the advice to princes (with the frequent use of the refrain "O Pryncis,
Pryncessis"),[101] are also useful to help the reader find a way in the
flow of the narration: the practice of briefly taking up the main
threads of the story that has just been told clarifies the structure of
the work and makes it easier to consult, supposing the reader to
have been interested in a particular story rather than in the whole
text; the choice presupposes in the reader the same attitude as in
the Middle English Palladius. In the prologue to Book II it is clearly
stated that this practice is suggested by Humphrey, and the passage,
which is here quoted in full, is strikingly similar to the analogous
passage at the end of Book II of the Palladius translation ("And now
my lord biholdith on his book . . ."), anticipating something of its
tone and images, particularly the idea of the patron wielding a pen:

---

p. 211, though even at a cursory glance it can be seen that the references to Ovid
are much more numerous than Schirmer notes.

[101] Nigel Mortimer reads also a political intention in the envoys: "Humphrey's
intention seems to have been that Lydgate's version of the *De casibus* should highlight the regiminal value of the work. Careful study of the sixty-nine envoys reveals
that Lydgate followed the terms of Humphrey's request closely: fifty-eight of the
passages consciously expound the significance of the preceding narrative for princes.
What emerges clearly, however, is that Lydgate's advisory idiom is broadly ethical
rather than specifically political or legal" (p. 63).

Anon afftir, I off entencioun,
With penne in hande faste gan me speede
As I koude, in my translacioun,
In this labour ferthere to proceede,
My lord cam forbi, and gan to taken heede;
This myhti prynce, riht manli & riht wis,
Gaff me charge in his prudent auys,
That I sholde in eueri tragedie,
Afftir the processe made mencioun,
At the eende sette a remedie,
With a lenvoie conueied be resoun,
And afftir that, with humble affeccioun,
To noble pryncis lowli it directe,
Bi othres fallyng thei myht themsilff correcte.
And I obeied his biddyng and plesaunce,
Vnder support off his magnyficence.
As I coude, I gan my penne auaunce,
Al-be I was bareyn off eloquence,
Folwyng myn auctour in substaunce & sentence:
For it suffised, pleynli, onto me,
So that my lord my makyng took at gre.
                    [141–61]

There is nothing similar in other books Lydgate wrote on commission, even when the patron was equally or more important than the
Duke of Gloucester. It may be true that the praise of the patron is
often generic, certainly less personal that in the Palladius translation;
but the constant intervention of the patron in the composition of
the text is a striking trait the two works have in common. Larry
Scanlon observes that "Commanding Lydgate to translate 'The noble
book off this John Bochas' (I.423) Humphrey shows not only that
he is in no real need of instruction, but can in fact take charge of
producing the very text by which instruction should take place.
Lydgate will cast him in this role in various ways throughout the
poem".[102] Scanlon, however, links this solely to the Lancastrian policy of literary propaganda, while it seems to me that the connection
with the Palladius text demonstrates that this desire to take charge
directly of the production of the work was a peculiar trait of Duke
Humphrey.

Humphrey's intervention does not seem to limit itself to the addition of references to Ovid to support the narration. At one point,

---

[102] Scanlon, *Narrative, Authority, and Power*, p. 334.

in Book II, l. 971, the poet mentions the Roman matron Lucretia, an excellent example of chastity and moral strength. As he has written in other occasions, he initially refers the reader to Chaucer, who "wrot off hir liff a legende souerayne" (l. 980). Chaucer told this story as well as the tragedy of Dido; Lydgate adds, with a characteristic modesty *topos*:

> Wherfore yiff I sholde my penne auaunce,
> Afftir his makyng to putte hem in memorie,
> Men wolde deeme it presumpcioun & veynglorie.
> [II, 992–4]

Since the modesty *topos* is drawn for four stanzas, and includes the story of Dido as well as that of Lucretia, the reader at this point expects the poet to move to a different subject. However, immediately after thus graciously yielding to Chaucer's superior poetry, Lydgate starts telling the story of Lucretia himself. "But at Lucrece stynte I will a while" (l. 1002). There is no other reference to Chaucer, and set in these terms the decision is somewhat unexpected, but shortly afterwards we are offered another, more convincing explanation than a sudden desire on the part of the poet to tell the story after all:

> Also my lord bad I sholde abide,
> By good auys at leiser to translate
> The doolful processe off hir pitous fate.
> [1006–8]

These three lines, concluding a stanza, are followed by "Folwyng the tracis of Collucyus". The EETS editor divides this last line from what precedes it by a full stop, but in so doing he creates an anacoluthon in the following stanza. I would rather think that the last line follows as part of a single sentence: his lord bade Lydgate not only to tell the story of Lucretia, but to follow "Collucyus" rather than Chaucer or Boccaccio. The hypothesis that Lydgate inserted the story of Lucretia independently of the original plan of his work is confirmed by the fact that on l. 1464 he resumes his narration (turning his attention to the story of Jeroboam King of Israel) with the phrase "next these stories". The use of the plural makes me think that he is referring to both the stories of Lucreetia and Dido, which he had decided not to tell. In Book III, ll. 932–1148, Lucretia's fate will be mentioned again, and this time the poet's attention will be focused not upon the story itself but upon Lucretia's complaint

before dying. Boccaccio is mentioned as the poet's source, together
with another writer:

> And for that Bochas remembreth pitousli
> Hir dedli sorwe and lamentacioun,
> Writ hir compleynt in ordre ceriousli,
> Which that she made for hir oppressioun,
> I folwe muste and make mencioun,
> Afftir myn auctour parcel rehersyng,
> Touchyng hir woordis said in hir deieng.
>
> Al-be-it so, be biddyng off my lord,
> Rehersed haue in my translacioun
> Afftir Pierius heer and ther a woord...
>   [III, 974–83]

Once again "my lord" has intervened in the process of composition
and modified the author's original intention, and both times his intervention is linked to an *auctoritas* not elsewhere mentioned in the
poem. The reference is to the humanist Linus Colucius Pierius, better known to modern readers as Coluccio Salutati, and to his *Declamatio
Lucretiae*. Eleanor Hammond was probably the first scholar to comment upon this insertion in *The Fall of Princes*,[103] and to compare
Lydgate's narration of Lucretia's tragedy with Salutati's. Everest-
Phillips later completed Hammond's observations by indicating the
manuscript in which Lydgate read Salutati, identifying it with
Humphrey of Gloucester's own copy.[104] The inference seems clear:
here, more notably than in other occasions, Humphrey directly intervened in Lydgate's work, suggesting the use of Salutati with such
determination that the result is a particularly awkward coexistence
of the deference to an *auctoritas*—Chaucer—with the use of another—
Salutati. The effect is of a rejection of Chaucer in favour of the
Italian humanist, who is clearly preferred here as Lydgate's source.
Perhaps then, the already quoted line "also my lord bad I sholde
abide" should not be read as a homage to the erudite patron, but
as an apology to the reader for an unhappy transition, and an imperfectly balanced passage in the book. Lydgate has often been criticised

---

[103] Eleanor Hammond, "Lydgate and Coluccio Salutati", *Modern Philology* 25:
1927–8, 49–57. See also Mortimer, pp. 65–83.
[104] The manuscript is now Manchester, Chetham's Library, Mun. A.3.131 (27929).
See Everest-Phillips, p. 142. A description of the manuscript can be found in
Sammut, pp. 111–2.

as too fond a lover of *amplificatio* in his translations, but it may be that in this case he was not the only culprit. As Peter Lucas observes, Humphrey's interest in this case "hardly falls short of interference, since it undoubtedly had an averse effect on the artistic integrity of the poem".[105]

David Wallace is probably right when he writes that "Lydgate plainly falls victim to the contradiction at the heart of his enterprise: that of trying to write of past *viri illustres* while a contemporary "myghty man" wields a pen and scraper at his side".[106] More self-conscious and autonomous though perhaps less talented in versifying than the Palladius translator, Lydgate suffers Humphrey's interventions less gladly, also because they often weigh upon an already frightfully complex structure. I have used the episode of Lucretia to demonstrate that Humphrey's commissions, unlike what happened with other members of the Lancastrian family, often entailed a direct participation of the patron in the organisation of the sources and disposition of the material, and I believe the poet's own words confirm my supposition; but a different conclusion may be also drawn, and that is that such participation on the part of the patron could be sometimes felt as an unwarranted interference even by the most compliant of poets. Besides, Lydgate's position was made even more difficult by the patron's status; the modern reader may think it an ironic coincidence that "Humphrey's own spectacular and brutally sudden fall"[107] would echo so appropriately the tragic cases his poet had described; but probably Lydgate, always attentive to the changing politics of his time, finely attuned to the currents of dissension among the nobility while obstinately longing for peace, felt it as an additional burden that his patron should be engaged in the same kind of political tension which he was describing in his work as the cause of the fall of so many princes.[108] It is not by chance that, in the eulogy of the Duke contained in the general prologue, he should

---

[105] Lucas, "The Growth and Development of English Literary Patronage", p. 233.

[106] Wallace, *Chaucerian Polity*, p. 333.

[107] James Simpson, "Bulldozing the Middle Ages", p. 234.

[108] Eleanor Hammond notes on this point that, though "the Fall of Princes allusions have some slender vitality in them, and for that vitality, I believe, Humphrey of Gloucester was largely responsible", "the heavy task which he assigned to his protégé did indeed crush Lydgate's verse and style to worse than a dead level much of the time" (*English Verse between Chaucer and Surrey*, p. 93).

observe that Humphrey's life is led "settyng a-side alle chaungis of Fortune" (l. 390). In a world dominated by the capricious mutability of Fortune, the *fortunys stabilnesse* is, or should be, a prerogative of the prince or of the ideal ruler, who has not defeated fortune (an impossible task) but is able effectively to ride it. Analysing some instances of Ricardian and Lancastrian poetry, Paul Strohm notes in the poets writing under the influence of Lancastrian patronage "a quality of unease, a kind of nervous reciprocity in which the adviser at once experiences a closer identification with his monarch, and a heightened uncertainty about the spirit in which even the most complicitous reassurances will be received".[109] I would contend that in the case of Lydgate's *Fall of Princes* this characteristic is enhanced by the patron's desire to be privy to the creative process.

Having seen such a clear instance of the patron's intervention in the case of the Lucretia episode, it may also be noted that a number of times, though less obtrusively, Lydgate inserts or mentions other poets besides his avowed *auctoritates*, and for these insertions Humphrey may be partly responsible. Thus Humphrey's influence, and the presence of his library, may be linked also to the mention of Dante's *Divine Comedy* in Book IV (ll. 136.40).[110] The same may be said as concerns the already mentioned references to Petrarch and his Latin works, or to passages in the prologue to the fourth book that seem indebted to John of Salisbury's *Policraticus*—another book that was in the Duke of Gloucester's library, since it appears in the list of the 1439 donation to Oxford. We might refer to the same source, though more tentatively, two fragments of Greek (III.1855 and IV.568), and connect them with the book described as "verba greca et interpretaciones lingue latine" appearing in Gloucester's third donation to the University of Oxford. Hammond sees also in the references to Aulus Gellius and Vincent de Beauvais an indication of Lydgate's use of Humphrey's library.[111] Humphrey's interventions are far from regular, and never so direct as in the case of the Lucretia story; so, for instance, while Book I is constantly interspersed with

---

[109] Paul Strohm, *England's Empty Throne: Usurpation and the Language of Legitimation 1399–1422*, New Haven and London: Yale University Press, 1998, p. 174.

[110] See Hammond, "Lydgate and Coluccio Salutati", p. 57, See also Paget Toynbee, *Dante in English Literature from Chaucer to Cary (c. 1380–1844)*, London: Methuen, 1909, p. 18.

[111] Hammond, *English Verse between Chaucer and Surrey*, p. 180.

references to Ovid, in Book II these references disappear, and apart from the insertion of the Lucretia story all mentions are exclusively of Boccaccio and occasionally of Chaucer. It seems that the patron's interest may have flagged, while Lydgate was composing Book II, and may have revived later, obliging the poet to insert Salutati's version in a book that was already completed. This hypothesis is substantiated by a "Letter to Gloucester" that seems to have accompanied a particularly difficult moment in the composition of the poem. Walter Schirmer notes that after Book II was completed, presumably in 1433, Lydgate momentarily interrupted his work, to dedicate his attention for a while to the *Life of St. Edmund and St. Fremund*, written at the request of his abbot, William Curteys. The critic believes this interruption to represent at least in part Lydgate's desire for respite from the weight of erudition Humphrey was piling up on him, and reads the almost contemporary "Letter to Gloucester" as almost an act of revenge on the part of the poet.[112] But as the letter itself shows, Lydgate was not only pressed with problems of compositions, but also with financial worries. The relatively easier writing of the *Life* might probably also have offered him a possibility of acquiring immediate if moderate wealth (or at least, the benevolence of his abbot, at whose request the work was written) while taking his mind momentarily off the monumental *Fall*. Lydgate himself was daunted by the magnitude of the task he had undertaken, as can be seen by the strangely moving prologue of Book III, in which the poet represents himself in the grip of a serious case of writer's block, and even kicking himself at the thought of having accepted this nearly impossible commission:

> Thus be my-selff remembryng on this book,
> It to translate how I hadde vndirtake,
> Ful pale off cheer, astonyd in my look,
> Myn hand gan tremble; my penne I felte quake . . .
> [III, 43–6]

The detail of the trembling hand appears again in the "Letter to Gloucester", echoing the line above with the expression "myn hand

---

[112] Schirmer, *John Lydgate*, p. 215. A.S.G. Edwards suggests that at this point, pressed as he was by financial worries, Lydgate may also have produced a shorter presentation version of the poem ("The McGill Fragment of Lydgate's 'Fall of Princes'", *Scriptorium* 28: 1974, 75–7).

I felte quake" (l. 4).[113] This short poem, however, is relatively uncon-
cerned with the troubles of composition, being a frank request for
money, though couched in the gentlest possible terms, with the gently
mocking refrain at the end of each stanza that bemoans the poet's
plight "oonly for lak of plate and of coignage". The request uses
successive sets of images, evidently chosen to please the patron: in
the second stanzas there are medical metaphors, which were sure to
catch Humphrey's fancy; then there is the image of a ship the poet
lacks, and without which he cannot continue his voyage, and in this
case Hammond correctly reads the allusion as referring to the ship
designed on the obverse of gold nobles, half-nobles, and quarter-
nobles. In the same vein are the references to a cross and a "vis-
age" at l. 30 (the designs on silver coins), and to Sol and Luna, to
be read as gold and silver, at l. 29.[114] The medical and financial
metaphors are joined by alchemical allusions, such as "aurum pota-
bile", indicated as the sovereign remedy for the poet at l. 46. As for
the allusion to "Bury toun" at l. 12, it may indicate that Lydgate
had temporarily gone back to his monastery. It may be remembered,
incidentally, that the *Life of St. Edmund* was composed for Henry VI,
who was visiting Bury St Edmunds at the time. We thus see Lydgate
engaged in two opposite types of mirror for princes literature at the
same time: on the one hand, the hagiographical portrait of the saint-
king, which underlines chastity and purity along with the martial
qualities of Edmund, dedicated to the saintly King Henry; on the
other, a series of models drawn from history or from classical antiquity, with very little or no religious reference, for the decidedly less
saint (and less chaste) Humphrey, while in roughly the same years
the latter was also commissioning a *Vita Henrici Quinti* to his Italian,
humanist secretary, thus proposing yet another and innovative model
of mirror for princes. The tone in which the poet addresses the two
powerful patrons is also very different; Lydgate's dedication to
Humphrey in the prologue of the *Fall of Princes* has already been
commented upon; in the *Life of St. Edmund* there is no dedication as
such, but the King is mentioned in the opening prayer to St Edmund:

---

[113] The poem is published in *John Lydgate. Minor Poems*, pp. 665–7.
[114] Eleanor P. Hammond, "Poet and Patron in the *Fall of Princes*: Lydgate and
Humphrey of Gloucester", *Anglia* 38: 1914, 121–36, p. 127.

This vertuous baner shal kepen and conserue
This lond from enmyes, daunte ther cruel pryde;
Off syxte Herry the noblesse to preserue,
It shal be born in werrys be his syde;
Tencresse his vertues, Edmund shal been his guyde,
By processe tenhaunce his Royal lyne.[115]

It can be easily seen that, though Lydgate's relationship to Humphrey may have been somewhat distant, yet there is a personal tone and a clear identification of the dedicatee in the *Fall of Princes* that is completely lacking here. Further references to Henry throughout the poem are equally generic. On the other hand, there are traces that, while writing the *Life*, Lydgate was thinking of the illustrious men and women on whom he had been working for many years: allusions to characters of Greek and Roman history appear, together with Biblical characters, and sometimes with little relevance to the story. There is even a reference to Petrarch's "Cosmographie" (l. 558), already mentioned in the *Fall*.

Eleanor Hammond rightly connects the contents of Lydgate's letter to the Duke to the prologue of Book III of *The Fall of Princes*, in which the poet acknowledged the Duke's generosity, which had given him new strength to continue his work. And indeed Book III does for a while strike the reader with the new energy and freshness of its tone. It is rather curious that there should be another request for money relatively soon in the same book, at ll. 3837–3871; this seems decidedly an ill omen. This time Lydgate is perhaps more pointed in his allusions: instead of pleasing the patron with nautical and medical images, he reminds him of the function of poets:

Ther cheeff labour is vicis to repreve
With a maner couert symylitude,
And non estat with ther langage greeve
Bi no rebukyng of termys dul and rude;
What-euer thei write, on vertu ay conclude,
Appeire no man in no maner wise:
This thoffise of poetis that be wise.
[III.3830–6]

Paul Strohm is probably right in reading these lines as evidence of a don't-rock-the-boat attitude on the part of the poet, since the latter

---

[115] Lines 41–6. The poem is published in *Altenglische Legenden. Neue Folge mit Einleitung und Anmerkungen*, ed. by C. Horstmann, Heilbronn: Henninger, 1881: 376–445.

was preparing his request for money;[116] but he has perhaps underestimated the threatening potential of the passage. Lydgate is conscious of the poets' usefulness to all estates, and of his being among
the "poetis that be wise". He is also telling Gloucester that his work
of propaganda and support is worth a recompense, since it may be
useful to the prince—a particularly apt observation in the case of a
patron so obsessed with his public image. But at this point we begin
to see in the poem the same pattern already noticed in the Palladius
translation: a decrease of active engagement in the work, corresponding to a diminishing size of the successive books. The prologues, too,
begin to disappear: there are none in books V, VI, VII and IX,
while book VIII present a rather unusual prologue: the poet is again
demoralised, but finds help not in the erstwhile munificent patron,
but in the poets of the past, such as Boccaccio and Petrarch. These
poets exhort Lydgate to continue, since he has passed "the se of
bookis seuene" (l. 135), promising him that when the work is completed he will find reward:

> Yit at the laste, thynk, for thi socour,
> Sum roial prince shal quyte thi labour.
> [146–7]

It is very surprising that these poets should encourage Lydgate mentioning the indefinite presence of "sum royal prince", while the reader
would expect Humphrey to come to the rescue as he had evidently
done at the beginning of Book III. But at this point the patron is
progressively fading from the scene, though he will reappear in the
obligatory final envoy.

Even as concerns the individual stories, Lydgate's interest and his
passion for *amplificatio* seem to have flagged, so that the tragedy of
Boethius, which by right should have fired his imagination, is narrated in little over thirty lines, while Laurent de Premierfait had
deemed it right in this case to expand Boccaccio's concise narrative
to inordinate length. The lack of interest does not seem to be connected with Boethius, since Lydgate was obviously interested in the
philosopher's work, and in the *Fabula Duorum Mercatorum* had chosen
to translate a fragment from *De Consolatione Philosophiae* (ll. 743–6). It
would seem more probable that the diminishing interest of the patron,

---

[116] Strohm, *England's Empty Throne*, p. 180.

together with the sheer magnitude and demanding nature of the work, counselled Lydgate to conclude it while the going was still relatively good. Seeing the similar fate of the Palladius translation, it is actually surprising that Lydgate should have managed to keep Gloucester interested for such a long time.

Humphrey's patronage of a poem in the *de casibus* tradition was almost certainly undertaken, at least initially, to perpetuate the monarchical image of the Lancastrians, and an image of himself as the perfect successor to his brother, though I find it difficult to believe that he was actually suggesting himself as the best candidate for the throne.[117] But what is probably more interesting is not the commission in itself, but the spirit in which it was directed throughout by the patron, even to the detriment of the final result. The patron's intervention forces the poet to alter his original plan, to change the structure of the work, to be often inconsistent in his advice.[118] The patron does not seem particularly concerned, however, as long as his personality is in strong relief.

Whether it was his connection with Duke Humphrey, or some aspects of his poetry that were to be gradually depreciated in time, Lydgate seems to have enjoyed a certain fame as a humanist in his own time, and in the following centuries. James Simpson makes this observation considering John Bale's treatment of the poet in his *Scriptorum Illustrium maioris Brytannie*:

> Bale praises him as the premier poet of his time. He creates for Lydgate a (wholly spurious) humanist's progress, including study periods in Padua and Paris, and a post as tutor to noble children; Lydgate, he says, sought to fill for the English the role Dante, Alain Chartier, and Chaucer had already played for their peoples. He recognizes both

---

[117] As Larry Scanlon thinks in his *Narrative, Authority and Power*, p. 325. It may be remembered, however, that this was a particularly problematic moment for the Lancastrian descent. Humphrey was heir apparent, but had no legitimate male offspring, and in the case of his and the King's death, it would have been difficult to find a claimant.

[118] Nigel Mortimer highlights this problem with particular reference to the envoys in the poem: "The problem with Lydgate's envoys is not just that they are unsystematic, but that there are genuine inconsistencies in his advice. Lydgate's exhortations to princes to regulate their moral behaviour frequently clash with his pathos-arousing laments on the inconstancy of Fortune and the ephemerality of human power" (p. 64). It may be added that these particular inconsistencies can often be found in the Italian humanists' production, and are probably to be connected to a similar cause.

Lydgate's metrical variety and wide learning, and says that 'after Chaucer he was certainly the greatest "illustrator" of the English language'. The greatest wonder for Bale is whence Lydgate managed to gain so much eloquence and erudition in 'so primitive an age' ('in aetate tam rudi'). Certainly the praise of Lydgate has not survived, but two aspects of Bale's placing of him have: firstly, Lydgate cannot be spoken of without reference to Chaucer, and secondly, he writes in a culturally impoverished age. It is also significant that Bale underplays Lydgate's monastic profession, stressing instead his humanistic achievement as 'artium omnium scientissimus'.[119]

Bale's description is probably as erroneous as the wholesale condemnation of more recent times. But in both attitudes there is some truth, and in seeing Lydgate as an instance of English humanism, and even inventing a spurious humanist biography for him, Bale was underlining some characteristics of Lydgate's poetry that are now undervalued, such as his curiosity for books, his attention to past and present history, his reverence for the literature of the past. All attitudes in which he found a powerful if somewhat overbearing ally in the Duke of Gloucester.

Commissioning literary and non-literary works

Patronage and propaganda were a well established practice in the Lancastrian household long before the commission of Lydgate's *Fall of Princes*. John Lydgate shares with a poet of the previous generation, Thomas Hoccleve, a complex and somewhat ambiguous relationship with the reigning dynasty. Paul Strohm rightly notes that neither was a court poet, neither lived at court or enjoyed consistent and continuative patronage from the members of the Lancaster family. Both are associated, however, to a privileged status that promoted them, even if temporarily, to the role of official chroniclers and celebrators of the Lancastrian fortunes.[120] Chronology would

---

[119] Simpson, "Bulldozing the Middle Ages", p. 218.

[120] Strohm, "Hoccleve, Lydgate and the Lancastrian Court", p. 640. There has been some confusion concerning Hoccleve's involvement with the Duke of Gloucester: Jane Chance, for instance, maintains that Gloucester requested the poet to translate Christine de Pizan's *Epistre au Dieu d'Amours*, but this translation, now known as the *Letter of Cupid*, was completed in 1402, when Humphrey was barely twelve and not yet a Duke (Jane Chance, "Christine de Pizan as Literary Mother. Woman's

require that Hoccleve be taken into consideration before Lydgate; but in the case of Humphrey of Gloucester his patronage of the latter, extending over a number of years and articulating itself into an uneasy relations with Lydgate's translation of *De casibus*, offers the modern scholar an opportunity to examine a particularly complex instance of the interaction of intellectuals and patrons, while the Duke's contact with Hoccleve is confined to a lesser episode of the patron's early years, and perhaps to the first instance we have of an English poem written for Humphrey, though perhaps not at his direct request.[121]

Thomas Hoccleve worked for the office of the Privy Seal, and was thus in some way a member, even if a very humble one, of the court. There is nothing in this poet of Lydgate's placid determination to live with his times and record them in obsequious observance of the wishes of his patrons, and of Lydgate's ability to ride with the ambiguity and uncertainty of the political situation: Hoccleve's status, both as a "proto-laureate" poet and as a member of the court, is forever uncertain, and his homage to the powers that be continually betrays an effort, as when he observes in the *Regement of Princes*, addressing Henry V:

> In al my book yee schul nat see ne fynde,
> That I youre deedes lakke or hem despreise.[122]

The poet may be said to be protesting too much. This is one of the factors that make the evaluation of his connection with Gloucester more difficult, together with the fact that Hoccleve's supposedly autobiographical *persona*, more decidedly intruding into his narrative than Lydgate's,[123] can occasionally confuse the issue for the reader looking for historical proof in his poems.

Authority and Subjectivity in 'The Floure and the Leafe' and 'The Assembly of Ladies'", in *The City of Scholars: New Approaches to Christine de Pizan*, ed. by M. Zimmermann and D. de Rentiis, Berlin: Walter de Gruyter, 1994: 245–59, p. 246).

[121] Strohm observes that "Hoccleve started his 'Series' in the hope but not the certainty of interesting the Duke of Gloucester" ("Hoccleve, Lydgate and the Lancastrian court", p. 641).

[122] Lines 4397–8. See *Thomas Hoccleve. The Regiment of Princes*, ed. by C.R. Blyth, Kalamazoo: Medieval Institute Publications, 1999.

[123] Or, as Derek Pearsall calls it, Hoccleve's "inveterate (and, as we shall see, calculated) self-referentiality" ("Hoccleve's *Regement of Princes*", p. 387).

His literary activity may be said to have begun in 1402, with the *Letter to Cupid*, so by the time Humphrey started exerting his literary patronage Hoccleve had already achieved a certain degree of fame. The best years of his early literary production are between 1409 and 1415, and at this point he can be associated with Henry V, for whom (while he had not yet ascended the throne) he wrote *The Regiment of Princes*, probably in 1410–12. Strohm speaks of this work as "wholly consistent with the prince's own programme of self-representation as a peerless exemplar of orthodoxy".[124] This association, together with Hoccleve's sustained attempt to become the official poetic voice of the Lancastrian household, makes it easy to understand his subsequent link with the Duke of Gloucester, though we possess only imperfect data concerning the latter's patronage in this case.

There is a clear allusion to Duke Humphrey in what is now known as Hoccleve's *Series*: a succession of poems linked by an autobiographical pretext, and including some of the poet's most fascinating meditations on himself and his writing.[125] John Burrow has conclusively demonstrated that the section of the *Series* that is of interest here, the *Dialogue*, was completed between December 1419 and February 1421.[126] The inclusion in the text of a clear reference to Duke Humphrey and his patronage is thus particularly interesting, since it shows that the Duke's intellectual activity did not begin, as has generally been assumed, as a reaction to his declining political

---

[124] Strohm, "Hoccleve, Lydgate and the Lancastrian Court", p. 644. On this poem, and on its relation with princely patronage, see also Larry Scanlon, "The King's Two Voices: Narrative and Power in Hoccleve's *Regiment of Princes*", in *Literary Practice and Social Change in Britain, 1380–1530*, ed. by L. Patterson, Berkeley: University of California Press, 1990: 216–47. The extraordinary complexity of the *Series* is underlined by its composition: a prologue, the *Complaint*, the *Dialogue*, an envoy, the *Tale of Jereslaus's Wife*, four linking stanzas, a prose moralisation of the preceding tale, *Lerne to Die*, three linking stanzas, a prose version of the ninth lesson for All Hallows' Day, a linking prologue, the *Tale of Jonathas*, a prose moralisation, and a final envoy of a single stanza (see John A. Burrow, "Hoccleve's *Series*: Experience and Books", in *Fifteenth-Century Studies: Recent Essays*, ed. by R.F. Yeager, Hamden, Conn.: Archon Books, 1984: 259–73, p. 259).

[125] The latest and best edition of the first two parts of the *Series*, the *Complaint* and the *Dialogue*, is *Thomas Hoccleve's Complaint and Dialogue*, ed. by J.A. Burrow, Early English Text Society, Oxford: Oxford University Press, 1999. Quotations from the text are taken from this edition.

[126] John A. Burrow, "Thomas Hoccleve: Some Redatings", *Review of English Studies* 46: 1995, 366–72.

fortunes, but had already started while his star was still very much in the ascendant, as a natural continuation of his brother Henry's own activity in the same direction—both Hoccleve's work and Lydgate's *Epithalamium* support this hypothesis. The *Dialogue* comments on what must have been the poet's long bout of mental illness, probably following a breakdown that had taken place in 1414 and interrupted the poet's activity for some years. The aftermath of this mental illness is described in the *Complaint*, the first book of the *Series*. The friend who takes part in the *Dialogue* encourages Hoccleve to write a story in praise of women, a palinode retracting the sentiments expressed in the misogynistic *Letter to Cupid*. The story could at the same time entertain Humphrey, Duke of Gloucester. The name of the patron is introduced almost casually in the course of the dialogue: the friend, encouraging Hoccleve to resume his literary activity, reminds him of a past promise:

'And of o thyng/now wel I me remembre,
Why thow purposist in this book trauaille.
I trowe þat in the monthe of Septembre
Now last, or nat fer from/it is no faille—
No force of the tyme/it shal nat auaille
To my mateere/ne it hyndre or lette—
'Vnto my lord/þat now is lieutenant,
My lord of Gloucestre/is it nat so?'
[526–34]

These lines make it clear that the promise is very recent; and it might be even more than a promise, since Hoccleve in his answer acknowledges his debt and says that "as by couenant He sholde han had it many a day ago" (ll. 535–6). The word *couenant* refers at least to an agreement, if not to an actual commission; in any case, it goes to indicate Humphrey's active role in this transaction. There follows a praise of the Duke, who has shown particular benevolence to the poet:

'Next our lord lige/our kyng victorious,
In al this wyde world/lord is ther noon
Vnto me so good ne so gracious,
And haath been swich/yeeres ful many oon.
[554–7]

The "kyng victorious" is of course Henry V, for whom Hoccleve had already written a major work; the mention of the King in connection with Humphrey highlights the role of both as patrons to the poet. It is true, as John Burrow notes, that the description of Humphrey that follows underlines his martial deeds rather than his studious inclination;[127] yet, if we consider that it was probably good policy to praise a patron telling him what he wanted to hear, we may assume that thus early in his career Humphrey preferred to hear himself celebrated as "Martys sone", as Lydgate was doing at roughly the same time in his *Epithalamium*. It is interesting to note that, while Lydgate uses the epithet "Martys sone", Hoccleve writes of "Bataillous Mars/in his natiuitee" (l. 592). Given Humphrey's interest in astrology and horoscopes, it is plausible that he liked to have it known that this planet had presided over his nativity. This hypothesis is confirmed by the Duke's preferred spelling of his name, *Homfrey*, which is interpreted by a marginal note in the Durham manuscript of the *Dialogue* "quasi homme feray"—a comment to Hoccleve's image of Mars saying "For Humfrey/as vnto myn intellect, 'Man make I shal'/in englissh is to seye".[128] The poet even imagines a biography of this paragon: "To cronicle his actes/were a good deede" (l. 603); this is what Tito Livio Frulovisi will eventually do with his *Hunfroidos*. These were the years in which Humphrey seemed destined to become a great soldier and leader of armies in his brother's wake—it is only later in his life that the poets' praise will rather insist on cultural achievements, when an allusion to politics and war could be more painful than otherwise to the patron. Hoccleve nicely blends the reader and the knight in his description, as he will later allude to his courtly qualities, and the choice of the books he mentions conforms to this attitude. Thus he thinks of translating Vegetius for the Duke, but reflects that a man of such knightly qualities would hardly need it; a nice touch, given the interest Humphrey showed in this author, and his possessing both a Latin and a French copy of his work. The reference to Vegetius is a pretext to introduce a list of Humphrey's glorious military deeds, with an allusion to the siege of Cherbourg; and the Duke is called a worthy descendant of "duc Henri", that is, his great-grandfather Henry of Lancaster, the author of that *Livre des seyntez medicines* of which Humphrey possessed a copy. Hoccleve's employment in the offices of the Privy Seal, next door to the Star Chamber where the King's Council met, obviously would

---

[127] Burrow, "Introduction", in *Thomas Hoccleve's Complaint and Dialogue*, p. lvi.

[128] Lines 596–7. See Burrow's note to this line and the marginal note in *Thomas Hoccleve's Complaint and Dialogue*, p. 103.

have made it possible for the poet to establish a reasonably close acquaintance with the Duke; it seems that these allusions are far from generic, and though he may be said to be less suave than Lydgate in his praise, he certainly shows, at this stage of Humphrey's life, a similar degree of intimacy with his patron. In a way the *Dialogue* substitutes, in an unusual form, the conventional dedication, generally embedded in a prologue.[129]

More difficult to interpret is Hoccleve's choice of a subject for his poem. Though during his *Dialogue* Hoccleve seems determined to write for the Duke "many a Balade" (l. 551), there seems to be little doubt that what he chooses in the end is the *Tale of Jereslaus's Wife and her False Brother-in-law*, a translation from the Anglo-Latin collection known as *Gesta Romanorum*; this translation will constitute the section of the *Series* that immediately follows the *Dialogue*. If this identification were certain, this would be the first work in English (significantly, a translation) written for the Duke of which we have sure knowledge.[130] The choice of the subject seems to be entirely in Hoccleve's hands, since, when his friend asks him about it, he answers that the Duke will not mind, provided that it be "mateere of honestee" (l. 627). If there was a commission on the part of Humphrey, apparently it did not extend to the choice of the subject or of the book, as was to happen in the case of Lydgate's *Fall of Princes* and of the Palladius translation. It is sufficient for the matter of the book to be "plesant and agreable" (l. 634), as well as virtuous. The final choice will concern more the poet than the patron, and resides with the friend, while Hoccleve apparently opposes it:

> Thow woost wel/on wommen greet wyt[e] & lak
> Ofte haast thow put/Be waar/lest thow be qwit.
> Thy wordes fille wolde a quarter sak
> Which thow in whyt/depeynted haast with blak.
> In hir repreef/mochil thyng haast thow write
> That they nat foryeue haue/ne foryite.
>
> 'Sumwhat now wryte in honour & preysynge
> Of hem/so maist thow do correccioun
> Sumdel of thyn offense and misberynge.
> [667–75]

---

[129] On this point see Everest-Phillips, p. 160.
[130] See Rundle, "Of Republics and Tyrants", p. 137, and H.S. Bennett, *Six Medieval Men and Women*, Cambridge: Cambridge University Press, 1955, p. 86.

As has been noted above, the work offending against women has been identified with Hoccleve's *Letter to Cupid*; it is less easy to determine how the *Tale of Jereslaus's Wife* would work as an apology, and how well it could please not only women but Duke Humphrey, who likes, says the friend,

> For his desport/& mirthe in honestee
> With ladyes/to haue daliance.
>   [705–6]

Daliance is meant as friendly or courtly conversation, and the whole image of Humphrey in pleasant conversation with ladies is courteous and flattering, if conventional. It should be remembered that in the same years matters were being arranged for Humphrey's marriage with Jacqueline of Hainault, and that other poets gravitating around the court, such as Lydgate, were eager to felicitate the Duke on his intended wedding. The rest of the *Dialogue* sets out in full the intended subject of the following work, and is addressed not to the patron but to the ladies.

The problem is that the *Tale* might well please previously misused ladies but seems singularly inopportune for a man who was trying to combine personal interest and political calculation in his marriage, since it tells of the abuse Jereslaus's wife has to suffer at the hands of her brother-in-law, in her husband's absence. As Lee Patterson rightly notes, "as an offering to Duke Humphrey, who was at this very time functioning as *custos* or lieutenant of England while his brother the King pursued his French ambitions, the *Tale* is thus a spectacularly tactless choice".[131] If this is indeed an error on the part of the poet, and not the result of a request on the part of the Duke, it may be explained with the fact that Hoccleve was trying to please two categories of potential readers at the same time, or that, having paid his homage to the patron through the spirited *Dialogue*, he let his own preferences override possible considerations on the political opportunity of the choice, or even the wishes of the distinguished prospective patrons.[132] This does not need to be

---

[131] Patterson, "What is Me", p. 448.

[132] One of the manuscripts of the *Series* was made for Joan Neville, Countess of Westmoreland, who can thus be considered another possible protector and patron for the poet. It may also be that Hoccleve had misgiving as far as Humphrey's generosity was concerned.

a conscious choice of political nonalignment on the part of the poet,[133] but simply a proof that he was less ready than Lydgate to use his pen to please his masters.

Of course, it must be remembered that the *Series* does not end with the *Tale of Jereslaus*, and it might be hypothesised that what Hoccleve promises to write for Humphrey is one of the other elements of the work: for instance, the *Tale of Jonathas*, though evidence in this case would be even weaker. The poet does not help us in the task of identification. The passage concerning Humphrey and his commission resolves itself into an address to women, that points to the *Tale of Jereslaus*, but does not solve the contradictions implicit in the presumed commission or dedication. Matters are further complicated by the fact that the whole *Series*, in the final envoy, is dedicated to Joan, Countess of Westmoreland, who also happened to be Humphrey's aunt; the book is commanded to present itself to her. As Burrow has noted, Hoccleve's own anxiety about the reception of his book intervened to complicate the issues of patronage and commission:

> Authors frequently express eagerness to please readers, not least wealthy and powerful patrons; but there is much more than mere convention or normal self-interest in Hoccleve's persistent expressions of concern about how his book will be received by his acquaintances, the Duke of Gloucester, the ladies, and the Countess of Westmoreland [. . .] His recovery from his breakdown (allowing him to have indeed recovered) has left him morbidly concerned about what people think of him and his work.[134]

The poet's own complex relation not only with patronage but with his own writing persona is a further addition to the difficulty of the issue. More than any other fifteenth-century English work, the *Series* is concerned with the act of composition and with the presentation of the self; and though one should bear it in mind and avoid identifying *tout court* the protagonist of the *Series* with the historical Thomas Hoccleve, it is a temptation to read the work as straight autobiography.[135] However, even if Hoccleve may be projecting a fictive

---

[133] As Patterson seems to believe (p. 449).

[134] Burrow, "Hoccleve's *Series*", p. 268.

[135] Again, Burrow seems to believe this when he writes: "In the world of Hoccleve's *Series*, books are part of life—patrons commission them, readers borrow them, authors

persona, and even playing with the notion of his own madness, his uneasy relation with his prospective or actual patrons would have made it difficult not to be as truthful as possible when describing commissions, though in this case the poet's wishful thinking might somewhat embellish the truth, transforming a manifestation of generic interest into a contract. However, if Hoccleve shows more than the usual concern for the patron's satisfaction, this very concern demonstrates that the patron, far from being a fiction or a projection of the poet's imagination, had a personality that required such a satisfaction.

It seems, in any case, that Hoccleve's effort to please bore fruit, since his petition for a stable source of income, a corrody in the priory of Southwick, Hampshire, was granted on 4 July 1424 by the Council, in the presence of Gloucester, who among others subscribed the petition.[136] On the other hand, the *Series* also marks the end of Hoccleve's efforts to identify his poetics with the requirements of the Lancastrian ideology.[137] Hoccleve's last bid for patronage is also his last surviving work; and it is striking that he should here evoke a patron who would be so important for the following generation of English poets.

There are other works commissioned by the Duke or related to him, though the interest they may raise as literary works is decidedly little. One such work is *The Libelle of Englyshe Polycye*. Included by Hakluyt in the second edition of his *Principal Navigations, Voyages, Traffiques and Discoveries of the English Nation* (1598–1600), it is almost forgotten now, having suffered the fate of most *Fachliteratur*. Yet its history and the circumstances of its composition are interesting, and, I believe, shed some light on the propaganda activity that found its ideological centre in the Duke of Gloucester. The apparition of the *Libelle* followed the uneasy peace established between Philip the Good, Duke of Burgundy, and Charles VII with the treaty of Arras in September 1435, and the ensuing hostility between Burgundy and England, culminating with Philip's attempt to besiege Calais in July

---

worry about them—and the *Series* itself strikes many readers as an almost painfully 'real' book" ("Hoccleve's *Series*", p. 269).

[136] The relevant section of document is published in John A. Burrow, *Thomas Hoccleve*, Authors of the Middle Ages, Aldershot: Variorum, 1994, p. 236.

[137] For an interesting analysis of the *Dialogue* and a commentary on the poet's relation with Lancastrian ideology, see also Paul Strohm, "Counterfeiters, Lollards, and Lancastrian Unease", in *New Medieval Literatures 1*, ed. by W. Scase, R. Copeland and D. Lawton, Oxford: Clarendon Press, 1997: 31–58.

1936. The repulse of Philip's Flemish soldiers on this occasion, though a minor episode in itself, was celebrated as a splendid victory on the part of the English army and, rightly of wrongly, of the Duke of Gloucester. It certainly moved the latter to continue his pro-war campaign: the angry political stalemate was not helped by a surprising flourishing of poems and ballads celebrating the English triumph of Calais, and reviling the Burgundians. The *Libelle* was written between 1436 and 1438, and its jingoistic tone reflects what was probably a widely shared feeling at the time.[138] The poem seems to have enjoyed some popularity even after its time, as is shown both by the number of surviving manuscripts (George Warner used nine for his edition, but there are at least sixteen preserving the poem) and by its appearing in a list, dated about 1479, of books possessed by Sir John Paston.[139] But the policy it advocated, though not concerned specifically with war, might not have been received with equal enthusiasm by the King's Council, to whom the work was expressly directed, as shown by the envoy (ll. 1142–9).

The poem does not limit itself to propaganda, but attempts to demonstrate that an English supremacy on the sea would bring both commercial and political benefits to the nation, and perhaps for the first time attempts to define England as a nation in geopolitical terms. It may be said to be the first treatise of political economy in English,

---

[138] On the dating of the poem, see George A. Holmes, "The 'Libel of English Policy'", *English Historical Review* 76: 1961, 193–216, p. 193. Holmes's article offers a full account of the political situation which generated the *Libelle*. In his edition of the poem, George Warner sets it earlier than 1438. See *The Libelle of Englyshe Polycye. A Poem on the Use of Sea-Power, 1436*, ed. by G. Warner, Oxford: Clarendon Press, 1926, p. x. The *Libelle* is also discussed in V.J. Scattergood, *Politics and Poetry in the Fifteenth Century*, pp. 90–5 and in his "*The Libelle of Englyshe Polycye*: The Nation and its Place", in *Nation, Court and Culture. New Essays on Fifteenth-Century English Poetry*, ed. by H. Cooney, Dublin: Four Courts Press, 2001: 28–49. Carol Meale argues for the *Libelle* not originating at court, but among the literate merchants in London; see her "*The Libelle of Englyshe Polycye* and Mercantile Literary Culture in Late-Medieval London", in *London and Europe in the Later Middle Ages*, ed. by J. Boffey and P. King, London: Centre for Medieval and Renaissance Studies, Queen Mary and Westfield College, University of London, 1995: 181–227.

[139] Andrew Breeze, "Sir John Paston, Lydgate, and *The Lybelle of Englyshe Polycye*", *Notes and Queries* 48: 2001, 230–1. Breeze notes that the fact that Paston possessed the *Libelle* "says something about his personality, as he must have felt this essay on 'strategic studies' was (for whatever reason) required reading. It also informs us on the tract's readership. Paston was willy-nilly involved in politics; his possession of the *Libelle* hence suggests it was valued as a policy statement long after it was written" (p. 231). See also Holmes, p. 194.

and its scope is carefully confined to the subject, since no comment is offered on the French wars; England's military policy is treated with great caution throughout. Great attention, on the other hand, is paid to the state of trade between a number of European countries: Spain, Flanders, Italy, France, Portugal, Denmark, Ireland, and of course England. The author shows himself very knowledgeable as concerns the wool and metal trade in particular, though his nationalistic bias is evident. Besides, the mention of the Flemish trade gives the writer an excuse to mock the Flemish both for their drinking habits and for their recent defeat at Calais. There was a point to this heavy irony: on 18 June 1434 Philip of Burgundy, in answer to the complaints of the Flemish cloth merchants, had prohibited the import of English cloth in his dominions; this, as the author of the *Libelle* realised, was bad policy, since the English exports were essential for the countries that received them; by levelling his attack at Philip and his Flemish soldiers rather than at the Flemish merchants, the writer showed his confidence on the growing hostility between Philip and his subjects.[140] As concerns home policies, the point of the whole treatise seems to be an exhortation to reinforce protective measures in favour of English trade, increasing levies and eventually proposing embargoes against too keen competitors such as the Venetians or the Florentines. A politically directed restraint upon foreign competition should encourage English merchants, as a means to increase the country's welfare and ultimately its power. Little allusion is made to the English monarchy and its role, but the ninth section of the poem includes a eulogy of three kings, Edgar, Edward III, and inevitably Henry V, who is set as an example to the present King, his son.

Unfortunately there has survived too little information on the author, and on the eventual commission of the book. It seems clear that the writer was well informed not only on the state of English, and indeed of European trade, but also that he knew the work of the Parliament and of the King's Council in this area. On the basis of internal evidence, the modern editor has proposed Adam Moleyns, afterwards Bishop of Chichester, as the probable author of the book,[141] but this hypothesis, though supported by a number of circumstances

---

[140] On this point, see Holmes, pp. 195–9.
[141] Warner, pp. xl–xlvi.

concerning Moleyns's life, is weakened by the central fact of his adherence to the party of the Bishop of Winchester, who was doing his utmost to establish a durable peace between England, Burgundy and France. Henry Beaufort, together with the King's Council, was determined to save Normandy, even if this meant to overlook the contrast with Burgundy; it is clear that, in a moment so decisive for foreign policy, they would hardly welcome a treatise advising him to reinforce hostilities in the name of international trade.

Though the poem addressed the members of the King's Council, it was clearly meant for the middle classes, particularly the merchants, and possibly for the Parliament, which on this issue was not on the side of the Council.[142] Its author showed a good knowledge of commerce, but his purpose was in the main a political appeal to the feelings of the traders. Such attitude is certainly more easily associated with the Duke of Gloucester than with the Bishop of Winchester, at least in those years. The Duke had seemed as critical of the policy of the Council on this point as he was on the Calais question: when Parliament and Council were at odds over the question of taking bonds from the cloth exporters, this remark had been attributed to him: "Som parlement hath be that the king hath no graunte".[143] Both the difficulties of the merchants and the defence of Calais were questions on which Gloucester disagreed with the Council, and both questions appealed powerfully to the middle classes and to Parliament.

It is impossible to ascribe the *Libelle* with any certainty to Humphrey's direct patronage, but there is little doubt that it was born of the same ideological attitude and of the same discontent. Though it is certainly more complex and knowledgeable than contemporary ballads and political poems on the same subject, there is an affinity between the tone of this treatise and much propaganda literature produced immediately after the Calais victory and already described in the third chapter of the present volume, including Lydgate's poems *A Ballade in Despyte of the Flemynges* and *The Debate of the Horse, Goose, and Sheep*. The association with Lydgate is not limited to the tone and purpose of these poems, but also to the fact that these, and other significant poems have been found in manuscripts together

---

[142] In January 1437 the Parliament "demonstrated the merchant's lack of sympathy with the council in a decisive way by the unusual step of exempting cloth exported by natives from the payment of poundage" (Holmes, p. 206).

[143] Quoted in Holmes, p. 207.

with the *Libelle*. Thus, in British Library, Harley 4011 we find the
treatise together with a number of Lydgate's secular and religious
poems, including what Warner describes as "L'Envoye to Humfray,
late duke of Glowceter";[144] a manuscript in the library of Mr. G.H.
Gurney, Keswick Hall, Norwick, includes the *Libelle* together with
Lydgate's *The Churl and the Bird*;[145] more important, Rylands English
995, discovered after Warner's edition, contained the *Libelle* and an
inscription added in a seventeenth-century hand: "Presented to ye
L. Archb. Chicheley by John Lidgate, anno domini 1436, 16 Henrici
6";[146] besides, the already mentioned list of books owned by Sir John
Paston included, along with the *Libelle*, works by Lydgate, such as
the *Fabula Duorum Mercatorum*. I would not say, as Holmes seems to
believe, that this is proof that Lydgate, in those years engaged in
the composition of the *Fall of Princes*, was the author of the *Libelle*;
but it certainly establishes a strong association, and shows that the
two writers, if two they were, supported similar views, which were
also championed by the Duke of Gloucester. A stylistic comparison
between Lydgate's works and the *Libelle* shows little similarity, with
the exception of the prologue and epilogue of the latter, written in
rhyme royal (as opposed to the heroic couplets employed in the body
of the poem), and presenting some of the lexical choices favoured
by Lydgate. Curiously enough, the poem, though apparently little
regarded in its own time, seems to have been more cherished after
1450, to judge from the surviving manuscripts; in this, it may be
said to have something in common with Duke Humphrey's own
fame. The link between the *Libelle* and Duke Humphrey is made
stronger by its subject matter: among the Anglicising forces in Calais
were the merchants of the Staple, first established there in 1363. As
David Grummitt notes, "the merchants of the Staple were probably
the most important and vocal of late-medieval pressure groups, a
pressure they exerted through their ability to lend the crown large
amounts of money".[147] Besides their objective political and economical

[144] Described in Warner, p. liii.
[145] Described in Warner, pp. lv–lvi.
[146] Quoted in Holmes, p. 214.
[147] David Grummitt, "'One of the mooste pryncipall treasours belongyng to his
Realme of Englande': Calais and the Crown, c. 1450–1558", in *The English Experience
in France c. 1450–1558. War, Diplomacy and Cultural Exchange*, Aldershot: Ashgate,
2002: 46–62, p. 49.

importance, they also had a special link with Humphrey, since among his servants there could be found prominent staplers such as Richard Whittingham and William Cantelowe. The *Libelle*, though speaking for national interest, is very much on the staplers' side; as Scattergood writes, it formulates "a definition of the nation by reference to a specific sectional interest".[148] In this sense it goes perhaps a step beyond Humphrey's own ideology, recognising as it does the importance of a military force for England but at the same time stressing that its real power lies in trade.

The attention Humphrey paid to propaganda as a means to enlist popular favour in his periodical clashes with the King's Council is probably part of a lesson he learned from both his older brothers. Henry V's attitude has already been discussed; it may be added that the Duke of Bedford was equally convinced of the use of propaganda as a means to enhance the stability of the dual Kingdom, and that he employed it unsparingly during his regency in France. Once again John Lydgate was among the poets called to help, but besides poems Bedford would make also use of the magnificence and pageantry of royal processions, and of coinage.[149] The Duke of Gloucester had neither the power nor the position to make use of coins and processions; besides, his propaganda seems to have taken a more personal direction than the simple support of the Lancastrian monarchy. Seeing the good use at which poems and books could be put, Gloucester employed his patronage, directly or indirectly, also to defend choices that proved unpopular or that were opposed by other members of the Council. *The Libelle of Englyshe Polycye* appears to be a case in point, together with a number of other poems and ballads that accompanied salient moments of his political life, such as the Calais expedition or his first marriage. Only later did his intellectual activity turn to less personal matters, and concerned itself with the commission or acquisition of books that would not bear directly on the Duke's personal fortunes. Some of the less elaborate and more topical political poems associated with Humphrey have been described in chapter three, and in the section devoted to Lydgate

---

[148] Scattergood, "*The Libelle of Englyshe Polycye*", p. 33.

[149] This has been the object of a specific study (J.W. MacKenna, "Henry VI and the Dual Monarchy: Aspects of Royal Political Propaganda, 1422–1432", *Journal of the Warburg and Courtauld Institutes* 28: 1965, 145–62).

of this chapter. There is little doubt that a similar purpose was behind
his commission to Tito Livio Frulovisi to write a life of his brother
Henry. Though the *Vita Henrici Quinti* has already been described in
chapter three, it may be useful to take up the discussion once again
at this point.[150]

In the chronology of Frulovisi's literary production, the *Vita* was
almost certainly preceded by the two last Latin comedies he wrote,
Peregrinatio and *Eugenius*.[151] They have been considered "the first
Renaissance plays to be written in England",[152] but have very little
literary merit, and there is no evidence that they were ever performed, as had happened instead with Frulovisi's earlier comedies,
or indeed that they were actually written in England, though some
allusions in the *Peregrinatio* seem to suggest it. In any case, they seem
to have been written without any prompting on the part of the Duke,
while on commission he had Frulovisi write pieces of historiography.
There is no proof that Humphrey was ever interested in drama. The
more interesting of the two comedies is certainly *Eugenius*, probably
written once Frulovisi had obtained his denization (formally declared
on 7 March 1437). The comedy includes a fervent praise of the
writer's patron, and presents him as one of the characters; the use
of allegory makes identification difficult, but if we identify Eugenius
with Duke Humphrey, then we can recognise in other characters of
the play Frulovisi himself, the Duke of Bedford, Henry VI, and members of Humphrey's household. Frulovisi here underplays his habitually satirical tone to turn his attention to allegory, though his
heavy-handed treatment of his material does not yield too fortunate
results.[153] The prologue also presents a praise of Humphrey (always

---

[150] For Frulovisi's work I have used the only available modern edition: *Titi Livii
Forojuliensis Vita Henrici Quinti Regis Angliae*, ed. by T. Hearne, Oxonii: E Theatro
Sheldoniano, 1716.

[151] Frulovisi had already written five Latin comedies in Venice, so his fame in
this field may have preceded him. For an overview of the two comedies written in
England, see Grady A. Smith, "'Languida Virtus Semper ad Extremum': Titus
Livius Frulovisi in England, 1437–39", *Fifteenth-Century Studies* 21: 1994, 323–33. An
analysis of Frulovisi's career as a playwright can also be found in Antonio Stauble,
"Le sette commedie dell'umanista Tito Livio De' Frulovisi", *Rinascimento: Rivista
dell'Istituto Nazionale di Studi sul Rinascimento* n.s. 3: 1963, 23–52.

[152] Grady A. Smith, "Medieval Drama, Work in Progress: Frulovisi's Peregrinatio
and Eugenius: An Introduction and Translation", *Fifteenth-Century Studies* 22: 1996,
192–93, p. 192.

[153] Together with the other comedies, the *De Republica* and the *Encomium Johannis*

supposing the identification to be correct) as a patron of letters, though the writer's financial worries and his desire for a recompense seem to override any other consideration, and probably deprive us of useful details on this patron. Another interesting point is an allusion to Dante's *Commedia* in the prologue of the *Eugenius*: speaking against the abhorred vice of avarice, in the context of a not-too-subtle appeal to his patron's munificence, Frulovisi adds "de tribus Dantes magnatum magis quid avaricia timuit".[154] In a note to Frulovisi's line, Previté-Orton explains this as an allusion to *Inferno* I.1, but it is an allusion to *Inferno* I.51–6, that is, the apparition of the third beast, a she-wolf, on the hill that the poet-narrator is trying to ascend. Dante says that this third beast is far more terrifying than the other two, though he does not offer an explicit interpretation of this apparition. Medieval commentaries, however, identified the she-wolf with *auaritia*, and Giovanni da Serravalle in particular described this vice at length as one of the worst for mankind.[155] However, this is not enough to prove that Frulovisi read Serravalle's commentary, or that he read it in the Duke's library.

The commission of the *Vita Henrici Quinti* was undoubtedly later than the *Libelle*, since Frulovisi entered the Duke's service probably in 1436,[156] and probably devoted himself first to the composition of his English comedies. Compared to the *Libelle*, the *Vita* also had altogether different intellectual ambitions. Whoever the author of the *Libelle* was, there is little doubt that Frulovisi's status as a writer would have been considered much higher, even if to a modern eye his actual achievements do not seem to amount to much; besides, his presence in the Duke's household as Latin secretary clearly indicated

---

Stafford, *Eugenius* is printed in *Opera Hactenus Inedita T. Livii de Frulovisiis de Ferraria*, ed. by C.W. Previté-Orton, Cambridge: Cantabrigiae typis Academiae, 1932: 221–86. For a more detailed discussion of the comedy and its relation with Duke Humphrey's patronage, I refer the reader to Previté-Orton's Introduction (pp. xiv–xxix).

[154] *Opera Hactenus Inedita*, p. 224. The allusion was first noted by Roberto Weiss in his "Per la conoscenza di Dante in Inghilterra nel quattrocento", *Giornale Storico della letteratura italiana* 108: 1936, 357–9, p. 357.

[155] *Fratris Ioannis de Serravalle ord. Min. Episcopi et Principis Firmani Translatio et Comentum totius libri Dantis Aldigherii cum textu italico Fratris Bartholomaei a Colle eiusdem ordinis*, ed. by M. da Civezza and T. Domenichelli, Prati: Ex Officina Libraria Giachetti, 1891, p. 31.

[156] For the date see Roberto Weiss, "Humphrey Duke of Gloucester and Tito Livio Frulovisi", in *Fritz Saxl 1890–1948. A Volume of Memorial Essays from his Friends in England*, ed. by D.J. Gordon, London: Nelson, 1957: 218–27, p. 219.

the patron's interest in the new approach to history coming from
Italian humanism, and clearly in asking him rather than an English
poet to write a biography of the dead King he meant on the one
hand to raise his brother's memory to European status, on the other
to acquire a work that would differentiate itself strongly from vernacular writings (or works by English writers) on the same subject.
The *Vita Henrici Quinti* seems to have been among the chief of
Frulovisi's duties, and perhaps his most successful work, since it was
copied and translated long after the patron's death.[157] It certainly
marked a change from the usual style of commemoration for a glorious King, and even from the traditional portrait of past kings in
the *Mirror of Princes* tradition. It is important to remember that shortly
before Frulovisi began writing this biography, Lydgate had written
his *Life of St. Edmund*, written for Henry VI just as the *Vita Henrici
Quinti* was to be meant for the same King, though the actual commission in both cases was coming from different people. Besides the
different attitude towards history, which will be discussed presently,
the important novelty of Frulovisi's work is that it creates and presents to Henry VI a triangular structure in which Henry V's example is presented through the mediation of Humphrey of Gloucester,
the new King's uncle but also the closest witness of the dead Henry's
deeds. It has been long recognised that the late 1430s and early
1440s were years in which the martial King's memory was cultivated in visual arts as well as literature: "Henry V came to embody
more explicitly an ethos of public life defined as the realization of
king-led war-enterprise".[158] I contend that Humphrey's role in this
case was decisive, and that he participated actively and consciously,
with his literary patronage, to this propaganda effort.

   Frulovisi's biography of Henry V was not the first account of the
King's life and deeds,[159] but for the first time we are faced with a

---

[157] The *Vita Henrici Quinti* was translated into Italian in 1463 by Pier Candido
Decembrio; the translation is dedicated to Francesco Sforza. This version seems to
have been very popular, to judge from the number of extant manuscripts.

[158] David Morgan, "The Household Retinue of Henry V and the Ethos of English
Public Life", in *Concepts and Patterns of Service in the Later Middle Ages*, ed. by A. Curry
and E. Matthew, Woodbridge: The Boydell Press, 2000: 64–79.

[159] It was preceded by the anonymous *Gesta Henrici Quinti*, written in 1416–7, and
by Thomas Elmham's *Liber Metricus de Henrico Quinto*, written in 1418 (see Antonia
Gransden, *Historical Writing in England, II, c. 1307 to the Early Sixteenth Century*, London:
Routledge & Kegan Paul, 1982, p. 195). Frulovisi may be indebted to the *Gesta*.

portrait in writing rather than a chronicle; it constitutes an attempt
to insert into the description of contemporary history a genre that
in England belonged almost exclusively to the lives of saints, and
rather than accounting for a number of years of English history, it
focuses upon a central figure around whom all events are grouped.
In short, Frulovisi is doing with Henry V what Lydgate was doing
with St Edmund, for the same audience but in different languages
and with a widely different purpose: moral and religious edification
in the case of Lydgate, an attempt at a humanist (in the wider sense)
education of a prince through recent history, through the account
of eye-witnesses, in the second. That Humphrey was a collector of
Vitae is clear not only from this commission, but also from the *Fall
of Princes*, and from a number of *Vitae* he collected and which were
dedicated to him: in particular, he received a number of translations
of Plutarch's *Lives*: Lapo da Castiglionchio dedicated to him his translation of Plutarch's *Vita Artaxerxis* in 1437, Antonio Beccaria sent him
a *Vita Romuli*, Antonio Pacini a *Vita Marii*; Humphrey also possessed
Pacini's translation of the *Vita Pelopide*; besides, the 1443 donation to
Oxford included "vitas triginta virorum illustrium", which Sammut
has indentified with a collection of Plutarch's works, Leonardo Bruni's
translation of *Vita Marcii Antonii*, Lapo da Castiglionchio's *Vita Camilli*,
and a *Vita Demetrii*.

The commission to Frulovisi then marks a new phase in Humphrey's
activity as a patron; for the first time we see how he attempted to
put at the service of his political and propaganda interests a new
intellectual attitude, in this case exemplified by the new, humanist
attitude towards the writing of history. Frulovisi's contribution both
to Italian humanism and to Duke Humphrey's patronage has often
been the object of ridicule, and it is true that his works are a serious disappointment to the modern reader; but the importance of his
role can be seen if we consider that he created a connection between
Humphrey's political activity and his literary interest by showing him
the possibility of exploiting the new intellectual trend imported from
Italy for his ideological purposes. As in the case of Lydgate's *Fall of*

Charles L. Kingsford believes that a Latin version of the *Brut* might also have been
among Frulovisi's sources; neither this nor the earlier biographies of Henry V appear
among Humphrey's books, but since he did have a collection of chronicles, it is
conceivable that he would possess these, too (Charles Lethbridge Kingsford, *English
Historical Literature in the Fifteenth Century*, Oxford: Clarendon Press, 1913, pp. 53–4).

Princes and of the Palladius translation, there is direct collaboration between patron and writer; but this time the contribution of each is not only essential, but blends harmoniously and contributes to create a singularly interesting biography, which in many ways anticipates English historical writing of the late fifteenth and early sixteenth century—Polydore Vergil was one of his later readers.[160]

The *Vita Henrici Quinti* concentrates on Henry's military campaigns, and particularly on those in which Humphrey had also taken part, which might confirm the hypothesis that the Duke's direct testimony was Frulovisi's main source, but might also mean that Humphrey was particularly interested in this side of his brother's portrait; the *Hunfroidos*, which shall be discussed presently, will use an almost identical criterion in selecting its narrative material. The martial Henry V becomes thus an *exemplum*; his brother is already conforming to it in the *Vita*, and will show himself a true successor of Henry in the *Hunfroidos*. The *Vita* never forgets the link between Henry and Humphrey, and underlines in the first lines that the latter has responsibility for the young prince who is supposed to grow up in his heroic father's image. As Henry V reaches the status of mythical hero, so is Humphrey compared, albeit more humbly, to the great men of antiquity: his charge of young Henry, involving moral and religious responsibility, is compared to Lycurgus's charge of his nephew, the son of Polydectes, King of the Lacedaemonians.[161] The comparison is also an occasion to introduce an encomium of Humphrey as a man of letters and a patron; it is at this point that we witness in its most explicit form the encounter between these two sides of Humphrey's personality; at the same time, it is probably in these years that his political fortunes began to decline, and that he devoted his energies more and more to his cultural activities.

While the *Vita Henrici Quinti* survives in a number of manuscripts and enjoyed popularity both in England and in Italy, the *Hunfroidos*,

---

[160] Tino Foffano considers the *Vita Henrici* Quinti a decisive influence in the renewal of English historical writing (see his "Charles d'Orléans e un gruppo di umanisti lombardi in Normandia", *Aevum* 41: 1967, 452–73, p. 452). Everest-Phillips writes: "The work represents an interesting fusion of the tradition Frulovisi and Gloucester were familiar with. Thus one can see patron and writer in successful and unusual collaboration; Frulovisi producing work in keeping with popular humanist trends which he would have inclined towards and been keen to try out for himself, and yet providing his patron with exactly the sort of work which would enhance his designs" (p. 203).

[161] On this point see also Gransden, pp. 211–2.

composed approximately at the same time or shortly afterwards, seems to have disappeared very soon. It is now extant in only one manuscript, re-discovered comparatively recently, and there is no mention of it after Humphrey's death. The manuscript is in Seville (Biblioteca Colombina 7.2.23, ff. 62r 84r), and it is unclear how it reached it, unless it was brought there by Frulovisi himself, who spent a few years in Spain before going back to his native Italy. Its rediscovery was announced by Roberto Weiss in 1957,[162] but the poem has excited little comment apart from a few observations on the very faulty quality of Frulovisi's Latin, and on the repetitive nature of his narrative. As had happened with the *Vita Henrici Quinti*, Frulovisi's attention is almost solely concentrated upon Gloucester's military prowess, and the poem is a description of the events from the congress of Arras in 1435 to Humphrey's return to England in 1436, after his triumphs in Calais and Flanders. Unlike the *Vita*, however, Frulovisi devises a mythical frame for the narration, imagining a council in the underworld in which Pluto laments a recent falling of the death rate on earth. This prompts him to summon the fury Alecto, who will go to the Duke of Burgundy and incite him to stir up war. The mythological setting is not meant to make the reader forget the present: the state of enmity between France and England is alluded to very early in the poem, and there is a reverent mention of Henry V as a harbinger of peace (l. 18). This awkwardly handed device, together with the choice to use Latin hexameters, indicates that the intent is somewhat different from the *Vita*: the eponymous hero is represented in a halo of classical glory, and the imitation of contemporary humanist poems such as Filelfo's *Sfortias*, Porcellio's *Feltria* or Tito Vespasiano Strozzi's *Borseide* is evident even in the title.[163] There are also direct classical influences: in particular,

---

[162] Weiss, "Humphrey Duke of Gloucester and Tito Livio Frulovisi". Documents preserved in the Warburg Institute, London, show that Weiss was already studying the manuscript in 1948, with the help of the Latin scholar Harold E. Butler (an epistolary exchange between Weiss and Butler, together with a partial, and partially annotated, transcription of the poem, can be found in the library of the Warburg Institute, under the shelfmark NAH 8320). Butler's commentary is headed "Some reflections on the work of a certain Tito Livio di Forli by one who is of opinion that either the aforesaid Tito or he himself should never have been born", which is an eloquent proof of what Butler thought of Frulovisi's work. The poem is transcribed, without any attempt at emendation, in Everest-Phillips, pp. 316–38. My quotations from the poem are taken from her transcription.

[163] A point already made by Weiss in his "Humphrey Duke of Gloucester and Tito Livio Frulovisi", p. 223.

it may be noted that the introductory debate in the underworld is
an imitation of the opening section of Claudian's *In Rufinum*. It has
been seen above that Claudian was one of the authors present in
Humphrey's library: it is possible that Frulovisi made use of this
library to compose his poem.

Yet the classical setting is abandoned once Humphrey enters the
scene, and at this point the poem shows more decided analogies
with the *Vita Henrici Quinti*. Once again Frulovisi's more direct source
appears to have been Humphrey himself, and the light in which he
is presented shows decided similarities with Henry V's portrait in
the *Vita*. There is no need to imagine one work to be the continuation of the other, but there is certainly a strong relation, especially
since the *Vita* had indirectly celebrated also Humphrey's early triumphs in war (particularly at Agincourt), so that the *Hunfroidos* could
be said to take up the threads of this narration. If the earlier mythological setting was very clumsily represented, Humphrey's appearance, delayed until almost one third of the poem, has a certain
dramatic impressiveness, even if his delayed arrival on the scene was
actually the result of bad timing on his part, and even if throughout the poem Henry V's shadow will loom behind him. He had
been alluded to as the subject of the poem in the opening lines,
which have a clear Virgilian ring:

> (M)agnanimum Humfredum, vires magnosque tropheos
> magnanime gentis britonum fraudesque philipi,
> hic canere incipiam atque ducis periuria seui
> burgondi.[164]

Once he appears, Humphrey is not so much a general but a soldier: his strength and bravery rather than any tactical subtleness are
the deciding factors of the battle. In true epic fashion, the whole
Calais episode is seen as a series of individual duels, though Humphrey
is not alone but accompanied by a number of individually named
peers, while the crowds are mainly depicted as passive and suffering.[165]
The choice presents some analogies with what happens in Lydgate's

---

[164] "I will begin here to sing of the magnanimous Humphrey, of the men and
of the great victories of the magnanimous people of England, of Philip's deception,
and of the perjury of the cruel duke of Burgundy".

[165] Though Humphrey is clearly the hero, the writer is careful not to make his
the absolute protagonist from beginning to end, but to stress rather his role as "regis
patruus", uncle of the King (l. 724).

Fall of Princes: individual men carry the burden of guilt, or are asked to rescue a nation, while the population is left to bear the disastrous effects of war, and to pray for peace. Even as the English triumphs are celebrated, there is a deprecating note:

> O furor o que sitis regnandi anxia cura
> Quorum mentes agitant hominum miserosque molestos
> Quot casus refferunt quos stulta superbia mouit.[166]
>
> [606–8]

Philip of Burgundy's greatest fault is his indifference at the waste and grief he has provoked; Humphrey's arrival at Calais is the answer to this public call for peace—a simple, if manichean, explanation of the hostility between Humphrey and the Duke of Burgundy. On the other hand, the writer shows a detailed knowledge of the diplomatic work that preceded Gloucester's arrival in Calais, and this detail shows his closeness to Humphrey, though from the literary point of view it is a jarring note in the poem.

If the poem was meant to present Humphrey as the ideal successor of his brother on the war field, this seems to exclude Henry VI, who was its direct addressee. More than the *Vita*, the *Hunfroidos* raises the question of its intended audience. Unless it was simply the answer to Humphrey's wish to see himself glorified in Latin hexameters like a classical hero or a humanist prince, it must have been meant for a wider (and less directly involved) audience than the Lancastrian court. The siege of Calais, though it raised much comment and interest in England, and generated a great amount of popular literature, was a minor episode in the continuing hostility between England, Burgundy and France. Through the metrical and stylistic choice of his poet Humphrey was perhaps trying to ennoble his deeds, to give them international status; or he may have wished simply to become the protagonist of a humanistic form of celebration, as had happened (through his patronage) to the memory of his brother. Calais was the last moment that saw the Duke of Gloucester protagonist of the political scene, and he probably used his patronage to promote this martial self-representation.

---

[166] Lines 606–8. "O rage, and thirst to reign with anxious care, upsetting the troubled and unhappy minds of men, how many cases they remember in which they were moved by blind pride".

This form of self-representation is also evident in the section of his library devoted to military treatises, and in another text that was written for him, Nicholas Upton's *De Studio Militari*.[167] A student of New College, Oxford, Upton became a subdeacon in 1420–1 and then entered the service of Thomas de Montacute, Earl of Salisbury, fighting against the French in Normandy. After his return to England, he became a protégé of the Duke of Gloucester, and thanks to his advice and influence was made precentor of Salisbury in 1446. There is no exact date for the composition of *De Studio Militari*, but it must have been written very near the end of Humphrey's life, since in his dedication Upton styles himself "Ecclesiarum Cathedralium Sar. & Wellie Canonicus", and alludes to himself as an old man. The dedication employs for Humphrey the usual appellation of "son, brother and uncle of kings" which can be seen not only in the correspondence with the University of Oxford, but in Lydgate and in the Palladius translation. Once again, as in other works written for Humphrey, there is evidence that in composing this treatise the writer is complying with the patron's wish: "Et quia de pertinentibus ad officium militare, prout in diversis actibus bellicis in *Francia* & alibi asseris diversa me vidisse, & visa in libellum redigi, tuoque desiderio postulas exhiberi".[168] Upton's book might thus be one of Humphrey's last commissions, showing his interest in military matters even after his semi-forced retirement from public affairs. Clearly divided in four parts corresponding to different aspects of the art of war, the treatise presents already in its dedication a summary of the contents, with a clear exposition of its structure; this device is similar, though in an abbreviated form, to the *tabula* in the presentation manuscript of the Palladius translation. As for its contents, Upton's clear exposition of the matter, particularly as concerns the third and fourth sections, devoted to heraldry, caused the treatise to be read with interest long after its author's death, if in 1654 the antiquarian and historian Edward Bysshe could decide to publish it as a useful guide

---

[167] The treatise is published in *Nicolai Vptoni De Studio Militari, Libri quatuor. Johan de Badoaureo, Tractatus de armis. Henrici Spelmanni Aspilogia*, ed. by E. Bysshe, Londinii: Typis Rogeri Norton, 1654.

[168] "And since you declare that I have seen various things concerning the military office, in various war acts in France and elsewhere, and having seen them you desire that I should write about them, in a little book, and show them according to your wish". *Nicolai Vptoni De Studio Militari*, p. 2.

to medieval warfare and heraldry. In his introductory pages Bysshe mentions Humphrey as "doctorum sui temporis Maecenas", though Upton makes no reference to Humphrey's intellectual pursuits. Discussing *De Studio Militari*, Everest-Phillips calls it "something of an anomaly, neither being in English nor a work of scholarship".[169] But I would contend that it springs from the same intellectual *milieu* that generated the Palladius translation, and that in former years had generated Frulovisi's historical works and Lydgate's *Fall*. The analogies with the Palladius text are not limited to the clearly defined structure: like the Middle English *De Re Rustica* this is a practical manual meant to be read for practical purposes, but it is not without literary ambitions; as in the *Hunfroidos*, there are references to a number of classical writers, from Valerius Maximus to Plinius, but with a constant attention to contemporary history; like Lydgate's work, it reconciles a classical with a medieval reference library by alluding also to John of Salisbury's *Polycraticus*, or to Isidore of Seville. On the other hand, Upton may not have been as close to his patron as the Palladius translator or Lydgate were.

There is at least another book which was certainly written for Duke Humphrey, and it is Gilbert Kymer's *Dietarium de sanitatis custodia*.[170] Kymer's position in the University of Oxford, and his role as mediator in the first of Humphrey's recorded donations of manuscripts to the University library, have been amply discussed in chapter 4. Kymer himself possessed a considerable collection of medical manuscripts, now in the Bodleian Library. He spent most of his life between Oxford and London, dividing his time between the University for which he was twice chancellor and the care of a noble or rich group of patients among whom perhaps the Duke of Gloucester was the most prominent; but he was not a household servant or retainer to the Duke, rather an independent practitioner.[171] Duke Humphrey

---

[169] Everest-Phillips, p. 172.

[170] British Library, Sloane 4, ff. 63–104. A selection of the *Dietarium* is published in *Liber Niger Scaccarii*, ed. by T. Hearne, Oxonii: E Theatro Sheldoniano, 1728, pp. 550–9.

[171] On this point see Jeremy Catto, "Master, Patrons and the Careers of Graduates in Fifteenth-Century England", in *Concepts and Patterns of Service in the Later Middle Ages*, ed. by A. Curry and E. Matthew, Woodbridge: The Boydell Press, 2000: 52–63, p. 61. For information on Kymer's career, see C.H. Talbot and E.A. Hammond, *The Medical Practitioners in Medieval England. A Biographical Register*, London: Wellcome Historical Medical Library, 1965, pp. 60–3.

employed another physician, Giovanni Signorelli, native of Ferrara.[172] Kymer then must be considered an independent professional and academic who sought Humphrey's favour, probably before involving him in the University affairs, since the *Dietarium* was written in 1424. The existence of this work, composed when the dedicatee was little over thirty, has been considered a proof of Humphrey's poor health, and of his undermining it by his excesses, and there are passages in which the writer addresses the Duke, with reference to his humours, and possibly to genital problems;[173] but the work itself is absolutely conventional in its advice, and it is difficult to consider it as relating to the infirmities of a specific patient; its perusal gives the reader the same sense of disappointment as the list of medical books Humphrey donated to Oxford: in both there is little that is new or that deviates from medieval conventions. C.H. Talbot is particularly severe in his analysis of this work and of its author:

> he was content to be a compiler and he says at the beginning 'I shall say nothing which has not been approved by authority, reason and experience', meaning the authority, reason and experience of others. Though the treatise is well written in good Latin, 'laying aside my mother tongue', and is logically drawn up, it contains not one iota of information which could not be found in the *Regimen Salernitanum* written more than two centuries earlier [. . .] It is obvious that his immediate source was the *Secretum Secretorum* attributed to Aristotle and that he was borrowing from the same source as the vernacular poems and treatises which were current among the bulk of the literate population.[174]

This conventionality is particularly surprising if we consider that Kymer seems to have been aiming at authentic renovation in the profession, and that he was acquiring notoriety in London alchemical circles.[175] In many ways, Gilbert Kymer remains a singularly

---

[172] He had apparently come to England at the Duke's request, and received denization in 1433. It is interesting, though probably of no significance, to note that both he and Frulovisi came from Ferrara, though there is no support to the hypothesis that Signorelli introduced Frulovisi to the Duke. For further information on Signorelli, see Talbot and Hammond, p. 182 (referred to as John De Signorellis).

[173] In particular this passage: "vestri autem renes & genitalia operis venereis immoderate frequencia aliquantulum debilitantur, quod liquiditas & paucitas vestri seminis denunciant" (p. 553; "your kidneys and genitals are weakened by immoderate abuse of veneral acts, as is shown by the scarcity and fluidity of your semen").

[174] C.H. Talbot, *Medicine in Medieval England*, London: Oldbourne, 1967, pp. 203–4.

[175] "Thomas Norton, in the *Ordinal of Alchemy* which he wrote about 1490, mentioned Kymer (who died in 1463) as the most prominent physician of this time.

problematic figure in the intellectual scene of fifteenth-century England, and the relative mystery that surrounds him is perhaps to be connected with a network of physicians, astronomers, mathematicians and alchemists that we see operating at various stages in Duke Humphrey's household, or near Eleanor Cobham. Most of them, included those who were involved in the Cobham scandal, had received their education in Oxford and had been or were in contact with Kymer. Humphrey himself has been attributed the composition of a *Prologus in tabulas* (now Cambridge University Library Ee.3.61, f. 108v), that is, astronomical tables, whose incipit is "Effectus planetarum proficientes probitos et futuros pronosticare".[176] To this same network might be connected a somewhat obscure reference that was found in 1856 in the registers of the Archbishops of York.[177] One William Byg alias Leech, charged with heresy in 1465, gave to the vicar-general of the Archbishop of York a full confession of his activity as a crystal-gazer, and in the course of this confession said he had left his books of magic in Greenwich "habuit libros suos apud Greynwiche cito post mortem ducis quondam Gloucestre in camera ejusdem apud Greynwich".[178] If, as I believe, "camera ejusdem" refers to Humphrey's own apartments,[179] then, whatever the truth of Byg's statement, we might infer that there was an exchange of suspicious books in Greenwich around the year of Humphrey's death. I have been unable to throw further light on this episode, but it seems to confirm my hypothesis of a centre of interest in medicine, astronomy and perhaps occult sciences in Greenwich in the 1430s and 1440s.

He claimed that Kymer failed in his pursuit of the philosopher's stone, but wrote on the subject even so" (F.M. Getz, "The Faculty of Medicine before 1500", in *The History of the University of Oxford, vol. 2: Late Medieval Oxford*, ed. by J.J. Catto and R. Evans, Oxford: Clarendon Press, 1992: 373–405, p. 404; see also *Thomas Norton's Ordinal of Alchemy*, ed. by J. Reidy, Early English Text Society, London: Oxford University Press, 1975, V. 1559–66). No trace has survived of Kymer's writings on alchemy.

[176] Lewis of Caerleon probably transcribed this work. See Pearl Kibre, "Lewis of Caerleon, Doctor of Medicine, Astronomer and Mathematician (d. 1494?)", *Isis* 43: 1952, 100–8, reprinted as ch. 15 of Kibre's *Studies in Medieval Science. Alchemy, Astrology, Mathematics and Medicine*, London: The Hambledon Press, 1984.

[177] What follows is taken from James Raine, "Divination in the Fifteenth Century by Aid of a Magical Crystal", *The Archaeological Journal* 13: 1856, 372–4.

[178] "He kept his books in Greenwich, shortly after the death of the Duke of Gloucester, in his room in Greenwich".

[179] Raines believes "ejusdem" to refer to Byg, but given the construction of the sentence one would have expect "sua" to be used in this case.

There are other allusions to Humphrey's patronage in other contemporary texts, but they tend to be extremely slight, and do not
refer to direct patronage. However, two of them may be of some
interest. One is to be found in George Ashby's *A Prisoner's Reflections*,
a poem probably composed in 1463:

> I gan remembre and revolue in mynde
> My bryngyng vp from chyldhod hedyrto,
> In the hyghest court that I coude fynd,
> With the kyng, quene, and theyr vncle also,
> The duk of Gloucetre, god hem rest do,
> With whome .I. haue be cherysshyd ryght well,
> In all that was to me nedefull euery dell.[180]

But is this case the allusion is too generic to be of definite interest,
though there is definite proof that Ashby was in the Duke's employment.[181] The other and earlier allusion comes from John Russell,
usher to Humphrey and author of a treatise on household management, the *Boke of Nurture*, written sometime before 1447. It might
be another instance of the practical manuals produced in Humphrey's
circle, and the hypothesis that Humphrey commissioned it has been
made, though there is very little to support it, apart from the fact
that the treatise is very clearly meant for the servant of a lord.[182] At
the beginning of his treatise (ll. 3–4) Russell writes:

> an vsshere y Am/ye may beholde/to a prynce of highe degre
> þat enioyethe to enforme & teche/alle þo thatt wille thrive and thee.[183]

---

[180] Lines 57–63. The poem is the first in *George Ashby's Poems Edited from Two 15th Century Mss. at Cambridge*, ed. by M. Bateson, Early English Text Society, London: Kegan Paul, 1899.

[181] A letter written by Queen Margaret in 1447 or 1448 mentions "George Asheby, clerc of our signet", in connection with payments of his wages "deue unto him by the Duc of Glouc. that last died" (*Letters of Queen Margaret of Anjou and Bishop Beckington and others. Written in the Reigns of Henry V. and Henry VI.*, ed. by C. Monro, Camden Society, London: Nichols, 1863, p. 114).

[182] The hypothesis is made by Keiser, pp. 484–5. Keiser notes that "of the five manuscripts in which the *Book of nurture* is found, three have other works produced under aristocratic patronage. One (1475–1500) contains John Lydgate's *Lyf of our lady*, commissioned by Henry V. Another (1450–75) contains, along with the *Canterbury Tales*, Lancastrian and Yorkist writings by Sir John Fortescue, and a poem cele-brating Edward IV's return to the throne in 1471. A third (1450–75) contains *Secrees of the old philosoffres*—a rime royal version of *Secretum secretorum*, begun by Lydgate and completed by Benedict Burgh for Henry VI—and the prose translation of Vegetius's *De re militari* made for Thomas IV, tenth Lord Berkeley, in 1408".

[183] "John Russell's Boke of Nurture", in *The Babees Book, Aristotle's ABC, Urbanitatis,*

It is not clear, however, whether "that" refers to himself or to Humphrey. At the end of the treatise the noble lord is alluded to again: the writers remembers his learning his art "with a prynce fulle royalle" (l. 1177). Gloucester is actually mentioned in the concluding lines of the poem (1229–30):

> pray for the sowle of Iohn Russelle, þat god do hym mede,
> Som tyme seruaunde with duke vmfrey, duc of Glowcetur in dede.

Everest-Phillips sees a link between the mention of the Duke of Gloucester and the attempt to give such an obviously practical manual a literary patina, and suggests "that Russell's debt to the atmosphere of literary encouragement in the Household was immense, if misplaced".[184] John Burrow also sees a relation between Russell's writing and the intellectual atmosphere in Humphrey's household, and highlights it humorously:

> In his *Boke of Nurture*, the former usher and marshal of the Duke's household, John Russell, describes how each of the four courses of an elaborate fish dinner may be accompanied by an elaborate "subtlety" or ornamental device. During their first course, diners were to contemplate the representation of a "galaunt yonge man, a wanton wight", standing on a cloud (air) at the beginning of the ver (spring), and named Sanguineus (blood). The second subtlety is to represent a "man of warre", standing in fire, red and angry (choler), and named Estas (summer). The third represents a "man with sikelle in his hande" in "þe thrid age of man", standing in a river (water and phlegm), and named Hervist (autumn). In the fourth and last subtlety, which came in with the spices and the wine, Yemps (winter) "with his lokkys grey, febille and old" sits on a cold hard stone (earth), "nigard in hert and hevy of chere" (melancholy). Each device is to be accompanied by a couplet from the Salernitan verses, setting out the characteristics of the appropriate humour. Thus, as Duke Humphrey's guests worked their way through this very unpenitentiary fish banquet, they were invited to see in it the four courses of their own life's feast.[185]

Stans Puer ad Mensam, The Lytille Childrenes Lytil Boke, The Bokes of Nurture of Hugh Rhodes and John Russell, Wynkyn de Worde's Boke of Kervynge, The Booke of Demeanor, The Boke of Curtasye, Seager's Schoole of Vertue, &c. &c. with some French & Latin Poems on Like Subjetcs, and some Forewords on Education in Early England, ed. by F.J. Furnivall, London: Trübner, 1868: 115–239.

[184] Everest-Phillips, p. 174.

[185] John A. Burrow, *The Ages of Man. A Study in Medieval Writing and Thought*, Oxford: Clarendon Press, 1986, pp. 29–30. Burrow is referring to ll. 719–94 of the *Boke*.

Russell's choice is interesting not only because of its wealth of classical allusions, but also because it connects a reflection on the ages of man with medical advice such as Kymer would have approved of. Other dinners are described with equal care, and accompanied by other "subtleties": thus a meat dinner can be accompanied by representations of the Annunciation, Nativity, and the coming of the Magi.[186] As Everest-Phillips maintains, Russell's words certainly might be evidence of a particularly charged intellectual atmosphere in Humphrey's household, though perhaps not of direct patronage.

I have left to the end of this section one of the most controversial instances of patronage, concerning John Capgrave. An Augustinian friar, theologian and historian, Capgrave has been considered for a long time very close to Duke Humphrey, and believed to have been his confessor and perhaps even his counsellor.[187] What actually happened was that some time before 1437 he sent the Duke copies of two Biblical commentaries, *In Regnum I* (= I Samuel) and *In Regnum III* (= I Kings), now lost. At this time he did not know the Duke and it is to be presumed that he was hoping to obtain patronage through these presentations. Even if his third work, a copy of his commentary *In Genesim*, was delivered by him personally and dedicated to Humphrey, he makes it clear in the Preface that even at this stage (1439) he knows the Duke only by report.[188] This time, however, the latter's response might have been more encouraging, because immediately afterwards Capgrave dedicated to him another commentary, *In Exodum*.[189] Subsequently the four volumes were

---

[186] Lines 686–718.

[187] The biography and bibliography of John Capgrave can be found in Alberic de Meijer, "John Capgrave, O.E.S.A. (1393–1464)", *Augustiniana* 5: 1955, 400–40, and "John Capgrave, O.E.S.A. (1393–1464)", *Augustiniana* 7: 1957, 118–48, 532–41. The two articles are, however, dated. Much of what they say about Capgrave's relation with Humphrey has been rectified in more recent times. See Peter J. Lucas, *From Author to Audience: John Capgrave and Medieval Publication*, The Library, Dublin: University College Dublin Press, 1997; Peter J. Lucas and Rita Dalton, "Capgrave's Preface Dedicating his Commentary *In Exodum* to Humfrey Duke of Gloucester", *The Bodleian Library Record* 11: 1982, 20–5. A more updated biography can be found in J.C. Fredeman, "The Life of John Capgrave, O.E.S.A. (1393–1464)", *Augustiniana* 29: 1979, 197–237.

[188] Lucas and Dalton, p. 20. The manuscript is now Oxford, Oriel College, 32. In *De Illustribus Henricis* Capgrave refers to Duke Humphrey as "inter omnes mundi proceres litteratissimus", but here too the praise is very generic (*Johannis Capgrave Liber de Illustribus Henricis*, ed. by F.C. Hingeston, Rolls Series, London: Longman, Brown, Green, Longmans, and Roberts, 1858, p. 109).

[189] Now Oxford, Bodleian Library, Duke Humfrey b.1.

included in the 1443 donation to Oxford. It seems clear, however, that in this case the Duke of Gloucester did not exercise that active and direct patronage that is to be witnessed in the case of Frulovisi, Lydgate or the Palladius translator. It has been believed that it was at the Duke's prompting that Capgrave wrote his *Chronicle of England* in the vernacular,[190] that he dedicated to the Duke another commentary, *Super Epistulas Pauli*, and that he wrote a *Vita Humfredi Ducis Glocestriae*, in the hope of obtaining the Duke's protection for the Augustinians, an order which had been founded in England by another Duke of Gloucester, Richard de Clare, in 1248. However, these suppositions are mostly the result of wishful thinking, or an effect of John Bale's somewhat embellishing the truth in his *Scriptorium Illustrium maioris Brytanniae*.[191] It is true that in his *Liber de Illustribus Henricis* Capgrave writes that he plans to compose a "specialem tractatulum" on the Duke, but there is no other reference to this mysterious work, nor is there particular attention to Humphrey in Capgrave's surviving historical works.[192]

We should thus think of Capgrave as a man attempting to obtain Humphrey's patronage, but being perhaps too late in his attempt, and employing a genre, the Biblical commentary, in which the Duke appeared no longer interested, though he had collected many examples of it in his library, and had been praised by Lydgate in the *Epithalamium* for his grasp of allegorical interpretation of the Scriptures. By the time Capgrave arrived with his volumes, Humphrey's interest had decidedly turned to the writing of history in its various forms, as attested by his commissions to Lydgate and Frulovisi, or to the need of a literature in the vernacular and thus to the commission of translations. Capgrave's Latin commentaries, with their discussions of religious or moral matters, or of priestly practices, were unlikely to excite his curiosity at this point, and the writer probably became aware of it quite soon, since further commentaries on Leviticus, Numbers and Deuteronomy which he had promised were apparently

---

[190] *John Capgrave's Abbreuiacioun of Cronicles*, ed. by P.J. Lucas, Early English Text Society, Oxford: Oxford University Press, 1983. The hypothesis concerning Humphrey's involvement is to be found in Karl Julius Holzknecht, *Literary Patronage in the Middle Ages*, New York: The Collegiate Press, 1923, p. 151.

[191] Some conclusive demonstration can be found in Peter J. Lucas, "John Capgrave and the *Nova Legenda Angliae*: A Survey", *The Library* 5th series, 25: 1970, 1–10, p. 7.

[192] *Johannis Capgrave Liber de Illustribus Henricis*, p. 109.

never delivered. However, the fact that Capgrave thought of Humphrey as a possible dedicatee, and went to the trouble and expense of having illuminated copies of his works made on purpose for him,[193] is interesting in itself, because it means that the Duke's fame as a literary patron was well established at this point. The two prefaces to the two surviving commentaries are eloquent on the subject; in the commentary *In Genesim* the writer maintains a rather generic tone, speaking of the Duke as somebody who peruses ancient authors "studiosissime";[194] but the preface to *In Exodum* shows how Capgrave had by this time become somewhat more acquainted with the Duke's inclination and activities, since he speaks of the Duke's patronage of scholars in his own house, and of how he has endowed the Oxford library with unheard-of generosity, giving it a great number of rare and necessary volumes. Unlike the previous preface, besides, this has a number of appropriate or inappropriate references to classical figures and medieval authors, with a particular attention to English writers. Capgrave stresses the bond that has always linked patron and writer, and seems even to insert a veiled request for money to this prospective patron. Altogether, this preface is more personal and pointed, but Capgrave's hopes must have been soon disappointed. Though Humphrey inscribed the second of the two books with his ex-libris, there is no proof that he actually read them before sending them to Oxford. Neither is there proof that the potential patron and the poet actually met: the ex-libris says "Cest livre est a moy Homfrey duc de Gloucestre du don Jehan Capgrave quy le me fist presenter a mon manoir de Pensherst le jour de lan [M] CCC-CXXXVIII".[195] John Capgrave's contribution to fifteenth-century English writing is of some importance, but his historical works, and especially his decision to use the vernacular for one of them, are certainly more important than his Biblical commentaries. J.C. Fredeman notes that though he was certainly known in his own time, Capgrave "was never as fashionable as John Lydgate nor did he enjoy a coterie fame comparable to that of his fellow friar, Osbern Bokenham".[196]

---

[193] Both *In Genesim* and *In Exodum* include portraits of the Duke, in the act of receiving the manuscripts.

[194] Both commentaries are printed in M.C. Seymour, *John Capgrave*, English Writers of the Middle Ages, Aldershot: Variorum, 1996, pp. 39–41.

[195] Sammut, p. 118.

[196] Fredeman, p. 223.

Fig. 5. The presentation scene of John Capgrave's *In Exodum*.

I believe his relation with Duke Humphrey is further proof of this statement.[197]

Humphrey's relative indifference for figurative arts, even as concerns the illumination of the manuscripts he commissioned or supervised, has already been discussed in the previous chapter. M.C. Seymour supposes that Hoccleve included a picture of himself and the duke on the presentation copy of his *Series*, but, if so, the manuscript has not survived.[198] The surviving portraits of Humphrey are actually very few, and none of them reliable: one of the interesting details about the presentation copies of *In Genesim* and *In Exodum* is that they both have a portrait of the duke receiving Capgrave's work, but since Capgrave's acquaintance with the duke was minimal, these portraits can show nothing more than the generic likeness of the conventional patron. Other presumed images of the duke can be found in other manuscripts, but never when Humphrey could directly supervise their composition, as in the case of the Palladius translation: thus we find one in a copy of Lydgate's *Fall of Princes*,[199] but the manuscript was very probably completed after the Duke's death. The only striking instance in which Humphrey probably desired an image of himself to be inserted in a manuscript is the Psalter discussed in chapter 4, in which there is a representation of the Duke kneeling before the Man of Sorrows. In this case, it may be argued that the image has a symbolic value; Humphrey then seems never interested in the merely decorative potential of an illumination, rather in its iconographic significance.[200]

---

[197] There have been other incorrect attributions concerning Humphrey's patronage: Jane Chance writes that Stephen Scrope dedicated to the Duke a copy of his translation of Christine de Pizan's *Epistre Othea*, but she is probably confusing this Humphrey with Humphrey Stafford, Duke of Buckingham (the manuscript is Cambridge, St John's College, H.5; see Chance, pp. 247–8). The editor of Scrope's text, however, maintains that Scrope did seek to enter Gloucester's service, though unsuccessfully (*The Epistle of Othea. Translated from the French Text of Christine de Pisan by Stephen Scrope*, ed. by C.F. Bühler, Early English Text Society, London: Oxford University Press, 1970, p. xx).

[198] M.C. Seymour, "Manuscript Pictures of Duke Humfrey", *The Bodleian Library Record* 12: 1986, 95–98, p. 95.

[199] Huntington Library HM 268, f. 18. The manuscript was completed *circa* 1460.

[200] Very few works of art, apart from the manuscripts, are connected with Duke Humphrey's patronage: Everest-Phillips lists the Duke's tomb in St Albans, a chalice he and Eleanor presented to Lady Margaret Beaufort, whose godfather Humphrey was (now in Christ's College, Cambridge), and possibly some stained glass in the churches of Greenwich and Cobham, now no longer surviving (p. 340).

The same interest in symbolic images can be seen in the Duke's tomb in St Albans Abbey, if it can be assumed that its decorations were manufactured during Humphrey's lifetime.[201] In an article published in 1946, T.D. Kendrick analyses these decorations, noticing a frequently repeated detail, a device of "daisies in a standing cup", or of "wheat-ears in vases on pedestals". Kendrick notes "the emphasis on the classical form of the vase [. . .] The badge was plainly intended to be an antique vase containing some unspecified kind of plant".[202] The badge appears to be connected with the Duke's literary tastes, and Kendrick quotes the Renaissance scholar John Leland and his hendecasyllabic poem *Cygnea Cantio*, published in 1545. In it a swan descends the Thames from Oxford to Greenwich, describing what he sees, and relates that it was Humphrey who first built a palace in Greenwich called Placentia (Plesaunce), adding:

> Sed quum Curia sustulisset illum
> Poli fraude, dolisque Sudovolcae
> Festas deposuit relicta cristas,
> Elugens Domini sui ruinam,
> Horti tunc perier Adonidisque,
> Quos insignia tanquam amoeniora
> Fatali omine pinxerat fenestris:
> Nimirum fragiles sciens honores,
> Et rerum instabiles vices novarum.[203]

The badge on the St Albans tomb should thus be referring to the Garden of Adonis, an emblem of mortality or of the insecurity of human affairs. The Garden of Adonis was the name given to "small pottery vases, or broken pots, filled with earth in which quick-growing plants (wheat, lettuce, fennel, etc.) were sown. Their planting was part of the Adonis ceremonies, and it was customary for them

---

[201] The details of the commission of Duke Humphrey's tomb can be found in London, British Library, Cotton Claudius A.VIII, ff. 195–8.

[202] T.D. Kendrick, "Humphrey, Duke of Gloucester, and the Gardens of Adonis", *The Antiquaries Journal* 26: 1946, 118–22, pp. 118–9.

[203] Kendrick, p. 120. Kendrick then translates the passage: "But after Bury St Edmunds had been the scene of his death/As a result of the mischievous plotting of William de la Pole, Earl of Suffolk,/Abandoned, the Plesaunce took down the Duke's proud plumes, /Mourning the ruin of its lord;/Then the Garden of Adonis faded and died,/The badges that, as though they had been propitious emblems,/Humphrey had displayed in his stained glass window, a fatal omen,/For he knew that honours are indeed transitory,/And politics beyond all reckoning".

to be attended to by women for the period during which they
flourished in luxuriance, and afterwards, as they began to fade, they
were carried away with images of the dead god thrown into the sea
or into springs".[204] There is actually no proof that this symbol was
know to fifteenth-century humanists, whether in Italy or in England,
but Kendrick's hypothesis (possibly supported by the same devices
in Antonello da Messina's "St Jerome in his Study") remains a fascinating one.

English humanists around Duke Humphrey: squaring the circle

The commissions, dedications and donations of manuscripts were the
highest goals of the intellectual activity around Duke Humphrey; but
his patronage seems to have extended also to scholars for whom
there is no proof of book production connected directly with the
Duke. Kathryn Kerby-Fulton and Steven Justice lament that a modern reader tends to identify a literary circle with a coterie, or a reading community, "constituted by nothing other than a shared and
exclusive knowingness about their own art";[205] but, though this may
be an exaggeration born of early twentieth-century notions of art for
art's sake, there is little doubt that there is an important component
of spiritual sharing and of basic and simple reading in any intellectual circle, a component that tends to be overlooked when, as in
the case of Duke Humphrey's, the modern scholar has to rely on
woefully insufficient evidence. Roberto Weiss attempted to judge
Humphrey's intellectual achievements by the manuscripts he possessed, supposing him to have read them all, and thus burdening
him with a task that no modern reader and library-owner has ever
accomplished; but though many of the manuscripts may never have
been perused by their owner, the collection itself, and the fact that
the Duke of Gloucester was obviously investing much time and money
in it, were bound to attract scholars, writers, or even simple readers.

---

[204] Kendrick, pp. 120–1.
[205] Kathryn Kerby-Fulton and Steven Justice, "Langlandian Reading Circles and
the Civil Service in London and Dublin, 1380–1427", in *New Medieval Literatures 1*,
ed. by W. Scase, R. Copeland and D. Lawton, Oxford: Clarendon Press, 1997:
59–83, p. 59.

Yet the definition of such a circle is a matter of some difficulty. Too often scholars seem to have been guided by enthusiasm in their definition of what at times seems the first humanist circle in England, and have included people who entertained no particularly close relation with the Duke. One such case may be Andrew Holes, Fellow of New College, Oxford, in 1414–20, and later king's proctor at the Papal Curia. Information on Holes is scanty and after Otto Schellenberg's partial reconstruction of his biography in 1912, there has been no attempt to investigate his role in English intellectual life in the fifteenth century.[206] The link between Holes and Gloucester is a copy of Coluccio Salutati's *De laboribus Herculis*, bearing the ex-libris "Cest livre est a moy Homfrey duc de Gloucester du don [maistre An]-drew Holes".[207] The manuscript has already been discussed in chapter 4, and it certainly shows that Holes at one point attempted to win the Duke's favour, or possibly received from him a direct commission to acquire this particular manuscript. But there is no other proof of Holes's enjoying Gloucester's patronage, though, as keeper of the Privy Seal in later years, he probably had frequent access at court. A somewhat similar case is that of Nicholas Bildeston, chancellor to Henry Beaufort, friend of Poggio Bracciolini, and Dean of Salisbury from 1435 to 1441 (the year of his death). As already noted in chapter 4, Bildeston gave Humphrey a manuscript of Petrarch's *De remediis utriusque fortunae*, including also Pietro Paolo Vergerio's *Vita Petrarce*, and Gloucester acquired after Bildeston's death a copy of Seneca's *Epistulae* from his testamentary executors. In neither case is there proof of a particular closeness between the two. Somewhat different is the case of Adam de Moleyns or Molyneux, Bishop of Chichester in 1446 and in his turn keeper of the Privy Seal. Like Holes, Moleyns has some claim to the title of humanist; David Rundle even considers him "the English equivalent to the clerical humanist who could make professional use of the *studia humanitatis*".[208] Unfortunately, very little of his work has survived, but one

---

[206] Otto Schellenberger, "Wer war Andrew Ols?", *Englische Studien* 46: 1912–13, 197–205. Schellenberger identifies him with the "Andrew Ols" known to Vespasiano da Bisticci and Flavio Biondo. Holes is one of three Englishmen who appear in Vespasiano da Bisticci's *Vite*.

[207] Biblioteca Apostolica Vaticana, Urbinate lat. 694, f. 179v. The manuscript is described in Sammut, pp. 123–4.

[208] David Rundle, "Polydore Vergil and the *Translatio studiorum*: The Tradition of Italian Humanists in England", in *Polidoro Virgili e la cultura umanistica europea*, ed. by R. Bachielli, Urbino: Accademia Raffaello—Urbino, 2003: 53–74, p. 23.

interesting detail is his donation of books to Oxford (once again, to
the University library) around 1450.[209] It would seem then that
Humphrey's great donations had driven others to emulate him, even
if on a smaller scale. In Moleyns's case, the connection with the
Duke of Gloucester is given by a letter written by Aeneas Silvius
Piccolomini to Moleyns in 1444, in which he praises Gloucester "qui
studia humanitatis summo studio in regnum vestrum recepit, qui,
sicut mihi relatum est, et poetas mirifice colit et oratores magnopere
veneratur."[210] The passage, already quoted in chapter 3, is perhaps
ill-timed and ill-directed: in these years the Duke's power was steadily
declining, and Moleyns had never been among his supporters. On
the contrary, three years later he would seal the warrant for the
arrest of the Duke, while in 1441 it had been his task to read the
articles accusing the Duchess of Gloucester of sorcery and necromancy. Piccolomini's praise, I believe, has simply led astray a number of historians and scholars. There are also tenuous connections
with William Say, Fellow of New College, and Thomas Chaundler,
also Fellow of New College and Bekynton's client;[211] Karl Julius
Holzknecht, in his turn, adds the names of Humphrey's secretaries
John Homme, Richard Wyot, John Everton, Henry Abingdon, "all
of whom copied books and found reward in his employ".[212]

Humphrey's relations with some important ecclesiastics of his time,
on the other hand, suggest greater closeness and the existence of
intellectual exchanges, and it is in these cases that the hypothesis of
an intellectual circle finds a more solid basis. One of these men is
Thomas Bekynton, yet again a fellow of New College, Oxford—it
seems possible that the Duke had special ties with this college.[213] In

---

[209] *Epistolae Academicae Oxonienses*, ed. by H. Anstey, Oxford: Clarendon Press, 1898,
vol. 1, pp. 281–2.

[210] "Who has welcomed humanist studies in your kingdom with great attention,
and reveres poets and orators". *Der Briefwechsel des Eneas Silvius Piccolomini*, ed. by
R. Wolkan, Wien: Alfred Holder, 1909, p. 325.

[211] J.B. Trapp, "The Humanist Book", in *The Cambridge History of the Book in Britain,
vol. 3: 1400–1557*, ed. by L. Hellinga and J.B. Trapp, Cambridge: Cambridge
University Press, 1999: 285–315, p. 296. Trapp also adds that "the connection with
Humfrey of a group associated with Balliol is, however, less close".

[212] Holzknecht, p. 151.

[213] Jeremy Catto notes that in the 1420s there were two distinguished lawyers
from New College in Duke Humphrey's service: dr John Fyton, who had been at
Pisa and Constance, and dr Thomas Bekynton, "a future intimate royal adviser"
("Masters, Patrons and the Careers of Graduates in Fifteenth-Century England",
p. 59). He adds: "These doctors of law were in no way beholden to their princely
employers, since they had other business to pursue. They were independent experts

1420, after resigning the fellowship, Bekynton entered Humphrey's service, and became the Duke's chancellor in 1423. He would later become Lord Privy Seal, and then Bishop of Bath and Wells.[214] Bekynton corresponded with learned men in England and Rome, such as Flavio Biondo, and knew some of Petrarch's works, as is shown in his treatise *De jure regum Anglorum ad regnum Francie*, written between 1443 and 1465.[215] The treatise, which includes a collection of texts (among which is Petrarch's *Bucolicum carmen*), was meant as a defence of Henry VI's pretences over the French territories. The insertion of Petrarch's text in particular was admired by contemporary Italian humanists as a good propaganda weapon, as shown by Francesco Piendibeni da Montepulciano's comment:

> Hec egloga nominatur conflictatio cuius materia est bellum Edwardi regis Anglorum et Iohannis regis Ffrancorum, anno domini M°CCC° quadragesimo sexto, qui sub istis nominibus introducuntur, scilicet Pan et Articus. Pan grecum vocabulum est a *pan* quod est totum vel Pan deo pastorum, nam ipse est pastor super pastores, scilicet rex Ffrancorum sic nominatus pereminet enim ceteris regibus. Articus Anglorum rex est, ab Artico stella septemtrionali sub qua est Anglia, vel ab Arturo Troiano origine sue rege.[216]

The use of classical, medieval and humanist texts for political propaganda is generally taken as a typically humanist trait, and may remind us of a practice begun by Duke Humphrey in some of his

---

who could be called on from time to time when their professional advice and expertise was required" (p. 59).

[214] David Wallace supposes that Bekynton might have brought to his seat of Bath and Wells a copy of Serravalle's commentary on Dante's *Divina Commedia*. See his "Dante in Somerset: Ghosts, Historiography, Periodization", in *New Medieval Literatures 3*, ed. by D. Lawton, W. Scase and R. Copeland, Oxford: Oxford University Press, 1999: 9–38.

[215] Nicholas Mann, "La prima fortuna del Petrarca in Inghilterra", p. 283. Mann refers in particular to a manuscript of Petrarch's *Bucolicum Carmen*, now Oxford, New College, 269.

[216] "This eclogue consists of a conflict; its subject matter is the war between Edward, King of England, and John, King of France, in 1346. They are introduced under these names, Pan and Articus. Pan derives from the Greek word *pan* which means either "everything" or Pan the god of shepherds, since he himself is a shepherd above any other, so the King of France who is thus named is eminent above all other kings. Articus is the King of England, deriving from the northern star Articus under which is England, or from Arthur its king, of Trojan origin". These lines are to be found in a manuscript of Bekynton's work, London, British Library, Cotton Tiberius B. XII, f. 58r, and have been transcribed by Nicholas Mann in his "Dal moralista al poeta: appunti per la fortuna del Petrarca in Inghilterra", p. 67.

controversies with the King's Council. During his years as Duke Humphrey's chancellor, Bekynton obviously had access to his library, and made good use of this opportunity, since he used the Duke's manuscripts to compile his own works. Thus we find letters related to Decembrio's translation of Plato in Bekynton's formulary, letters that he could access and copy in the Duke's collection.[217] Bekynton might be one of the early English humanists creating a link between the Duke of Gloucester's intellectual activity and the following generation of English humanists, such as John Tiptoft.[218]

More complex and at the same time more tenuous are Humphrey's links with another, less fortunate bishop, Reginald Pecock. He owed Humphrey the early promotions and preferments in his career; his *Repressor* alludes to his residence in the rectory of St Michael in Riola, London, in 1431; Pecock had obtained at that time the mastership of Whittington College, thanks to the Duke's intercession, and here he began to study the controversy between the Lollards and the official church—ironically enough, a study that would in the end result in a trial for heresy. Pecock is one of the most surprising minds of fifteenth-century England: the first to realise that Lollardy could be more effectively fought through persuasion and instruction than through dogma, the first to write in English to defend orthodoxy (thus, incidentally, becoming an easy target for censorship and ecclesiastical persecution), a man who in his writings maintains a precarious balance between scholasticism and a sense of relativity that is typical of the humanist frame of mind.[219] Apart from the protection alluded to above, there is no further proof of a connection, and especially an intellectual one, between Pecock and the Duke of Gloucester, but it is tempting to think that the sense of history that emerges from Pecock's writings found its roots in the approach to history and to classical texts promoted by Duke Humphrey.

---

[217] See David Rundle, "Humanism before the Tudors: On Nobility and the Reception of *studia humanitatis* in Fifteenth-Century England", in *Reassessing Tudor Humanism*, ed. by J. Woolfson, Basingstoke: Palgrave Macmillan, 2002: 22–42, p. 39. The letters copied by Beckington are now to be found in Oxford, Bodleian Library, Ashmole 789, ff. 218–19.

[218] On this point see Roberto Weiss, *Humanism in England During the Fifteenth Century*, Oxford: Blackwell, 1941 (3rd ed. 1967), pp. 72–3.

[219] An interesting discussion on this point can be found in Arthur B. Ferguson, "Reginald Pecock and the Renaissance Sense of History", *Studies in the Renaissance* 13: 1966, 147–65.

The closest relationship certainly was with John Whethamstede, who became abbot of St Albans in 1420, and resigned in 1440, when Humphrey's fortune was beginning to decline, only to be re-elected in 1451, and remain abbot until his death, in 1465. Whethamstede was one of the first Englishmen to come into direct contact with Italian humanism, and there are frequent exchanges between him and Humphrey: books and gifts were given on both sides, together with mutual support. The Palladius translator includes his name in his prologue, when describing the intellectual work going on in Humphrey's household, and though he is not always a reliable witness, there is evidence of a correspondence between Whethamstede and Pietro del Monte;[220] as has already been noted in chapter 4, the abbot gave Gloucester a copy of the *Historia Anglorum* by Matthaeus Parisiensis, together with the last part of the *Chronica Majora 1254–9*,[221] and a miscellaneous collection of philosophical, medical and astrological texts including Albertus Magnus's *De divinatione*, Raymond de Marseille's *Liber cursum planetarum* and Aristotelian or pseudo-Aristotelian texts, Plato's *Phaedo* and *Meno*, and a commentary on Timaeus.[222] The *Annales Monasterii Sancti Albani* also record that a *Cato Glossatus* was prepared for and donated to the Duke, the expense amounting to £6. 13s. 8d.: a very expensive item.[223] Besides, Humphrey's last recorded donation to Oxford includes a copy of Whethamstede's *Granarium*, which also was probably given to the Duke by the abbot. The Duke was equally generous: in the *Annales Monasterii Sancti Albani* for the year 1438 it is shown that he was considered the prime donor and benefactor of the abbey, since he had given it precious ornaments for the altar and church, as well as costly vestments.[224] Besides, Gloucester's influence probably helped the abbot to obtain grants from the crown of several estates, after former grants in the abbey's favour had been annulled. There may be doubts on Whethamstede's achievements as a humanist: commenting upon his

---

[220] Roberto Weiss, "Piero del Monte, John Whethamstede, and the Library of St. Albans Abbey", *English Historical Review* 60: 1945, 399–406.

[221] The manuscript is now London, British Library, Royal 14 C. VII. Described in Sammut, p. 106.

[222] Now Oxford, Corpus Christi College, 243. Described in Sammut, pp. 115–6.

[223] *Annales Monasterii Sancti Albani a Johanne Amundesham, Monacho, ut videtur, conscripti, (A.D. 1421–1440)*, ed. by H.T. Riley, Rolls Series, London: Longman & Trübner, 1870–71, vol. 2, p. 268.

[224] The donation is described in detail in *Annales Monasterii Sancti Albani a Johanne Amundesham, Monacho, ut videtur, conscripti (A.D. 1421–1440)*, vol. 2, pp. 186–90.

friendship with Pietro del Monte, Weiss writes that the latter must have "shuddered with horror at that rude and ungrammatical Latin",[225] but this would not be the first time that the scholar's judgement has been heavily biassed by his appreciation of humanist Latin (and implicit condemnation of medieval Latin). On the other hand, the *Granarium* reads more like a medieval encyclopedia than a humanist historiographical treatise; yet among the sources Whethamstede used there are Petrarch's *De viris illustribus*, Boccaccio's *Genealogia*, and Bruni's translation of Plutarch's lives of Antony and Cato,[226] as well as Coluccio Salutati's *De fato*, a text that immediately precedes the *Declamatio Lucretiae* in the manuscript of Salutati's works belonging to the Duke.[227] Once again we see many of the contradictions inherent in the first generation of English humanists, and the fundamental continuity they preserved with the medieval cultural inheritance. Humphrey and Whethamstede shared an intense love of learning and repeated efforts to collect a library (in the case of Whethamstede, the library of St Albans) that would reflect not only the medieval world of learning from which they came, but also the new impulse offered by humanism. It is possible they helped each other in their activity as book collectors; they shared an interest in Plutarch's *Lives*;[228] they both patronised the same poet, since at the abbot's request John Lydgate translated into English the life of St Alban. Evidence of Whethamstede having access to Humphrey's library is provided not only by his *Granarium*, but also by another work, the *Palearium*, in which there are allusions to Dante's *Divina Commedia* and to Serravalle's commentary on the same work: once again, there is little doubt that the abbot consulted the manuscripts in the Duke's possession. In the *Manipularium*, Whethamstede intriguingly alludes to Dante's *Monarchia*: and this, the first English allusion to this text, opens interesting possibilities on other manuscripts either Humphrey or Whethamstede might have possessed.[229]

---

[225] Weiss, "Piero del Monte, John Whethamstede, and the Library of St. Albans Abbey", p. 401.

[226] On this point see E.F. Jacob, "*Florida Verborum Venustas*. Some Early Examples of Euphuism in England", *Bulletin of the John Rylands Library* 17: 1933, 264–90, p. 281.

[227] Manchester, Chetham's Library, Mun. A.3.131 (27929). See Mortimer, p. 190.

[228] In 1437 Whethamstede received from Pietro del Monte a collection of the *Lives* translated into Latin by various humanists. See Weiss, "Pietro del Monte, John Whethamstede, and the Library of St. Albans Abbey", pp. 400–01.

[229] Weiss, "Per la conoscenza di Dante in Inghilterra nel quattrocento", p. 359.

The friendship between Duke Humphrey of Gloucester and Abbot John Whethamstede provides a fitting conclusion to this work, as well as an excellent symbol of early humanism in England. Unlike later generations of humanists, these two did not and could not consider intellectual life a profession; yet they devoted much energy and enthusiasm to it, not only for themselves, but for a number of poets and writers they patronised, and, in the case of Duke Humphrey, for the students of the University of Oxford. In a recent article, David Rundle is rather sceptic on the existence of a scholarly circle like the one evoked by the Palladius translator in his prologue: "what, it might be questioned, is a circle if not a figure nought?".[230] The reconstruction of Humphrey's activity, in particular as concerns his collection of books, goes to show that he was far from the passive centre, the unaware target of scholarly appeals; his efforts, though occasionally misguided or doomed to failure, tended towards the construction of a centre of learning that could first serve his own political purposes, and then contribute to the intellectual development of a nation. Much of the ideological purpose of his work has been made obscure to us by his sudden political decline and his spectacular fall; yet the works he commissioned in the 1430s demonstrate that his intellectual activity was meant to give active support to his difficult role in English public life. It is for this reason that he intervened so often and sometimes so tactlessly in the composition of the works, as we have seen in the case of Lydgate's *Fall of Princes*; far from being interested solely in the magnificent image his patronage created, he also wanted this patronage to propose a new, more sophisticated and intellectually aware version of propaganda. Humphrey meant to propose an image of himself as the true, spiritual inheritor of Henry V's legacy; especially during the minority of Henry VI, he attempted to gain the favour of the Parliament and the middle classes, and to win the hostility of the King's Council, by evoking the memory of a king to whom he had been especially near. Some of the young King's or of the Council's decisions, such as the liberation of Charles d'Orléans, were felt by the Duke as actual betrayals of his brother's wishes; at the same time he used, or attempted to use, the image of the victorious King in order to impose his own, often not very palatable policies.

---

[230] Rundle, "Humanism before the Tudors", p. 29.

In later years, when his declining fortunes made him realise the substantial failure of his project, his attention turned to less personal matters: thus his patronage and very generous gifts to the University of Oxford, however they may have been timed to coincide with critical moments in the Duke's public life, also reveal an interest in the development of a public community of learning, in the enhancement of what was to become the symbol of academic teaching and scholarly research in England and all over the world; almost forcing the University to provide itself with adequate room in order to house the collection he had donated, Humphrey had at least the merit of notable foresight. At the same time, his commissions of books seem to indicate that he was also interested in the question of the affirmation of the vernacular; what his brother had begun to do to favour the ascendance of English as the language of chancery and public life, he imitated by turning his efforts towards what he could do best, a library. One of the effects of this multi-faceted activity is the formation of an intellectual circle, changeable and sometimes unstable as all intellectual circles, composed of English poets and Italian humanists, attention-seeking monks and protection-seeking professionals, aspiring courtiers, noblemen and ecclesiastics. They were not all at Humphrey's service, and they did not reside necessarily in Greenwich; but at one point or another they all established contact with the duke, exchanged manuscripts, made use of his library. Different levels of intimacy are shown by a different tone or a different mode of address in the dedications, or in the correspondence, and often we see a conventional or stereotyped formula put to different uses. The various attempts at defining and describing this circle and its components have not perhaps taken into sufficient account variations and differences in relations that could be friendly, professional, or sometimes servile. We can also impute to the Duke a lack of critical judgement, perhaps a presumptuous assurance that did not allow him to see the shortcomings of many of the poets and scholars he patronised. Yet it is among his great merits to have encouraged learning in a manner that did not only open a way for Italian humanism into England, but also helped English intellectual life to find a new, autonomous identity.

Towards the end of the fourteenth century Leonardo Bruni professed a great admiration for Thomas of England, an Augustinian monk who had been to Florence to purchase manuscripts, and had lectured there; with a rather barbed compliment, he said that the

English scholar could admire and appreciate the new Italian humanism *quantum illa natio capit*, as much as one of his nation was able to
understand it.[231] In spite of anything that has been written to the
contrary, it may be argued that Humphrey taught his nation not
only a greater understanding of intellectual movements coming from
abroad, but also a greater appreciation of the English nation's own
intellectual resources.

---

[231] Quoted in Lewis Einstein, *The Italian Renaissance in England. Studies*, New York:
The Columbia University Press, 1902, p. 5.

BIBLIOGRAPHY

Manuscripts

Bruxelles, Bibliothèque Royale
9627-8 (volume including *La quête du saint Graal* and *La mort au roi Artus*)

Cambridge, Corpus Christi College
285 (Tito Livio Frulovisi's *Vita Henrici Quinti*)

Cambridge, Gonville and Caius
183/216 (Seneca's *Epistulae*)

Cambridge, King's College
27 (St Athanasius's *Orationes contra Arianos*)

Cambridge, Pembroke College
243 (*Knyghthode and Bataile*)

Cambridge, St John's College
C.10 (Tito Livio Frulovisi's Latin comedies)
H.5 (Stephen Scrope's translation of Christine de Pizan's *Epistre Othea*)

Cambridge University Library
Ee.2.17 (Jean de Vignay's version of Vegetius's *De re militari*)
Ee.3.61 (f. 108v, an astronomical table sometime attributed to Duke Humphrey)
Gg.4.27 (collection of Chaucer's works)
Gg.i.34(i) (the Scipio-Caesar controversy)

Florence, Biblioteca Riccardiana
827 (Pier Candido Decembrio's correspondence)

Glasgow, University Library
Hunter 104 (Middle English translation of Palladius's *De Agricultura*)

Gloucester, Cathedral Library
21 (astrological treatise by Roger Bolingbroke)

Leiden, Bibliotheek der Rijksuniversiteit
Or. 4726 (Hebrew psalter)

London, British Library
Additional A.369 (abridged version of the Middle English translation of Palladius's
  De Agricultura)
Additional 11814 (Middle English translation of Claudian's *De Consulatu Stilichonis*)
Additional 34360 (collection of Lydgate's poems)
Additional 48031 (John Lydgate's *Serpent of Division*)
Arundel 66 (medical treatise sometime attributed to Caerleon)
Ashmole 66 (geomancy written for Duke Humphrey)

Cotton Claudius A.VIII (ff. 195–8, the details of the commission of Duke Humphrey's tomb)
Cotton Nero E.V (miscellaneous volume including the Acts of the Council of Constance)
Cotton Tiberius B.XII (collection of Thomas Bekynton's works)
Harley 33 (William of Ockham's *Dialogus inter magistrum et discipulum de heresi et hereticis*)
Harley 2251 (collection of Lydgate's poems)
Harley 2278 (presentation copy of John Lydgate's *Life of St Edmund and St Fremund*)
Harley 4011 (collection of Lydgate's poems)
Royal 1.e.ix (illuminated Bible possibly belonging to Henry IV)
Royal 2.b.i (choice of Latin psalms)
Royal 5.f.ii (St Athanasius's theological treatises)
Royal 14.c.vii (Matthaeus Parisiensis's *Historia Anglorum*)
Royal 16.g.iv (*Chronique de France ou de Saint Denis*)
Royal 19.a.xx (*Le livre de linformacion de princes*)
Royal 19.c.iv (*Le Songe du Vergier*)
Sloane 4 (ff. 63r–98v, Gilbert Kymer's *Dietarium*)
Sloane 248 (Latin version of an Arabic *Antidotarium*)
Sloane 407 (set of planetary tables attributed to John Randolf, ff. 223–6)
Yates Thompson 14 (Latin psalter)

LONDON, COLLEGE OF ARMS
Arundel 12 (Tito Livio Frulovisi's *Vita Henrici Quinti*)

LONDON, SION COLLEGE
(olim) Arc. L40.2/L.28 (collection of bestiaries, now in private hands)

MANCHESTER, CHETHAM'S LIBRARY
Mun. A.3.131 (27929) (Coluccio Salutati's *Declamatio Lucretiae*)

MILAN, BIBLIOTECA AMBROSIANA
I 235 inf. (correspondence of Pier Candido Decembrio)
R 88 sup. (ff. 172v.173r, list of Latin volumes compiled by Pier Candido Decembrio)

OXFORD, BODLEIAN LIBRARY
Ashmole 59 (collection of Lygate's poems)
Ashmole 789 (ff. 218–9, Bekynton's formulary)
Auct. F. inf. 1.1 (Valerius Maximus's *De dictis et factis memorabilibus*)
Bodley 294 (collection of John Gower's works)
Duke Humfrey b.1 (John Capgrave's *In Exodum*)
Duke Humfrey d.2 (Middle-English translation of Palladius's *De Agricultura*)
Hatton 36 (S.C. 4082) (Albucasis's *Antidotarium*)
Lat. Misc. d. 34 (Antonio Beccaria's version of Giovanni Boccaccio's *Corbaccio*)

OXFORD, CORPUS CHRISTI COLLEGE
243 (collection of astrological, medical and philosophical texts)

OXFORD, NEW COLLEGE
269 (Francesco Petrarca's *Bucolicum Carmen*)

OXFORD, ORIEL COLLEGE
32 (John Capgrave's *Super Genesim*)

Paris, Bibliothèque Mazarine
1729 (Jean du Vignay's version of Jacopo da Varazze's *Legenda Aurea*)

Paris, Bibliothèque Nationale
franç. 2 (Pierre Le Manguer's *La Bible Historiée ou Les Histoires écolâtres*)
franç. 12421 (Laurent de Premierfait's version of Giovanni Boccaccio's *Decameron*)
franç. 12583 (*Le roman de Renart*)
lat. 7805 (collection *Duodecim Panegyrici Latini*)
lat. 10209 (Francesco Petrarca's *De remediis utriusque fortunae* and Vergerio's *Vita Petrarce*)

Paris, Bibliothèque de Sainte Geneviève
franç. 777 (Pierre Bersuire's translation of Livy's *Histories*)

Reims, Bibliothèque Municipale
570 (Frère Laurent's *La somme du roi Philippe ou Somme des vices et des vertus*)

San Marino, Huntington Library
HM 268 (John Lydgate's *Fall of Princes*)

Seville, Biblioteca Colombina
7.2.23 (ff. 62r–84r, Tito Livio Frulovisi's *Hunfroidos*)

Vatican City, Biblioteca Apostolica Vaticana
Urbinate lat. 694 (Coluccio Salutati's *De laboribus Herculis*)
Vatic. Lat. 10669 (Pier Candido Decembrio's translation of Plato's *Republic*)

Primary sources

Anecdota Oxoniensia. Index Britanniae Scriptorum, Quos ex variis bibliothecis non parvo labore collegit Ioannes Balaeus, cum aliis, ed. by R.L. Poole and M. Bateson, Oxford: Clarendon Press, 1902.
Annales Monasterii Sancti Albani a Johanne Amundesham, Monacho, ut videtur, conscripti (A.D. 1421–1440), ed. by H.T. Riley, Rolls Series, London: Longman & Trübner, 1870–71.
The Brut or the Chronicles of England, ed. by F.W.D. Brie, Early English Text Society, London: Kegan Paul, Trench, Trübner, 1906–8.
Chronicles of London, ed. by C.L. Kingsford, Oxford: Clarendon Press, 1905.
The Court of Sapience, ed. by E.R. Harvey, Toronto Medieval Texts and Translations, Toronto: Toronto University Press, 1984.
The Earliest English Translation of Vegetius' De Re Militari, ed. from Oxford MS Bodl. Douce 291, ed. by G. Lester, Middle English Texts, Heidelberg: Carl Winter—Universitätsverlag, 1988.
An English Chronicle of the Reigns of Richard II, Henry IV, Henry V, and Henry VI, ed. by J.S. Davies, Camden Society, London: Nichols, 1856.
The Epistle of Othea. Translated from the French Text of Christine de Pisan by Stephen Scrope, ed. by C.F. Bühler, Early English Text Society, London: Oxford University Press, 1970.
Epistolae Academicae Oxonienses, ed. by H. Anstey, Oxford: Clarendon Press, 1898.
Foedera, conventiones, literae, et cujuscumque generis acta publica, inter reges Angliae, et alios quosvis imperatores, reges, pontifices, principes, vel communitates, ab ineunte saeculo duodecimo, viz. ab Anno 1101, ad nostra usque tempora, habita aut tractata, ed. by T. Rymer, Hagae comitis: Apud Joannem Neaulme, 1741.

Hall's Chronicle; Containing the History of England, During the Reign of Henry the Fourth, and the Succeeding Monarchs, to the End of the Reign of Henry the Eighth, ed. by H. Ellis, London: Rivington et al., 1809.

The Historical Collections of a Citizen of London in the Fifteenth Century, ed. by J. Gairdner, Camden Society, London: Nichols, 1876.

Historical Poems of the XIVth and XVth Centuries, ed. by R.H. Robbins, New York: Columbia University Press, 1959.

Knyghthode and Bataile. A XVth Century Verse Paraphrase of Flavius Vegetius Renatus' Treatise "De Re Militari", ed. by R. Dyboski and Z.M. Arend, Early English Text Society, London: Oxford University Press, 1936.

Letters and Papers Illustrative of the Wars of the English in France during the Reign of Henry the Sixth, King of England, ed. by J. Stevenson, Rolls Series, London: Longman et al., 1864.

Letters of Queen Margaret of Anjou and Bishop Beckington and others. Written in the Reigns of Henry V and Henry VI, ed. by C. Monro, Camden Society, London: Nichols, 1863.

The Libelle of Englyshe Polycye. A Poem on the Use of Sea-Power, 1436, ed. by G. Warner, Oxford: Clarendon Press, 1926.

Liber Niger Scaccarii, ed. by T. Hearne, Oxonii: E Theatro Sheldoniano, 1728.

The Middle-English Translation of Palladius De Re Rustica, ed. by M. Liddell, Berlin: E. Ebering, 1896.

The Mirror for Magistrates. Edited from Original Texts in the Huntington Library, ed. by L.B. Campbell, Cambridge: Cambridge University Press, 1938.

Munimenta Academica, or Documents Illustrative of Academical Life and Studies at Oxford, ed. by H. Anstey, Rolls Series, London: Longmans, Green, Reader and Dyer, 1868.

Palladius on Husbondrie, ed. by B. Lodge, Early English Text Society, London: Trübner, 1873.

Paston Letters and Papers of the Fifteenth Century, ed. by N. Davis, Oxford: Clarendon Press, 1976.

Poems of Cupid, God of Love. Christine de Pizan's Epistre au dieu d'Amours and Dit de la Rose. Thomas Hoccleve's The Letter of Cupid, ed. by T.S. Fenster and M. Carpenter Erler, Leiden: Brill, 1990.

Political Poems and Songs Relating to English History, Composed during the Period from the Accession of Edw. III to the of Ric. III, ed. by T. Wright, Rolls Series, London: Longman, Green, Longman and Roberts, 1859–61.

Three Fifteenth-Century Chronicles, ed. by J. Gairdner, Camden Society, London: Nichols, 1880.

Three Prose Versions of the Secreta Secretorum, ed. by R. Steele, Early English Text Society, London: Kegan Paul, Trench, Trübner, 1898.

[Ashby, George], *George Ashby's Poems Edited from Two 15th Century Mss. at Cambridge*, ed. by M. Bateson, Early English Text Society, London: Kegan Paul, 1899.

Bale, John, *Scriptorum Illustrium maioris Brytanniae, quam nunc Angliam & Scotiam uocant: Catalogus*, Basileae: apud Ioannem Oporinum, 1557.

Bracciolini, Poggio, *Opera Omnia*, ed. by R. Fubini, Torino: Bottega d'Erasmo, 1969.

[Bracciolini, Poggio], *Poggio Bracciolini. Lettere. I: Lettere a Niccolò Niccoli*, ed. by H. Harth, Istituto Nazionale di Studi sul Rinascimento, Firenze: Olschki, 1984.

[Bruni, Leonardo], *Leonardi Bruni Arretini Epistularum Libri VIII*, ed. by L. Mehus, Florentiae: Ex Typographia Bernardi Paperinii, 1741.

[Bruni, Leonardo], *Leonardo Bruni Aretino. Humanistisch-philosophische Schriften mit einer Chronologie seiner Werke und Briefe*, ed. by H. Baron, Leipzig: Teubner, 1928.

[Bruni, Leonardo], *Opere letterarie e politiche di Leonardo Bruni*, ed. by P. Viti, Torino: Unione tipografico-editrice torinese, 1996.

[Capgrave, John], *The Chronicle of England by John Capgrave*, ed. by F.C. Hingeston, Rolls Series, London: Her Majesty's Stationery Office, 1858.

[Capgrave, John], *Johannis Capgrave Liber de Illustribus Henricis*, ed. by F.C. Hingeston, Rolls Series, London: Longman, Brown, Green, Longmans, and Roberts, 1858.

[Capgrave, John], *John Capgrave's Abbreuiacioun of Cronicles*, ed. by P.J. Lucas, Early English Text Society, Oxford: Oxford University Press, 1983.

Chaucer, Geoffrey, *A Treatise on the Astrolabe*, in *The Riverside Chaucer*, ed. by L.D. Benson, Oxford: Oxford University Press, 1987: 661–83.

[Drayton, Michael], *Englands Heroicall Epistles*, in *The Works of Michael Drayton, volume II*, ed. by J.W. Hebel, Oxford: Blackwell, 1961.

[Drayton, Michael], *The Miseries of Queene Margarite*, in *The Works of Michael Drayton, volume III*, ed. by J.W. Hebel, Oxford: Blackwell, 1961.

[Fabyann, Robert] *The New Chronicles of England and France. In Two Parts. By Robert Fabyann. Named by Himself the Concordance of Histories*, ed. by H. Ellis, London: Rivington et al., 1811.

Foxe, John, *Acts and Monuments*, ed. by G. Townsend, New York: AMS Press, 1965.

[Frulovisi, Tito Livio], *Titi Livii Forojuliensis Vita Henrici Quinti Regis Angliae*, ed. by T. Hearne, Oxonii: E Theatro Sheldoniano, 1716.

[Frulovisi, Tito Livio], *Opera Hactenus Inedita T. Livii de Frulovisiis de Ferraria*, ed. by C.W. Previté-Orton, Cambridge: Cantabrigiae typis Academiae, 1932.

[Grafton, Richard], *Grafton's Chronicle; or History of England*, London: Johnson, Rivington, et al., 1809.

[Henry of Lancaster], *Le Livre des Seyntz Medicines. The Unpublished Devotional Treatise of Henry of Lancaster*, ed. by E.J. Arnould, Anglo-Norman Text Society, Oxford: Blackwell, 1940.

[Hoccleve, Thomas], *Hoccleve's Works. The Minor Poems*, ed. by F.J. Furnivall and I. Gollancz, Early English Text Society, London: Oxford University Press, 1937 (rev. ed. 1970).

[Hoccleve, Thomas], *Selections from Hoccleve*, ed. by M.C. Seymour, Oxford: Clarendon Press, 1981.

Hoccleve, Thomas, *The Regement of Princes*, ed. by C.R. Blyth, Kalamazoo: Medieval Institute Publications, 1999.

[Hoccleve, Thomas], *Thomas Hoccleve's Complaint and Dialogue*, ed. by J.A.W. Burrow, Early English Text Society, Oxford: Oxford University Press, 1999.

Holinshed, Raphaell, *The Third Volume of Chronicles*, London: Johnson et al., 1808.

James I of Scotland, *The Kingis Quair*, ed. by J. Norton-Smith, Medieval and Renaissance Texts, Leiden: Brill, 1971.

[Leland, John], *Commentarii de Scriptoribus britannicis, auctore Joanne Lelando Londinate*, ed. by A. Hall, Oxonii: E Theatro Sheldoniano, 1709.

Lydgate, John, *S. Edmund und Fremund*, in *Altenglische Legenden. Neue Folge mit Einleitung und Anmerkungen*, ed. by C. Horstmann. Heilbronn: Henninger, 1881: 376–445.

[Lydgate, John], *Lydgate and Burgh's Secrets of Old Philosoffres*, ed. by R. Steele, Early English Text Society, London: Kegan Paul, Trench, Trübner, 1894.

[Lydgate, John], *Lydgate's Reson and Sensuallyte*, ed. by E. Sieper, Early English Text Society, London: Kegan Paul, Trench, Trübner, 1901–3.

[Lydgate, John], *Lydgate's Troy Book*, ed. by H. Bergen, Early English Text Society, London: Kegan Paul, Trench, Trübner, 1906.

[Lydgate, John], *The Serpent of Division by John Lydgate the Monk of Bury*, ed. by H.N. MacCracken, London: Oxford University Press, 1911.

Lydgate, John, *Minor Poems. Vol. 1: Religious Poems. Vol. 2: Secular Poems*, ed. by H.N. MacCracken, Early English Text Society, Oxford: Oxford University Press, 1934.

[Lydgate, John], *Lydgate's Fall of Princes*, ed. by H. Bergen, Early English Text Society, Oxford: Oxford University Press, 1923–27.

[Lydgate, John], *The Gouernaunce of Kynges and Prynces. The Pynson Edition of 1511. A Translation in Verse by John Lydgate and an Anonymous Poet from the Latin of the Secretum Secretorum*, ed. by D.T. Starnes, Gainesville: Scholars' Facsimiles and Reprints, 1957.

Lydgate, John, *Poems*, ed. by J. Norton-Smith, Oxford: Clarendon Press, 1966.

Middleton, Christopher, *The Legend of Humphrey Duke of Glocester*, London: Printed by E.A. for Nicholas Ling, 1600.

More, Thomas, *A Dialogue Concerning Heresies*, The Complete Works of St. Thomas More, ed. by T.M.C. Lawler, G. Marc'Hadour, et al., New Haven and London: Yale University Press, 1981.

[Norton, Thomas], *Thomas Norton's Ordinal of Alchemy*, ed. by J. Reidy, Early English Text Society, London: Oxford University Press, 1975.

[Piccolomini, Aeneas Silvius], *Der Briefwechsel des Eneas Silvius Piccolomini*, ed. by R. Wolkan, Wien: Alfred Holder, 1909.

[Piccolomini, Aeneas Silvius] *Selected Letters of Aeneas Silvius Piccolomini*, ed. by A.R. Baca, Northridge: San Fernando Valley State College, 1969.

[Piccolomini, Aeneas Silvius], *Pii II Commentarii rerum memorabilium que temporis suis contigerunt*, ed. by A. van Heck, Città del Vaticano: Biblioteca Apostolica Vaticana, 1984.

[Piccolomini, Aeneas Silvius], *Enee Silvii Piccolomine postea Pii PP.II De viris illustribus*, ed. by A. van Heck, Città del Vaticano: Biblioteca Apostolica Vaticana, 1991.

Russell, John, *John Russell's Boke of Nurture*, in *The Babees Book, Aristotle's ABC, Urbanitatis, Stans Puer ad Mensam, The Lytille Childrenes Lytil Boke, The Bokes of Nurture of Hugh Rhodes and John Russell, Wynkyn de Worde's Boke of Kervynge, The Booke of Demeanor, The Boke of Curtasye, Seager's Schoole of Vertue, &c. &c. with some French & Latin Poems on Like Subjetcs, and some Forewords on Education in Early England*, ed. by F.J. Furnivall. London: Trübner, 1868: 115–239.

[Serravalle, Giovanni Bertoldi da], *Fratris Iohannis de Serravalle ord. min. Episcopi et Principis Firmani Translatio et Comentum totius libri Dantis Aldigherii cum textu italico Fratris Bartholomaei a Colle eiusdem ordinis*, ed. by M. da Civezza and T. Domenichelli, Prati: Ex Officina Libraria Giachetti, 1891.

Scogan, Henry, "A Moral Balade", in *Chaucerian and Other Pieces*, ed. by W.W. Skeat. Oxford: Clarendon Press, 1897: 237–44.

[Upton, Nicholas], *Nicolai Vptoni De Studio Militari, Libri quatuor. Johan de Badoaureo, Tractatus de armis. Henrici Spelmanni Aspilogia*, ed. by E. Bysshe, Londinii: Typis Rogeri Norton, 1654.

[Vergil, Polydore] *Three Books of Polydore Vergil's English History, Comprising the Reigns of Henry VI, Edward IV, and Richard III*, ed. by H. Ellis, Camden Society, London: AMS Press, 1844.

Studies

Duke Humfrey and English Humanism in the Fifteenth Century. Catalogue of an Exhibition Held in the Bodleian Library Oxford, Oxford: Bodleian Library, 1970.

Duke Humfrey's Library and the Divinity School 1488–1988. An Exhibition at the Bodleian Library June–August 1988, Oxford: Bodleian Library, 1988.

Adamson, J.W., *The Illiterate Anglo-Saxon and Other Essays on Education, Medieval and Modern*, Cambridge: Cambridge University Press, 1946.

Ambrosoli, Mario, *The Wild and the Sown. Botany and Agriculture in Western Europe: 1350–1850*, transl. by M. McCann Salvatorelli, Cambridge: Cambridge University Press, 1997 (original edition *Scienziati, contadini e proprietari. Botanica e agricoltura nel'Europa occidentale 1350–1850*, Torino: Einaudi, 1992).

Arnould, E.J., "Henry of Lancaster and his *Livre des seintez medicines*", *Bulletin of the John Rylands Library* 21: 1937, 352–86.

———, *Étude sur le Livre des saintes médecines du duc Henry de Lancastre*, Paris: Didier, 1948.

Barber, M.J., "The Books and Patronage of a Fifteenth-Century Prince", *The Book Collector* 12: 1963, 308–15.

Barker-Benfield, B., "Alfonso Sammut, *Unfredo duca di Gloucester e gli umanisti italiani*", *The Library* 6th series, vol. 4: 1982, 191–94.

Barratt, Alexandra, "Dame Eleanor Hull: A Fifteenth-century Translator", in *The Medieval Translator: The Theory and Practice of Translation in the Middle Ages*, ed. by R. Ellis, Cambridge: D.S. Brewer, 1989: 87–101.

Baswell, Christopher, "*Troy Book*: How Lydgate Translates Chaucer into Latin", in *Translation Theory and Practice in the Middle Ages*, ed. by J. Beer, Kalamazoo: Western Michigan University, 1997: 215–37.

Bell, H.E., "The Price of Books in Medieval England", *The Library* 4th series, 17: 1937, 312–32.

Bennett, H.S., *The Pastons and their England. Studies in an Age of Transition*, Cambridge: Cambridge University Press, 1932.

——, *Chaucer and the Fifteenth Century*, Oxford: Clarendon Press, 1947.

——, "The Production and Dissemination of Vernacular Manuscripts in the Fifteenth Century", *The Library* 5th series, 1: 1947, 167–78.

——, *Six Medieval Men and Women*, Cambridge: Cambridge University Press, 1955.

Benson, C. David, *The History of Troy in Middle English Literature: Guido Delle Colonne's Historia Destructionis Troiae in Medieval England*, Woodbridge: D.S. Brewer, 1980.

Berndt, Rolf, "The Period of the Final Decline of French in Medieval England (Fourteenth and Early Fifteenth Centuries)", *Zeitschrift für Anglistik und Amerikanistik* 20: 1972, 341–69.

Blackwell, C.W.T., "Humanism and Politics in English Royal Biography: The Use of Cicero, Plutarch and Sallust in the *Vita Henrici Quinti* (1438) by Titus Livius de Frulovisi and the *Vita Henrici Septimi* (1500–1503) by Bernard André", in *Acta Conventus Neo-Latini Sanctandreani: Proceedings of the Fifth International Congress of Neo-Latin Studies*, ed. by I.D. McFarlane, Binghamton: Medieval & Renaissance Texts & Studies, 1986: 431–40.

Blake, N.F., "The Fifteenth Century Reconsidered", *Neuphilologische Mitteilungen* 71: 1970, 146–57.

Boffey, Julia, "English Dream Poems of the Fifteenth Century and their French Connections", in *Literary Aspects of Courtly Culture*, ed. by D. Maddox and S. Sturm-Maddox, Cambridge: D.S. Brewer, 1994: 113–21.

Borsa, Mario, "P.C. Decembrio e l'umanesimo in Lombardia", *Archivio Storico Lombardo* 20: 1893, 5–75, 358–441.

——, "Correspondence of Humphrey Duke of Gloucester and Pier Candido Decembrio", *English Historical Review* 19: 1904, 509–26.

Breeze, Andrew, "Sir John Paston, Lydgate, and *The Lybelle of Englyshe Polycye*", *Notes and Queries* 48: 2001, 230–1.

Brewer, Derek, *English Gothic Literature*, London: Macmillan, 1983.

Brie, Friedrich, "Mittelalter und Antike bei Lydgate", *Englische Studien* 64: 1929, 261–301.

Briggs, Charles F., *Giles of Rome's De Regimine Principum. Reading and Writing Politics at Court and University, c. 1275–c. 1525*, Cambridge: Cambridge University Press, 1999.

Brusendorff, Aage, *The Chaucer Tradition*, London: Oxford University Press, 1925.

Bullough, Vern L., "Duke Humphrey and His Medical Collections", *Renaissance News* 14: 1961, 87–91.

Burrow, John A., "Hoccleve's *Series*: Experience and Books", in *Fifteenth-Century Studies: Recent Essays*, ed. by R.F. Yeager, Hamden, Conn.: Archon Books, 1984: 259–73.

——, *The Ages of Man. A Study in Medieval Writing and Thought*, Oxford: Clarendon Press, 1986.

——, "Autobiographical Poetry in the Middle Ages: The Case of Thomas Hoccleve", in *Middle English Literature: British Academy Gollancz Lectures*, ed. by J.A. Burrow, Oxford: Oxford University Press, 1989: 223–46.

——, *Thomas Hoccleve*, Authors of the Middle Ages, Aldershot: Variorum, 1994.

——, "Thomas Hoccleve: Some Redatings", *Review of English Studies* 46: 1995, 366–72.

——, "'Alterity' and Middle English Literature", *The Review of English Studies* 50: 1999, 483–92.

Bush, Douglas, *The Renaissance and English Humanism*, Toronto: The University of Toront Press, 1939.

Calvino, Italo, "Books of Chivalry—Libros de caballerias", in *Tesoros de España. Ten Centuries of Spanish Books. Catalogue of an Exhibition in the New York Public Library, October 12–December 30, 1985*, New York: The New York Public Library, 1985: 231–2.

Campana, Augusto, "The Origin of the Word 'Humanist'", *Journal of the Warburg and Courtauld Institutes* 9: 1946, 60 73.

Campbell, Lily B., "Humphrey Duke of Gloucester and Elianor Cobham His Wife in the *Mirror for Magistrates*", *The Huntington Library Bulletin* 5: 1934, 119–55.

Carey, Hilary M., "Astrology at the English Court in the Late Middle Ages", in *Astrology, Science and Society: Historical Essays*, ed. by P. Curry, Woodbridge: The Boydell Press, 1987: 41–56.

——, *Courting Disaster. Astrology at the English Court and University in the Later Middle Ages*, London: Macmillan, 1992.

Caspari, Fritz, *Humanism and the Social Order in Tudor England*, Chicago: University of Chicago Press, 1954.

Catto, Jeremy, "Masters, Patrons and the Careers of Graduates in Fifteenth-century England", in *Concepts and Patterns of Service in the Later Middle Ages*, ed. by A. Curry and E. Matthew, Woodbridge: The Boydell Press, 2000: 52–63.

Chance, Jane, "Christine de Pizan as Literary Mother. Woman's Authority and Subjectivity in 'The Flower and the Leafe' and 'The Assembly of Ladies'", in *The City of Scholars: New Approaches to Christine de Pizan*, ed. by M. Zimmermann and D. de Rentiis, Berlin: Walter de Gruyter, 1994: 245–59.

Chrimes, S.B., "The Pretensions of the Duke of Gloucester in 1422", *The English Historical Review* 45: 1930, 101–3.

Coleman, Joyce, "Lay Readers and Hard Latin: How Gower May Have Intended the *Confessio Amantis* to Be Read", *Studies in the Age of Chaucer* 24: 2002, 209–35.

Connolly, Margaret, *John Shirley. Book Production and the Noble Household in Fifteenth-Century England*, Aldershot: Ashgate, 1998.

Cooper, Helen, "Introduction", in *The Long Fifteenth Century. Essays for Douglas Gray*, ed. by H. Cooper and S. Mapstone, Oxford: Clarendon Press, 1997: 1–14.

Copeland, Rita, "Lydgate, Hawes, and the Science of Rhetoric in the Late Middle Ages", *Modern Language Quarterly* 53: 1992, 57–82.

Craster, H.H.E., "Index to Duke Humphrey's Gifts to the Old Library of the University in 1439, 1441, and 1444", *Bodleian Quarterly Record* 1: 1914–16, 131–35.

——, "Duke Humphrey's Dante, Petrarch, and Boccaccio MSS.", *Times Literary Supplement* 13 May: 1920, 303.

Creighton, Mandell, "Some Literary Correspondence of Humphrey, Duke of Gloucester", *English Historical Review* 10: 1895, 99–104.

Cross, Claire, "Oxford and the Tudor State from the Accession of Henry VIII to the Death of Mary", in *The History of the University of Oxford, vol. 3: The Collegiate University*, ed. by J. McConica, Oxford: Clarendon Press, 1987: 117–49.

Davenport, Tony, "Fifteenth-century Complaints and Duke Humphrey's Wives", in *Nation, Court and Culture: New Essays on Fifteenth-Century English Poetry*, ed. by H. Cooney, Dublin: Four Courts Press, 2001: 129–52.

Davies, Martin C., "Friends and Enemies of Poggio: Studies in Quattrocento Humanist Literature", D.Phil., Oxford, 1986.

De la Mare, A.C., "The Return of Petronius to Italy", in *Medieval Learning and Literature. Essays Presented to Richard William Hunt*, ed. by J.J.G. Alexander and M.T. Gibson, Oxford: Clarendon Press, 1976: 220–54.

——, "Duke Humfrey's English Palladius (MS. Duke Humfrey d.2)", *The Bodleian Library Record* 12: 1985, 39–51.

——, "Manuscripts Given to the University of Oxford by Humfrey, Duke of Gloucester", *The Bodleian Library Record* 13: 1988, 30–51, 112–21.

Deanesly, M., "Vernacular Books in England in the Fourteenth and Fifteenth Centuries", *Modern Language Review* 15: 1920, 349–58.

Delany, Sheila, *Impolitic Bodies. Poetry, Saints, and Society in Fifteenth-Century England. The Work of Osbern Bokenham*, New York, Oxford: Oxford University Press, 1998.

Doig, James A., "Propaganda, Public Opinion and the Siege of Calais in 1436", in *Crown, Government and People in the Fifteenth Century*, ed. by R.E. Archer. Stroud: Sutton, 1995: 79–106.

Doyle, A.I., "English Books in and out of Court from Edward III to Henry VII", in *English Court Culture in the Later Middle Ages*, ed. by V.J. Scattergood and J.W. Sherbourne, New York: St Martin's Press, 1983: 163–81.

Doyle, A.I. and M.B. Parkes, "The Production of Copies of the *Canterbury Tales* and the *Confessio Amantis* in the Early Fifteenth Century", in *Medieval Scribes, Manuscripts and Libraries. Essays Presented to N.R. Ker*, ed. by M.B. Parkes and A.G. Watson, London: Scolar Press, 1978: 163–210.

Edwards, A.S.G., "The McGill Fragment of Lydgate's 'Fall of Princes'", *Scriptorium* 28: 1974, 75–7.

——, "The Influence of Lydgate's *Fall of Princes* c. 1440–1559: A Survey", *Medieval Studies* 39: 1977, 424–39.

——, "The Middle English Translation of Claudian's *De Consulatu Stilichonis*", in *Middle English Poetry: Texts and Traditions: Essays in Honour of Derek Pearsall*, ed. by A.J. Minnis, York: York Medieval Press, 2001: 267–78.

—— and Derek Pearsall, eds., *Middle English Prose: Essays on Bibliographical Problems*, New York: Garland, 1981.

—— and Derek Pearsall, "The Manuscripts of the Major English Poetic Texts", in *Book Production and Publishing in Britain 1375–1475*, ed. by J. Griffiths and D. Pearsall, Cambridge: Cambridge University Press, 1989: 257–78.

Einstein, Lewis, *The Italian Renaissance in England. Studies*, New York: The Columbia University Press, 1902.

Everest-Phillips, L.C.Y., "The Patronage of Humphrey, Duke of Gloucester. A Re-evaluation", Ph.D., York, 1983.

Ferguson, Arthur B., "Reginald Pecock and the Renaissance Sense of History", *Studies in the Renaissance* 13: 1966, 147–65.

Fisher, John H., "Chancery and the Emergence of Standard in Written English", *Speculum* 52: 1977, 870–99.

——, "A Language Policy for Lancastrian England", *Publications of the Modern Language Association* 107: 1992, 1168–80.

——, *The Emergence of Standard English*, Lexington: University Press of Kentucky, 1996.

Foffano, Tino, "Charles d'Orléans e un gruppo di umanisti lombardi in Normandia", *Aevum* 41: 1967, 452–73.

Forster, Leonard, *The Poet's Tongues: Multilingualism in Literature. The de Carle Lectures at the University of Otago 1968*, London: Cambridge University Press, 1970.

Fredeman, J.C., "The Life of John Capgrave, O.E.S.A. (1393–1464)", *Augustiniana* 29: 1979, 197–237.

Freeman Sandler, Lucy, "The Illustration of the Psalms in Fourteenth-Century English Manuscripts: Three Psalters of the Bohun Family", in *Reading Texts and Images. Essays on Medieval and Renaissance Art and Patronage*, ed. by B.J. Muir, Exeter: University of Exeter Press, 2002: 123–51.

Fumagalli, Edoardo, "Francesco Paolo Luiso, *Studi su l'epistolario di Leonardo Bruni*", *Aevum* 56: 1982, 343–51.

Getz, F.M., "The Faculty of Medicine before 1500", in *The History of the University of Oxford, vol. 2: Late Medieval Oxford*, ed. by J.J. Catto and R. Evans, Oxford: Clarendon Press, 1992: 373–405.

Gransden, Antonia, *Historical Writing in England, II, c. 1307 to the Early Sixteenth Century*, London: Routledge & Kegan Paul, 1982.

Gray, Douglas, "Humanism and Humanisms in the Literature of Late Medieval England", in *Italy and the English Renaissance*, ed. by S. Rossi and D. Savoia, Milano: Unicopli, 1989: 25–44.

Green, Richard Firth, *Poets and Princepleasers: Literature and the English Court in the Late Middle Ages*, Toronto: University of Toronto Press, 1980.

——, "The *Familia Regis* and the *Familia Cupidinis*", in *English Court Culture in the Later Middle Ages*, ed. by V.J. Scattergood and J.W. Sherborne, London: Duckworth, 1983: 87–108.

Griffiths, Ralph A., "The Trial of Eleanor Cobham: An Episode in the Fall of Duke Humphrey of Gloucester", *Bulletin of the John Rylands Library Manchester* 51: 1968–9, 381–99.

——, *The Reign of King Henry VI*, London: Sutton Publishing, 1981.

——, *King and Country. England and Wales in the Fifteenth Century*, London: The Hambledon Press, 1991.

Grummitt, David, "'One of the mooste pryncipall treasours belongyng to his Realme of Englande': Calais and the Crown, c. 1450–1558", in *The English Experience in France c. 1450–1558. War, Diplomacy and Cultural Exchange*, Aldershot: Ashgate, 2002: 46–62.

Hallmundsson, May Newman, "Chaucer's Circle: Henry Scogan and his Friends", *Medievalia et Humanistica* 10: 1981, 129–39.

Hammond, Eleanor Prescott, "Lydgate and the Duchess of Gloucester", *Anglia* 27: 1904, 381–98.

——, "Two British Museum Manuscripts (Harley 2251 and Adds. 34360). A Contribution to the Bibliography of John Lydgate", *Anglia* 28: 1905, 1–28, 143–44.

——, "A Reproof to Lydgate", *Modern Language Notes* 26: 1911, 74–6.

——, "Poet and Patron in the *Fall of Princes*: Lydgate and Humphrey of Gloucester", *Anglia* 38: 1914, 121–36.

——, "The Nine-syllabled Pentameter Line in some Post-Chaucerian Manuscripts", *Modern Philology* 23: 1925, 129–52.

——, *English Verse between Chaucer and Surrey*, London: Duke University Press, 1927.

——, "Lydgate and Coluccio Salutati", *Modern Philology* 25: 1927–28, 49–57.

Hanawalt, Barbara and David Wallace, eds., *Bodies and Discipline: Intersections of Literature and History in Fifteenth-Century England*, Minneapolis: University of Minnesota Press, 1996.

Harriss, G.L., "Henry Beaufort, 'Cardinal of England'", in *England in the Fifteenth Century: Proceedings of the 1986 Harlaxton Symposium*, ed. by D. Williams Woodbridge: The Boydell Press, 1987: 111–27.

——, *Cardinal Beaufort: A Study of Lancastrian Ascendancy and Decline*, Oxford: Clarendon Press, 1988.

Harriss, Kate, "Patrons, Buyers and Owners: The Evidence for Ownership and the Role of Book Owners in Book Production and the Book Trade", in *Book Production and Publishing in Britain 1375–1475*, ed. by J. Griffiths and D. Pearsall, Cambridge: Cambridge University Press, 1989: 163–99.

Harvey, Margaret, *England, Rome and the Papacy 1417–64. The Study of a Relationship*, Manchester: Manchester University Press, 1993.

Hay, Denys, "England and the Humanities in the Fifteenth Century", in *Renaissance Essays*, London: The Hambledon Press, 1988: 169–231 (reprinted from *Itinerarium Italicum*, ed. by H.A. Oberman and T.A. Brady, Leiden: Brill, 1975, pp. 305–67).

Heath, Peter, *Church and Realm, 1272–1461: Conflict and Collaboration in an Age of Crisis*, Fontana History of England, Glasgow: Fontana Press, 1988.

Hellinga, Lotte and J.B. Trapp, eds., *The Cambridge History of the Book in Britain, vol. 3: 1400–1557*, Cambridge: Cambridge University Press, 1999.

Holmes, George A., "The 'Libel of English Policy'", *English Historical Review* 76: 1961, 193–216.

Holzknecht, Karl Julius, *Literary Patronage in the Middle Ages*, New York: The Collegiate Press, 1923.

Hortis, Attilio, *Studj sulle opere latine del Boccaccio con particolare riguardo alla storia della erudizione nel Medio Evo e alle letterature straniere*, Trieste: Julius Dase, 1879.

Howlett, D.R., "Studies in the Works of John Whethamstede", D.Phil., Oxford, 1975.

——, "The Date and Authorship of the Middle English Verse Translation of Palladius' *De Re Rustica*", *Medium Aevum* 46: 1977, 245–52.

Hudson, Anne, "Some Aspects of Lollard Book Production", in *Schism, Heresy, and Religious Protest. Papers Read at the Tenth Summer Meeting and the Eleventh Winter Meeting of the Ecclesiastical History Society*, ed. by D. Baker, Cambridge: Cambridge University Press, 1972: 147–57.

Hudson, Anne and H.L. Spencer, "Old Author, New Work: The Sermons of MS Longleat 4", *Medium Aevum* 53: 1984, 220–38.

Jacob, E.F., "*Florida Verborum Venustas*. Some Early Examples of Euphuism in England", *Bulletin of the John Rylands Library* 17: 1933, 264–90.

——, *The Fifteenth Century, 1399–1485*, Oxford History of England, Oxford: Clarendon Press, 1961.

James, M.R., "Bury St. Edmunds Manuscripts", *English Historical Review* 41: 1926, 251–60.

Johnston, Andrew James, *Clerks and Courtiers: Chaucer, Late Middle English Literature and the State Formation Process*, Heidelberg: Universitätsverlag C. Winter, 2001.

Jones, William R., "Political Uses of Sorcery in Medieval Europe", *The Historian* 34: 1972, 670–87.

Kantorowicz, Ernst H., *The King's Two Bodies: A Study in Medieval Political Theology*, Princeton: Princeton University Press, 1957.

Keiser, George R., "Serving the Needs of Readers: Textual Division in Some Late-Medieval English Texts", in *New Science out of Old Books. Studies in Manuscripts and Early Printed Books in Honour of A.I. Doyle*, ed. by R. Beadle and A.J. Piper, Aldershot: Scolar Press, 1995: 207–26.

Kelsall, Jane, *Humphrey Duke of Gloucester, 1391–1447*, St Albans: The Friends of Saint Albans Abbey, 2000.

Kendrick, T.D., "Humphrey, Duke of Gloucester, and the Gardens of Adonis", *The Antiquaries Journal* 26: 1946, 118–22.

Ker, Neil Ripley, *Medieval Libraries of Great Britain*, London: Offices of the Royal Historical Society, 1941; 2nd ed. 1964.

——, "Salisbury Cathedral Manuscripts and Patrick Young's Catalogue", *Wiltshire Archaeological and Natural History Magazine* 53: 1949–50, 153–83 (reprinted in *Books, Collectors and Libraries. Studies in the Medieval Heritage*, ed. by A.G. Watson, London: The Hambledon Press, 1985, pp. 175–208).

——, "The Chaining, Labelling, and Inventory Numbers of Manuscripts Belonging to the Old University Library", *The Bodleian Library Record* 5: 1955, 176–80.

——, "Oxford College Libraries before 1500", in *The Universities in the Late Middle Ages*, ed. by J. Ijsewijn and J. Paquet. Louvain: Louvain University Press, 1978: 293–311 (reprinted in *Books, Collectors and Libraries. Studies in the Medieval Heritage*, London: The Hambledon Press, 1985, pp. 301–20).

——, "The Provision of Books", in *The History of the University of Oxford, vol. 3: The Collegiate University*, ed. by J. McConica, Oxford: Clarendon Press, 1987: 441–77.

Ker, Neil Ripley and Alan J. Piper, *Medieval Manuscripts in British Libraries*, Oxford: Clarendon Press, 1969–82.

Kerby-Fulton, Kathryn and Steven Justice, "Langlandian Reading Circles and the Civil Service in London and Dublin, 1380–1427", in *New Medieval Literatures 1*, ed. by W. Scase, R. Copeland and D. Lawton, Oxford: Clarendon Press, 1997: 59–83.

Kibre, Pearl, "The Intellectual Interests Reflected in Libraries of the Fourteenth and Fifteenth Centuries", *Journal of the History of Ideas* 7: 1946, 257–97.

——, "Lewis of Caerleon, Doctor of Medicine, Astronomer and Mathematician (d. 1494?)", *Isis* 43: 1952, 100–8 (reprinted as ch. 15 of Kibre's *Studies in Medieval Science. Alchemy, Astrology, Mathematics and Medicine*, London: The Hambledon Press, 1984).

Kingsford, Charles Lethbridge, *English Historical Literature in the Fifteenth Century*, Oxford: Clarendon Press, 1913.

——, *English History in the Fifteenth Century and the Historical Plays of Shakespeare*, London: National Home-Reading Union, 1914.

——, *Prejudice and Promise in Fifteenth Century England*, Oxford: Clarendon Press, 1925.

Klinefelter, Ralph A., "'The Siege of Calais': A New Text", *Publications of the Modern Language Association* 67: 1952, 888–95.

——, "A Newly-discovered Fifteenth-century English Manuscript", *Modern Language Quarterly* 14: 1953, 3–7.

Kraye, Jill, ed., *The Cambridge Companion to Renaissance Humanism*, Cambridge: Cambridge University Press, 1996.

Kristeller, Paul Oskar, "Humanism and Scholasticism in the Italian Renaissance", *Byzantion* 17: 1944–45, 346–75 (reprinted in *Renaissance Thought and its Sources*, New York: Columbia University Press, 1979).

——, "The European Diffusion of Italian Humanism", *Italica* 39: 1962, 1–20.

Lawton, David, "Dullness and the Fifteenth Century," *ELH* 54: 1987, 761–99.

Lièvre, Marion, "Notes sur le manuscrit original du 'Songe du Vergier' et sur la librairie de Charles V", *Romania* 77: 1956, 352–60.

Lucas, Peter J., "John Capgrave, O.S.A. (1393–1464), Scribe and 'Publisher'", *Transactions of the Cambridge Bibliographical Society* 5: 1969, 1–35.

——, "John Capgrave and the *Nova Legenda Angliae*: A Survey", *The Library* 5th series, 25: 1970, 1–10.

——, "The Growth and Development of English Literary Patronage in the Later Middle Ages and Early Renaissance", *The Library* 6th series, 4: 1982, 219–48.

——, "An Author as Copyist of his own Work: John Capgrave OSA (1393–1464)", in *New Science out of Old Books. Studies in Manuscripts and Early Printed Books in Honour of A.I. Doyle*, ed. by R. Beadle and A.J. Piper, Aldershot: Scolar Press, 1995: 227–48.

——, *From Author to Audience: John Capgrave and Medieval Publication*, The Library, Dublin: University College Dublin Press, 1997.

—— and Rita Dalton, "Capgrave's Preface Dedicating his Commentary *In Exodum* to Humfrey Duke of Gloucester", *The Bodleian Library Record* 11: 1982, 20–5.

Luiso, Francesco Paolo, *Studi su l'epistolario di Leonardo Bruni*, Roma: Istituto storico italiano per il Medio Evo, 1980.

MacCracken, Henry Noble, "Vegetius in English", in *Anniversary Papers by Colleagues and Pupils of George Lyman Kittredge*, Boston and London: Ginn, 1913: 389–403.

MacFarlane, K.B., *Lancastrian Kings and Lollard Knights*, Oxford: Clarendon Press, 1972.

Machan, Tim William, "Textual Authority and the Works of Hoccleve, Lydgate, and Henryson", in *Writing After Chaucer: Essential Readings in Chaucer and the Fifteenth Century*, ed. by D.J. Pinti, New York: Garland, 1998: 177–99.

——, "Politics and the Middle English Language", *Studies in the Age of Chaucer* 24: 2002, 317–24.

MacKenna, J.W., "Henry VI and the Dual Monarchy: Aspects of Royal Political Propaganda, 1422–1432", *Journal of the Warburg and Courtauld Institutes* 28: 1965, 145–62.

MacRay, W.D., "Early Dedications to Englishmen by Foreign Authors and Editors", *Bibliographica: Papers on Books, their History and Art* 1: 1895, 324–47.

Manheim, Michael, "Duke Humphrey and the Machiavels", *American Benedictine Review* 23: 1972, 249–57.

Mann, Nicholas, "Petrarch's Role in Humanism", *Apollo* 94: 1971, 176–83.

——, "La prima fortuna del Petrarca in Inghilterra", in *Il Petrarca ad Arquà. Atti del convegno di studi nel VI centenario (1370–1374)*, ed. by G. Billanovich and G. Frasso, Padova: Antenore, 1975: 279–89.

——, "Petrarch Manuscripts in the British Isles", *Italia Medioevale e Umanistica* 18: 1975, 139–509.

——, "Dal moralista al poeta: appunti per la fortuna del Petrarca in Inghilterra", in *Atti dei Convegni dei Lincei: Convegno Internazionale Francesco Petrarca*, Roma: Accademia Nazionale dei Lincei, 1976: 59–69.

——, "Il Petrarca e gli inizi del Rinascimento inglese", *La Cultura* 15: 1977, 3–18.

——, *Petrarch*, Oxford: Oxford University Press, 1984.

Marchi, Gianpaolo, "L'umanista Antonio Beccaria alla Corte di Humphrey di Gloucester e di Ermolao Barbaro", *Annali della Facoltà di Lingue in Verona dell'Università di Padova* 2, 1: 1966–67, 3–41.

Meale, Carol M., "Patrons, Buyers and Owners: Book Production and Social Status", in *Book Production and Publishing in Britain 1375–1475*, ed. by J. Griffiths and D. Pearsall, Cambridge: Cambridge University Press, 1989: 201–38.

——, "*The Libelle of Englyshe Polycye* and Mercantile Literary Culture in Late-medieval London", in *London and Europe in the Later Middle Ages*, ed. by J. Boffey and P. King, London: Centre for Medieval and Renaissance Studies, Queen Mary and Westfield College, University of London, 1995: 181–227.

Medcalf, Stephen, ed., *The Later Middle Ages*, New York: Holmes & Meier, 1981.

Meijer, Alberic de, "John Capgrave, O.E.S.A. (1393–1464)", *Augustiniana* 5: 1955, 400–40.

——, "John Capgrave, O.E.S.A. (1393–1464)", *Augustiniana* 7: 1957, 118–48, 532–41.

Moore, R.I., "Literacy and the Making of Heresy *c.* 1000–*c.* 1150", in *Heresy and Literacy, 1000–1530*, ed. by P. Biller and A. Hudson, Cambridge: Cambridge University Press, 1994: 19–37.

Moore, Samuel, "General Aspects of Literary Patronage in the Middle Ages", *The Library* 3rd series, 4: 1913, 369–92.

Morgan, David, "The Household Retinue of Henry V and the Ethos of English Public Life", in *Concepts and Patterns of Service in the Later Middle Ages*, ed. by A. Curry and E. Matthew, Woodbridge: The Boydell Press, 2000: 64–79.

Morgan, Nigel, "Patrons and Devotional Images in English Art of the International Gothic c. 1350–1450", in *Reading Texts and Images. Essays on Medieval and Renaissance Art and Patronage*, ed. by B.J. Muir, Exeter: University of Exeter Press, 2002: 93–121.

Mortimer, Nigel, "A Study of John Lydgate's *Fall of Princes* in its Literary and Political Contexts", D.Phil., Oxford, 1995.

Moule, H.J., "A MS. of the Metrical Translation of Palladius 'De Re Rustica'", *Athenaeum*: 1888, 664.

Munby, A.N.L., "Notes on King's College Library in the Fifteenth Century", *Transactions of the Cambridge Bibliographical Society* 1: 1951, 280–86.

Mynors, R.A.B., *Catalogue of the Manuscripts of Balliol College, Oxford*, Oxford: Clarendon Press, 1963.

Newman, W.L., "The Correspondence of Humphrey, Duke of Gloucester, and Pier Candido Decembrio", *The English Historical Review* 20: 1905, 484–98.

Nicholson, E.W.B., "Annual Report of the Curators of the Bodleian Library", *Oxford University Gazette* 24: 1894, 443–50.

Nolan, Maura B., "Necromancy, Treason, Semiosis, Spectacle. The Trial of Eleanor Cobham, Duchess of Gloucester", *Proteus* 13: 1996, 7–11.

Nolcken, Christina von, "Lay Literacy, the Democratization of God's Law, and the Lollards", in *The Bible as Book: The Manuscript Tradition*, ed. by J.L. Sharpe and K.V. Kampen, London: The British Library, 1998: 177–95.

North, J.D., "The Alfonsine Tables in England", in *Prismata: Naturwissenschaftsgeschichtliche Studien. Festschrift für Willy Hartner*, ed. by Y. Maeyama and W.G. Saltzer, Wiesbaden: Franz Steiner Verlag, 1977: 269–301.

——, *Horoscopes and History*, London: The Warburg Institute, 1986.

Owst, G.R., "Some Books and Book-Owners of Fifteenth-Century St. Albans", *Transactions of the St Albans and Hertfordshire Architectural and Archaeological Society*: 1929, 176–95.

Parkes, M., "The Provision of Books", in *The History of the University of Oxford, vol. 2: Late Medieval Oxford*, ed. by J.J. Catto and R. Evans, Oxford: Clarendon Press, 1992, 2: 407–83.

Patterson, Lee, *Chaucer and the Subject of History*, London: Routledge, 1991.

——, "Making Identities in Fifteenth-Century England: Henry V and John Lydgate", in *New Historical Literary Study: Essays on Reproducing Texts, Representing History*, ed. by J.N. Cox and L.J. Reynolds, Princeton: Princeton University Press, 1993: 69–107.

——, "'What is me?': Self and Society in the Poetry of Thomas Hoccleve", *Studies in the Age of Chaucer* 23: 2001, 437–70.

Pearsall, Derek, *John Lydgate*, London: Routledge & Kegan Paul, 1970.

——, "Lydgate as Innovator", *Modern Language Quarterly* 53: 1992, 5–22.

——, "Hoccleve's *Regement of Princes*: The Poetics of Royal Self-Representation", *Speculum* 69: 1994, 386–410.

——, *John Lydgate (1371–1449): A Bio-bibliography*, English Literary Studies Monograph Series, University of Victoria: English Literary Studies, 1997.

——, ed., *Chaucer to Spenser. An Anthology of Writings in English 1375–1575*, Oxford: Blackwell, 1999.

——, "The Idea of Englishness in the Fifteenth Century", in *Nation, Court and Culture. New Essays on Fifteenth-Century English Poetry*, ed. by H. Cooney, Dublin: Four Courts Press, 2001: 15–27.

Perkins, Nicholas, "Musing on Mutability. A Poem in the Welles Anthology and Hoccleve's *The Regement of Princes*", *The Review of English Studies* 50: 1999, 493–8.

Petrina, Alessandra, *The Kingis Quair of James I of Scotland*, Padova: Unipress, 1997.

——, "The Middle English Translation of Palladius's De Agricultura", in *The Medieval Translator. Traduire au Moyen Age 8*, ed. by R. Voaden, R. Tixier, T. Sanchez Roura and J.R. Rytting, Tournhout: Brepols, 2003: 317–28.

Pratt, Samuel M., "Shakespeare and Humphrey Duke of Gloucester: A Study in Myth", *Shakespeare Quarterly* 16: 1965, 201–16.

Raine, James, "Divination in the Fifteenth Century by Aid of a Magical Crystal", *The Archaeological Journal* 13: 1856, 372–4.

Regoliosi, Mariangela, "Alfonso Sammut, *Unfredo duca di Gloucester e gli umanisti italiani*", *Aevum* 56: 1982, 352–4.

Renoir, Alain, *The Poetry of John Lydgate*, London: Routledge & Kegan Paul, 1967.

—— and C. David Benson, "John Lydgate", in *A Manual of the Writings in Middle English 1050–1500*, ed. by A.E. Hartung, New Haven: The Connecticut Academy of Arts and Sciences, 1980, 6: 1809–1920.

Richardson, Malcolm, "Henry V, the English Chancery, and Chancery English", *Speculum* 55: 1980, 726–50.

Rigg, A.G., *A History of Anglo-Latin Literature 1066–1422*, Cambridge: Cambridge University Press, 1992.

Robbins, Rossell Hope, "An Epitaph for Duke Humphrey (1441)", *Neuphilologische Mitteilungen* 56: 1955, 241–49.

——, "A Middle English Diatribe against Philip of Burgundy", *Neuphilologus* 39: 1955, 131–46.

——, "Medical Manuscripts in Middle English", *Speculum* 45: 1970, 393–415.

Rodgers, R.H., *An Introduction to Palladius*, London: University of London Institute of Classical Studies, 1975.

Root, Robert K., "Publication before Printing", *Publications of the Modern Language Association of America* 28: 1913, 417–31.

Rosenthal, Joel T., "Aristocratic Cultural Patronage and Book Bequests, 1350–1500", *Bulletin of the John Rylands University Library of Manchester* 64: 1981–2, 522–48.

Roskell, J.S., *Parliament and Politics in Late Medieval England*, London: The Hambledon Press, 1981.

Rossi, Sergio, "Enrico V dalla cronaca alla poesia", in *Ricerche sull'Umanesimo e sul Rinascimento in Inghilterra*, Milano: Società Editrice Vita e Pensiero, 1969: 1–25.

Rundle, David, "On the Difference between Virtue and Weiss: Humanist Texts in England during the Fifteenth Century", in *Courts, Counties and the Capital in the Later Middle Ages*, ed. by D.E.S. Dunn, New York: St Martin's Press, 1996: 181–203.

——, "Of Republics and Tyrants: Aspects of Quattrocento Humanist Writing and Their Reception in England, c. 1400–c. 1460", D.Phil., Oxford, 1997.

——, "Two Unnoticed Manuscripts from the Collection of Humfrey, Duke of Gloucester", *The Bodleian Library Record* 16: 1998, 211–24, 299–313.

——, "Humanism before the Tudors: On Nobility and the Reception of *studia humanitatis* in Fifteenth-Century England", in *Reassessing Tudor Humanism*, ed. by J. Woolfson, Basingstoke: Palgrave Macmillan, 2002: 22–42.

——, "Polydore Vergil and the *Translatio studiorum*: The Tradition of Italian Humanists in England", in *Polidoro Virgili e la cultura umanistica europea*, ed. by R. Bachielli, Urbino: Accademia Raffaello—Urbino, 2003: 53–74.

Sabbadini, Remigio, "Tito Livio Frulovisio umanista del sec. XV", *Giornale Storico della Letteratura Italiana* 103: 1934, 55–73.

Sammut, Alfonso, *Unfredo duca di Gloucester e gli umanisti italiani*, Padova: Antenore, 1980.

——, "Tra Pavia, Milano e Oxford: trasmissione di codici", in *Vestigia. Studi in Onore di Giuseppe Billanovich*, ed. by R. Avesani, M. Ferrari, T. Foffano, G. Frasso and A. Sottili, Roma: Edizioni di Storia e Letteratura, 1984, 2: 613–22.

——, "Per una storia della critica sulla fortuna inglese del Petrarca", in *Il passaggiere italiano. Saggi sulle letterature in lingua inglese in onore di Sergio Rossi*, ed. by R.S. Crivelli and L. Sampietro, Roma: Bulzoni, 1994: 41–57.

Saygin, Susanne, *Humphrey, Duke of Gloucester (1390–1447) and the Italian Humanists*, Leiden: Brill, 2002.

Scanlon, Larry, "The King's Two Voices: Narrative and Power in Hoccleve's *Regement of Princes*", in *Literary Practice and Social Change in Britain, 1380–1530*, ed. by L. Patterson, Berkeley: University of California Press, 1990: 216–47.

——, *Narrative, Authority, and Power: The Medieval Exemplum and the Chaucerian Tradition*, Cambridge: Cambridge University Press, 1994.

Scattergood, John, "*The Libelle of Englyshe Polycye*: The Nation and its Place", in *Nation, Court and Culture. New Essays on Fifteenth-Century English Poetry*, ed. by H. Cooney, Dublin: Four Courts Press, 2001: 28–49.

Scattergood, V.J., *Politics and Poetry in the Fifteenth Century*, London: Blandford Press, 1971.

Schellenberg, Otto, "Wer war Andrew Ols?", *Englische Studien* 46: 1912–13, 197–205.

Schirmer, W.F., "The Importance of the Fifteenth Century for the Study of the English Renaissance with Special Reference to Lydgate", *English Studies Today* 1: 1951, 104–10.

——, *Der englische Frühhumanismus. Ein Betrag zur Englischen Literatur-Geschichte der 15. Jahrhundert*, Leipzig: Bernherd Tauchnitz, 1931.

——, *John Lydgate, a Study in the Culture of the Fifteenth Century*, London: Methuen, 1961.

Schofield, A.N.E.D., "The First English Delegation to the Council of Basel", *The Journal of Ecclesiastical History* 12: 1961, 167–96.

——, "England, the Pope and the Council of Basel, 1435–1449", *Church History* 33: 1964, 248–78.

——, "The Second English Delegation to the Council of Basel", *The Journal of Ecclesiastical History* 17: 1966, 29–64.

Scott, Kathleen L., "A Mid-Fifteenth-Century English Illuminating Shop and its Customers", *Journal of the Warburg and Courtauld Institutes* 31: 1968, 170–96.

——, "*Caveat Lector*: Ownership and Standardization in the Illustration of Fifteenth Century English Manuscripts", in *English Manuscript Studies 1100–1700, vol. 1*, ed. by P. Beal and J. Griffiths, Oxford: Blackwell, 1989: 19–63.

Seaton, Ethel, *Sir Richard Roos (c. 1410–1482), Lancastrian Poet*, London: Rupert Hart-Davis, 1961.

Seymour, M.C., "Manuscript Pictures of Duke Humfrey", *The Bodleian Library Record* 12: 1986, 95–98.

——, "The Manuscripts of John Capgrave's English Works", *Scriptorium* 40: 1986, 248–55.

——, *John Capgrave*, English Writers of the Middle Ages, Aldershot: Variorum, 1996.

Simonini, R.C., *Italian Scholarship in Renaissance England*, Chapel Hill: The University of North Carolina, 1952.

Simpson, James, "Bulldozing the Middle Ages: The Case of 'John Lydgate'", in *New Medieval Literatures 4*, ed. by W. Scase, R. Copeland and D. Lawton, Oxford: Oxford University Press, 2001: 213–42.

Skeat, Walter W., "Palladius on Husbondrie", *The Academy* 4: 1873, 315–17.

Smith, Grady A., "'Languida Virtus Semper ad Extremum': Titus Livius Frulovisi in England, 1437–39", *Fifteenth-Century Studies* 21: 1994, 323–33.

——, "Medieval Drama, Work in Progress: Frulovisi's Peregrinatio and Eugenius: An Introduction and Translation", *Fifteenth-Century Studies* 22: 1996, 192–93.

——, "Frulovisi, Humanist Writer: A Career Abandoned", *Fifteenth-Century Studies* 24: 1998, 231–41.

Smith, Jeremy J., "Chaucer and the Invention of English", *Studies in the Age of Chaucer* 24: 2002, 335–46.

Starkey, David, "England", in *The Renaissance in National Context*, ed. by M. Teich and R. Porter, Cambridge: Cambridge University Press, 1992: 149–63.

Stauble, Antonio, "Le sette commedie dell'umanista Tito Livio De' Frulovisi", *Rinascimento: Rivista dell'Istituto Nazionale di Studi sul Rinascimento* n.s. 3: 1963, 23–52.

Stephen, Leslie and Sidney Lee, eds., *The Dictionary of National Biography*, Oxford: Oxford University Press, 1993.

Storey, R.L., "University and Government 1430–1500", in *The History of the University of Oxford, vol. 2: Late Medieval Oxford*, ed. by J.J. Catto and R. Evans, Oxford: Clarendon Press, 1992: 709–45.

Straker, Scott-Morgan, "Rivalry and Reciprocity in Lydgate's *Troy Book*", in *New Medieval Literatures 3*, ed. by D. Lawton, W. Scase and R. Copeland, Oxford: Oxford University Press, 1999: 119–47.

Stratford, Jenny, "The Manuscripts of John, Duke of Bedford: Library and Chapel", in *England in the Fifteenth Century: Proceedings of the 1986 Harlaxton Symposium*, ed. by D. Williams, Woodbridge: The Boydell Press, 1987: 329–50.

Stratford, Jenny, "The Royal Library in England before the Reign of Edward IV", in *England in the Fifteenth Century. Proceedings of the 1992 Harlaxton Symposium*, ed. by N. Rogers, Stamford: Paul Watkins, 1994: 187–97.

——, *The Bedford Inventories. The Worldly Goods of John, Duke of Bedford, Regent of France (1389–1435)*, London: Society of Antiquaries, 1993.

Strohm, Paul, "The Trouble with Richard: The Reburial of Richard II and Lancastrian Symbolic Strategy", *Speculum* 71: 1996, 87–111.

——, "Counterfeiters, Lollards, and Lancastrian Unease", in *New Medieval Literatures 1*, ed. by W. Scase, R. Copeland and D. Lawton, Oxford: Clarendon Press, 1997: 31–58.

——, *England's Empty Throne: Usurpation and the Language of Legitimation 1399–1422*, New Haven and London: Yale University Press, 1998.

Strong, Patrick and Felicity, "The Last Will and Codicils of Henry V", *The English Historical Review* 96: 1981, 79–102.

Struever, Carl, *Die Mittelenglische Übersetzung des Palladius. Ihr Verhältnis zur Quelle und Ihre Sprache*, Halle: Ehrhardt Kanas, 1887.

Talbot, C.H., *Medicine in Medieval England*, London: Oldbourne, 1967.

——, and E.A. Hammond, *The Medical Practitioners in Medieval England. A Biographical Register*, London: Wellcome Historical Medical Library, 1965.

Taylor, Frank, "Some Manuscripts of the 'Libelle of Englyshe Polycye'", *Bulletin of the John Rylands Library* 24: 1940, 3–45.

Taylor, John, "Notes on the Rise of Written English in the Late Middle Ages", *Proceedings of the Leeds Philosophical Society* 8: 1956, 128–36.

Thompson, John J., "Reading Lydgate in Post-reformation England", in *Middle English Poetry: Texts and Traditions. Essays in Honor of Derek Pearsall*, ed. by A.J. Minnis, York: York Medieval Press, 2001: 181–209.

Thorndike, Lynn and Pearl Kibre, *A Catalogue of Incipits of Medieval Scientific Writing in Latin*, Cambridge, Mass.: The Medieval Academy of America, 1963.

Torti, Anna, *The Glass of Form: Mirroring Structures from Chaucer to Skelton*, Cambridge: D.S. Brewer, 1991.

Toynbee, Paget, *Dante in English Literature from Chaucer to Cary (c. 1380–1844)*, London: Methuen, 1909.

——, "The Dante MSS. Presented to Oxford by Duke Humphrey", *The Times Literary Supplement* 18 March: 1920, 187.

——, "Duke Humphrey's Dante, Petrarch, and Boccaccio MSS.", *The Times Literary Supplement* 22 April: 1920, 256.

Trapp, J.B., "Il libro umanistico tra Italia e Inghilterra dal '400 al primo '500", *Scrittura e civiltà* 22: 1998, 319–37.

Ullman, Berthold L., "Manuscripts of Duke Humphrey of Gloucester", in *Studies in the Italian Renaissance*, Roma: Edizioni di Storia e Letteratura, 1955: 345–55.

Ullman, Berthold L. and Philip A. Stadter, *The Public Library of Renaissance Florence. Niccolò Niccoli, Cosimo de' Medici and the Library of San Marco*, Padova: Antenore, 1972.

Vickers, Kenneth H., *Humphrey Duke of Gloucester. A Biography*, London: Archibald Constable, 1907.

Voigts, Linda Ehrsam, "Scientific and Medical Books", in *Book Production and Publishing in Britain 1375–1475*, ed. by J. Griffiths and D. Pearsall, Cambridge: Cambridge University Press, 1989: 345–402.

Wallace, David, *Chaucerian Polity: Absolutist Lineages and Associational Forms in England and Italy*, Stanford: Stanford University Press, 1997.

——, ed., *The Cambridge History of Medieval English Literature*, Cambridge: Cambridge University Press, 1999.

——, "Dante in Somerset: Ghosts, Historiography, Periodization", in *New Medieval Literatures 3*, ed. by D. Lawton, W. Scase and R. Copeland, Oxford: Oxford University Press, 1999: 9–38.

Warton, Thomas, *History of English Poetry from the Close of the Eleventh to the Commencement of the Eighteenth Century*, London, 1774–81.

Watson, Nicholas, "Censorship and Cultural Change in Late Medieval England: Vernacular Theology, the Oxford Translation Debate, and Arundel's Constitutions of 1409", *Speculum* 70: 1995, 822–64.

——, "Conceptions of the Word: The Mother Tongue and the Incarnation of God", in *New Medieval Literatures 1*, ed. by W. Scase, R. Copeland and D. Lawton, Oxford: Clarendon Press, 1997: 85–124.

Watts, John, *Henry VI and the Politics of Kingship*, Cambridge: Cambridge University Press, 1996.

Weiss, Roberto, "Per la conoscenza di Dante in Inghilterra nel quattrocento", *Giornale Storico della letteratura italiana* 108: 1936, 357–9.

——, *Humanism in England During the Fifteenth Century*, Oxford: Blackwell, 1941 (3rd ed. 1967).

——, "Piero del Monte, John Whethamstede, and the Library of St. Albans Abbey", *English Historical Review* 60: 1945, 399–406.

——, "New Light on Humanism in England during the Fifteenth Century", *Journal of the Warburg and Courtauld Institutes* 14: 1951, 21–33.

——, "An Unnoticed MS of Humfrey, Duke of Gloucester", *The Bodleian Library Record* 5: 1955, 123–24.

——, "Humphrey Duke of Gloucester and Tito Livio Frulovisi", in *Fritz Saxl 1890–1948. A Volume of Memorial Essays from his Friends in England*, ed. by D.J. Gordon, London: Nelson, 1957: 218–27.

——, "The Private Collector and the Revival of Greek Learning", in *The English Library before 1700*, ed. by F. Wormald and C.E. Wright, London: The Athlone Press, 1958: 112–35.

——, "Portrait of a Bibliophile XI: Humphrey, Duke of Gloucester, d. 1447", *The Book Collector* 13: 1964, 161–70.

Wilkinson, B., *The Later Middle Ages in England 1216–1485*, London: Longmans, 1969.

Wogan-Browne, Jocelyn, Nicholas Watson, et al., eds., *The Idea of the Vernacular: An Anthology of Middle English Literary Theory, 1280–1520*, Exeter: University of Exeter Press, 1999.

Wolffe, Bertram, *Henry VI*, London: Eyre Methuen, 1981.

Wood, Anthony à, *The History and Antiquities of the University of Oxford*, Oxford: John Gutch, 1792–96.

Wright, Elizabeth Cox, "Continuity in Fifteenth-Century English Humanism", *Publications of the Modern Language Association of America* 51: 1936, 370–6.

Wright, Sylvia, "The Author Portraits in the Bedford Psalter-Hours: Gower, Chaucer, and Hoccleve", *British Library Journal* 18: 1992, 190–201.

Wylie, J. Hamilton, "Decembri's Version of the *Vita Henrici Quinti* by Tito Livio", *The English Historical Review* 24: 1909, 84–9.

INDEX

BRILL'S STUDIES
IN
INTELLECTUAL HISTORY

82. McCALLA, A. *A Romantic Historiosophy.* The Philosophy of History of Pierre-Simon Ballanche. 1998. ISBN 90 04 10967 6
83. VEENSTRA, J.R. *Magic and Divination at the Courts of Burgundy and France.* Text and Context of Laurens Pignon's *Contre les devineurs* (1411). 1998. ISBN 90 04 10925 0
84. WESTERMAN, P.C. *The Disintegration of Natural Law Theory.* Aquinas to Finnis. 1998. ISBN 90 04 10999 4
85. GOUWENS, K. *Remembering the Renaissance.* Humanist Narratives of the Sack of Rome. 1998. ISBN 90 04 10969 2
86. SCHOTT, H. & J. ZINGUER (Hrsg.). *Paracelsus und seine internationale Rezeption in der frühen Neuzeit.* Beiträge zur Geschichte des Paracelsismus. 1998. ISBN 90 04 10974 9
87. ÅKERMAN, S. *Rose Cross over the Baltic.* The Spread of Rosicrucianism in Northern Europe. 1998. ISBN 90 04 11030 5
88. DICKSON, D.R. *The Tessera of Antilia.* Utopian Brotherhoods & Secret Societies in the Early Seventeenth Century. 1998. ISBN 90 04 11032 1
89. NOUHUYS, T. VAN. *The Two-Faced Janus.* The Comets of 1577 and 1618 and the Decline of the Aristotelian World View in the Netherlands. 1998. ISBN 90 04 11204 9
90. MUESSIG, C. (ed.). *Medieval Monastic Preaching.* 1998. ISBN 90 04 10883 1
91. FORCE, J.E. & D.S. KATZ (eds.). *"Everything Connects": In Conference with Richard H. Popkin.* Essays in His Honor. 1999. ISBN 90 04 110984
92. DEKKER, K. *The Origins of Old Germanic Studies in the Low Countries.* 1999. ISBN 90 04 11031 3
93. ROUHI, L. *Mediation and Love.* A Study of the Medieval Go-Between in Key Romance and Near-Eastern Texts. 1999. ISBN 90 04 11268 5
94. AKKERMAN, F., A. VANDERJAGT & A. VAN DER LAAN (eds.). *Northern Humanism between 1469 and 1625.* 1999. ISBN 90 04 11314 2
95. TRUMAN, R.W. *Spanish Treatises on Government, Society and Religion in the Time of Philip II.* The 'de regimine principum' and Associated Traditions. 1999. ISBN 90 04 11379 7
96. NAUTA, L. & A. VANDERJAGT (eds.) *Demonstration and Imagination.* Essays in the History of Science and Philosophy Presented to John D. North. 1999. ISBN 90 04 11468 8
97. BRYSON, D. *Queen Jeanne and the Promised Land.* Dynasty, Homeland, Religion and Violence in Sixteenth-Century France. 1999. ISBN 90 04 11378 9
98. GOUDRIAAN, A. *Philosophische Gotteserkenntnis bei Suárez und Descartes im Zusammenhang mit der niederländischen reformierten Theologie und Philosophie des 17. Jahrhunderts.* 1999. ISBN 90 04 11627 3
99. HEITSCH, D.B. *Practising Reform in Montaigne's* Essais. 2000. ISBN 90 04 11630 3
100. KARDAUN, M. & J. SPRUYT (eds.). *The Winged Chariot.* Collected Essays on Plato and Platonism in Honour of L.M. de Rijk. 2000. ISBN 90 04 11480 7
101. WHITMAN, J. (ed.), *Interpretation and Allegory:* Antiquity to the Modern Period. 2000. ISBN 90 04 11039 9
102. JACQUETTE, D., *David Hume's Critique of Infinity.* 2000. ISBN 90 04 11649 4
103. BUNGE, W. VAN. *From Stevin to Spinoza.* An Essay on Philosophy in the Seventeenth-Century Dutch Republic. 2001. ISBN 90 04 12217 6
104. GIANOTTI, T., *Al-Ghazālī's Unspeakable Doctrine of the Soul.* Unveiling the Esoteric Psychology and Eschatology of the Iḥyā. 2001. ISBN 90 04 12083 1
105. SAYGIN, S., *Humphrey, Duke of Gloucester (1390-1447) and the Italian Humanists.* 2002. ISBN 90 04 12015 7
106. BEJCZY, I., *Erasmus and the Middle Ages.* The Historical Consciousness of a Christian Humanist. 2001. ISBN 90 04 12218 4
107. BRANN, N.L. *The Debate over the Origin of Genius during the Italian Renaissance.* The Theories of Supernatural Frenzy and Natural Melancholy in Accord and in Conflict on the Threshold of the Scientific Revolution. 2002. ISBN 90 04 12362 8
108. ALLEN, M.J.B. & V. REES with M. DAVIES. (eds.), *Marsilio Ficino: His Theology, His Philosophy, His Legacy.* 2002. ISBN 90 04 11855 1
109. SANDY, G., *The Classical Heritage in France.* 2002. ISBN 90 04 11916 7
110. SCHUCHARD, M.K., *Restoring the Temple of Vision.* Cabalistic Freemasonry and Stuart Culture. 2002. ISBN 90 04 12489 6

111. EIJNATTEN, J. VAN. *Liberty and Concord in the United Provinces*. Religious Toleration and the Public in the Eighteenth-Century Netherlands. 2003. ISBN 90 04 12843 3
112. BOS, A.P. *The Soul and Its Instrumental Body*. A Reinterpretation of Aristotle's Philosophy of Living Nature. 2003. ISBN 90 04 13016 0
113. LAURSEN, J.C. & J. VAN DER ZANDE (eds.). *Early French and German Defenses of Liberty of the Press*. Elie Luzac's *Essay on Freedom of Expression* (1749) and Carl Friedrich Bahrdt's *On Liberty of the Press and its Limits* (1787) *in English Translation*. 2003. ISBN 90 04 13017 9
114. POTT, S., M. MULSOW & L. DANNEBERG (eds.). *The Berlin Refuge 1680-1780*. Learning and Science in European Context. 2003. ISBN 90 04 12561 2
115. GERSH, S. & B. ROEST (eds.). *Medieval and Renaissance Humanism*. Rhetoric, Representation and Reform. 2003. ISBN 90 04 13274 0
116. LENNON, T.M. (ed.). *Cartesian Views*. Papers presented to Richard A. Watson. 2003. ISBN 90 04 13299 6
117. VON MARTELS, Z. & A. VANDERJAGT (eds.). *Pius II – 'El Più Expeditivo Pontefice'*. Selected Studies on Aeneas Silvius Piccolomini (1405-1464). 2003. ISBN 90 04 13190 6
118. GOSMAN, M., A. MACDONALD & A. VANDERJAGT (eds.). *Princes and Princely Culture 1450–1650*. Volume One. 2003. ISBN 90 04 13572 3
119. LEHRICH, C.I. *The Language of Demons and Angels*. Cornelius Agrippa's Occult Philosophy. 2003. ISBN 90 04 13574 X
120. BUNGE, W. VAN (ed.). *The Early Enlightenment in the Dutch Republic, 1650–1750*. Selected Papers of a Conference held at the Herzog August Bibliothek, Wolfenbüttel 22–23 March 2001. 2003. ISBN 90 04 13587 1
121. ROMBURGH, S. VAN, *"For My Worthy Freind Mr Franciscus Junius."* An Edition of the Correspondence of Francis Junius F.F. (1591-1677). 2004. ISBN 90 04 12880 8
122. MULSOW, M. & R.H. POPKIN (eds.). *Secret Conversions to Judaism in Early Modern Europe*. 2004. ISBN 90 04 12883 2
123. GOUDRIAAN, K., J. VAN MOOLENBROEK & A. TERVOORT (eds.). *Education and Learning in the Netherlands, 1400-1600*. 2004. ISBN 90 04 13644 4
124. PETRINA, A. *Cultural Politics in Fifteenth-Century England: The Case of Humphrey, Duke of Gloucester*. 2004. ISBN 90 04 13713 0
125. SCHUURMAN, P. *Ideas, Mental Faculties and Method*. The Logic of Ideas of Descartes and Locke and Its Reception in the Dutch Republic, 1630–1750. 2004. ISBN 90 04 13716 5